Japanese Workers and the Struggle for Power
1945–1947

Japanese Workers and the Struggle for Power
1945–1947

Joe Moore

The University of Wisconsin Press

Published 1983

The University of Wisconsin Press
114 North Murray Street
Madison, Wisconsin 53715

The University of Wisconsin Press, Ltd.
1 Gower Street
London WC1E 6HA, England

First printing

Printed in the United States of America

For LC CIP information see the colophon

ISBN 0-299-09320-4

For Tomoko and Erika, with love

Contents

List of Tables and Figures

Tables

Figures

Acknowledgments

The research and writing of this book were done in stages over the past ten years in three different places: Tokyo, the University of Wisconsin–Madison, and the Australian National University in Canberra. The idea of making production control the topic of my doctoral dissertation originated in conversations with several people in Tokyo in 1972. Among them was Professor John W. Dower, who subsequently supervised the writing of my dissertation at the Department of History at the University of Wisconsin. He provided the best of guidance at that time, and has since continued to give me the benefit of his careful criticism.

Professor Yamamoto Kiyoshi of the Tokyo University Institute of Social Science also encouraged me in my study at the outset and has been more than generous with his own collection of materials on the postwar workers' movement. His extensive work on the early occupation has been a constant stimulus and example to me. I would also like to express my thanks to Professor Noguchi Tasuku of Keio University and Nimura Kazuo of the Ōhara Institute for Social Research at Hōsei University.

While studying in Madison I profited from the knowledge of Professor Solomon B. Levine and Professor Sumiya Mikio, both of whom read parts of my dissertation and commented helpfully. At the same time, James Hastings of the National Archives and Record Service in Washington, D.C. greatly aided my research in the mountain of SCAP materials.

Another basic collection of materials on the occupation is located at the University of Maryland. I would like to thank Professor Frank Shulman and his staff for assisting me in going through the Gordon S. Prange Collection in McKeldin Library.

This book could not have been written, however, without the generous financial and academic support of the Australian National University in Canberra where I held a two-year postdoctoral fellowship in 1979–81. My special appreciation goes to Professor E. Sydney Crawcour and Professor Andrew Fraser, who read and commented on various versions of the material in this book. While in Canberra I also had the pleasure of finding first-rate collections of materials in two places: the Oriental Language Collection of the National Library of Australia, presided over by Sydney Wong, Chief Librarian, and the Australian Archives, where Graham Joyner worked hard to locate materials on the occupation.

To Professor William McMahon Ball, British Commonwealth Member to the Allied Council for Japan during the early occupation, and Eric Ward, his extremely perceptive economic adviser and a participant in the writing of the land reform program, I owe particular thanks. They not only agreed to be interviewed by me about their experiences in Japan but also generously gave me access to their collections of important materials on the occupation.

It is impossible to convey in words the obligation I feel to a number of friends and colleagues who have read what needed to be read and been there to talk about and react to the argument elaborated in this book as it developed. My thanks go to Professor Matsuda Takeshi, Professor Robert Marks, Paul Winnacker, Professor Timothy Wright, and Professor Rob Steven.

The tremendous task of getting this manuscript typed fell to Ms. Marian Saville, the very capable secretary of the Department of Far Eastern History at the Australian National University. For the skill and good humor with which he edited my manuscript for the University of Wisconsin Press, I want to thank Brian Keeling.

Introduction

In any nation's history there are watersheds, short periods of height-ened change which contain the potential for fixing a new course for the future. The Russian and Chinese revolutions are obvious ex-amples. In the modern history of Japan, the postwar occupation was a watershed comparable to these in its origins and its possibilities, but one that ended in a restoration and not a revolution. It was closer in its resolution to the Meiji Restoration, the controlled, conservative "revolution" from above that set Japan on the course to industrial power and ultimately war.

The Meiji period was characterized by a controlled restructuring of Japanese society that contained the impulse toward radical social change from below within a framework responsive to new conditions, but knit together with traditional elements. The postwar occupation, similarly, saw a successful attempt from above to stabilize serious social contra-dictions made explosive by defeat in total war, and to reconstruct the essence of the prewar social order. The Japanese leadership's success stands in striking contrast to the failures of the Russian Tsarist autoc-racy and the Chinese Guomindong, which were swept away following disastrous wars that aided the rise of new classes to power.

When World War II ended, it was unclear what direction Japan would take. It might seem in retrospect that, given the American decision to occupy Japan, the only real possibility for Japan was the type of bourgeois-democratic reform that actually took place. Yet at the time there were many in both countries who feared an early return of fas-cist repression, while others were equally alarmed about the possibil-ity of a communist revolution.

Although the Japanese have taken such concerns seriously, Western scholars have not. Virtually transfixed by the Japanese "economic mir-acle," they have concentrated on finding the secret formula for Japan's postwar "modernization" and "liberalization." Indeed, some scoff at the suggestion that there might have been some other outcome, pre-ferring to ignore the ambiguous legacy of the period of fascism and the postwar reaction of the Japanese people to the long decades of oppression. The consequence of this "success-story" approach to the postwar history of Japan has been a distressing absence of the sensitivity the scholar ought to have to paths not taken and possibilities unfulfilled. What eventually did happen has come to be regarded as what had to happen.

The charge of writing history without people has been made in other contexts, but has truly been the case here. The flesh and blood of mass firings and joblessness, destitution and hunger, massive strikes and union busting, class struggle and state repression have been submerged in dry statistics and abstract theory. The revolutionary ferment of the times has not come through, and the depth of the postwar crisis of capitalism in Japan has yet to be appreciated.

The year and a half from the surrender in August 1945 to the failure of the 1 February 1947 general strike was the crucial time. War and occupation had created a situation of flux by breaking the hold of the old leaders on the economy and politics of Japan and by giving the working class freedom of action. The ensuing confrontation of labor and capital admitted of a number of different resolutions ranging from the restoration of the prewar capitalist order to the creation of a democratic people's republic. The most likely path for Japan in the months and years after the war changed in direct response to changes in the strength and perceptions of the three major participants in the battle to control the immediate course of Japan's reconstruction—the Supreme Command for the Allied Powers (SCAP), the conservative economic and political establishment (the "old guard"), and the working class. While working-class radicalism was at its height during the first nine months of occupation, the socialist alternative to the old guard's program of straightforward restoration was a living possibility, and was at the center of the battle between labor and capital. During the succeeding nine months, when the old guard began reestablishing its ascendancy with SCAP support, the working class shifted to defense of its class interests *within* the capitalist economic reconstruction that was then seen as inescapable.

The orthodox interpretation of the occupation glosses over these first two periods and focuses on the 1 February general strike, which it depicts as the peak of a narrowly based and easily thwarted revolutionary movement. SCAP's prohibition of the strike marked the decisive defeat of this movement, and turned the tide in favor of the essential moderation and conservatism of the Japanese people. SCAP's intervention is also viewed as the beginning of a policy transition from the early stress on democratization to a concentration on economic reconstruction. In such an interpretation, the U.S. government and SCAP are the active elements, defining not only the conditions for the conservative resurgence but also those for the left-wing challenge in the first place by extending to the Japanese through "democratization" an unaccustomed freedom which was used irresponsibly.

It is not necessary to be Japanese to wonder if the Japanese people were truly as passive and malleable as the orthodox interpretation implies. That the Japanese appear to come onstage and retreat to the wings in response to the prompting of SCAP says less about Japanese "docility" than it does about the failings of a problem consciousness and periodization which places SCAP's activities and U.S. interests at center stage.

A different periodization will be used here, one focusing on the working class as it experienced the broad economic and social changes taking place within Japanese society. Although the last of the three periods will not be taken up in this book, an overview that includes it is presented in order to give a sense of the wider context within which my argument is posed.

Period One: Workers' Control and the Revolutionary Upsurge

Yoshida Shigeru, who became prime minister in May 1946, later characterized the period in which he came to power as revolutionary. In so doing, he had several things in mind—among them the resurgent Communist party and the huge street demonstrations of spring 1946—but the main object of his concern was workers' seizure and operation of mines, factories, and offices. Production control (*seisan kanri*) was not at all something peculiar to post-surrender Japan, but corresponded to the factory occupations in Leningrad, Berlin, and Turin of some twenty-five years before, and the workers' councils that sprang up in Germany at the moment of the Nazi defeat. In parallel with the situation following the two world wars in Europe, Japanese workers after World War II stood up to protest their lot, to make the radical demand for workers' control, and to take over and run their enterprises through their own system of councils.

By spring 1946, large numbers of workers and ordinary citizens were challenging the old guard by way of factory takeovers and popular seizures of food-distribution depots, while hundreds of thousands took to the streets to express their opposition to the old order. Alarmed, General MacArthur condemned the popular movement in May, threatening intervention by occupation authorities to control a situation which, he said, was a menace to orderly government.

The crisis of the old order was played out in circumstances of seemingly bewildering complexity. Big business was divided into conflicting conservative and progressive camps, and the governing bureaucracy was similarly split. Communists and socialists fought among themselves while battling the old guard for control of the government. The U.S. occupation headquarters loosed a flood of directives for democratizing Japanese society. Workers, farmers, and city people sought collective relief in the desperate times by organizing in unions and councils, through them groping toward a new, populist order. Yet, one issue cut through the complexity and provided a point of reference for the political coalitions being formed on the left and on the right: how to deal with accelerating economic chaos.

The economic breakdown in 1945–46 was catastrophic. Big-business leaders—adamantly opposed to "economic democratization"—hesitated to cooperate in reconstruction under disadvantageous terms. Badly crippled by zaibatsu retrenchment, industrial production failed to meet the bare minimum of goods needed to feed, clothe, and house the suffering populace, who—facing the possibility of mass starvation—had to search for new answers.

The workers' answer was production control. Production control was highly rational from the workers' and the public's viewpoint since it increased output even while securing the workers' livelihood. It brought on a confrontation between workers and the old guard, however, because it flouted traditional rights of private property.

Stimulated by the workers' example and by necessity, farmers and city people in midwinter began to demand control over production and distribution of food. As spring approached, these related struggles began to coalesce. The combined mass movement brought down the Shidehara cabinet in April 1946 and blocked the formation of another conservative cabinet for an entire month, while political and economic power seemed about to devolve into popular hands at the point of production and distribution.

The society toward which the working class was moving in the spring of 1946 when production control was rapidly spreading cannot be fully known, for the simple reason that this drive for radical change was turned back. After all, the workers' movement developed within a capitalist and an occupied Japan and can therefore give only a partial indication of what promised to become an alternative form of social organization. An indication can be seen, nonetheless.

Period Two: Industrial Unionism

MacArthur's condemnation of "mass violence" came in May 1946. SCAP's intervention threw the left-wing leaders into confusion, leaving the popular movement on its own, and stiffened the resolve of the old guard, whose counterattack was not long in coming. The participants in the struggles in the villages, on factory floors, and in local neighborhoods drew the conclusion that while conservative control continued, caution was required. Whether caution was dictated by a fear of retaliation or by the necessity of just surviving when the old guard still controlled the distribution of food and other necessities of life, there was a general turning away from radical answers toward making the best accommodation possible within the existing order. This was nowhere more apparent than among the working class in the succeeding period, when it abandoned production control. A more orthodox industrial union movement, which centered on the right to organize and to bargain collectively over wages and working conditions, became the main arena for the conflict with big business thereafter.

However obvious it might have been to Japanese workers that they needed strong industrial unions to defend their interests, it was not so obvious to the old guard that they would have to adopt an approach to reconstruction that would be sufficiently progressive to win it at least the tacit support of unionized labor. On the contrary, the Yoshida cabinet that was formed as a result of the SCAP intervention in May chose to take SCAP's action as both a repudiation of the workers' movement and an endorsement of its reactionary program for reconstruction—reactionary in the sense that it was intended to recreate the essence of the "laissez-faire" economy of the twenties when the zaibatsu were strong, the state pliable, and labor weak and cheap.

If underlying the first period was the fundamental question of whether Japan was to have a capitalist or socialist reconstruction, then the second period saw a drastic narrowing of the ground of conflict to the question of what kind of a capitalist reconstruction it was to be—conservative "laissez-faire" or progressive "modified" (shūsei) capitalism. The former was the program of the old guard which looked back to the twenties when planning was all but nonexistent and an oppressed work force underwrote capitalist expansion by providing for cheap textile exports and rapid capital accumulation for the zaibatsu. When the Yoshida cabinet came to power, it attempted to carry out the conservatives' economic program by means of inflationary handouts intended to recapitalize the zaibatsu and a counteroffensive against the new unions in order to provide an abundant supply of cheap labor. Furthermore, big-business and government leaders, whether progressive or conservative, had already shown their common determination not to knuckle under to the national federations of the unions, and were trying to make the enterprise the fundamental unit for bargaining with unionized labor.

The left-wing unions reacted in the second half of 1946 with a powerful wave of strikes, through which they intended to secure labor's rights and to perfect the national system of industrial unions in the process of formation. The strike wave gave the old guard a severe setback and blocked its economic program. Because the stockpiles of critical raw materials were being wasted in production of non-essential consumer goods while the producer-goods sector of the economy stagnated, a long-term standoff preventing the revival of production could have but one result, an economic collapse even more severe than the one of winter 1945–46.

The possibility of a "March crisis" and a workers' revolt of immense proportions sent a shudder through the ranks of big business and government in late October, and the old guard began to reconsider its conservative economic program. As winter came on, fear of an imminent economic collapse produced an atmosphere of crisis conducive to the formation of a consensus in late 1946 behind the reform program being put forward jointly by the progressives in big business and government and the right wing of organized labor. In contrast to the conservatives, they accepted the need for comprehensive economic planning and for economic concessions to unionized labor in exchange for increases in productivity.

Although the Yoshida cabinet agreed to comprehensive economic planning in December, it resisted concessions to labor, economic or otherwise. The cabinet fought the winter offensive of the unions of public employees, through which these workers attempted to catch up with their counterparts in private industry. This hard line precipitated the general strike movement of January 1947 which aimed at toppling Yoshida and the conservatives. The political crisis the Yoshida cabinet had brought on itself did have one hoped-for result. Labor's political involvement provoked SCAP once again to intervene. The SCAP prohibition of the general strike discredited the militant industrial unions that had organized it and tipped the balance in the labor movement in favor of the right wing.

There can be no doubt that there was a reverse course in labor reform in Japan, or that it began in May 1946, not February 1947 or July 1948, though these dates mark succeeding stages of it. The reverse course began when SCAP became alarmed about the revolutionary potential of the working-class movement in the spring of 1946 and, over the objections of Labor Division, encouraged the Yoshida cabinet to curb labor's power. The decision to step in openly to save the Yoshida cabinet was to be followed a year later by even more drastic steps to end the troublesome militance of the left-wing unions.

Period Three: Enterprise Unionism

The period from early 1947 to 1950 encompassed the breaking of the industrial unions and the establishment from above of Japan's "unique" contribution to industrial relations, the enterprise union. From 1947 the left-wing labor leaders sustained attacks from within their unions by so-called democratization leagues, which claimed to represent rank-and-file discontent with the policies of left-wing leaders. There undoubtedly was dissatisfaction with the left wing and resentment over communist influence, but the splits and recriminations resulting from the democratization movement benefited the old guard far more than anyone else, except perhaps for labor's right wing. These internal difficulties were compounded in 1948 by anti-labor legislation designed to hobble the strong unions of government workers that were the mainstay of the left wing and to permit big-business and government employers to make mass dismissals as part of a program of economic retrenchment now deemed to be essential before recovery could begin.

The left-wing labor federations were not able either to overcome their internal disunity or to fend off the damaging changes in labor laws and the mass firings of union members that followed. The new attack on the labor movement abetted the splitting of the left-wing unions by the democratization leagues working in close cooperation with management. This frequently resulted in the setting up of rival, "second" unions at the enterprise level to which management at once granted sole recognition. The period closes with an open red purge in 1949 and 1950 that put out of action those left-wing party and labor leaders who had been leading the resistance to the reverse course in labor reform. The attempt to establish industrial unionism went down to defeat, and Japanese workers were driven back into the framework of weak and isolated enterprise unions.

The events of the early occupation that are chronicled in this book have a special place in the labor history of Japan. They show that, contrary to the Western stereotype of Japan as the land of labor-capital harmony and worker docility, classes and class conflict underlie labor-capital relations in Japan, just as they do elsewhere in the industrialized world.

   MacArthur and Yoshida were confirming by their very actions against
the workers' movement in 1946 and 1947 that Japanese society was
riven by fundamental conflicts of interest between labor and capital,
and that the working class was on the move, determined to secure its
economic and political rights in the new society to be built. Whether
in their move toward revolutionary change during the first nine months
of occupation or in their drive for social-democratic reforms thereafter, the Japanese workers' anti-capitalist activism following the war
is incontestable—and fundamental to an understanding of the real history of the Japanese working class before and since.

*Japanese Workers and the Struggle for Power
1945–1947*

1

The Old Guard Digs In

Toward the end of the war the civilian leaders within Japan's ruling class began to fear that the specter of working-class revolution that had been haunting them for fifty years would come to life in the moment of defeat. From the time that capitalism had called a working class into existence, the leaders of big business and government had cooperated in the systematic suppression of worker efforts to organize, in explicit recognition of the hostility underneath all the talk of harmony and cooperation between labor and capital. Under no circumstances could they allow the hostility bred by miserable wages and working conditions and wasted lives to erupt into the class war which they feared would put an end to capitalism in Japan. Yet in 1945 their ability to keep social order and stability was under threat from two sides—from the chaos sure to follow a last-ditch fight on the home islands and from the Allied policy of economic and political democratization announced at Potsdam.

Ridden by fear of social revolution and apprehensive about Allied intentions, certain members of the civilian leadership had early begun to consult among themselves about how best to meet the coming disaster. The Konoe Memorial of February 1945, which Yoshida Shigeru had a part in drafting, took as its basic premise that: "More than defeat itself, what we must be most concerned about from the standpoint of preserving the *kokutai* [national polity, i.e., the family state with the emperor as its supreme symbol and head] is the communist revolution which may accompany defeat."[1] The Memorial urged an early surrender as the best chance for staving off the revolutionary uprising that they anticipated should there be an Allied invasion, but it offered no plan toward that end.

The atomic bombing of Hiroshima and Nagasaki, followed by the U.S.S.R.'s entry into the war, brought the early surrender, and U.S. forces found a functioning government solidly in command upon their belated landing two weeks afterwards. The contrast with Germany— where as the Allied armies advanced factory soviets and anti-fascist committees had sprung up to assert popular control over the government and the economy in the wake of the disintegrating Nazi apparatus—is instructive. Because of the early surrender, the apparatus of oppression in Japan remained intact at the crucial moment, laying to rest the specter of communism rising out of the ashes of total defeat that had so worried Japan's civilian leaders and many Western ones as well. But now the leaders of big business and government had the contradictory task before them of reasserting their traditional privileges and powers over the Japanese people even while trying to demonstrate to the American occupiers their indispensability to the reconstruction of a democratic and peace-loving country.

Japan's ruling class—having for several decades been a shifting coalition of the leaders of big business, government, and the military— underwent a change in composition at the end of World War II. The military disappeared as a major partner in the coalition, to be replaced by conservative party politicians who quickly gained in power as the Americans carried out a series of political reforms. The members of this reconstituted ruling coalition soon became known as the "old guard" after their role as determined defenders of the old regime. They had deep roots in the prewar structure of economic and political power and they adhered as strictly as circumstances would permit to prewar conservatism in their planning for postwar Japan.

The old guard hoped to convince the American occupiers that they could bring to fruition the "democratic" traditions of the 1920s, when party politics enjoyed a brief moment of liberalization, and could therefore be trusted to live up to the ideals of Potsdam. They hoped that the Allies would forget that the liberalism of the twenties had evaporated in the thirties almost without a trace, when the world depression started Japan's plunge into the "dark valley." The strong steps taken at that time to preserve Japan's position in the world revealed that political power lay in the emperor system and economic power in the *zaibatsu*—the great financial and industrial combines corresponding to the corporate giants of the U.S. and Europe.

That the old guard in the moment of military defeat would turn to the expedients of the past to demonstrate Japan's civilization and enlightenment to a skeptical West was both natural and predictable. But the tactic of erecting the old liberal and democratic facade over the enduring political framework of elite rule and monopoly control was not likely to work unless the old guard had the good will of the American occupiers. And that they would not have for some time.

Nevertheless, big-business and government leaders could do much to prepare for their own survival in the days between surrender and the actual onset of Allied control. They took a number of defensive actions in August and September that would have lasting consequences for Japan's democratization. Their political goals were to disassociate the emperor from the war and identify the imperial institution with the people's hopes and needs, to display enough of the democratic trappings of Taishō to satisfy the Allies, to prevent an outbreak from below by a calculated intensification of police activity, and to entrench the power of the administrative bureaucracy. Economically the old guard sought to dismantle the system of wartime controls over the economy, to recapitalize and resupply the zaibatsu with government funds and stockpiles of raw materials, and to promote the retrenchment and rationalization of the economy in preparation for an anticipated zaibatsu revival.

The Political Response

Refurbishing the Emperor System

The Suzuki cabinet accepted responsibility for the military defeat and resigned on the day of the broadcast of the Imperial Edict on the End of the War. The emperor designated his uncle, Prince Higashikuni Naruhiko, an army general, to organize a transition cabinet to prepare for the arrival of the occupation forces. This choice was made in part to forestall a military rebellion against the edict of surrender. But much more important was to be the cabinet's role in bolstering the emperor system by simultaneously presenting it to the Allied powers as a liberal and benevolent institution in Japanese society and mobilizing it to provide ideological justification for the sacrifice and suppression of the interests of the Japanese people.

The Higashikuni cabinet was a vague non-party coalition representing the prewar "liberalism" of the old guard, and its resemblance to the transcendent national unity cabinets of the thirties was strong. The national interest the cabinet stood for was not unity behind impending war, but unity in defeat in defense of an inviolable national polity purged of military extremism. The liberal pose the Higashikuni cabinet struck was for the edification of the Allied policy makers, especially for the "Japan crowd" in the State Department clustered around the prewar ambassador, Joseph Grew. The old guard looked to the Japan crowd for succor because it advocated lenient treatment of Japan and the restoration of the prewar liberals to power. Figures with ties to the Japan crowd like Shigemitsu Mamoru (the Foreign Minister) and Yoshida Shigeru (who soon replaced him) were to be the leaders in the postwar liberalization of Japanese politics. Ex-bureaucrats for the most part, such men hardly constituted an independent liberal element in its own right.[2]

More representative of the spirit of the Higashikuni cabinet were its more notorious figures like Home Minister Yamazaki Iwao (a wartime police official and one-time high official in the secret police) and Special Cabinet Advisers Kodama Yoshio and Ishiwara Kanji. The "liberal" Higashikuni cabinet rallied to the defense of the emperor and national polity and did not hesitate to use the political police against popular stirrings and the efforts of the left to organize.[3]

Since the throne had been an impregnable barrier against which earlier attempts to extend liberalism and democracy had broken, it was crucial for the old guard to absolve the emperor from any tinge of popular blame for the disastrous policies of the past. The emperor's advisers with the aid of the Higashikuni cabinet began a propaganda campaign designed to demonstrate that the emperor had all the while been suffering deeply at the people's sorrows and trials and steadfastly looking out for their welfare.[4]

This had been the message of the Imperial Edict on the End of the War (broadcast 15 August), which fairly oozed with the emperor's paternal solicitude for his good and loyal subjects. He identified himself with their inmost feelings, and spoke of the solemn obligation which had been handed down by his ancestors to strive for the security and well-being of his subjects. He said that he was protecting the national polity and strongly admonished his loyal subjects, in whose sincerity he trusted, that it was "of the greatest importance not to become agitated and allow your emotions to overflow, to fall recklessly into fraternal strife, to depart from the great moral principles, or to lose the confidence of the world, but to hold firmly to the inheritance of posterity of the whole nation as one family." He called for further sacrifices in the name of the national polity, and exhorted his subjects to devote their collective strength to construction for the future.[5]

That had only been the opening shot. On 20 August the public was informed that the emperor had ordered Higashikuni to devote attention to improving the public welfare. Constant expressions of imperial concern over the critical shortages of food and housing followed, as did well-publicized examples of imperial largesse.[6] In a rescript on 24 August calling for the convening of an extraordinary session of the Diet for 4 September, the emperor called on the Japanese people to "make manifest the innate glory of Japan's national polity."[7] In his address to the Diet session he "stated that his relationship with all Japanese as one family had been preserved."[8]

The Higashikuni cabinet took pains to shift the blame for defeat upon the Japanese people, an imputation it encapsulated in the official phrase *ichioku sō zange* (collective confession of guilt of the 100 million).[9] Higashikuni, in his first cabinet press conference on 28 August, said "I believe that collective confession of guilt by the whole nation is the first step toward our country's reconstruction, the first step toward our country's unity."[10] Despite the mistakes made by the government and the military, no single person or group, least of all the emperor, should be singled out for blame. The primary responsibility rested not with the military, the bureaucracy, or the zaibatsu, but with the people, who had failed in their determination. According to Higashikuni the true cause of defeat lay inward, in "a lowering of national morality," and henceforth officials and the people in general must unite and strive to preserve the national polity.[11]

The Apparatus of Control

Ideology alone would not be enough. Above all, the old guard had to keep its administrative grip on the populace. This it could do because at the most critical time after surrender it was able to turn to its advantage a system of controls reaching far down into the individual household. Figure 1.1 depicts the situation in late September 1945, when SCAP (Supreme Command for the Allied Powers) was just beginning to organize and the old instiutions as yet remained virtually intact. These channels of elite control would not disappear instantaneously with the issuance of a directive of dissolution by SCAP. Their dissolution was a long drawn-out process in most instances, and business and government leaders were making effective use of many of them—formally or informally—as late as the formation of the Katayama cabinet in May 1947.

Certain elements of the pre-surrender power structure are omitted from the chart: the military for obvious reasons and the politicians and palace officials because they ultimately depended upon others for access to the levers of power. Moreover, the cabinet, the political capstone of this structure, was less a true decision-making body than the organ for articulating and implementing policies hammered out between big-business leaders and top government bureaucrats in the

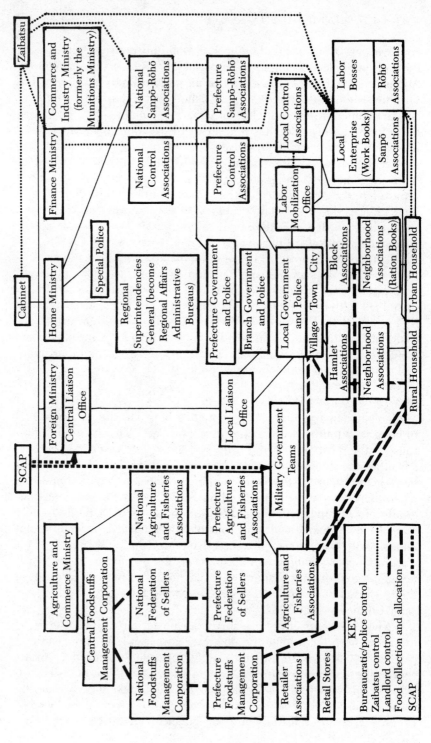

Figure 1.1. The Apparatus of Control.

various ministries.[12] (On the other hand, the channels of control available to the landlords, merchants, and local officials at the village level as well as [to a lesser extent] to their urban counterparts are depicted, because the ability of those local men of power to maintain social order and stability was absolutely vital to Japan's rulers.) Also, since both the ordinary police and the secret police were centralized under the Home Ministry and closely coordinated with government administrative offices at all levels down to the locality, they are not shown separately on the chart.[13]

Figure 1.1 is intended to depict, therefore, the bare bones of the apparatus of elite control over Japanese society at a time when the ruling class faced two equally grave challenges—from the Japanese people and from the Allied occupation. Just how effectively the old guard used the resources still available to them after the surrender will be seen.

The linchpin of the structure was the Home Ministry, with its ability to control social and political life through the local government and police. The 220,000 to 240,000 neighborhood associations blanketing the country, to which the authorities assigned rural and urban households under a system of collective responsibility, made it extremely difficult to express opposition. The petty bosses appointed by the authorities to head the urban block associations and the local men of power who dominated the rural hamlet associations had face-to-face contact with the member constituent households, and availed the government and police of their intimate knowledge of local conditions.[14]

Urban neighborhood associations had more power over the household than did the rural ones because the government used them as rationing agencies for staple foods (which were naturally more abundant in the countryside) and other scarce commodities. Since the associations held the ration books and distributed the food, the bosses' leverage over local inhabitants increased with the severity of the food shortages.[15] But although the rural neighborhood associations might have been less effective as instruments of control than urban ones, that was compensated for by the fact that personalized top-down control had long existed in the traditional organs of local government and in the agricultural organizations. Both were dominated by the landlord stratum and were amenable to the government's manipulation.

The landlord stratum gained new powers during the war when the government combined the prewar Producers' Cooperatives and Farmers' Associations into a national system of Agricultural Associations under the Agriculture and Forestry Ministry. These the government used for collection of staple foods for urban rationing. The central government set the national quotas for staple-food collections and assigned them to the prefectures, which in turn assigned them to village authorities for actual levying of quotas upon individual households. The household had to sell its quota to a designated purchasing agent, almost always the local Agricultural Association, at the offical price. Landlord manipulation of quotas was common, and the poorer peasants carried the heaviest burden, even though government efforts to subsidize non-landlord production late in the war somewhat improved the economic position of tenants and owner-cultivators. The system allowed much produce to be diverted, with official connivance, into the black market, and local men of power made considerable profits.[16]

Another agency reaching into all households was the labor-mobilization office, which allocated labor to industry through the local control associations. In order to cope with increasing labor shortages in industry, the government carried out a national registration of the labor force eventually extending to all males aged twelve to sixty and all females aged twelve to forty.[17] The Home Ministry administered the mobilization office, which was generally located in the local police station. This office kept one of the labor workbooks which all workers were required to have; the employer held the other. The national registration and the workbook gave the police and local government a valuable tool for surveillance and control that could be coordinated with the neighborhood associations to put pressure on the recalcitrant by threatening them with conscription.[18]

The police also organized and supervised *Sanpō* (Sangyō Hōkoku Kai, Patriotic Industrial Association) and *Rōhō* (Rōmu Hōkoku Kai, Patriotic Labor Association) in cooperation with enterprise management and labor bosses. Rōhō amounted to the semi-official recognition of the prewar labor-boss system that controlled casual labor for zaibatsu employers; and Sanpō represented the institutionalization of the prewar zaibatsu-sponsored works councils. Originating in the desire of business and government leaders to counter the growing trade union consciousness in the twenties and thirties, the works-council movement had promoted labor-capital collaboration by means of an ideology portraying the firm as one big family. The right-wing labor leaders and bosses found both the ideology and organizational structure congenial, easing the government's task of integrating their organizations into Sanpō and Rōhō. Sanpō enrolled the more or less permanent employees in an enterprise and Rōhō handled the casual workers dominated by the labor bosses, thus preserving the existing division of power.[19]

Professor Ōkōchi Kazuo has described the system as follows:

Sanpō units were organized in every workshop by the military clique, right-wing bureaucrats, and great war industrialists, with the collaboration of right-wing labor leaders, using coercive methods on the lines of the Nazi Labor Front. There was no pretense of voluntary action. The object of the organization was to compel the workers to submit unconditionally to forced labor, overwork, and low wages in war time. It included all the employees of every establishment, and, like its Nazi counterpart, was run on military lines, with a hierarchy of rank and with discipline strictly enforced. Such discipline was barely maintained until the end of the war by the strong arm of the "thought" police or political high police and military police, reinforced by appeals to ultra-nationalistic and imperialistic ideology.[20]

Since Sanpō encompassed approximately 6.4 million industrial workers and Rōhō about 2 to 2.5 million casual laborers, the police were able between the two of them to exercise control over the great bulk of the industrial labor force, which approximated 10 million in 1945.[21]

It is striking that the police were charged with both labor surveillance and labor mobilization. The zaibatsu relied on the Home Ministry to mobilize the industrial labor force and coerce it into working under the worst of conditions. Business leaders were only too happy to have the Home Ministry take responsibility for assuring a docile and available labor force, and the Home Ministry was not reluctant to do so since the mechanism of economic control overlapped with and strengthened the government's social and political controls.[22]

Big business retained its managerial prerogatives throughout the war, with the exception of certain defense plants taken over by the military directly. But personnel management became a major concern as the war dragged on, especially in respect to labor indoctrination, discipline, and productivity. Under wartime conditions workers fared badly in almost every way, suffering increasing shortages, reductions in real wages, and lengthening of the work day. Understandably, the will to work flagged, and what had at first been accepted as the normal difficulties of life for workers degenerated into cruel deprivation and harsh exploitation. To compound the problem for management, the labor force changed in composition as the government conscripted able-bodied skilled male workers for military service and allocated women, men unfit for military service, the young and elderly, and even Koreans and Chinese as replacements.[23]

In an attempt to overcome these problems, big business used Sanpō for indoctrinating workers with corporate notions about the structure of industry. In accordance with an ideology in which the enterprise was another embodiment of Japan's unique family system, the Sanpō hierarchy paralleled the enterprise hierarchy, with the head of the enterprise being the head of the local Sanpō association. All employ-

ees and company officials—management, white-collar, blue-collar—
were to join and assume their prescribed places in the hierarchy. That
conflicts might arise between the paternalistic managers and their dependent workers was specifically denied. Sanpō supposedly obviated
class-based organizations like unions, since it resolved the petty self-
ishness of classes into a greater harmony of labor-capital collaboration
in service of the emperor and the national polity. Regardless of whether
or not the ideas peddled through Sanpō convinced the workers, the
organization gave employers another means to keep a watchful eye on
workers and an ideological justification for their efforts to tighten factory discipline and increase work loads.[24]

No doubt many in industry and government would have liked to
retain Sanpō and Rōhō as weapons against postwar worker militance,
but in the end they had no choice but to let Sanpō die, which it did
on 30 September 1945. First of all, SCAP was sure to mark Sanpō for
abolition as an undemocratic organization. More practically, big business had little economic need of a state organization for mobilizing
labor power in a time of wholesale factory closures and mass unemployment. After all, the zaibatsu could always try to reorganize the
associations into company unions and hem them in by such features of
prewar industrial relations as works councils and labor bosses. Many
zaibatsu made the attempt, thereby helping to bequeath the doctrine
of labor-capital collaboration that Sanpō and Rōhō had promoted during the war to a wide variety of conservative unions and to the boss-
controlled labor organizations outside the enterprise.[25]

Continued Political Repression

The uncanny quiet of the first weeks of occupation was due more to
the continued enforcement of the authoritarian controls than to anything else. The old guard had never wholly trusted ideological means,
and had long ago made recourse to an efficient apparatus of oppression
centralized in the state bureaucracy and police. Accordingly, in the
moment of defeat, the government backed up its ideological appeals
for loyalty and forbearance with an attempt to intensify police enforcement of laws against dissent and to heighten police suppression of
communists and potential radicals.[26]

These acts were not merely the last twists and turns of the military
or the Suzuki cabinet which had resigned on 15 August. The cabinet
which Higashikuni organized on 17 August not only reaffirmed the
validity of the Peace Preservation Law (Chian Iji Hō) on 23 August,
but also decided to expand and reinforce the power of the police preparatory to military demobilization.[27]

SCAP was slow to act against the police and the power of the authorities to suppress dissent. No doubt many Japanese took this as evidence that the power of the old guard would continue after the war. Although SCAP issued a statement declaring freedom of speech and the press as early as 10 September, it accomplished little substantial dismantling of authoritarian controls until October. For example, SCAP did not get around to the abolition of the *Tokkō* (Tokubetsu Kōtō Keisatsu Bu, Special Higher Police Section), the Military Police (Kempeitai), and other political police until the week following the resignation of the Higashikuni cabinet on 5 October, two months after Japan's surrender.[28]

SCAPIN-93, the famous civil liberties directive composed in Washington ordering the removal of restrictions on political, civil, and religious liberties, was not issued until 4 October, seven weeks after surrender, thus giving the old guard a critical interlude in which to consolidate its position. In accordance with SCAPIN-93, the Peace Preservation Law of 1925 and its revision in 1941, the Public Peace Police Law of 1900 (Chian Keisatsu Hō), the Protection and Surveillance Law for Thought Offenses of 1936 (Shisō Han Hogo Kansatsu Hō), and many (but not all) similar laws were abrogated on October 15.[29]

SCAPIN–93 was much more than a "bill of rights," as it has been called, ordering elimination of restrictions on civil liberties. It also required: 1) release by 10 October of all political prisoners and all persons whose freedom was restricted in any way under provisions of such laws; 2) abolition of all organizations or agencies created to carry out provisions of those laws; and 3) a purge of and prohibition against future activity by all high government and police officials and the personnel of those agencies engaged in enforcing restrictions on political, civil, and religious liberties. The directive prohibited mistreatment of all persons currently imprisoned or restricted under the laws, and ordered the preservation and protection of all records of the agencies involved.[30] This last stipulation showed some SCAP awareness of the bureaucracy's deliberate and systematic destruction of potentially incriminating government and police records.

The promulgation of SCAPIN-93 on 4 October provided the occasion for the press to force Home Minister Yamazaki to admit publicly on that same day that indeed "the secret police are at present still in action."[31] The cabinet's reaction to the directive was little short of frantic. It dispatched former Prime Minister Konoe Fumimarō to plead (in vain) with MacArthur for delay in the democratization policy and in the enforcement of SCAPIN–93 on the grounds that the result would be an immediate communist takeover. The cabinet appealed to the emperor for a stay of the SCAP order to release political prisoners, but he could do nothing. Before resigning on 5 October, the cabinet even requested permission from SCAP to expand the police, which SCAP refused on 11 October.[32]

The SCAP attack on Yamazaki and the police apparatus which he headed presented the government with an unresolvable dilemma. Ogata Taketora, Chief Cabinet Secretary, argued that the cabinet could hardly punish Yamazaki for carrying out a policy the cabinet members all supported.[33] Rather than making Yamazaki the scapegoat, the cabinet chose to resign over the principle of SCAP restrictions on the use of police powers. The cabinet resignation underscored the seriousness with which the government viewed the dismantling of the social controls that had been painstakingly erected over some fifty years. It was not so much the abrogation of wartime laws and controls that distressed the cabinet. They had already allowed important parts of the wartime controls to lapse in advance of SCAPIN-93. What they could not tolerate was destruction of the legal foundation stones of elite rule that had been laid down by peacetime governments from 1900 to 1930—that is, the Public Peace Police Law, the Peace Preservation Law, and the regulations and agencies providing for their enforcement. These laws had provided the bedrock of big-business and government control right through the "liberal" era of Taishō democracy, when the political police under Home Ministry guidance began in earnest to fill jail cells with leftist political prisoners.

Next to these restrictions on their police powers, the old guard feared the result of the SCAP-ordered release of political prisoners and the lifting of restraints on the activity of those who were politically suspect. SCAPIN-93 ordered that this be done by 10 October, and Higashikuni's fruitless attempts to hinder release only delayed matters slightly. The succeeding Shidehara cabinet acted upon the directive, but deliberately misconstrued the meaning of the term "political prisoner" that had been used in the directive to mean only that very small number who had been convicted for organizing or belonging to an illegal political party. This they did in order to lay the blame for freeing communists at SCAP's feet, while crediting the emperor with the pardon of all the others.

On 10 October the government released the 2,500 to 3,000 persons who fitted their definition, out of whom perhaps 800, most of them communists, had actually been in jail. The rest had been under house arrest or some lesser form of detention.[34] A State Department report dated 30 November 1945 pointed out, "In contrast some 320,000 prisoners were pardoned by an Imperial amnesty of 17 October 1945 . . . In addition, more than 600,000 others who had previously been released were restored to their civil rights."[35] It is easy to understand why the old guard might have feared the resumption of activity by nearly a million dissenters.

The Bureaucratic Defense

Among the first steps the government took to protect important bureaucrats and the reemerging "liberals" was the destruction of incriminating records.[36] Next came extensive shifting about of administrative personnel in order to prevent SCAP from gathering compromising information from local people. The government internally reshuffled officials like prefectural governors and school officials on a large scale, but gave the police special attention, transferring over two-thirds of them.[37]

When the government learned in September that SCAP would issue a purge directive in early October aimed at key officials and agencies like the police and Sanpō (but especially the Tokkō), it resorted to external transfers as well as to encouraging discreet resignations followed by reappointment to unrelated government posts.[38] These tactics were so effective that top Tokkō officials soon reappeared in important posts in the Ministries of Education, of Commerce and Industry, and of Welfare (including the post of chief of the Labor Division). They even got back into the Home Ministry, notwithstanding the SCAP ban on reappointments to this and other police-related organizations.[39]

The old guard greatly feared the corrosive effect of rule by an Allied military government, and the government sought to limit official contact between SCAP and the Japanese people, and to control the channels available to occupation authorities for policy implementation. The framework set up to achieve these ends was the War Termination Central Liaison Bureau organized under the Shigemitsu Foreign Ministry on 26 August. After Yoshida Shigeru became Foreign Minister on 17 September, he reorganized this bureau as the Central Liaison Office. Yoshida understood the critical importance of monopolizing the liaison machinery, and accordingly expanded the office's functions and set up a system of Local Liaison Offices throughout the country. Even though the Central Liaison Office was purely Japanese in inspiration and organization, SCAP accepted it as its medium for control without apparent objection.[40]

SCAP described its purpose in this way: "The Supreme Commander transmits his instruction through directives and memoranda to the Japanese Government. Directives and memoranda are transmitted through the Liaison Officer, G-2, to the Central Liaison Office (CLO) of the Japanese Government. The latter directs the proper course of instructions to the appropriate ministries for compliance."[41] This organization was in a strategic position, and under Yoshida's guidance became an effective barrier between SCAP and the Japanese.[42]

The Central Liaison Office was able to monopolize channels of communication and authority between SCAP and the Japanese people because SCAP was critically short of qualified administrative personnel, not to speak of administrators competent in Japanese.[43] SCAP's own description of the relationship of its civil affairs teams to the Japanese government makes the point quite well. The civil affairs duty of the commanders in the field was basically to check compliance with SCAP directives routed through the Central Liaison Office, and not to "issue orders to, administer, or direct the operation of any agency of the Japanese Government."[44] For checking compliance, teams were established "in each of the forty-six prefectures and one in each of the eight regional headquarters created for administrative purposes. Some 500 officers, 500 civilian specialists, and 2,300 enlisted men staffed these teams."[45]

John M. Maki has called the Central Liaison Office "a brilliant administrative and political device" which served the bureaucracy well. In Maki's experience, far from the least of its services was intelligence.

Not only is it privy to all matters currently of interest to GHQ [General Headquarters], SCAP: it is also in a position to maintain at least informal dossiers on each and every official with whom it deals—and even a knowledge of the pro- or anti-Japanese attitudes of certain officials can be of great use to the Japanese Government. Naturally, it is also in a key position to observe the individual and administrative rivalries and conflicts in GHQ, SCAP.[46]

In contrast to the indirect and inefficient way in which SCAP attempted to carry out the Allied mandate, the old guard had the use of a highly centralized governmental structure that reached down to the neighborhood associations and pulled together in one chain of command the various strands of authority that the central government held over the local groups binding the individual households to the state. SCAP was aware of the anti-democratic potential of the whole edifice of control from the Home Ministry through the Regional Superintendencies General on down to the neighborhood associations, and planned to abolish all three.[47]

In anticipation of SCAP abolition of the Superintendencies, the Japanese government on 28 September requested permission to establish Regional Affairs Administrative Bureaus in their stead. Although this amounted to little more than a change of names, SCAP granted final approval of it on 3 November.[48] SCAP's understanding of the purposes of the new Bureaus was:

Although the affairs of the bureau are under the supervision of the Ministry of Home Affairs, the Prime Minister and Cabinet Ministers give directions to these officials. Supplanting the function of a wartime organization the present bureaus are to coordinate and adjust within each respective region all the industrial, economic and all peacetime aspects of local administration.[49]

Sweeping powers indeed!—for which SCAP's justification was that the Regional Bureaus were potentially useful.[50]

The neighborhood associations persisted essentially unchanged as the lowest level of government administration well past the first year of occupation. A State Department study written in November 1945 reflected an early awareness that the associations continued to wield considerable influence and represented a danger to democratization,[51] but SCAP did not abolish them until April 1947. The associations' power during the occupation derived, much as before, from being the distribution agency for rationed goods. When families depended upon rationing for survival, the association bosses and their government superiors had virtual life-and-death powers over them.[52]

The Home Ministry, too, retained a large measure of its far-reaching administrative powers long after October 1945 when SCAP issued the "bill-of-rights" directive. SCAP finally abolished it at the remarkably late date of 31 December 1947. In truth, the Home Ministry—through the Regional Affairs Administrative Bureaus, the prefectural governors' offices, and the neighborhood associations—was the agency that "coordinated and adjusted" all facets of local political and economic activity for the central government, including the police.[53]

The Economic Response

Big Business Calls for Laissez-Faire

During the war, the readiness of big business to defer to state efforts to centralize and make more total the means of popular repression and mobilization stood in sharp contrast to its resistance against bureaucratic attempts to control and rationalize the national economy for the war effort. T. A. Bisson has argued that the wartime economic controls were nothing like a harnessing of the zaibatsu to a military-dominated, all-out war economy. Rather, the zaibatsu wrote their own program for economic mobilization. Instead of industry being subordinated to bureaucratic and military control under supervision of the cabinet ministries, the existing zaibatsu cartels were turned into official Control Associations with powers over the allocation of materials, labor, and capital.[54] When Prime Minister Tōjō Hideki later succeeded in centralizing government administrative control over war industry in the Munitions Ministry in 1943, top zaibatsu executives again filled the key posts and used the new machinery for their own interests.[55]

Zaibatsu domination in this area was exceedingly important, according to Bisson, because:

Priorities, the factor of life and death for enterprises in a controlled economy, would be available in largest measure for industries engaged in this sector of the national economy. Raw materials, machine tools labor, motive power, and capital—all were being channeled into this field. Here, moreover, the door was wide open to the big companies for the most drastic program of absorption of smaller competing or subsidiary firms.[56]

Even the nationalization of industry that the cabinet of General Koiso Kuniaki carried out in 1945 merely enabled the zaibatsu to shift financial responsibility for wartime destruction of plant to the treasury and to obtain a government guarantee of profits.[57]

Dr. Sherwood Fine, who served SCAP throughout the occupation as Director of Economics and Planning in the Economic and Scientific Section and had detailed knowledge of the workings of the economy, has confirmed Bisson's view.

Ties with the government and military were close and the impact of the zaibatsu upon Japanese economic policy was marked even though numerous conflicts developed with the overventuresome military clique not properly sensitive to the stable political and economic framework required by large-scale industry. The partnership between the government and the zaibatsu was mutually satisfactory entailing assured profits, markets and sources of raw material supply in exchange for an expanding political prominence and military sway. While it is difficult to characterize the Japanese economy, it appeared to represent a form of "totalitarian state capitalism" wherein industry while operating under profit incentives nonetheless was obligated to serving [sic] the ends of the state.[58]

Yet, to a troublesome degree, the wartime controls placed shackles on zaibatsu freedom to seek profits and expansion as they saw fit. Even the shrewdest manipulation of the economic controls by zaibatsu executives could not reverse the shortages, unpredictably changing priorities, and complicated bureaucracy of a wartime economy. The military and administrative bureaucracies were formidable rivals of the zaibatsu throughout the war, constantly maneuvering to increase their ability to direct the economy at zaibatsu expense. What success they achieved was owing to their use of the control legislation and the implementing legislation as their weapons. So from the war's end to the beginning of the Shidehara cabinet in early October, demands to abolish bureaucratic controls and return to a "free" economy guided by the principles of "laissez-faire" swept the business world.[59]

Besides being a quite natural principle to turn to after years of regulation, laissez-faire appealed greatly to business leaders who associated it with the economic prosperity of Taishō. In the economy, no less than in politics, Taishō "liberalism" appeared to be the answer. The demand for the revocation of controls in the name of competitive private enterprise in a free-market economy in fact expressed the desire to restore the ability of the zaibatsu to dictate the terms of market exchange by means of their immense economic power.

A return to a free economy might have seemed a straight forward matter of abolishing controls and returning to a reliance upon the market,[60] but that was not so. When it came to what actual steps should be taken toward the resurrection of a free economy, the task became difficult, for the gap between ideology and reality yawned wide. Yet the ideology cannot be dismissed out of hand. It did provide a rallying cry which in the early postwar months united the business world behind a program (however vague) with potential appeal to the Allies.

First of all, in the same way that government leaders hoped to curry favor with the Allies by resurrecting the formal but empty liberalism of Taishō, so zaibatsu leaders hoped to find favor for Taishō-style laissez-faire and forestall an attack on the zaibatsu. Their optimism was encouraged, no doubt, by their prewar contracts with American business and politics in which the ideological keynote had always been free private enterprise operating in unregulated markets, while the reality had always been toleration for the powers of corporate monopoly.

More important, as a practical matter a return to Taishō-style economic liberalism offered a considerable degree of self-protection: protection against domination by the government bureaucracy itself and against SCAP or a leftist government using the economic controls for its own ends. As long as the basic state machinery for centralized economic planning and regulation remained intact, the zaibatsu were vulnerable to economic and political threats from all three directions.

Zaibatsu leaders had no intention of relinquishing the tremendous power over the economy that had accrued to them as private businessmen through the operation of the wartime controlled economy.

They considered government regulation to be perfectly compatible with a free economy so long as private business applied it through its monopolies, cartels, and business organizations, but they wanted to rid themselves of the state controls for coordinating and directing a command economy that the bureaucracy had used in an attempt to wrest control of war production from private hands. It was not the existence of state economic agencies per se that worried them, but the locus of economic power. In fact, as long as private business ran the economy, business leaders were quite ready to use parts of the state control machinery for their own ends—which is exactly what they eventually did.

In any event, the nucleus of the control apparatus was destroyed, though certain subordinate parts of it remained for some time. That the centralizing legislation and agencies went first made it exceedingly difficult if not impossible for SCAP to influence the economy, much less be in command of events. Instead it was constantly reacting to situations created by big-business and government leaders, who closed ranks when confronted by SCAP's program of economic democratization. Selective decontrol as it happened did shift economic power decisively into private hands. Big-business leaders thereby gained an advantage in the battle to decide who would determine the course of economic recovery—SCAP, a popular government, or big business.

Allied Economic Policy

Several items in the Potsdam Declaration boded ill for the leaders of the zaibatsu, particularly paragraph eleven, which read:

11. Japan shall be permitted to maintain such industries as will sustain her economy and permit the exaction of just reparations in kind, but not those industries which would enable her to re-arm for war. To this end, access to, as distinguished from control of raw materials shall be permitted. Eventual Japanese participation in world trade relations shall be permitted. [61]

The industries which would enable Japan to rearm for war were those on which the zaibatsu had come to rest during the previous decade. To reduce chemicals, iron and steel, ship-building, mining, refining, and other war-related industry to an ancillary position in a truncated Japanese economy would strike at the heart of zaibatsu power, for it meant the permanent institutionalization of a low-level economy based on light industry and agriculture, with access to raw materials and world trade only on sufferance of the victorious Allies, the U.S. in particular.

Whatever the lack of precision with which the Allies declared their plans for the reconstruction of Japan's economy, it is difficult to believe that business leaders failed to understand U.S. intentions in respect to the international economy. Before the war the Americans had spelled out their terms for Japan's reintegration into the world economy in the series of notes that the U.S. sent to the Japanese government in 1941 reiterating its long-standing policy of subordinating Japanese economic interests in a U.S.-dominated Asia.[62]

After the war the Americans pursued this end in a sophisticated way through a policy of combined economic and political democratization for Japan. From the American point of view, what could be better than furthering U.S. international economic interests through the democratization of Japanese society, especially since the latter would be sure to find Allied favor for American intentions? Effecting a partial transfer of economic and political power to farmers, workers, the urban middle class, and small- and medium-sized businesses promised permanently to cut the zaibatsu and their government allies down to size by erecting internal barriers against the continuance of the cheap labor that had been a central element in the zaibatsu rise to international economic power in the interwar period.[63] In part, the U.S. intended to attain its economic interests in Asia by forcing completion of Japan's bourgeois-democratic revolution.

The old guard approached surrender in the spirit of compromise. Believing the U.S. to be fundamentally opposed to Japan's communization and cognizant of the revolutionary potential of radical reform, government and business leaders tried to present themselves as the only bulwark of liberalism and capitalism in Japan. They were ready to accept a degree of economic and political subordination to the U.S. as the price for their own retention of power, but should the Americans turn out to be serious about democratization, this hoped-for compromise would be destroyed. This accounts for the shock that members of the old guard like Yoshida felt when SCAP showed it was serious about democratization by releasing communists from prison and encouraging unionization in October.[64]

Allied policy might have directed the carrying out of sweeping economic reforms such as zaibatsu dissolution, encouragement of labor organization, disbanding of cartels, and relaxation of state controls, but SCAP saw its overall responsibility for Japan's economy as distinctly limited: "In supervising Japan's peaceful economic activities the major considerations are: (1) maintaining a minimum peacetime economy, (2) controlling all foreign trade and (3) continuing such economic controls and rationing systems as are necessary to avoid acute economic distress and to assure a fair distribution of domestic and imported supplies."[65] In pursuance of the third objective, SCAP issued Directive Number 3 on 22 September, which among other things "instructed the Japanese Government to stimulate the immediate maximum production of all commodities essential to the feeding, clothing and housing of the population, and of producers goods necessary to the output of these commodities."[66] SCAP clearly had no intention at the outset of assuming responsibility for economic recovery. Stated policy was to leave responsibility in the hands of the Japanese.[67]

"Laissez-Faire" in Action

On 3 September, the day after the signing of the surrender, Minister of Commerce and Industry Nakajima Chikuhei submitted a long list of wide-ranging questions to the heads of Japan's four major business associations, asking their views on the best way to approach the economic problems brought about by the defeat. Nakajima was one of the sons who together controlled the Nakajima Aircraft Company and the family conglomerate to which it belonged, the fifth largest of the zaibatsu.[68] He was certainly not presenting a plan to business for ratification, but asking business leaders to devise one for adoption by the government. The four associations were: *Nihon Keizai Renmei Kai* (Japan Economic League), *Jūyō Sangyō Kyōgikai* (Essential Industry Council), *Zenkoku Shōkō Keizai Kai Kyōgikai* (Commerce and Industry Economic Association), and *Shōkō Kumiai Chūō Kai* (Central Association of Commerce and Industry Groups).

Nakajima had divided the questions into two groups, one on "emergency matters" and a second on "basic matters." Due to the all-inclusiveness of the questions and the short time to answer, the four associations stated that they would limit themselves to answering only the first two items under "emergency matters." Nevertheless, their answer clearly foreshadowed the stand the business world would take toward most of the other issues raised by Nakajima.

Nakajima's long list of questions can be summarized briefly. The "emergency matters" concerned short-range problems associated with economic stabilization: 1) negotiations with the Allies and how best to present business needs; 2) war industry (reconversion, government financial policy, and indemnities); 3) civilian industry; 4) demobilization and unemployment; 5) finance (prices and administration); and 6) reparations (especially in connection with mining and manufacturing). The "fundamental matters" dealt with questions of long-range planning for economic reconstruction. They focused on: 1) priorities in planning economic recovery (especially the interrelationship of trade and the desired priorities in industrial reconstruction); 2) economic controls (policy toward existing rationing and distribution systems, and toward controls in general if deemed necessary); 3) attitudes concerning the founding of a central, autonomous business organization for purposes of continuing economic control and guidance; 4) functioning of local economies in Japan; and 5) business views of officialdom (its organization and operation).

The business organizations' joint answer on 8 September[69] showed that they saw the entire list of separate items outlined by Nakajima as an interrelated whole whose permanent solution would depend on two preconditions: rapid reentry into world trade, and internal industrial reconstruction on the basis of the development of a strong export industry (textiles) and expansion in heavy industry. As they saw it, access to world trade was imperative—for the import of raw materials for industry and food to make good Japan's agricultural deficiencies, as well as for the export of finished goods in order to pay for reparations and also vital imports.

They considered production for the domestic consumer market and for agriculture as primarily subsidiary concerns, important in relation to their contribution to economic and social stability. Stability, and not expansion of the consumer market, was their basic concern, and the four business organizations expressly emphasized light exports and heavy industry as the engines of postwar economic growth, as they had been in prewar years. Accordingly textiles, coal, electric power, and transport were singled out as priority sectors for economic reconstruction.[70]

Though not detailed in the business proposals, two roles were to be played by heavy industry. First, it would provide the base upon which a strong light export industry could be built; second, it would become the mainstay of Japan's economic power in the future. Light industrial exports would contribute to the growth of heavy industry as they did in Japan's early industrialization, by stimulating demand for heavy industrial products and by earning foreign exchange. Obviously, the four organizations were rejecting the Potsdam Declaration assumption of a low-level economy with a limited heavy industry.

Other proposals urged vehement opposition to the use of military scrip by the occupying powers, prompt release of war industry materials and equipment for use in reconstruction, and adoption of a strong, well-prepared stance in negotiations with the Allies, all the while insisting on the principle of Japan's autonomy in accordance with the Potsdam Declaration. Last, the four economic organizations concurred with the call for constructing a united and autonomous business association to exert guidance and control over the economy.

The *Keizai Dantai Rengō Keizai Taisaku Iinkai* (Federation of Economic Organizations' Policy Committee)—the parent organization of the most powerful of the postwar business organizations, Keidanren—was duly organized on 18 September. The Keizai Dantai Rengo Iinkai (Keidanren Committee), as it was soon renamed, went right to work conducting studies on a number of problems and set about framing the first detailed, written plans for reconstruction. The makeup of the Keidanren Committee was exactly what might be expected, a composite of the most important figures from the four business organizations Nakajima had approached and other top zaibatsu figures. Their blueprint for reconstruction stressed textile exports, and explicitly "expressed a positive zeal for an autonomous industrial reconstruction,"[71] that is, one under the direction of big business, and freed from bureaucratic control.[72]

In short, laissez-faire was to be the heart of the postwar reconstruction. Big business leaders intended to stimulate recovery by abolishing all price and distribution controls, and by massive capital investment in industry. They expected rationalization of war-related industries as they reconverted to peacetime production to create conditions for using the capital most effectively, and assumed that most of the funds for investment would come from government indemnity payments to war industries, a major demand of the Keidanren Committee.

The plans that these zaibatsu representatives made in September revealed that they intended cheap labor to be central once again in underwriting exports and capital accumulation by big bisiness. The very choice of the labor-intensive textile industry as the key for reviving the economy meant that they did not intend to use the expansion of the internal consumer economy to promote growth on the model of the New Deal. Rather, they saw the restoration of a "free" labor market as the counterpart of the restoration of private control over capital and resources—that is, a labor market marked by the absence of both government regulation and union organization.

In this sense, free labor is synonymous with cheap labor, since a worker without state protection and without unions must bargain with the buyers of labor—whether the business enterprise, the government, or a labor boss—individually. The worker is free to accept or reject the terms of employment offered by those immeasurably more powerful, but not to organize to improve those terms. But establishing free labor implied the need for measures of control—for cheap labor would no more just happen in postwar Japan because big business expressed a need for it than it had before the war—and measures of control would be sure to bring conflict with labor and with SCAP.

The views that the zaibatsu leaders expressed in September were unrealistic in many ways—about Allied policy on trade, reparations, and labor, for instance, and about the efficacy of the steps they proposed to take toward recovery. Their early optimism is difficult to explain since they were after all aware of the content of the Potsdam Declaration and ought to have appreciated the extent of the Allied plans to limit and reform Japan's economy. Perhaps it was little more than wishful thinking born of the times, but it did exist and influence their plans.[73]

Fujiyama Aiichirō, whose long big business career began in the twenties and outlasted the occupation, recalled "the feeling of relief that the Americans would work a severe penalty upon the military leaders and the police, so that industrial circles would be secure." He also noted that another cause of jubilation was anticipation of an early resumption of economic relations with the U.S. As for the business attitude toward America, "many industrialists in Karuizawa uncorked their champagne bottles and toasted the coming of a new 'industrialists' era'" upon hearing that the occupying power would be the U.S.[74]

The specific plans big-business and government leaders laid in September came to nothing as a result of SCAP's onslaught of democratization in late 1945. They were important, nonetheless, because they anticipated the position that the mainline conservatives would defend as the leaders of big business sought a workable program for a capitalist reconstruction. That the plans they made in September and October 1945 could not be accomplished at once did not mean that the goals behind them would be given up. In fact, the tenacity with which the conservatives held to the goal of a free economy constricted their vision and prevented their easy adaptation to the radically changed circumstances imposed by the SCAP reforms. The inability to make rapid adjustments contributed to the ad hoc economic slowdown that zaibatsu leaders resorted to during the first winter of occupation as the true scope and nature of SCAP's reforms became known.

The urgent tactical steps big business was pressing on the Higashikuni government were primarily to protect the zaibatsu from the consequences of the lost war and to lay the groundwork for their future preeminence in the revival of a peacetime economy. Those steps were essentially three: payment of indemnities, abolition of controls, and distribution of materials. Big business was in effect urging the government to liquidate the war ecomomy by turning all the proceeds over to private hands in order to finance and generally facilitate a capitalist reconstruction centered on textile exports and a buildup of heavy industry.

Indemnities

Following hard upon the recommendations of the four business federations to Nakajima concerning the postwar economic situation, the Committee on the Liquidation of the Munitions Companies (organized within the Nihon Keizai Renmei Kai) produced on 15 September a major document detailing the business program for government liquidation of war industry.[75] The Committee began by declaring this to be "the greatest problem," one demanding great haste in resolution. The Committee was aware that implementation of their proposals would intensify inflation, but urged the government to action anyway. Item 1 called for immediate wholesale liquidation of government insurance and other liabilities in cash. Item 3 called for the speedy release to private industry of the materials once slated for use by the munitions industry, if necessary by abolishing the distribution and control system for such strategic goods. The crux of the nine-point document was simple—the government should write off its financial claims on private industry resulting from liquidation of the munitions industry so that private industry could receive payment (in cash wherever possible) for their claims arising out of wartime operations. Furthermore, the government should divert useful stockpiles and materials to private industry before the Allies assumed control.

Controls

The prime targets of the zaibatsu push to abolish controls were the National General Mobilization Act, the control associations, and the Munitions Ministry. The Mobilization Act theoretically gave the government unlimited powers to regulate all aspects of industry including production, distribution, prices, wages, foreign trade, and stockpiling, and the control associations were used to decide actual priorities and allocations. The Munitions Ministry was set up later in the war in order to concentrate the authority over the operation of the war economy that had been divided among the services and ministries into one agency responsible for policy planning and decision making. The government also had enacted various laws and regulations for blocking bank accounts, controlling wages and prices, ordering collection of staple foods for rationing, and outlawing the black market. The system was far from perfect and began to break down under the strain of the deteriorating military situation near the end, but it was capable of being made to work—and that was why big business was anxious to do away with it.

In response to the demand for decontrol, the government set about reorganizing the administrative agencies concerned with economic planning, and either abolished or ceased to enforce the laws regulating the allocation of capital and materials. The Mobilization Act remained on the books for a time, but became a dead letter. The Munitions Ministry was abolished and replaced by the Ministry of Commerce and Industry when the Higashikuni cabinet was formed, and Nakajima was appointed minister. The government could dismantle the control machinery without greatly impairing the de facto zaibatsu coordination of the economy because big business still could have recourse to the combinations and agreements it had used for the same purposes before the controls were in place. One of Minister Nakajima's main purposes for calling the 3 September meeting of the four business organizations was to accomplish the full return to informal zaibatsu operation of the economy.

By SCAP's direct order, however, the control associations were not abolished. Instead they were returned to their pre-1943 status under which zaibatsu leaders fixed intra-industry allocations and in effect operated the control associations for the Ministry of Commerce and Industry.[76] The government also repeatedly attempted to abolish all price and distribution controls during the Higashikuni and Shidehara cabinets, regardless of the harm to ordinary consumers. SCAP refused to allow it, but the government's lax enforcement accomplished nearly the same thing, to which the flourishing black market bore witness.[77]

Notwithstanding the fears of big business, retention of the control associations did not enable SCAP to exert its control over the economy. SCAP was unprepared to direct the economy, having neither the personnel nor the technical capacity to supervise the uses to which the associations would be put. SCAP's failure to use the associations gave to the zaibatsu by default a nearly unbreakable hold on the economy. Such wartime constraints as the bureaucracy and the military had managed to place on zaibatsu autonomy had been abolished, yet the means for the zaibatsu to direct public economic policy and programs had been left intact.[78]

Distribution of Stockpiled Materials and Government Funds

The immediate distribution of war industry materiel and payment of government liabilities was the third action that big business urged upon the Higashikuni cabinet. The zaibatsu leaders intended to use the goods and capital obtained thereby to underwrite their plans for reconversion to peacetime production. By cornering essential raw materials and manufactured goods of all kinds, the zaibatsu would also place themselves in position to carry out a radical retrenchment if necessary, abandoning production and sitting back comparatively well insulated against inflation and economic chaos. Whatever it would be, early reconversion or retrenchment first, as many goods as possible had to be distributed before the Allied assumption of authority. Much was done between surrender on 14 August and the formal signing of terms on 2 September. The government in that time handed out vast quantities of goods and twelve billion yen in currency, mostly to the great zaibatsu concerns.[79]

The Suzuki cabinet took the first steps toward recapitalization of the zaibatsu on 14 August when, just before resigning, it authorized, in willful misinterpretation of Allied instructions, the opening of military arsenals and warehouses for distribution of their stores to local authorities and zaibatsu firms. This was accompanied by destruction of the pertinent documents.[80] Between 14 and 28 August, when the Higashikuni cabinet rescinded the authorization on direct order from General MacArthur, the government allowed a large proportion of these stockpiles to disappear with barely a trace, most of it into zaibatsu warehouses. The plunder has been estimated at a minimum of fifty billion yen, and its immensity can be gauged by the fact that currency in circulation on 1 August was only 28.5 billion yen.[81]

The loot ran the gamut from medical supplies to gold, from machine tools to textiles, and as a result the bulk of industrial materials and finished commodities available at the time of surrender passed into zaibatsu hands. Unknown quantities of foodstuffs also disappeared, enough to have significantly alleviated the sufferings of the Japanese people had they been available through rationing channels at official prices.[82]

SCAP did take possession of the remainder of the military materiel, mostly armaments and other war goods, the total value of which has been estimated at 240 billion yen. Perhaps two-fifths of this was of some use to the civilian economy, and by November 1946 SCAP had turned over goods amounting to over 100 billion yen in value to the Home Ministry for allocation.[83] SCAP directed that: " . . . the supplies, materials, and equipment returned to your Government are for the purpose of civilian relief, and for use towards restoration of Japanese civil economy to the extent that it can provide the essentials of food, clothing and shelter for the Japanese civilian population. The use of these supplies for any purposes other than the above is expressly forbidden."[84]

That was hardly how it turned out. Collusion between government and big business in any society can seldom be documented beyond the shadow of a doubt, since it is not in the interests of either party to keep permanent records of dubious dealings. Some records do exist in this instance, however, and perhaps the best-documented example was the "Arms Disposal Committee" case concerning disposal of these materials after SCAP turned them over to the Japanese government. It was uncovered by the Katō Committee, which was formed in the Diet on 25 July 1947 under the chairmanship of Katō Kanjū for the express purpose of investigating the concealed and hoarded goods scandal then breaking. The Katō Committee found that the "Arms Disposal Committee" was a front for a group of big businesses—Japan Steel Company, Sumitomo, Asano, Furukawa, and Kawasaki—and had no legal standing for concluding the "contract" it had made with the Home Ministry. That contract established the committee as "the Government's agent in the sale and distribution of surrendered goods and materials returned to the Government by the Occupation Forces to relieve want and distress."[85] As the investigators discovered, only big business "want and distress" was relieved.[86]

When the investigators later began to uncover hoards of materials, the first large one—nine billion yen worth of essential items like machinery, metals, and oil—was found in March 1948 at the plants of the former Nakajima Aircraft Company. It will be recalled that Nakajima Chikuhei, a top zaibatsu figure, had held the post of Minister of Commerce and Industry in the Higashikuni cabinet.[87]

The concealed goods trickled into the economy over the next several years through sale on the black market or diversion to other illegal uses in which fantastic profits could be realized, and by which the zaibatsu could obtain large sums of money when needed. One of the uses of such funds was to provide the financial backing that the conservative parties needed to combat the leftist parties in the elections of 1946–47, as the Katō Committee later discovered.[88] The intimate relationship among big business, the government, and the conservative parties that the Katō Committee uncovered helps to explain official tolerance of the wide-open black markets—and why when SCAP pressure brought about salutary crackdowns the victims invariably were small-time operators.

Big business also benefited from the immense sums paid out from 15 to 31 August for war damage, military procurements, contract indemnities, and industrial reconversion. Most of the payments came from extraordinary, military budget funds, but other government disbursing offices also emptied their coffers. The exact size of the payments made during late August cannot be known, but it can be estimated from the fact that in those sixteen days the note issue of the Bank of Japan increased by more than twelve billion yen, from 30.282

billion to 42.3 billion. One account puts the total of the indemnity payments to the zaibatsu in a little over three months after surrender at 26.6 billion yen.[89]

Given this release of huge amounts of money in an economy already showing strong inflationary pressures deriving from the war years, there was little point for anyone to hold on to cash. The only rational course was the one the zaibatsu took, when in the fall of 1945 they devoted "their major efforts to converting liquid assets into any type of machinery, raw materials or finished goods available."[90]

Labor

Big business felt little pressure at first to formulate an explicit policy toward labor, since that matter did not demand such immediate action as did the need for materials and funds and for decontrol of the economy. At the time of the Higashikuni cabinet the repressive laws and agencies inherited from the previous half century were still largely intact and in force, apparently adequate for the task of containing worker discontent for the moment.

Discontent there would be, and a letdown in labor discipline and the will to work. The danger was not so much that labor would be demoralized, but that workers might find a rationale for their feelings and a guide to action in anti-capitalist ideas. That possibility would become more and more likely if unemployment rose too high and lasted too long. That worried big-business and government leaders, some of whom were predicting that unemployment, swollen by military demobilization and repatriation of Japanese abroad, could rise to thirteen million—a staggering number considering the population was in the neighborhood of seventy-two million.[91]

Because labor recruitment would simply not be a problem in a time of rising unemployment and a slowdown of production, big business was unconcerned about the loss of techniques for labor mobilization per se. The erosion of their authority vis-à-vis labor subsequent to government repeal of certain legislation pertaining to labor control they took far more seriously, especially after the dissolution of the Sanpō associations in late September. The government had withdrawn its support from Sanpō and Rōhō on 27 August. Then, in anticipation of SCAP orders, they dissolved themselves on 30 September, thereby making employer surveillance and indoctrination of the workforce much more difficult.

The disappearance of the local Sanpō association often left a hole in personnel management, and industries that continued production on any considerable scale, like coal mining, felt the loss the most. Accordingly, coal was one of the industries in which Sanpō officials—in coordination with employers and, like as not, right-wing socialists—tried to reorganize the associations into company unions. SCAP prohibited this and ordered Sanpō's assets turned over to the government. Nevertheless, at the local level business had some success in converting the associations into pliable "unions."[92]

A more direct tie with the past can be seen in Rōhō. With SCAP's blessing, Rōhō immediately reconstituted itself after its dissolution as the Laborers' Association, so that it might continue to supply labor to the government for allocation to SCAP. The new association covered some 2 to 2.5 million casual workers. It was in turn dissolved in December 1945, and a number of unions sprang up in its place, headed by labor bosses. These were the same bosses who had formed and run Rōhō in the first place, and they maintained their control over casual labor unimpaired right through the winter of 1945–46 and the entire occupation.[93]

Certain other aspects of the government's apparatus of surveillance and control survived in other guises. The Employment Offices, which had administered the mobilization of labor out of the local police stations during the war, operated under the Home Ministry's control until spring 1946, after which they were put under the Welfare Ministry. Even after that, the offices maintained close ties with the labor bosses, and whatever labor recruitment was going on was coordinated by the government's administrative bureaucracy and the labor bosses.[94]

2

The Workers Stand Up

When the occupation began in September 1945, the labor front was quiet. Measures for control of labor dating back to the Meiji period, and periodically extended as events called forth sterner measures, were still in effect in the immediate post-surrender weeks. The fact that surrender took place before war had destroyed the basis of the established social order as it had in Russia in 1917 had far-reaching effects. One of these was that the old guard retained its grip and saw to it that the police continued to be active in enforcing the repressive political and economic controls until the fall of the Higashikuni cabinet in early October. With few exceptions the first weeks after surrender did not see uprisings of workers, for the long decades of oppression had succeeded in uprooting workers' organizations and in undermining the will to resist.

In short, the surrender had not brought home to the working class as a whole that a new era was at hand. That realization spread only in the last three months of 1945, after it had become clear just how vulnerable the old political and business leaders were, and how greatly the old social order had been weakened by the disastrous war. SCAP made its contribution to kicking the props out from under the old regime through abolishing many of the repressive laws and organizations in October, thereby clearing the way for the long-pending confrontation between capital and labor. But the real stimulant to workers' action was after all the utter misery to which the rule of the old guard had reduced them.

The Rush to Organize

The Foreign Miners

It was only natural that the coal mines witnessed the first drive to organize. Working conditions and pay for coal miners had been among the worst in Japan from the time the country began to industrialize, and World War II intensified the miners' misery many times over. The draft and the running down of equipment created a labor shortage, and the government resorted to putting foreigners to work at forced labor, chiefly Koreans, but also Chinese and a few Caucasian prisoners of war. About 140,000 foreigners were in the mines at the end of July 1945, 35 percent of the total labor force of nearly 400,000.[1] In Hokkaidō, where conditions were very bad and wartime labor turnover greatest, 45 percent of the miners were foreigners.[2] The mine operators assigned the great majority of them to underground work where they outnumbered the Japanese and did the most difficult and dangerous jobs under the supervision of Japanese overseers in an atmosphere suffused with racial contempt. The toll of starvation rations and overseer brutality was high, and many died. The foreign miners were nothing more than slave laborers, and when Japan's defeat saved them from almost certain death in the mines from malnutrition and overwork, they rose against their exploiters.[3]

The government authorities and the mine owners attempted in vain to divert attention from themselves by fanning the fires of racism in the hope that the Japanese workers would discharge their discontent in violent outbursts against the Koreans and Chinese. Instead, the sheer fact of resistance coming from a group so exploited served as an object lesson to the Japanese workers and emboldened them to stand up and fight for their own rights. Beyond that, the political consciousness that the Chinese and Koreans exhibited had its effects, especially in Hokkaidō.[4] The influence of the foreign miners in stimulating the Japanese miners to rise up convinced the government and the coal companies that their best interests lay in the most rapid repatriation possible. By October less than half of the foreign workers were still in the mines, and by the end of the year not even a thousand were left.[5] Evidently, those in Hokkaidō were among the last to leave, perhaps because they accounted for the bulk of the underground workers—

rising above 80 percent in at least one mine—and were essential to continued operation.[6]

The Chinese became active first.[7] Unlike the Koreans, who were "contract" labor, the Chinese were primarily prisoners who had been captured in the fighting in North China. Chinese Communist party members from the Eighth Route Army led the Chinese miners when they stopped work at the end of the war and began liberating their barracks and forming self-governing councils. Their first targets were their old overseers in the pits and the barracks, whom they drove out or tried in workers' courts. Delegations also began going out to establish contact with other Hokkaidō mines in September, sometimes meeting strong police resistance. As they established communications toward the end of September, the Chinese began to demand better treatment, more food, and rapid repatriation.

In some cases, the Chinese seized company and police officials and had bloody clashes with Japanese authorities. When deaths resulted on both sides in late September, SCAP, which by that time was becoming increasingly concerned about coal production, stepped in on the side of the authorities, often with armed force. On 26 September, SCAP issued a proclamation on the maintenance of order in the mines that sanctioned establishing order by firing on and imprisoning the rebellious Chinese, if need be. The authorities, however, tried concessions as a means for preventing the spread of radical influence of the Chinese through the mines.

The Koreans continued to work for a time, but the coal companies greatly feared their uniting with the Chinese, and displayed SCAP's proclamation of 26 September before the Koreans' barracks. Nevertheless, in early October the Koreans in Hokkaidō commenced a series of strikes, slowdowns, and violent incidents. The first action, a strike, took place at the Hokutan Yūbari mine where the coal company soon found itself in the odd position of encouraging the Korean miners to form a union in the hope of quieting the situation. SCAP took this dispute very seriously and did its part by extending the authority of the military police to cover union activities and by dispatching a representative of the Korean Provisional Government to the mine. Although the strike was settled on 9 October, afterwards both attendance at work and productivity fell steeply.

By now the Koreans were getting together with the Chinese throughout Hokkaidō and presenting the companies with joint demands. One common demand was for distribution of stores that management had taken from the workers' allotments and hidden away. SCAP, faced with the coalescence of the Chinese and Korean miners' uprisings, issued a proclamation on 1 November specifically addressed to them which declared, in effect, that they were required to dig coal for the occupation forces. The foreign miners resisted enforcement of the back-to-work orders, and clashes occurred such as the one at the Mitsubishi Bibai mine, where on 6 November Chinese miners not only beat the personnel section chief but also subsequently occupied the personnel office and submitted company officials to negotiations from which only SCAP intervention extricated them. The resistance was so great that on 13 November the authorities gave up and decided to repatriate the remaining foreign miners at once. On 17 November SCAP ordered that American military vessels be lent to the Japanese government for that purpose, and soon afterward repatriation from the Hokkaidō mines went forward at high speed.

In the Jōban mines in eastern Honshū there were no Chinese, and the Koreans initiated the fight against the coal companies. Their struggle began on 7 October when the just-formed association of Koreans at one of the mines decided to refuse to work starting the next day. Their demands centered on the single point of early repatriation. The mine authorities tried to enforce a return to work with threats of violence and a suspension of the food ration, to which the Koreans responded by contacting other mines and causing further refusals to work. The American army now appeared and demanded a return to work, but the miners still refused to dig coal.

Around the middle of October, three representatives of the Korean miners in the Jōban mines went to Tokyo together with the head of the company personnel section in order to fix a date for repatriation. There the Koreans attended the founding conference of *Chōren*—the communist-led League of Koreans in Japan (Zainichi Chōsenjin Renmei)—and reported to it on the situation in the Jōban coal fields. Chōren decided to send ten people from their staff to the mines at once. From this point on, the struggle advanced under the lead of the Chōren organizers, whose hand was evident in street speeches, handbills, and pamphlets, which insisted, "The enemy is the Emperor system, and both the Korean people and the Japanese people are victims in common. The Japanese people want to understand and to support the struggles of the Korean people."[8]

The Japanese Miners

Even before the first shock of defeat and dislocation had passed, some Japanese coal miners had begun to organize.[9] The first actions took place in Hokkaidō, where 180 workers at the Ibana Kami Utashinai mine struck on 11 September and the miners at the Mitsui Ashibetsu mine formed a union on 6 October. From the beginning of the occupation, coal was in the forefront of the workers' movement, and the Hokkaidō mines were in the forefront of the coal industry.

During the last ten days of September Hokkaidō miners were engaging in informal conferences throughout the coal fields. Quite without outside leadership at first, they began to organize and form the first unions at the enterprise level. Their efforts often benefited from the example of the Chinese and Koreans, but also owed much to the presence of Japanese miners with prewar experience in the labor movement. Although both the coal companies and labor organizers from the outside encouraged unionization—for completely different reasons—the impetus to organize came from below, generated by the terrible conditions in the mines.

The workers' solidarity and will to act arose from their having shared experiences and from facing the same uncertain future. Consequently, the workers almost always confronted the operators with a common set of demands: more pay, shorter hours, union recognition, establishment of the right of collective bargaining, increased and equitable distribution of rations (especially food), abolition of worker-staff discrimination in treatment, expulsion of labor bosses, and reform of semifeudal labor conditions. This combination of hard-headed economic demands and less precise demands for democratization of the enterprise was typical, and indicative of the tension that was soon to arise in the labor movement between the advocates of business unionism and the supporters of a socialist transformation of Japanese industry.

The miners' consciousness was not free from ideological ambiguity. Even in hard-fought battles, overtones of Sanpō-like attitudes might appear. For example, as late as 23 December, the union at the Sumitomo Hashi Betsu mine presented a program which listed increased production and promotion of techniques of increased efficiency as tasks for the union to undertake under management's lead for the good of the enterprise. As time went on, such remnants of the philosophy of class collaboration that the operators had pushed by way of Sanpō disappeared, and demands for democratization became increasingly prominent.

The process of union organization showed a basic similarity from mine to mine in Hokkaidō, though the specifics of each dispute naturally differed. Events at the Mitsubishi Yūbari mine might be taken as typical. There the more activist miners formed a "comrades' association" (dōshikai) on 2 October which had its founding conference on 23 October. The members formulated demands, held negotiations with the company, and obtained a satisfactory settlement on the 26th. While the leaders were reporting to the membership on the next day, about thirty people who appeared to be members of the semi-official young men's association still surviving from the war burst in and interrupted the meeting. During the ensuing struggle between the two groups, Murakami Yūkari of the Communist party came to the mine as an organizer and became the leader of the comrades' association.

On 30 October the miners attended a meeting of the association at which the company manager reported on the condition of the enterprise and Murakami reported on the international situation and explained the significance of establishing a union. The company said it approved of unionization, and the comrades' association, joined by a number of other workers, decided to form a union. At the same time, the company was secretly encouraging a more conciliatory group of workers to convene at once their own preparatory conference for a union. After an unpleasant fight, the two groups joined together and on 10 November formed a union. The union at once presented these demands: 1) recognition of the workers' rights to form a union, engage in collective bargaining, and strike; 2) immediate distribution of hoarded goods; 3) an absolute guarantee of provisions at official prices, with the company assuming liability for the difference; 4) normalization of commodity rationing; 5) an eight-hour workday and a 7:00 A.M. starting time for entering the pits; 6) immediate dismissal of corrupt officials; and 7) abolition of the attendance allowance and payment of a staple-commodity price allowance of five yen per day (apparently intended to help make up the difference between black-market and official prices of staple foods like rice).

After the company rejected the first item on 14 November, the union broke off negotiations and began a slowdown. In order to force a settlement, the workers took direct action and put the company manager up on a stage to negotiate with the union in the presence of all. Within four days after the dispute had begun, the union forced the company to accept item 1 and the majority of its other demands. The "public negotiations" broke the resistance of the company and foreshadowed the use of such techniques as mass negotiations and people's courts in the greater struggles that so shocked business and government leaders in early 1946.

Very early the Hokkaidō miners felt the need for a union organization that would not be confined to one mine or one enterprise, but would encompass all mines. This idea was first broached at Mitsubishi Bibai when in early October the miners held a meeting to discuss forming a union. At a later preparatory meeting (31 October), they drafted a union program, bylaws, and list of demands. Speakers—among whom were such important figures in later labor organization as Mizutani Takashi[10]—explained that unions were necessary for obtaining an eight-hour day, wage increases, collective agreements, and worker control of the distribution of commodities. Nevertheless, the miners stopped short of taking the step of constituting a union and presenting demands. Meanwhile, the company announced the election of twenty-five representatives to a company-sponsored "harmony society" which was to replace the Sanpō association. In response, the miners expressed their determination to take over any such society and found a real union. At this juncture, Mizutani met with the leader of the Chinese miners at nearby Jōbandai, Zhang Shaowei of the Eighth Route Army, and asked his help. Zhang urged a workers' liberation movement and gave him a ¥3,000 contribution toward that end.

The miners founded their union on 4 November and adopted a progressive program which, with one exception, later became the model for the program of the national federation to be organized by Mizutani. That single exception read: "We resolve to realize a true labor-capital collaboration in a relationship of equality between self-conscious labor and self-reflective capital." This sentence revealed the difficulty that the new unions had in shaking off the ideology of the collaborationist Sanpō associations. It also suggested what was going to happen when it became clear that the leaders of business and government had no intention of recognizing the workers' demand for an equal partnership in industry. It was but a short step to take from the rejection of the demand for labor-capital equality to the radical demand for the ascendancy of self-conscious labor over unrepentant capital.

The new union presented its demands on 13 November, and asked for such things as higher wages, the eight-hour day, and control over distribution of commodities. Negotiations began on 20 November in the reception room of the company office. The union members surrounded the office, and overhead flew a handmade red flag. When Mizutani revealed during the negotiations that company officials had stores of hoarded goods in their houses, the union began preparations for a strike. After four hours the union got everything it demanded without having to begin a dispute.

The coal company was unhappy, and when the government took action to place guidelines on wages in the coal industry, in December it unilaterally retracted part of the wage increases it had agreed to. This precipitated a long and bitter fight which the miners won by seizing and trying top company officials in the famous people's court incident during their takeover and operation of the mine at Mitsubishi Bibai in February 1946. (See chapter 5.)

Coal mine operations everywhere had first reacted to the end of the war and the dissolution of Sanpō by trying to maintain the existing

TABLE 2.1
Growth of Unions in Coal Mining, October 1945–December 1946

Year	Month	Percentage of Mines with Organized Unions				
		All Japan	Hokkaidō	Eastern Honshū	Western Honshū	Kyūshū
1945	Oct	2.5	5.4	0.0	0.0	2.8
	Nov	18.1	52.6	0.9	0.0	10.7
	Dec	35.4	74.7	15.1	1.0	28.8
1946	Jan	52.9	81.3	48.5	16.3	48.0
	Feb	72.1	88.0	64.3	34.7	72.4
	Mar	79.9	91.1	73.1	65.8	78.8
	Apr	82.8	92.1	73.7	78.6	81.6
	May	86.4	92.2	75.9	81.8	86.8
	Jun	87.9	92.2	75.9	83.0	89.1
	Dec	92.1	94.3	86.1	86.7	92.7

Source: Nihon Tankō Rōdō Kumiai, ed. *Tanrō Jūnen Shi* (Tokyo: Rōdō Junpōsha, 1964), p. 41.

order in the mines by reconstituting the Sanpō associations as company unions. This tactic had some success outside Hokkaidō. In the other islands the rate of unionization lagged two months behind (see table 2.1), and even the independent unions exhibited a strong tendency toward labor-capital collaboration.

One reason for this was that the composition of the work force in the mines was different. In Kyūshū, the other major coal-producing region in Japan, the percentage of foreign workers was small, women workers were many, and new wartime entrants to the mines were few. Since labor turnover had not been as great, wartime changes had neither disrupted the *oyabun-kobun* (patron-client) relationships typical of the prewar Sōdōmei (Nihon Rōdō kumiai Sōdōmei, Japan General Federation of Labor, the largest and most conservative of the prewar union federations) nor greatly undermined the Sanpō ideology. Since the old labor bosses and union leaders were still around, their brand of unionism rapidly regained its dominance. There were a number of instances in which miners organized under non-Sōdōmei unionists put forth strong demands and formed unions, but the general situation in Kyūshū was the reverse of that in Hokkaidō.

These different regional developments led to the formation of competing regional organizations of coal miners' unions on the left and right, with a large third group of independents in the middle. The first to organize was the Hokkaidō Federation of Mine Workers' Unions (Hokkaidō Kōzan Rōdō Kumiai Rengōkai) on 10 November. At its second conference on 3 February, the federation became a unitary regional organization for Hokkaidō and was renamed the Hokkaidō Federation of Coal Miners' Unions (Hokkaidō Tankō Rōdō Kumiai). Mizutani was chosen as president and Murakami as secretary general. The conference pressed the need for a united national organization and appealed to the unions of all regions to unite. A national council of representatives of the coal workers' unions followed on 10 February in Tokyo, for the purpose of setting up a national federation. Mizutani went to Tokyo in early February to take part in the organization of the national union. According to SCAP's account of this meeting, four resolutions were passed: "(1) to secure labor union participation in management; (2) to relieve the food problem; (3) to oppose company unionism; and (4) to secure the funds and facilities formerly belonging to Sanpō." [11]

The Tokyo council of the coal workers' unions soon affiliated with the Council of Industrial Unions' Preparatory Conference (Sanbetsu Kaigi Junbikai) at its inauguration on 20 February, and went on to found on 22 April the All-Japan Federation of Coal Miners' Unions (Zen Nihon Tankō Rōdō Kumiai, or Zentan). Mizutani was chosen president. Zentan membership rose to nearly 100,000 in 1946, and it became one of the central unions of Sanbetsu. [12]

In Kyūshū, a group of prewar Sōdōmei leaders formed the Kyūshū Regional Mine Workers' Union (Kyūshū Chihō Kōzan Rōdōsha Kumiai, or Kyūkō) on 16 December. Most of the affiliated unions were from small-to-medium-sized mines, because the executives of Kyūkō had antagonized the workers in the large mines by showing a tendency toward labor-capital collaboration and self-seeking—as, for example, in giving help to one of the prewar leaders for his campaign to be elected to the Diet. Kyūkō allied itself with the conservative national federation, Sōdōmei, that was being organized at the time. In November 1946, it changed its name to the Japan Mine Workers' Union (Nihon Kōzan Rōdō Kumiai, or Nikkō).

Another Kyūshū regional federation established itself in opposition to Kyūkō. It professed neutrality at first, but moved toward Zentan and became the nucleus of the Zentan organization in Kyūshū. While the Zentan and Kyūkō unions struggled for supremacy, many of the large mines formed enterprise-based rather than regional federations. These affiliated with neither side, but in October 1946 formed a "neutral" federation which advocated the unification of labor in a single, national body. Though outnumbered by the Kyūkō and Zentan unions, this group actually came to hold the balance of power in Kyūshū. [13]

Left-right divisions appeared within the coal miners' movement at the moment of its birth, and have persisted to this day. In this way, events in the coal industry anticipated trends and problems that would plague the entire labor movement. The split between the miners' unions—on the one hand a vanguard of the radical left wing, and on the other a bastion of right-wing social democracy—would soon be reproduced in most sectors of industry.

The Course of Unionization

Coal mining was not the only industry undergoing labor organization in the fall of 1945. The first national union to organize was not in mining at all, but shipping. The All-Japan Seamen's Union (Zen Nihon Kaiin Kumiai) which reorganized on 5 October, had been the largest and most right-wing union in prewar Japan. Far from being revived from below by ordinary workers, the Seamen's Union was reimposed from the top down by the joint efforts of the old Kaiin labor bosses and the zaibatsu operators in shipping. Shipping had been notoriously boss-ridden for decades, the union under the control of the great labor bosses in Ōsaka, Kōbe, and Kita Kyūshū. When their union was dissolved during the war the Kaiin executives had simply shifted over to become the directors of the control associations in shipping and continued to wield their power over labor in the industry. Once the war ended, the bosses resuscitated the union and installed a certain Koizumi Hidekichi as head. Considering Koizumi's history as the prewar head of the Merchant Marine Officers' Association (Kaiin Kyōkai), ship captain, director of Mitsui shipping, and president of Mitsui Wooden Ships, it is clear that the Seamen's Union was not only boss-ridden and undemocratic, but perilously close to being an out-and-out company union.[14]

The distinction between spontaneous worker self-organization and outside organization from the top down can be seen clearly in the cases of coal and shipping, where left-right divisions were sharp. Even when the outside organizers were left-wing socialists or communists with a commitment to worker activism, the top-down style of unionization still left its mark on future attitudes toward worker autonomy. It implied a certain distrust of the organizational ability of production workers, a readiness to assume that the leadership usually knew best what strategy and tactics ought to be followed in conflicts between labor and capital. That attitude eventually opened a dangerous gap between the national leadership and the rank and file. In the early months, however, mutual trust and understanding characterized the relationship between the left-wing organizers and workplace movements; for the left-wing socialist and communist organizers understood full well that worker solidarity in intent and action was a requirement for successful unionization. It had to be, if only because the left could not gain employer cooperation and had to rely on the workers' initiative to provide the impetus to unionize.

TABLE 2.2
Growth of Unions and Union Membership throughout Japan, August 1945–February 1947 (cumulative end-of-month totals)

Year	Month	Unions	Membership
1945	Aug	0	0
	Sep	2	1,177
	Oct	9	5,072
	Nov	75	68,530
	Dec	509	380,677
1946	Jan	1,517	902,751
	Feb	3,243	1,537,606
	Mar	6,538	2,568,513
	Apr	8,531	3,023,979
	May	10,541	3,414,699
	Jun	12,007	3,681,017
	Jul	12,923	3,814,711
	Aug	13,341	3,875,272
	Sep	14,697	4,122,209
	Oct	15,172	4,168,305
	Nov	16,171	4,296,589
	Dec	17,265	4,849,329
1947	Jan	17,972	4,922,918
	Feb	18,929	5,030,574 [a]

Source: Japan Prime Minister's Office, Cabinet Bureau of statistics, *Japan Statistical Year-book* (Tokyo: Cabinet Bureau of Statistics, 1949), p. 717.
[a]Membership first exceeded six million in December 1947.

In contrast, the right-wing socialists who sought to set up unions according to prewar concepts were out of touch with the workers' needs. They took a narrow economic view of the limits of worker interests and at best promoted a conservative brand of unionism that made a virtue of cooperation with employers. At worst, they aided and abetted the formation of company unions. Such organizers frequently solicited the cooperation of employers with the argument that installation of a moderate union now would prevent the appearance of a red union later. The participation of the workers to be organized was minimal where the right-wing socialists took control, and the union bureaucracy subsequently devoted much of its time to containing worker activism. (For specific examples, see the discussion in the passages on the Japan Socialist Party in chapter 4.) Workers who organized from the shop floor up showed a surprising readiness for radical experimentation, as the previous examples taken from the coal industry show, although they, like the others, often framed their demands in traditional terms.

The statistics of unionization—impressive as they are—do not re-

TABLE 2.3

Growth of Unions and Union Membership in the Basic Industries and Services, August 1945–February 1947 (cumulative end-of-month totals)

Year	Month	Manufacturing		Mining		Transportation and Communications		Government and Professions	
		Unions	Members	Unions	Members	Unions	Members	Unions	Members
1945	Aug	0	0	0	0	0	0	0	0
	Sep	1	1,046	1	31	0	0	0	0
	Oct	4	1,980	2	1,270	2	1,652	0	0
	Nov	44	43,633	18	20,538	6	3,079	3	244
	Dec	282	214,276	82	69,996	107	76,876	12	1,578
1946	Jan	846	456,710	157	131,493	361	254,121	79	23,147
	Feb	1,086	776,503	267	211,409	769	409,121	244	73,255
	Mar	3,530	1,223,086	511	316,146	1,488	868,518	613	200,036
	Apr	4,561	1,437,539	597	333,641	1,880	799,916	859	254,984
	May	5,665	1,620,440	674	348,129	2,130	874,295	1,224	332,739
	Jun	6,432	1,751,609	724	357,525	2,284	903,243	1,548	396,060
	Jul	6,859	1,794,705	754	361,802	2,389	923,813	1,774	432,868
	Aug	7,065	1,828,727	776	368,381	2,440	921,119	1,865	448,161
	Sep	7,733	1,929,916	819	378,522	2,664	978,002	2,126	498,675
	Oct	7,935	1,939,847	839	382,103	2,688	981,304	2,281	521,291
	Nov	8,905	1,989,205	863	388,380	2,770	997,446	2,558	561,830
	Dec	8,905	2,323,199	847	420,570	2,645	1,091,083	3,106	661,284
1947	Jan	9,172	2,346,678	852	420,969	2,691	1,103,913	3,362	687,998
	Feb	9,581	2,384,563	869	422,688	2,760	1,120,478	3,672	722,606

Source: Japan Prime Minister's Office, Cabinet Bureau of Statistics, *Japan Statistical Year-book* (Tokyo: Cabinet Bureau of statistics, 1949), pp. 718–19, 720–21.

flect such important schisms within the labor movement, and give only the aggregate numbers of unions formed and workers organized. (See table 2.2.) The greatest increase in unionization took place in the first six months of 1946, when 3.3 million workers in the basic industries and services organized. Table 2.3 compares participation of the different sectors in the initial burst of unionization, and indicates that the largest enterprises unionized first—the zaibatsu firms and government enterprises. The slowing of the pace after June reflected the difficulties of organizing in small- and medium-sized enterprises.[15] Table 2.4 contrasts the numbers of the unionized with the number employed in the basic services and industries and shows that the rate of unionization reached 30 percent as early as the end of May 1946.

This phenomenal performance concealed problems, however. Although many of the two to three million casual workers once in Rōhō had been unionized, it was in name only, since the union leaders were the same bosses who had always run the labor gangs. Big business and government controlled the bosses through their powers to award private or government work, and in reality it made no great difference to most casual workers whether they were unionized or not. Nor did efforts by some left-wing socialists and communists to organize the millions of unemployed accomplish much. Discharged workers left for the countryside in droves, while the rest drifted around the cities trying to survive through odd jobs, street businesses, or black marketeering. Furthermore, unionization made little headway in the innumerable medium- and small-sized businesses that often depended on zaibatsu orders. They were traditionally hard to organize, and were all the more so after the war when they were going bankrupt in large numbers. Thus, a large part of the non-agricultural labor force was either out of the labor movement altogether, or, if unionized, under the thumb of big business and government.

While the coal miners were unionizing locally and nationally, the coal mine operators were not sitting on their hands. They, too, felt the necessity to coordinate nationally. The Essential Industry Council, one of the four major business organizations that had come together to form the Keidanren Committee, was headed by a Kyūshū coal magnate, Matsumoto Kenjirō. Matsumoto chaired a Keidanren subcommittee in February whose purpose was to organize the business world to combat the workers' movement, and his efforts eventually culminated in the organization of Nikkeiren (Nihon Keiesha Dantai Renmei, Japan Federation of Employers' Associations). Matsumoto's prominence in these efforts indicates the high importance zaibatsu executives attached to their ability to control the coal industry and labor in general.[16]

TABLE 2.4
Employment and Union Membership in Basic Industries and Services, 1944–January 1947 (cumulative end-of-month totals in thousands)

Year	Month	Manufacturing		Mining		Transportation and Communications		Government and Professions		Totals		Percentage Organized
		Union-ized	Em-ployed	Union-ized	Em-ployed	Union-ized	Em-ployed	Union-ized	Em-ployed	Union-ized	Em-ployed	
1944	(ave.)	0	9,363	0	788	0	1,615	0	2,849	0	14,615	0
1945	Dec	214	4,526	70	478	77	1,923	2	2,269	363	9,196	4
1946	May	1,620	5,708	348	572	874	1,940	333	2,325	3,175	10,545	30
	Oct	1,940	6,211	382	625	981	1,993	521	2,361	3,824	11,190	34
1947	Jan	2,347	6,006	421	643	1,104	1,986	678	2,374	4,550	11,009	41

Sources: Japan Prime Minister's Office, Cabinet Bureau of Statistics, *Japan Statistical Year-book* (Tokyo: Cabinet Bureau of Statistics, 1949), pp. 717, 720–21; Japan Ministry of Finance and Bank of Japan, *Statistical Year-Book of Finance and Economy of Japan, 1948* (Tokyo: Ministry of Finance Printing Office), p. 589.

On 18 December the first association of mine owners, the Hokkaidō Coal Industry Federation (Hokkaidō Sekitan Kōgyō Renmei), comprising the principal mines of Hokkaidō, was established. Nikkeiren, in its official history of the period, dates its beginnings back to this very organization.[17] The key figures behind its formation were Fukugawa Masao of the Mitsui mines and Maeda Hajime of the Hokutan mines, a Mitsui subsidiary. One of the federation's main purposes, as expressed in its bylaws, was to "work for liaison in the control of labor problems in the Hokkaidō coal mining industry." Among its other functions, it listed "investigation and research and tendering of intelligence concerning labor problems as well as the disposition and settlement of coal mine labor-capital strife (including settlement by collective bargaining)." In Tokyo and Kyūshū, on 1 and 15 April respectively, analogous federations were set up. The mine owners' associations must be understood primarily as zaibatsu organs expressing the extreme anti-labor attitudes of the Keidanren Committee advocates of the free economy.[18]

For its part, the government did establish a Coal Board in late December under SCAP pressure "to investigate and make recommendations to stimulate productions,"[19] but judging from coal production figures it accomplished practically nothing to that purpose. More than likely, its main activities were surveillance of the mine workers' movement and coordination of coal policy with the zaibatsu coal companies. As the coal struggles in 1946 were to show, the Coal Board was active in obstructing the miners' struggles.

The postwar situation in the mines called for greater sophistication and coordination in labor management than this, if Sōdōmei-type business unionism was to prevail over more radical currents. As coal company attitudes at the time of union formation typically showed around the end of 1945, the beleaguered operators on the spot were coming around grudgingly to accepting unions as stable bargaining agencies with which they could deal on a business-like basis in contrast to the only other alternative, which was rank-and-file organizations of angry miners ready to take direct action to accomplish their goals. Given the gravity of the situation, any means for containing worker discontent, even something as repugnant as unions, commended itself to the operators. The early tactic of preempting the workers' drive to organize by establishing company unions had failed by midwinter. Above all, big business was coming to the conclusion that outright oppression was not then possible.[20]

The coal company tactic of encouraging moderate unions as the lesser evil while at the same time setting up management organization on an inter-enterprise, regional level dedicated to repression of the miners' movement was contradictory, of course. But a policy based straightforwardly on the proposition of cheap, "free" labor and a rollback of union gains would have been likely to end up alienating all but the most compromising company unions, and bringing on a violent confrontation with the miners. A more rational policy was clearly needed.

Union recognition fitted in well with the labor relations machinery being reluctantly set up by the government under SCAP pressure in the winter of 1945–46. But it may be noted that the weaving of a "web of rules" binding capital and labor in predictable channels of behavior through a complex set of agencies and regulations began to look more and more appealing, and not only for the hard-beset mine owners. The use of force against such unruly elements as the miners, the policy most consistent with the free economy notions still prevalent among conservative business leaders like the zaibatsu coal executives, had temporarily been ruled out by SCAP.

Great pressure was being brought to bear on big business and government to reconsider the accepted wisdom of laissez-faire and free labor. The old guard would have to come up with national policies more in keeping with the actual tactical recognition of unions on the plant level. Labor would have to be accorded its due as a legitimate interest group in whatever program for a capitalist reconstruction should replace the increasingly anachronistic free economy policy. The devising of new policies became a matter of utmost urgency when workers in many critical industries broke through the bounds of capitalist trade unionism in January by taking over control of production in plant after plant to force the employers to give in to their demands.

First Steps toward Taking Control of Production

Despite these qualifications, the postwar Japanese workers' movement must be given its due as one of the most remarkable advances in labor history. It bears witness to the tremendous strength of their desire to organize. Examples abound of workers spontaneously taking action to unionize far in advance of the pace of SCAP's labor reforms and to fight back against what might be called the Japanese employers' "divine right" to rule the work force. One of the most original and effective of the tactics workers used to obtain their rights and their demands was production control (seisan kanri), worker seizure and operation of an enterprise. The employees of the *Yomiuri* newspaper originated this form of struggle as part of their fight to democratize their paper, a paper most assuredly in need of democratizing.

Democratizing the Yomiuri

War Responsibility

The link between the official ideology of the state and the point of view of the leading newspapers had been drawn closer than ever once war broke out in China. The defense of Japan's national interest soon seemed to require omission of certain kinds of news and eventually the printing of outright falsehoods about Japan's situation at home and abroad. The *Yomiuri* stood in the forefront of the controlled press, following the enthusiastic lead of its president, Shōriki Matsutarō.[21]

Shōriki's readiness to cooperate with the authorities was not surprising. In the early 1920s he had been Director of the Secretariat of the Metropolitan Police Board of Tokyo and a key figure in the surveillance and suppression of activities of the Communist party in particular, but also of labor, left-wing groups, and Koreans. His position afforded him access to influential people in business as well as in government and politics, contacts that he used in 1924 to buy control of the faltering *Yomiuri*. Through a combination of tightening control over the employees in order to cut labor costs and raise productivity and adopting a policy of sensational "yellow" journalism, Shōriki made the *Yomiuri* into one of the three largest newspapers in Japan by the late 1930s. He was an ultra-nationalist, a collaborator with the wartime leaders, and played an important role in controlling and using the Japanese press for state purposes. In managing the *Yomiuri*, Shōriki showed a preference for former policy or intelligence figures who were staunch anti-communists like himself.[22]

During the war, reporters, printers, and newspapermen in general were exceptional for having both the intellectual training and the access to hard news that would enable them to pass judgement on operation of their companies' activities. And pass judgement they did at the *Yomiuri*, despite having to go along with the Shōriki regime. The employees bitterly resented the reactionary editorial policy that subordinated news reporting to the propaganda purposes of the state, and a highly authoritarian system of personnel management intended to extract maximum work from each employee for minimum pay. When the war ended, both aspects of direction came under sharp attack, and the *Yomiuri* employees put forward demands for pursuit of war responsibility and internal democratization of the paper, regarding them as at least as important as economic demands for better pay and benefits.[23]

The first *Yomiuri* dispute broke out on 13 September 1945 when forty-five editorial employees presented a "statement of views" to Shōriki. Their main requests were for democratization of the company's organization, a shakeup of personnel, acceptance of war responsibility by company officials, and better pay for employees. Shōriki merely replied that he did not object to the purport of the statement and that he would reform those points that would be for the betterment of the company, but that he had no intention of making a shakeup of management. At about this time Suzuki Tōmin, who had been forced into retirement in his home village for daring to speak out during the war, returned to the newspaper office in Tokyo. Suzuki, a "fighting liberal," joined with the other dissidents on the paper—who ranged in views from mildly social democratic to revolutionary Marxist and anarchosyndicalist—to become the center of the ensuing democratization movement.[24]

The "Democratic Study Group" that Suzuki and the others set up as a preliminary to the organization of a union met with Shōriki on 19 October and put forth essentially the same demands as before. Shōriki reacted angrily, told them they were free to pursue study on their own but that they must submit any opinions they might have in regard to the paper to the head of the research bureau of the newspaper, and terminated the interview.[25] The next day Shōriki called together all officials from the assistant department chiefs up and said: "I will not permit employees selfishly to set up an organization within the company. If you set one up against my will, I will have your resignations. It is outrageous that some wrong-headed employees are using democracy as an excuse to conspire for something else. This company is mine, and I am utterly determined not to let you do it."[26]

The reaction of the employees to Shōriki's threats was to solidify their organization as the means for achieving their demands in full. The Democratic Study Group scheduled a mass meeting of all *Yomiuri* employees for 23 October for the purpose of creating a union preparatory committee. At just this time a similar dispute that had been going on at the *Asahi* newspaper ended with the collective resignation of the paper's executives in acknowledgement of their responsibility for promoting war policies. This gave the *Yomiuri* struggle added stimulus, and the workers turned out en masse on 23 September, over 1,000 out of a total of 1,875 employees. The workers acted resolutely, endorsing demands for collective resignation of all bureau chiefs and higher executives including Shōriki on grounds of war responsibility. They also put forth four items as necessary for the establishment of a democratic system at the paper: formation of an employees' union, thoroughgoing democratization of the company's organization, better pay for the employees and respect for them as human beings, and formation of an independent consumers' union and mutual aid association.[27]

Shōriki had no intention of giving in to these demands, believing them to be merely excuses for a communist scheme to seize control of the company. Rather, he was determined to break through and establish a pattern at the *Yomiuri* for the settlement of disputes throughout Japan henceforth. For him the *Yomiuri* was in the front line battling against a communist conspiracy to take over Japanese industry. Shōriki was wholeheartedly supported in these beliefs and in his refusal to settle except on his own terms by such important business figures as Fujiwara Ginjirō, the ultra-nationalist creator of the Ōji Paper Co.[28]

Shōriki and Fujiwara typified the conservative majority among business leaders in much the same way that Yoshida Shigeru—who was to play a key role in the second *Yomiuri* dispute—represented the conservative political leaders. All detested unions almost as much as they did communists, and had feared the resurgence of both after the end of the war. Their ideal of proper labor relations was that of prewar Japan, when government oppression kept labor fragmented and weak, and therefore cheap. Such men were unwilling or unable to distinguish militant unionism from communism, and insisted that any erosion of the rights of private property would contribute to the communist goal of destroying the whole capitalist system. Thus Shōriki insisted that his authority must be absolute within the *Yomiuri*, and that the workers' organization being set up was nothing but a front for a communist conspiracy.[29]

Shōriki and Fujiwara notwithstanding, the Communist party had nothing to do with the origins of the first *Yomiuri* dispute, even though a small number of Marxists in the editorial bureau were among the leaders of the dispute. More important by far than Marxist theory in shaping the workers' response to the situation at the *Yomiuri* was the unique situation of the Japanese press during the early occupation.

Origins of Production Control

In the fall of 1945 SCAP was promoting the democratization of the press at the same time that it was insisting that production of newspapers must continue because they were an essential vehicle for Allied policy in general.[30] On the one hand, SCAP was saying workers must not strike, especially newspaper workers, but, on the other, Shōriki was categorically rejecting all demands for democratization. This placed the *Yomiuri* workers in a difficult spot. To strike invited trouble, since both the government and SCAP would oppose it. Far worse, even if suppression did not come, a strike could end in the complete closure of the paper, which Shōriki considered more desirable than handing the company over to the employees.[31]

What could be done? If the dispute was to be won a solution had to be found. The answer came out of an informal gathering of *Yomiuri* workers at a restaurant on the evening of 23 October, after the mass meeting of employees had served far-reaching demands on Shōriki. One of those present proposed that, if it was no good to strike, then: ". . . ,why don't we put out the paper by ourselves? If we do that we don't have to worry about bankrupting the company. And if we gain the support of the readers by putting out an excellent newspaper, then we can reconstruct the *Yomiuri* as a democratic paper . . . "[32] At that a lively discussion ensued that touched on such things as the prewar Italian and French examples of factory occupation and control. The result was that the editorial staff resolved, if need be, to take control over the editing, printing, shipping, and distribution of the *Yomiuri*.

When Shōriki summoned Suzuki and five other employees to his office the next day to receive his "final answer," he summarily rejected the demands and ordered the resignation of Suzuki and four others whom he considered to be ringleaders. Shōriki now stood revealed to the *Yomiuri* workers as a steadfast and unrepentant supporter of the old order, a symbol of what was wrong with prewar Japan. Shōriki and his supporters refused to admit any kind of war guilt or to allow the company's democratization.[33]

Suzuki and the others left after Shōriki's "final answer," and went back to the editorial office to report to the workers gathered to hear the results. On the spot a second employees' meeting was convened. Suzuki reported, and ended by saying, "We are entering a dispute in order to achieve our demands. And from the 25th, we are going to put out the paper independently by our own hand." In order to carry this out, the assemblage elected a "supreme struggle committee" with Suzuki as chairman, and decided that supporting struggle committees would be elected in every department. When the meeting ended, the workers, raising shouts of victory, occupied the editorial office and evicted the bureau chiefs. With this the *Yomiuri* newspaper production-control struggle began, the first in postwar Japan.[34]

The onset of production control hardened Shōriki's conviction that a communist conspiracy lay behind his troubles. Until the end of the dispute he continued to insist, "How this dispute is settled is not a problem for the *Yomiuri* alone, but one of whether or not Japan's industry is to be seized by the JCP."[35] Unfortunately for Shōriki, he was ahead of his time. His was later to become the view adopted by American and Japanese authorities alike when the second *Yomiuri* dispute broke out some six months later.[36]

The day after production control began, 25 October, a meeting of workers set up the *Yomiuri* Newspaper Employees' Union and elected Suzuki chairman. The meeting also formulated demands, one of the

major ones being for participation in management by the union, but
in the struggle that followed the union played no active role at all.
From the outset, real authority lay in the system of struggle committees through which production control was being carried out. The superior position of the struggle committees at the *Yomiuri* in relationship to the union is clearly illustrated in a diagram prepared by Professor
Yamamoto Kiyoshi.

The union members and executive committee acted merely as one
of the constituent parts of the struggle committee, and the union
chairman and standing executive committee had no function. Furthermore, decision making and executive functions in the struggle committee system were not separated, as the diagram might imply, but
merged. Whenever a problem came up requiring some kind of action,
the struggle committee would call together as many of the workers
concerned as it could to discuss the matter. Those at the mass meeting
would make a collective decision, and collectively carry it out. In short,
the struggle committee system operated on the basis of direct, partic-
ipatory democracy, in which the struggle committee's basic role was,
more than anything else, to elicit the decision of the workers.[37]

Arbitration and Settlement

Under production control the *Yomiuri* took a progressive stance edi-
torially and overnight became the most left-leaning and outspoken of
Japan's major newspapers. The new policy gained public approval,
and circulation rose sharply.[38] Many outside organizations rallied to
the side of the *Yomiuri* workers, such as the other newspaper unions,
the JSP (Japan Socialist party), and the JCP (Japan Communist party).
But Shōriki was not to be moved. Instead, on 30 October he asked
the authorities that indictments be brought against the production
control leaders on the grounds of illegal occupation of premises and
interference with business operations; but the indictments were dismissed after a short investigation in mid-November. There was little
movement until late November when the newly created Labor Dispute Arbitration Committee (Rōdō Sōgi Chōtei Iinkai) in Tokyo decided to take up the *Yomiuri* dispute at Shōriki's request. The *Yomiuri*
workers would not submit their case for arbitration to the committee,
which was openly reactionary in membership. Its chairman, for example, Kawarada Kakichi, was a former Home Minister, and one of
the management members, Shinagawa Shūkei, was a former chief of
the Secretariat of the Metropolitan Police Board.[39]

In response to the protests over the committee's makeup, the authorities set up a special arbitration subcommittee to which the *Yomi-*

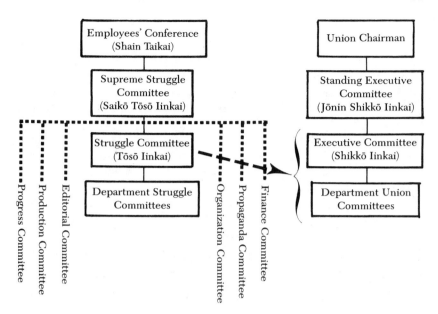

Figure 2.1. Struggle-Committee Structure at the *Yomiuri* Newspaper. Sources: Ya-mamoto Kiyoshi, *Sengo Rōdō Undō Shiron* (Tokyo: O-Cha no Mizu Shobō, 1977), vol. 1, *Sengo Kiki ni okeru Rōdō Undō*, p. 263; Tōkyō Daigaku Shakai Kagaku Kenkyū-jo, ed., *Shiryō* (Tokyo: Tōkyō Daigaku Shakai Kagaku Kenkyū-jo, 1973), vol. 6, *Sengo Kiki ni okeru Rōdō Sōgi: Yomiuri Shinbun Sōgi*, p. 34.

uri workers nominated the three labor members: Kikunami Katsumi (chairman of the *Asahi* newspaper employees' union), Suzuki Mōsa-burō (a JSP executive committee member), and Tokuda Kyūichi (secretary-general of the JCP). Three other members represented management, and Suehiro Izutarō (a law professor from Tokyo Impe-rial University) represented the public interest. There was some ob-jection to the nomination of Tokuda from white-collar staff in the *Yom-iuri* union, but the final decision on 26 November was strongly in Tokuda's favor. Now that a more equitable arbitration body had been constituted, Shōriki reversed himself and refused to submit to arbi-tration.[40]

It was only after SCAP—in an unrelated move[41]—on 2 December listed Shōriki as one of the suspected war criminals it was ordering the government to arrest that Shōriki agreed to arbitration. Nine days later, on 11 December, the day before he was imprisoned at Sugamo, Shō-riki signed the agreement hammered out in arbitration. The agree-ment provided that: (1) Shōriki would resign and sell all shares he owned in excess of 30 percent of the total stock of the *Yomiuri*; (2) the company would be reorganized as a corporation, allowing a wider distribution of shares; (3) Baba Tsunego was to be the new publisher (Shōriki had urged this right-wing socialist and staunch anti-communist who had once been editor of the *Yomiuri* Sunday Review to take leadership of the paper); and (4) a management council (keiei kyōgikai) having equal representation of management and employees would be set up to consult on important matters concerning editing and business operations. Other items dealt with such specifics as further consideration of pay raises, withdrawal of dismissals for dispute activities, union recognition, collective bargaining, and conclusion of a contract.[42]

This compromise agreement was worked out only at the last minute. The hardest bargaining went on between Shōriki and Tokuda over what degree of workers' control over the paper was to be permitted. Although the union had earlier presented a demand for participation in management, the point had not come to the fore as the central issue. The employees apparently presumed that the control they were currently exercising over the paper through production control would continue by virtue of the other concessions Shōriki had made, and felt that no formal mechanism for workers' control was needed. At any rate, the arbitration subcommittee came up with the management council as a means for effecting a compromise between the two extremes.[43]

Tokuda and Kikunami, two of the labor members on the subcommittee, demanded the establishment of a management control council through which the workers would run the *Yomiuri* alone. They were in essence demanding that the system of production control be made permanent, as the action program put forth by the Fourth JCP Congress on 1 December called for. Shōriki wanted precisely the opposite. Though he called it "management participation," he proposed merely appointing union representatives to the board of directors where they would be powerless before a management still in full possession of all its old powers. Shōriki and the business members of the subcommittee, then, were advocating labor-capital collaboration of the prewar variety.[44] Suehiro and Suzuki argued for the establishment of a joint organization in which representatives of capital and labor would amicably cooperate on an equal basis to solve the important problems of the enterprise.[45]

Tokuda argued vehemently for workers' control, but in the end went along with the other labor members in withdrawing his proposal, presenting another calling for the creation of a "management council" with equal membership of management and employees. This was the

basic proposal that ended up in the final settlement. Apparently Tokuda's thought on the compromise was: sacrifice the name but keep
the reality. He later explained that at the time of the *Yomiuri* settlement the workers were still weak, and that if they had tried to get
everything at once, it would have given an opening to the company to
use a strategy to split the workers and prevail. Since the *Yomiuri* after
the settlement came very much under the sway of the employees in
the editorial bureau through the management council, Tokuda's tactical compromise seems to have been sound. Certainly neither Shōriki
nor Suehiro anticipated that the employees would gain the upper hand,
and that workers' control would come into being at the *Yomiuri*. [46]

Two conclusions can be drawn concerning the effects on postwar
Japan of the first *Yomiuri* struggle. First, the *Yomiuri* struggle points
up the underlying theme of the workers' fight in postwar Japan for
greater control over the work process at the point of production. The
Yomiuri union had asked for the right of participation in management,
but their own actions belied those moderate-sounding words both
during and after production control. Spearheaded by the editorial bureau, the struggle committees had simply seized total control over
production and distribution for the duration; and once the struggle
was over, the workers in the editorial bureau came to dominate the
paper, this time through the union and the management council. The
tendency of the workers' representatives on the management council
was toward steadily enlarging their power at the expense of the owners and managers, who were effectively frozen out. The point is crucial, because it suggests that the premise of joint and equal labor-
management participation which the Arbitration Committee had laid
out in the settlement was in reality impossible.

Second, the influence of production control attracted great attention. Even while the dispute was going on, workers and organizers
streamed to Tokyo *Yomiuri* headquarters from all parts of Japan to learn
at first hand how to organize themselves and take action. And of course
the *Yomiuri*, with its wide national circulation, carried the message to
uncounted others unable to make the pilgrimage to Tokyo. The *Yomiuri* employees had won their dispute, without going out on strike and
without interrupting production, by the novel step of dispossessing
the owners and managers. The lesson seemed clear. Production was
critically needed but so was radical social and economic change. If
employers resisted worker demands, victory could still be had by seizing and operating the enterprise. [47]

Equal labor-capital cooperation was inherently unstable for one basic reason—the pursuit of capitalist profits and the pursuit of workers'

control were contradictory. The fundamental premises behind them differed too drastically. Profits demanded the extension of tight management control: over editorial and business policy in order to make the most of whatever economic opportunities there might be, and over workers in order to keep labor costs down and productivity high. The *Yomiuri* workers' goals of democratization and assignment of war responsibility were not reducible to enlisting labor cooperation in maximizing profits in the marketplace, for what they wanted was dignity and justice in their life and work. Capitalist profits *or* workers' self-realization—one could not have both; and joint labor-management participation in capitalist enterprise as a means for pursuing *production* on a *democratic* basis remained an illusion.

Workers' Control at the Keisei Electric Railway

The *Yomiuri* dispute and settlement directly stimulated the second production control struggle to break out, but at the Keisei Electric Railway intellectuals like Suzuki Tōmin were few, and ordinary workers conducted the fight.[48]

The Keisei Electric Railway was already during the war a "hunger railway," one of those which Tokyo dwellers took to the agricultural regions surrounding the city in their daily search for food. The Keisei line ran from Ueno in Tokyo to Narita in Chiba prefecture, and employed about 2,500 people. The Keisei Labor Union was formally inaugurated at a conference on 5 December, at which time the 2,000 employees attending unanimously adopted three demands: a fivefold wage increase, recognition of the right of collective bargaining, and opening of the account books for rationed goods. The newly elected thirteen-person negotiating committee, accompanied by two lawyers, ran a special express train to the Ueno company main office, where they learned that the account books had been burned. Furthermore, the company officials replied to their demands with remarks such as, "The right of collective bargaining, what's this?"

When the negotiating committee reported back, the angered workers at the Keisei union headquarters promptly added the following demands to their list: immediate resignation of those guilty of war responsibility and of those supervisors who had distributed rationed goods corruptly, and an explanation of why the company had burned the ration account books. They demanded that a reply be made at their headquarters by noon 8 December. On that day the company offered a twofold increase in pay and recognized the right of collective bargaining, but denied any fraud in the distribution of rations. The company showed no further will to negotiate after that, more than once simply not showing up at an appointed time.

Although the workers' first impulse was to strike, concern over the hardship which stopping of service would work on the passengers, especially those using the train in their search for food, led them to institute production control from 11 December. Further, the workers decided not to charge fares, a tactic apparently used to gain public support, while they temporarily withdrew a large number of dangerous cars from service for repairs. The famed "free-ride" trains continued for three days, after which fares were charged once again, and service was increased substantially over previous levels. The union handled the receipts from fares, depositing them in a bank in the company's name. Production control went smoothly, the white-collar staff and union members cooperating to continue operations much as usual. For example, repair materials were supplied by the company, and there was no diversion of fares to the union for its needs. Despite the successful production control, the agitated company officials made no concessions, and tried unsuccessfully to find a way to suppress the workers by government or SCAP intervention. The union, in turn, advanced a further demand on 22 December: the establishment of a management council of equal company-employee representation that would "conduct the entire management" of the company.

The company responded to the new demand by finally coming up with a compromise proposed on 23 December which offered a threefold increase in base pay and similar increases in a number of allowances, but did not respond to the other union demands. The union rejected the company offer. At that, an old and well-liked company official came to union headquarters on 26 December and informally consented to the granting of the following package of demands:

1. Recognition of the right of collective bargaining
2. Immediate fivefold raise of the basic wage
3. Immediate resignation of the three accused supervisors
4. Recognition of union participation in a management council (a council to be composed of thirteen members from each side which was to conduct the entire management of the company)
5. Shortening of the work day to eight hours
6. A considerable simplification of company organization
7. Payment of dispute expenses by the company

The company did not honor its informal agreement, however, and its formal proposal on the 27th fell far short of it, offering only: a fivefold wage increase; recognition of the right of collective bargaining; a provision that the official who had made the informal agreement be entrusted with the details of the resignation of the three supervisors; and the establishment, not of a management council, but of a round-table conference on operations.

For the union, the management council was the issue—more than wages, more than resignation of corrupt company officials, more than all the other demands. The workers got set to fight to the bitter end on that issue, for they realized that establishment of the kind of management council they envisioned meant a dramatic increase in their power at the expense of company officials. On 27 December the union held an extraordinary employees' conference which decided, first, to realize all demands, and second, to pay very large bonuses and allowances to the workers out of the fare receipts from production control.

The latter step shook company officials, who immediately requested that the union suspend its plans to pay out the production control receipts since the company was going to make a special payment equal to five months' wages. When on 28 December the union asked the company to pay the whole sum to the union, the company refused. After that, on the same afternoon about fifty angry union members forced their way into the main office and began grilling the corrupt supervisors about the rationed goods matter. After several hours they brought the three supervisors to union headquarters where they subjected them to "mass negotiations" that continued on through the night until 6:00 P.M. the next day, when the company conceded the union demands.

As the Keisei dispute had dragged out and appeared headed into a dead end after the company's unsatisfactory response on 27 December, the workers' reaction was twofold, as related above. They took direct action (mass negotiations) in the hope of forcing an immediate and favorable settlement, and they decided to deepen the production control struggle by illegally paying the workers out of funds accumulated from fares. One thing these very different tactics had in common was the surfacing of the workers' will to take illegal action, to break the hobbles of the capitalist legal order, if that were necessary to attain their goals. In another fundamental respect they were quite different. Direct action aimed at an immediate solution by breaking the will of the employers to resist, but even so it implied a settlement within the existing order. Appropriation of funds pointed toward a long struggle during which the workers would have to provide for their own needs by successfully operating the company in all respects and did not necessarily anticipate a final settlement within the existing order at all.

Direct action might provoke state oppression. The appropriation of funds seemed less likely to do so, but possession of funds was no guarantee that supplies could be obtained elsewhere in the face of big-business and government hostility. Thus there were limits to both tactics. Although these limits did not become apparent at Keisei, since the company gave in to the workers' demands, the success of a long-term struggle would necessarily have depended on the forging of alternative channels of distribution and exchange. A lengthening struggle would have entailed the continuous expansion of the sphere of the struggle-committee type of control structure within the company. Only in this way could the union overcome its fatal dependence on the owners for funds, wages, supplies, and so forth. That, in fact, was the underlying threat that had brought the company to settle.

Miners' Control of Production at Mitsui Bibai

Unlike many industries after the war, which were able to lay off workers en masse and virtually cease operations pending adoption of a policy on economic reconstruction in line with the wishes of the business leaders, the coal industry had to maintain the minimum output necessary to stave off complete economic paralysis, even though it might fall far short of the people's needs. That meant that coal was among the few key industries in which a strike still had meaning. Yet SCAP, in the name of the general welfare, had outlawed the coal miners' use of the strike. The miners were not anxious to strike in the first place, being concerned over their own security and over maintaining production. It was natural, therefore, that the miners too by spring 1946 had turned to using production control in their clashes with employers.

By taking control of production from the foot-dragging coal companies, the coal miners served the public interest by increasing and not crippling production, and this of course pleased SCAP. At the same time, it served the miners' demands for better working and living conditions and higher pay. The actual struggle to implement production control generated among the workers greater awareness about why production was needed and why it had not been adequately maintained. Production control was, therefore, to become a tremendously effective weapon for breaking through the barrier of zaibatsu sabotage. Worse yet from capital's point of view, production control accomplished all these things while making a direct attack on private property, and in the process called into question the capitalist system itself. All the implications of production control were not fully realized at once, of course, and the first production control struggle in coal was a decidedly limited action.

The first production control struggle in coal mining took place at the Mitsui Bibai mine[49] under the leadership of Murakami Yūkari, but also under the influence of Mizutani Takashi from the Mitsubishi Bibai mine, who as chairman of the Hokkaidō miners' union federation had come to assist in the struggle. The Mitsui Bibai union presented a list of demands on 14 November: a wage raise, abolition of the contract system, assurance of provisions, and purging of corrupt executives. Negotiations made no progress, and the union went on strike 6 December. The Chinese and Korean workers' outburst here had been violent and had included the kidnapping and holding for ransom of the company manager, who naturally enough became extremely fearful of mass actions. He disappeared from the site while the dispute was going on. All the officials of the union favored a strike, but Mizutani was aware of the two production control struggles then going on in Tokyo at the *Yomiuri* newspaper and Keisei Electric Railway and argued for production control. A strike, he argued, would stop coal production and the company would receive no funds with which to pay wages; in the meantime, inflation would accelerate, and since the company would benefit by keeping idle, a strike might go on indefinitely and cause much pain and suffering among the miners. Mizutani later described his reasoning: "The workers themselves must shoulder the burden of industrial reconstruction for a new Japan . . . I therefore thought of production control, taking the production-control incidents at *Yomiuri* and Keisei Dentetsu as our precedents . . . "[50] Mizutani argued, however, for careful adherence to legality in conducting operations. Of Mizutani's role at Mitsui Bibai, Sumiya Mikiō writes:

Mizutani at this time was not a Communist party member, so it does not seem as if he was acting according to party policy, and all the Communist party members among the others had been insisting upon a strike. As can be understood from these points, production control in this case was something which grew up spontaneously based on the peculiarities of Japan's economic situation after the lost war and on the position into which the working class had been placed.[51]

The union officials, convinced after hearing a concrete explanation of just what would be involved, decided to enter into production control 14 December. During the twelve days in which production control was practiced, the miners at Mitsui Bibai greatly increased labor productivity and coal output despite cutting the hours of work from twelve to eight, and were able to double output over what it had been just before the dispute. The one countermeasure the company was able to come up with was to obstruct the supply of coal cars to the mine, so that coal began to pile up. It should be stressed that the white-collar staff did not participate, and the scope of the action never extended beyond the mining of coal to its transport and sale. As the coal piled up and payday approached, neither side was complacent: the miners saw the strike as heading into a dead end, and the company was getting more and more worried over the length of the action. Hokkaidō government officials at this stage saw and took the opportunity to step in. With their mediation, a settlement was signed on 26 December in which the union achieved nearly all its aims.

This production control struggle strongly influenced the Hokkaidō labor movement, since the entire fight from start to finish had been carried out by the production workers through their union. Company officials were completely excluded, as were most of the white-collar staff, who took the company's side.

Allied Labor Policy

The most suitable workers' organization for the Japanese, according to American policy makers, was a moderate union which did not trouble itself too deeply about politics or the internal affairs of management. For many in SCAP, especially outside of Labor Division, the closest model to this idea was the more constricted "business union" that confined its activities to the pursuit of economic, job-oriented goals: higher wages, job security, better working conditions, and the like.[52] This kind of union acted solely in defense of those workers organized by it or federated with it, avoided representing workers as a class, and conducted a "businesslike" operation that recognized no basic conflict of interest between itself and the business enterprise.

Labor unions had gained general acceptance in the U.S. during the Roosevelt years of depression and world war, when the federal government accorded labor broad recognition as a legitimate interest group within American capitalism. This was part of the joint effort of big government and big business to overcome the failings of laissez-faire corporate capitalism through increased regulation of the economy. Recognition of labor's economic interests was intended to serve two purposes: first, to defuse a volatile situation of labor-capital confrontation by bringing labor into the system; second, to create increased demand for the products of American industry through the resulting rise in wages.

More specifically, the New Deal approach to labor involved the spinning of a "web of rules"—to borrow a phrase from a later theorist of American industrial relations, John Dunlop—binding labor to the modified capitalist order through legislation and union-employer contracts, the effect of which was to recognize labor's right to organize, strike, and bargain collectively over terms of employment. To realize their program, the FDR administration and its supporters in business and labor circles had to contest the conventional wisdom of their day, represented by conservative business, whose labor program amounted to encouraging company unions at best, or engaging in union busting at worst.

The contrasting liberal and conservative views of labor in America had an interesting parallel in postwar Japan. Some business leaders there shared the New Deal enthusiasm for updating capitalism while others staunchly advocated untrammeled free enterprise. The former were ready, indeed by spring 1946 often eager, to recognize unions as a means for stabilizing relations between capital and labor, while the old-fashioned conservatives in both countries fought unions as a vicious evil. SCAP, however, by erecting the framework of unionism in accordance with the view of American policy makers, ruled out very early the possibility of a complete return to the former anti-union repression of Japan's labor movement.

Whatever the intentions of U.S. policymakers in introducing labor reforms in the first place, the basic ideas of business unionism appealed more to the zaibatsu leaders, who were greatly interested in spinning their own web of rules and in containing worker discontent. Like corporate capitalists everywhere, the zaibatsu leaders needed predictability and stability in labor relations in order to plan rationally, regardless of whether or not they were emotionally prepared to accept unionization. A carefully circumscribed recognition of business unions held out that promise, and liberal members of the business world would come to just that conclusion in early 1946.

Policy Formation

Sometime in 1945, a certain Dave Denson was put to work in Washington, D.C., drafting a Civil Affairs Guide on Japanese labor for the State-War-Navy Coordinating Committee. This was but one of many policy guides written concerning sensitive problems anticipated in the occupation of Germany, Japan, and Korea. In spring 1945 an informal review committee composed of representatives of the Foreign Economic Administration, Office of Strategic Services, Treasury Department, Agricultural Department, and State-War-Navy Coordinating Committee rejected Denson's draft. The Foreign Economic Administration representative was Theodore Cohen, who, after a stint with the Office of Strategic Services, had become chief of the Japanese Labor Section in the Foreign Economic Administration's Enemy Branch. Although Cohen was a very young man and practically fresh out of college, his thesis work as a student distinguished him as the only person at all informed about Japanese workers and unions. Accordingly, Cohen was asked to prepare a new draft.

Cohen later recalled of Denson that: " . . . he didn't know anything about Japan. His specialty was Germany. And also, as far as I could tell, he was a Stalinist. There were quite a few of them around in Washington at the time. And his proposed Guide certainly sounded like a handbook on revolution."[53] Speaking of his own views, Cohen said that he personally "was violently anti-communist all through the war and for years before." Mark Gayn described Cohen as "a young man with a pathological fear of being labelled red (though Lord knows he is not)."[54]

While in the Foreign Economic Administration, Cohen worked directly under Irving Brown, chief of the Labor Division of the Foreign Economic Administration's Enemy Branch. An associate of George Meany, Brown had been nominated by the American Federation of Labor (AFL) to that agency. Brown "was a very strong anticommunist," Cohen said of his boss.[55] This was undoubtedly true, since Brown became notorious later for his successful operation, funded by the CIA through the AFL, to split the European labor movement and isolate the left wing.[56] This Brown did in close cooperation with people like Jay Lovestone of the rabidly anti-communist Free Trade Union Committee of the AFL, who coordinated a worldwide AFL offensive against left-wing labor movements immediately after World War II. Working closely with Brown, Cohen wrote a new draft for the policy guide on Japanese labor. Cohen later said that preparation of the guide was not an individual operation, "not just a composition by one person."[57] Cohen and Brown's efforts yielded the official Civil Affairs Guide on Japanese labor under the title, "Trade Unions and Collective Bargaining in Japan."

The specific recommendations of the guide were incorporated almost word for word into the State-War-Navy Coordinating Committee policy paper on Japanese labor, entitled "Treatment of Japanese Workers' Organizations," written in the labor provisions in both of the key U.S. government directives to SCAP: the "U.S. Initial Post-Surrender Policy for Japan" of 29 August, and the "Basic Directive for Post-

Surrender Military Government in Japan" (JCS 1380/15) of 3 November. There was, therefore, through Brown and Cohen, deep AFL involvement in formulating U.S. policy toward Japanese labor.[58]

The State-War-Navy Coordinating Committee paper on labor was written in the State Department's Office of International Labor Affairs by Philip B. Sullivan, and in addition to specific statements of policy drawn from Cohen's guide, included a lengthy appendix. This was an explicit justification for the stated policy that the growth of labor organizations should be encouraged by SCAP and by the Japanese government, and that these organizations should be "encouraged to bargain collectively with employers" over the terms of employment including wages, hours, and working conditions.[59] Sullivan's paper was adopted officially in December 1945 and transmitted to SCAP as policy, but had been informally made the basis of policy almost as soon as it was written. The content of "Treatment of Japanese Workers' Organizations" went far beyond Cohen's guide, however, in that the arguments Sullivan used to justify Cohen's recommended policies stated with exceptional clarity and forthrightness the relationship of the establishment of American-style business unionism in Japan to major political and economic goals of U.S. foreign policy.

Several points were made. U.S. policy makers anticipated that Japanese workers' organizations "might assist materially in the reconstruction of the country's political structure along democratic lines and in the reorientation of its economy towards peace and stability." Politically, the union movement was expected to provide a bulwark against the revival of fascism by becoming the "guardian of civil liberties," and by giving positive support to or becoming directly involved in responsible party politics. Economically, it was hoped labor organizations would be capable of promoting the emergence in Japan of "a welfare economy through which labor's living standards may be raised to the highest levels possible," thereby eliminating the "unfair advantage" of cheap labor Japan's exporters had held.[60]

As soon as conditions are favorable, the Japanese trade unions, both by day-to-day negotiation with the employers and by pressure for national legislation, will undoubtedly press for an increase in the general wage level and the elimination of sub-standard wages. The achievement of such an objective could have important results internationally. Pre-war Japan's foreign trade policies and practices had aroused widespread resentment. With relatively high technical efficiency in many lines of production and extremely low labor costs due to the low wages paid to even the really skilled among her workers, she was able to undersell her commercial rivals in a wide range of goods in many parts of the world. This low wage level, it should be understood, was a product of the peculiar political, social and economic forces existing in the country, among which should be listed the violent opposition by government to genuine labor organizations that has already been discussed. Unions were persecuted not only because of their political and social potentials but because it was feared they might be able to force increases in wages. Such increases, by raising labor costs, would have tended to diminish the volume of or the profit margin on Japanese exports, reduce foreign balances, and prevent the importation of those machines and materials vital to Japan's plans for armament and conquest. What Nazi-Germany accomplished largely by exchange controls and (frequently forced) bilateral trade agreements, Japan accomplished in the main by keeping the real income of her workers and farmers low. The over-all evidence on this point was the phenomenon obvious to all close observers of Japan's economy, that Japanese industrial workers were not only unable to afford foreign goods, but that quantities of home produced goods were either not offered for sale in Japan, or were priced beyond their means. Much of Japan's price undercutting in foreign markets, therefore, was based not on superior technical advantages, but on the exploitation of what may be called "sweated" labor and the fact that the "sweating" was nationwide in this case and not limited to a few shops or industries only, does not make the term any less appropriate. Higher labor costs, therefore, would not only move in the direction of eliminating the unfair advantage long enjoyed by the Japanese manufacturing and exporting interests, an advantage maintained to the detriment of the laboring classes in that country as well as to the legitimate business and labor interest of other lands, but the redistribution of income resulting from it would be a step in the desired direction of turning Japanese productive energies toward meeting the long neglected demands of the domestic consumer. The improbability that any appreciable amount of consumers' goods will be imported for some time to come will make this shift all the more likely as well as desirable.[61]

The paper, as might be expected, dealt only briefly with the practical details of implementing that policy.

Policy Implementation

An integrated picture of the operational policies of SCAP can be gained by comparing the SWNCC paper with three other basic documents on labor: the Cohen Civil Affairs Guide; the "First Interim Report on Treatment of Workers' Organizations since the Surrender," presented in June 1946 to SCAP by its Advisory Committee on Labor; and the Far Eastern Commission's "Statement of Principles for Japanese Trade Unions," adopted December 1946. The extent of agreement on basics among them, even including identical working in many places, reveals remarkable formal unanimity on labor policy.[62] That policy was to encourage labor organization and collective bargaining over terms and conditions of employment through: 1) enactment of protective legislation and abrogation of restrictive laws; 2) extension of full civil rights to labor; 3) dissolution of Japanese government agencies obstructing labor (especially the police) and a purge of the individuals involved; 4) dissolution of undemocratic labor organizations; and 5) release of people imprisoned for labor offenses. SCAP, however, reserved the right to ban strikes directly prejudicial to the needs of the occupation.

In implementation of policy, SCAP pursued two overlapping lines of action: clearing away restrictions and building an institutional framework for organized labor, a "web of rules." A major step toward the dismantling of barriers was taken on 4 October when SCAP issued SCAPIN-93,[63] which had the purpose or removing restrictions on civil rights. It required the abrogation of oppressive laws, abolition of agencies of oppression within the Japanese government (including the special police forces), placing of severe limitations on the functions of the regular police, and release of political prisoners. Although not directed specifically at labor, the order greatly affected labor developments, mainly because so much of the oppressive apparatus of Imperial Japan had been directed at labor, and because a number of committed Communist party members were among the political prisoners released, notably Tokuda Kyūichi and Shiga Yoshio.

Subsequently, on 11 October, MacArthur made a statement to the Japanese government directing it to undertake, among other things, "the encouragement of the unionization of labor." This step reinforced SCAPIN-93 and indicated to the Shidehara cabinet and Japanese business that SCAP would not tolerate obstruction of labor organization. Last came the 4 January 1946 purge directive. How effective it was in removing anti-labor personnel (temporarily or permanently) from public agencies is open to question, but that was a part of its intent. In any case, it probably restrained such functionaries from blatantly anti-labor actions during the early occupation.

The first action taken pursuant to MacArthur's directive to the Shidehara cabinet to encourage unionization was the setting up on 24 October of a Diet Committee to write new union legislation. The committee produced a Trade Union Law that passed the Diet 21 December, the first piece of legislation looking toward the establishment of an American-style system of labor relations. Without waiting for passage, SCAP had already obtained on 2 November the setting up of temporary labor-employer arbitration committees which were to operate at the national and prefectural levels. The Trade Union Law gave legal status to unions and collective bargaining. It defined unions solely as economic entities working for the economic betterment of their membership. It also established the dispute settlement agencies mentioned above, the Central Labor Relations Committee and its prefectural counterparts, on a permanent basis. Their functions were to be spelled out more fully under a succeeding law.

That law, the Labor Relations Adjustment Law, was also drafted by the Diet Committee. The preliminary draft was completed in January, but completely rewritten in April 1946 by Theodore Cohen and four other Americans. This version was passed by the Diet in September over the opposition of the labor movement, which condemned it as a step backward. It was designed to enforce settlement of labor disputes through conciliation, mediation, and arbitration procedures when collective bargaining failed. The crown to SCAP's labor-relations edifice was supplied by the new Japanese Constitution, which placed a guarantee of the rights of workers to organize, bargain, and act collectively under chapter 3, "Rights and Duties of the People."[64]

Once having accomplished its two immediate tasks of sweeping away obstacles to labor organization and seeing to the legislation of a "web of rules," SCAP took an attitude of benign neglect toward the workers' movement. The balance between capital and labor was being righted, and the proper stance now was non-interference. This became apparent in SCAP's attitude in early 1946, when workers engaged in actions that in the United States would have resulted in an immediate government crackdown. Though U.S. policy makers' (and therefore SCAP's) toleration of worker actions was broad, it had its limits, as would become increasingly apparent as the first winter of occupation wore on into spring.

It is often said that "political unions" were precisely what U.S. policy makers wanted to avoid in Japan, and that it was the workers' and labor unions' political involvement that eventually brought down the wrath of SCAP. It can easily be shown that this is a gross oversimplification. For example, on 28 August, 1945, Philip Sullivan wrote an interesting memo as State Department member of the Committee on Economic Policy, which was then reviewing for the last time the labor section of the document shortly to be issued to General MacArthur as the "Basic Directive for Post-Surrender Military Government in Japan." Concerning the nature of the Committee's recommended revisions of the labor sections of JCS 1380/15, Sullivan observed:

Moreover the talk now is that the political sections of the report are going to be interpreted in such a way that democratic movements of all kinds, insofar as they are not directed against our operations, even if they result in extensive social unrest and disorder, are not going to be interfered with by the occupation forces. "Let the pot brew what it may" so long as it is properly seasoned with popular sentiment and not too highly flavored with the spice of Communism. Under such conditions we may get a real labor movement started.[65]

Phrases with much the same meaning appeared in JCS 1830/15. SCAP, in its monthly Labor Division reports, viewed the close ties between the left-wing political parties (including the JCP) and the labor unions with surprising equanimity and impartiality, at least up until mid-1946. Even as late as May Day, 1946, SCAP described the big demonstrations approvingly, concluding that "They demonstrated the new freedom which the Occupation has given to the Japanese people and the political vitality of the working class which, properly guided, can be a potent force in the democratic reconstruction of Japan."[66] By that time, however, a major reevaluation of SCAP policy toward the labor movement was going on at the highest levels.

Two conclusions may be drawn from the above. First, there was little difference between SCAP and Washington on labor policy, and SCAP was clearly following Washington's lead. Second, the original policy and SCAP's implementation were much more flexible and pragmatic about political activity by labor than might at first be thought. It even appears that Washington and SCAP had some hopes of using the left in reconstructing a liberal but capitalist Japan. As early as November, the monthly summation stated that the JCP had launched a union-organizing campaign, and that "Party leaders assert that they will discourage strikes because direct action will hinder the reconversion of industry."[67] There were in fact very few strikes during the first year of occupation, and SCAP officials are reported to have often asked the JCP labor leaders to prevent strikes in 1945–46.[68]

On the other hand, should the workers' movement or the JCP transgress the limits of toleration, the means and rationale for suppression of radical worker actions had already been provided for in a clause of JCS 1380/15. It gave MacArthur authority "to prevent or prohibit strikes or other work stoppages" when he considered this necessary for military or other occupation reasons.[69] MacArthur's interpretation of the directive can be seen in his 17 November command letter to the armies of occupation entitled "Civilian Labor Employed by Occupation Forces."

Strikes, lock-outs, or other work stoppages which are inimical to the objectives of military occupation are prohibited. . . . A labor dispute "inimical to the objectives of military occupation" is one which jeopardizes the safety of Allied troops, interferes with troop supply, disrupts services or production necessary to the maintenance of public order, public service and public health or adversely affects other purposes of the occupation.[70]

After citing these passages in its "First Interim Report" of June 1946, the SCAP Advisory Committee on Labor went on:

In practice, transportation, communication, coal mining, public utilities, repatriation service and Occupation Forces' projects have been considered essential. This limitation has been communicated orally by Economic and Scientific Section, GHQ/SCAP, to the Japanese Government, employers and labor unions on numerous occasions and has prevented several serious stoppages in those categories.[71]

An even fuller explanation appears in a SCAP summation of events in December 1945:

SCAP has adopted the following policies in the handling of labor disputes:
Strikes, lock-outs and other work stoppages which are inimical to the objectives of military occupation are prohibited.
Mediation and arbitration of labor disputes which are not inimical to occupation objectives are responsibilities of the Japanese Government. The prefectural mediation committees established by a Ministry of Welfare order of 2 November are designated as appropriate agencies to intervene in such disputes.
Government and union leaders have been informed of the above policies and an explanation has been given of those production activities and services considered to be essential to the occupation objectives. Government officials have been advised to further the development of agencies and administrative procedures capable of taking corrective measures prior to disputes resulting in work stoppages. Labor leaders have been advised to develop responsibility and stability in their organizations and urged not to resort to strike action without first exhausting the possibilities of negotiations and mediation procedures. Parties concerned realized that indiscriminate work stoppages would hamper the economic reconstruction of Japan and an earnest effort appears to have been made to adopt and to adhere to an "avoid strikes" policy.[72]

In short, any worker action that interfered with the reconstruction of the Japanese economy as it then existed, that is, as capitalist, would be banned.

The question for U.S. policy makers and SCAP was not whether strikes were to be permitted, or even whether political involvement was to be tolerated. Rather, it was how to prevent the effective political use of the workers' weapons against the liberal, capitalist regime the U.S. was trying to construct in Japan. SCAP was trying in effect to draw a fine line separating the "normal" political concerns of labor within a capitalist economy from "revolutionary" actions of workers combining in a movement to wrest economic and political control from capitalist hands entirely. Production control seems not to have registered with the occupation authorities as a particularly radical action at first. There was little open concern over the politicization of labor, anyhow, until the mass demonstration in April and May 1946 alarmed U.S. policy makers, who suddenly found conditions too highly seasoned with the spice of communism indeed.

After the initial clearing away of obstructions, SCAP's implementation of Allied labor policy consistently lagged behind events. The Japanese working class was well on the way to unionization even before its legal basis was secured by the coming into effect of the new Trade Union Law. Moreover, production control—direct action of a fundamentally radical and anti-capitalist kind with implications outstripping anything envisaged in the Allied labor reforms—had captured the imagination of workers by midwinter and bid fair to overshadow the Allied reforms completely. The surge of the working class far in advance of SCAP was quite natural. The abstract principles of American-style business unionism had little to offer workers attempting to salvage their livelihood and to keep their families from being crushed by a capitalist society in disintegration.

3

Capitalist Sabotage and the Winter Crisis

From Retrenchment to "Sabotage"

The Bankruptcy of Laissez-Faire

The plans the Keidanren Committee elaborated following Minister of Commerce and Industry Nakajima's invitation to big business to devise a policy for economic recovery did not long outlive the Higashikuni cabinet. Before the year was out, the old guard suddenly found itself with no coherent plan for getting through the difficult days ahead.

Labor's unchecked rise signaled the end of the historic edge Japan had held in the competition for foreign markets with the resource-rich nations of the West, an edge which had only been possible because of severe restrictions on wages and internal consumption. Unions and the higher wages they would bring threatened to rule out the old strategy of using exports of labor-intensive light industry like textiles as the springboard for growth of heavy industry. SCAP compounded the labor troubles of the old guard by virtually ending foreign trade, earmarking heavy industry for reparations, and slating the zaibatsu for dissolution.

In effect, postwar conditions only permitted the shifting of idle zaibatsu resources into production of civilian consumer goods. Before, the zaibatsu had produced for export or for the state, leaving the depressed and meager internal consumer market to small- and medium-sized business. The risky capital investment needed to expand production for the internal market and the prospect of smaller profits than in their traditional overseas and state markets was discouraging enough to the zaibatsu, but much more than profits was at stake. A rapid economic recovery based on conversion to the production of consumer goods—many of which were products of light industry like textiles, food processing, and household or farm goods—would simultaneously strengthen labor and give the Allied Powers ample justification for following through with their demands for economic democratization and reparations. Failure of the economy to recover, however, might well have the opposite effect. Given such considerations, it is plain to see that big business had little to gain by hastening the revival of the civilian economy.

The Keidanren Committee had earlier seen the recapitalization and rationalization of the zaibatsu as the preconditions for early recovery. The pruning of unprofitable operations and the reorganization of business on a sound basis for future expansion were simply phases in industrial reconversion and reentry into world trade. Now these steps had degenerated into a defensive retrenchment. Retrenchment was no longer a means to an end, but the end itself. It had indeed become "sabotage," an ad hoc program of withdrawal from production and a shift to large-scale speculation in essential commodities on the black market. Capital had gone on a sit-down strike.[1] Moreover, although sabotage was primarily an economic tactic resorted to by the zaibatsu because of their inability to develop a positive program for economic revival, it also had a political dimension, and would have been much less effective without the cooperation of the government.

Some would deny the culpability of the leaders of business and government for the postwar economic crisis and simply maintain that government bureaucrats were incompetent and businessmen so paralyzed by events that they were in a "state of despondency" (kyodatsu jōtai). Utterly discouraged and fearful of SCAP intentions, the old guard was supposedly incapable of taking the initiative to resume production and commence with reconstruction. Without doubt, government incompetence and business despondency did exist, but when it suited their purposes, as it had in liquidating the munitions industry, the Japanese leadership was more than capable of coordinated and purposeful effort. Capital's sit-down would not have been possible, in fact, had the old guard failed to decontrol the economy and recapitalize the zaibatsu in the first weeks. Once that was done, neither SCAP nor the Japanese were able to do much about it when big business, in anticipation of worse to come, closed up shop, discharged employees, and sat back with its hoards to wait out the bad times.

What was involved was no vague malaise, no indefinable loss of will among the leadership. On the contrary, the very intensity with which they had seized on laissez-faire and the free economy as the panacea for the foreign and domestic threats before them led to the practice of sabotage. This was not the result of a general collapse of morale at all. It was a specific form of economic resistance arising from all too strongly held beliefs.

The Political Dimension

As winter approached, Japan above all needed a government determined to marshall existing resources behind the maximum production and equitable distribution of essential consumer goods, but that was not what it got.[2] The Shidehara cabinet, which governed Japan from 9 October 1945 to 22 April 1946, was somewhat of a contradiction. It was headed by a "bureaucratic" prime minister who advocated extreme small business free private enterprise even while implementing the free economy policies of big business, and who ended his brief tenure as premier trying to reimpose controls on the economy.

Part of the difficulty of evaluating the Shidehara cabinet lies in the temptation to ascribe greater initiative and autonomy to cabinets and prime ministers than is justified. Cabinets in Japan have always been heavily dependent upon big business funds and bureaucratic expertise for retention of power and execution of policy. The Shidehara cabinet was no exception, and even if it had had the will to step in to organize production for civilian needs, it is doubtful that it possessed the power. For to do so would have required it to demand that big businesses make sacrifices, surrender their precious hoards, and in effect disarm themselves before the dangers of the rising workers' movement and the Allied economic democratization. As the creature of others, it comes as no surprise that the Shidehara cabinet faithfully reflected the change away from the free economy back to economic controls and planning when the business and bureaucratic consensus changed in February.

On 9 October, Shidehara published a message on the occasion of his assumption of office outlining his cabinet's policies on major problems which made the predictable obeisance to democracy and popular welfare.[3] Alongside the Higashikuni cabinet's slogan of "preservation of the national polity," Shidehara now advanced slogans of political and economic democratization as if to snatch the initiative from SCAP.[4]

That the cabinet would fail to steal a march on SCAP became a foregone conclusion after General MacArthur's famous 11 October communication to Shidehara, the "Statement to Japanese Government Concerning Required Reforms." After listing five reforms to be carried out as rapidly as possible—emancipation of women, organization of labor, democratization of education, abolition of repressive institutions, and democratization of the economy—MacArthur concluded by calling for " . . . vigorous and prompt action on the part of the Government with reference to housing, feeding and clothing the population in order to prevent pestilence, disease, starvation, or other major social catastrophes. The coming winter will be critical and the only way to meet its difficulties is by the full employment in useful work of everyone."[5]

Outflanked ideologically by SCAP, and unable to withstand the pressure for prompt action on political reform, the Shidehara cabinet nonetheless fought a surprisingly effective rear-guard action on the economic front against both SCAP and the Japanese people. Its repeated efforts to abolish controls, to give away commodities and supply cash subsidies to industry, to aid the "rationalization" of labor even to the extent of engaging in governmental layoffs,[6] all contributed to the capitalist sit-down and the economic stagnation.

The enthusiasm for laissez-faire that swept big business in August and September had never been total, of course. It began to wane in October in counterpoint to the rising tempo of economic directives issuing from SCAP and the deepening of the economic collapse as retrenchment degenerated into sabotage and contributed to the worrisome increase in popular unrest. The more progressive managerial stratum in big business began to press for a return to economic controls and planning. The changing climate of opinion in business was reflected in politics when in early November the two major conservative parties formally organized—the Liberal party on 9 November and the Progressive party on 16 November.

The Liberal party program held to the conventional wisdom of the mainline conservatives as formulated in the early weeks, pledging "to strengthen finances, promote free economic activity, and reconstruct agriculture, commerce, manufacturing, and all industries to build up the national economy."[7] The third and fifth of its "emergency policies" revealed solid agreement with the Keidanren Committee.

Number 3, Administration
1. To overthrow bureaucratism, and resolutely to carry out a fundamental revolution in the existing system of government officials.

. . . .

Number 5, Economy, Industry
1. To abolish totally all controls, outside of necessary and unavoidable voluntary controls, to restore a free economy, and to take the following measures in order to promote national industrial activity.
   (a) The prompt abolition of the National Mobilization Act and all laws and ordinances based on it

(b) Immediate abolition of the Timber Control Act
(c) Abolition of the system of economic police
2. We pledge rapid participation in international trade, and to strive for the cultivation of export industries like silk thread, textiles, handicrafts, and industrial arts.

The nominal Liberal party position on labor was recognition of labor's rights to protective legislation and better treatment, but events would show the party in reality to be resolutely anti-labor. Far from enhancing labor's economic and social position, the party worked hand in hand with the big business conservatives typified by Keidanren which wanted to keep labor atomized, weak, and cheap.

The Progressive party took a very different line on economic policy, and pledged in its program to ". . . work for equity of distribution and flourishing production through an industrial balance permeated by the free activities of all, erect a new economic structure, and make secure the existence of the whole nation."[8] A general statement of its position appeared at the end of the long introductory declaration:

If we base our philosophy on the improvement of public welfare, we must be dedicated to the construction of a new society, such as will take as its goals improvement of the standard of living and the stability of public welfare by full employment; will establish a new economy which will obtain a proper balance under an industrial plan which would coordinate and regulate agriculture, industry, and commerce; will check "inflation" by eliminating bureaucratic controls and stabilizing finance; will secure foodstuffs; further, will increase production by bringing in science and technology throughout our administration; and will eradicate zaibatsu monopoly over enterprise.[9]

There was no separate section on labor and unions, but Progressive party policy can be gathered from statements like these: "we must rectify the disparity of wealth and poverty, resolutely enforcing a thoroughgoing social policy"; "[we must] develop a consensus through joint organizations and realize labor-capital solidarity."[10]

The Progressive party platform foreshadowed the working out of a radically different approach to economic reconstruction. The basic element can already be seen here, namely, a return to national economic regulation and planning which would be coordinated and carried out through both public and private agencies, that is, through government administrative agencies and through private business associations.

The Liberal party's promotion of textile exports and expansion of heavy industry as the engines of recovery was conspicuously absent in the Progressive platform. Instead, the program promised to promote civilian industry through the planned, balanced development of agriculture, commerce, and industry, and to obtain greater equity of distribution through full employment and a rise in the standard of living. The Progressive party was tentatively bringing together the expansion of internal consumer demand and greater production of consumer goods as the mechanism for resuming economic growth. Accordingly, labor—which the Liberals saw as just one of the factors of production to be gotten as cheaply as possible—now gained recognition as consumers, whose effectiveness in stimulating "flourishing production" depended on their attainment of purchasing power through "equity of distribution." The Progressives were beginning to see that without either of the two previous stimuli to economic growth—light industrial exports and war expenditures—business would have to turn to the domestic consumer economy.

The Progressive party was decidedly not advocating a return to full-fledged, bureaucratic controls of the wartime variety, or the building of a strong and independent union movement. Bureaucratic expertise was needed, but business leadership had to remain dominant. Nor can the strong flavor of prewar labor-capital collaboration be missed. If need be, labor might be more generously rewarded, but it had to be obedient.

The Capitalist Sit-Down in Industry

While the leaders of big business and government purposefully intensified the severity of the postwar collapse by their economic policies, they also worried over the impossibility of feeding the people of Japan with indigenous resources, the dangers of inflation, and unemployment, which was projected to reach thirteen million.[11] They hoped their policies would lead to an early recovery and to solutions to the grave problems facing the country before the populace was goaded beyond endurance. But recovery did not come.

The Scope of the Economic Collapse

Statistics alone cannot convey the human suffering of the years of economic collapse and agonizingly slow recovery. They can, however, put across some feeling for the magnitude of the tragedy that was visited upon the Japanese people (see table 3.1). Industrial activity after surrender fell below 10 percent of the 1935–37 average,[12] rising only to about 13 percent during the winter. The stoppage resulted in severe shortages of all kinds and contributed to a major inflation that cut deeply into wages already below survival levels.

TABLE 3.1
Index of Industrial Production, April 1945–1948 (1935–37 = 100)

Year	Month	Textiles	Chemicals	Iron and Steel	Machinery	Coal	Mining and Manufacturing	Mining	Consumer Goods	Producer Goods
1945	Apr	6.5	37.7	44.8	12.1	103.8	24.7	21.7	14.5	52.0
	Jun	4.1	32.5	31.3	4.4	101.3	18.1	15.6	11.4	40.6
	Aug	6.1	7.7	5.4	4.0	48.3	8.5	7.5	26.7	12.1
	Sep	6.0	11.1	3.0	1.3	25.7	9.0	8.4	31.6	7.7
	Oct	6.1	15.1	2.6	12.1	17.1	13.0	12.7	32.5	10.4
	Nov	6.6	16.5	3.4	9.0	16.0	13.6	13.5	29.3	11.1
	Dec	5.0	15.0	4.2	11.5	24.7	13.4	13.2	25.1	13.1
1946	Jan	3.9	12.8	4.2	16.6	34.3	13.4	12.9	23.4	13.7
	Feb	5.4	14.8	4.9	22.4	39.0	15.6	15.1	23.2	15.2
	Mar	6.2	19.1	6.8	29.4	47.4	18.8	18.2	25.1	21.5
	Apr	7.2	22.4	6.9	38.4	47.2	21.8	21.3	28.3	25.0
	May	8.1	25.9	7.0	43.0	49.3	25.2	24.7	34.9	26.7
	Jun	8.7	27.8	6.6	43.2	46.3	25.7	25.2	38.9	29.0
	Aug	12.1	27.5	6.6	47.8	51.8	29.6	29.0	48.2	29.4
	Oct	15.7	29.0	7.1	46.4	51.7	29.4	28.8	45.5	30.0
	Dec	17.9	27.0	7.0	46.7	63.3	27.7	26.8	34.1	29.0
1947	(ave.)	15.8	31.6	10.9	49.4	65.1	31.5	30.6	32.1	25.6
1948	(ave.)	17.7	43.0	24.6	86.7	81.1	44.2	43.3	38.8	39.4

Source: Japan Ministry of Finance and Bank of Japan, *Statistical Year-Book of Finance and Economy of Japan, 1948* (Tokyo: Ministry of Finance Printing Office), pp. 558–59; Bank of Japan, Statistics Department, *Economic Statistics of Japan (Annual), 1948* (Tokyo: Bank of Japan), pp. 172–73.

A full year after surrender, in August 1946, the index of industrial production was only approaching 30 percent of the 1935–37 average, and in 1948 the yearly average was still below half of the base period, at 44.2 percent. Recovery to prewar levels, even those of the relatively good years of 1935–37, would not have meant recapturing some high prewar standard of affluence. Even in the mid-thirties—the best years that Japanese workers had ever had—the standard of living was still very low, not far above a bare minimum for most.[13]

Industry during the winter of 1945–46 fell far short of providing even the necessities for the seventy-two million people crowded into the four main islands. Furthermore, when production recovered to the level of 25–30 percent in the last half of 1946, it stagnated there. The dismal economic performance soon compelled the U.S. to supply aid on a large scale, with foodstuffs first being imported in the spring of 1946 to prevent starvation.

It is often said that the economic collapse was the unavoidable result of the confusion and destruction attendant upon the military defeat. But to prove that Japan's *war* economy had been shattered by blockade and bombing does not in itself prove that maintenance of a modest but adequate level of production in the *civil* economy was beyond reach. On the contrary, this was quite within Japan's capabilities.[14]

War destruction of physical plant as a decisive limiting factor can be dismissed at the outset. Productive capacity in key industries like steel, aluminum, coal, power, chemicals, and machine tools remaining after the end of the war was actually greater than 1935–37 levels, more than adequate for supplying the minimum needs of the postwar civilian economy.[15] For example, according to SCAP statistics, total estimated capacity for steel production in late 1945 was nearly 10.7 million metric tons. Of this, 8.5 million tons was the potential output in major industrial areas; even after accounting for damage to physical plant, these areas were capable of producing 6.7 million tons. Since little damage occurred outside the major areas, actual capacity after surrender was in the neighborhood of 8 to 9 million tons, well in excess of the average annual production for 1935–37 of 5.6 million tons (a figure that includes production in Korea and Manchuria. These figures make a startling contrast to actual steel production in 1946 of 375,000 metric tons.[16]

Even if deterioration of plant meant that these figures for capacity were greatly inflated, it is inconceivable that real plant capacity was less than the 3.5 million tons that the Allies proposed as Japan's annual postwar output. SCAP sources make it quite clear that they did not believe that steel production was impeded by lack of productive capacity, but by shortages of coal, coking coal, and iron ore, of which coal was the crucial bottleneck.[17] Indeed, shortages are most often cited as the root cause of Japan's economic problems—shortages of raw materials, labor, transport, fuel, and even working capital.[18] Only one of these factors was truly outside the control of business and government leaders: the acquisition of raw materials not found in quantity in Japan, such as coking coal, petroleum, and bauxite.

The sizeable stockpiles of critical materials handed out at the end of the war may have contained enough steel, iron, aluminum, and other essentials to have fed a substantial peacetime economy for a couple of years.[19] As one indication, according to estimates made by Japanese authorities and used by SCAP, the total quantity of usable steel stock on hand at the end of hostilities was nearly one million metric tons; and that was only a fraction of the large hidden stockpiles that existed.[20] Arisawa Hiromi pointed out in his 1949 study of the problem of economic recovery that only the existence of concealed stocks can explain why the machine industry recovered to nearly half its 1935–37 average output within a year while iron and steel production languished at around 7 percent.[21]

Even had all possible resources been mobilized behind reconstruction, bottlenecks would soon have appeared, no doubt, and recovery would have been limited by Japan's restricted ability to obtain certain crucial imports. Even so, the Japanese people would have reaped benefits through improvement in their daily lives, instead of the zaibatsu taking speculators' profits as actually happened. Furthermore, SCAP was anxious enough to get the economy moving again before six months were out to devise a program to allow imports of cotton from the U.S. on credit as early as February 1946 as a means for stimulating textile production.[22] Imports of other essential commodities followed as 1946 wore on, indicating that the U.S. would not have allowed bottlenecks in the supply of raw materials to block recovery. The heart of the problem was that big business was unwilling to use its reserves for all-out production.

Since industry was operating at a small fraction of capacity and unemployment was endemic, business complaints of shortages of labor, skilled or unskilled, simply reveal that wages and working conditions in the industries claiming to be affected were so bad as to be worse than unemployment itself. Labor productivity was very low, but this cannot be considered a cause of the lagging recovery so much as a reflection of the deterioration of plant and a work force sapped of the will and ability to work by hunger and deprivation.

In regard to transport, overseas and coastal shipping had sustained heavy war damage. Steel merchant shipping of over 500 gross tons had declined to only 557,000 tons by the end of the war, but according to government estimates of total tonnage, in the fall of 1945 80 percent of the needed 2.5 million gross tons was available. The disastrous wartime attempts at industrial dispersal to escape attack had intensified the overburdening of local transport shuttling between shipping and rail heads and factories. Motor vehicle transport was also badly crippled by shortages and under-maintenance, and fuel was short for the mere 30,000 to 40,000 trucks that were usable, necessitating increasing reliance on horse and hand carts. However, the existence of considerable overcapacity in almost every sector of industry meant that the worst strain on local transport caused by industrial dispersal could be overcome rather quickly by shifting production back to centrally located plants.[23]

Little need be said about the supposed shortage of working capital. Except for small- and medium-scale industry without zaibatsu connections—accounting for only a fraction of industrial capacity—the so-called shortage was an insignificant factor; for the government turned over to its big business creditors staggering sums in partial payment of wartime liabilities..

The Example of the Coal Industry

Japan in the forties depended on coal far more than on petroleum for industry, power generation, and transportation. While Japan's coal is of rather low quality and difficult to mine, deposits were large enough to supply as much fuel as industry could have used. Nonetheless, contemporary accounts of economic stagnation in 1945–46 repeatedly stress the coal shortage, and the mine owners' culpability.[24] The list of industries crippled by lack of coal included virtually every type of enterprise, beginning with the means for shipping the coal, the railroads. The limitations imposed upon production of chemical fertilizers, textiles, iron and steel, and cement were extremely damaging. Recovery in coal was essential to recovery everywhere.[25]

Average monthly production from 1935 to 1946 and actual monthly output in the first year of occupation appear in table 3.2. The effects of the low production on allocation to key industries can be seen in table 3.3. The situation was even worse than these figures suggest, for the quality of the coal produced had fallen drastically.

SCAP was well aware of the crucial importance of the coal industry, and on 15 September directed the Japanese government to take steps to increase production. Because the mines were run-down and in need of cable, timber, cement, and many other items including labor, the industry was to be accorded preferential treatment thenceforth. SCAP's directive had little effect, however, because mine owners and the gov-

TABLE 3.2
Coal Production, 1935–August 1946 (metric tons)

Year[a]	Average Monthly Production (1,000 tons)[b]	Month	Monthly Production (1,000 tons)[c]
1935	3,142		
1936	3,484		
1937	3,772		
1938	4,057		
1939	4,367		
1940	4,776		
1941	4,634		
1942	4,515		
1943	4,628		
1944	4,111		
1945	1,861		
		Apr	3,597
		May	3,676
		Jun	3,513
		Jul	2,787
		Aug	1,673
		Sep	890
		Oct	593
		Nov	553 [d]
		Dec	856
1946	1,877		
		Jan	1,197
		Feb	1,349
		Mar	1,643
		Apr	1,637
		May	1,710
		Jun	1,603
		Jul	1,631
		Aug	1,794

[a] 1935–39—calendar year; 1940–46—April to March fiscal year.

[b] Rōdō Sōgi Chōsa Kai, Sengo Rōdō Sōgi Jittai Chōsa (Tokyo: Chūō Kōron-sha, 1957), vol. 1, Sekitan Sōgi, pp. 10–11.

[c] Japan Ministry of Finance and Bank of Japan, Statistical Year-Book of Finance and Economy of Japan, 1948 (Tokyo: Ministry of Finance Printing Office), p, 646.

[d] The lowest monthly production in the twentieth century. SCAP, General Headquarters, Summation, no. 3, pp. 66–67.

ernment were indifferent to increasing production beyond a bare minimum.

Four zaibatsu dominated the industry—Mitsubishi, Mitsui, Furukawa, and Sumitomo, in descending order—and operated the largest, most modern and productive mines.[26] Their mines in Hokkaidō were especially hard hit by the revolts of the foreign miners after the surrender, and the manner in which the operators and the government

TABLE 3.3
Allotment of Coal to Selected Industries, 1935–37 and 1944–46 (thousands of metric tons)

Year[a]	Iron and Steel	Chemicals	Textiles	Occupation Forces	Total
1935	5,259	2,506	5,449		44,616
1936	6,129	3,295	6,387		49,201
1937	6,639	3,958	6,968		53,092
1944	11,242	4,600	1,026		51,148
1945	3,309	1,856[b]	582	293	24,765
1946	1,448	1,916[c]	736	835	22,389

Source: Japan Ministry of Finance and Bank of Japan, *Statistical Year-Book of Finance and Economy of Japan, 1948* (Tokyo: Ministry of Finance Printing Office), pp. 647–49.

[a] 1935–37—calendar year; 1944–46—April to March fiscal year.
[b] Fertilizers—294; other chemicals—1,562.
[c] Fertilizers—1,237; other chemicals—679.

dealt with the ensuing labor problems is a revealing example of sabotage.

Most of the Korean and Chinese forced laborers who made up approximately 40 percent of the entire work force in the coal industry were removed in October and November. They would have to be replaced before production could begin to recover. Obviously a prerequisite to their replacement was to remedy the appalling situation that had existed in the mines by providing decent pay, food, housing, and working conditions, but the operators and the government did little, and recruitment lagged badly. Life as a coal miner was so bad that it was hard to get people to go to the mines to work, regardless of mass unemployment and great want, even starvation.[27] Those zaibatsu leaders in a position to do something about it clearly did not think that increased coal production was urgent enough to divert a portion of their multi-billion yen profits from munitions to improve conditions for the miners. SCAP had to order the government to take action.[28]

The U.S. Civil Affairs Guide on working conditions in Japan printed in September 1945 set forth SCAP's position on coal mining and miners as follows:

The main concern of Military Government in connection with working conditions in mines will be the problem of securing maximum coal production to supply military needs and civilian requirements. It is very doubtful that even fair production will be forthcoming unless something is done to improve the situation of the miners. In this respect, mining is likely to prove the critical industry in peace as in war, and special measures may be required in order to secure a satisfactory relationship between the mine workers and Military Government and a resulting adequate output of coal. . . .

Special measures planned and carried out by Military Government to increase production in coal mines ought to be carefully considered in the light of the ultimate objective: willing cooperation on the part of the Japanese workers. If conditions in mines are bad, production may temporarily be increased by the use of force to coerce the miners, but in the end the cooperation of the miners and of other workers may be permanently lost. It is therefore recommended that an inquiry be made into conditions in Japanese mines (by inspection tours to selected mines), and if it is clear that a revival of prewar standards will not materially improve them, special orders should be prepared immediately to bring conditions in the most important mines up to a reasonably high standard. If necessary, special food rations or other measures may be authorized for miners, and, if substantial numbers of Korean workers remain, special relief measures may be taken in their behalf.[29]

Despite the phrases about securing cooperation from the miners, SCAP's reaction to the Korean and Chinese uprisings quite straightforwardly came down to a policy of coal production first, at the price of SCAP military intervention if need be.[30] The Japanese government and mine owners were willing to use police force against the uprisings, but when suppression failed, the government simply abdicated responsibility, turning the situation over to the coal company officials on the spot, who had no choice but to make concessions to the miners' demands. As soon as it became obvious that the foreign miners were not going to settle down and dig coal even if force were used, SCAP and the Japanese cooperated in rushing repatriation.[31]

When SCAP realized in November that the foreign miners were not being replaced, it directed the government to assume responsibility for recruitment and institute the following measures:

(1) Recruitment of volunteer labor through various propaganda media. Advice and facilities of this headquarters [SCAP] have been made available.

(2) Increase of food rations for miners and families, increase of wages, clothing and footgear and special food bonuses of sweet potatoes, sake and oil.

(3) Improvement of working conditions and repair of mine living quarters.[32]

The government did not carry out these measures,[33] and SCAP's retrospective assessment of the recruitment drive indicates some of the reasons for the failure.

The recruiting effort of the Government to offset the loss of the foreign laborers was not successful. The long hours and the hard and dangerous work as well as the low labor standards associated with the mines discouraged the unemployed from seeking work in the coal fields. Moreover, the Government failed to keep its promises. In some districts the efficiency of the miners was lowered because the Government failed to deliver not only the promised special food rations but the basic food rations. Labor morale was further lowered by the Government's recruitment method of assigning a quota to each employment exchange and then exerting great pressures on it to meet the quota. On several occasions vagrants were rounded up in the large cities and offered the choice of working in the coal mines or going to jail. Absenteeism in the mines increased as workers left for the country in search of food. In *December* 1945 and again in *January* 1946 SCAP sharply criticized the Government for its failure to execute a satisfactory recruitment program, and demanded that the Government indicate the progress made toward increasing miners' wages and food and clothing rations.

As a result of SCAP criticism, the Government intensified its recruiting efforts and tried to reduce absenteeism by raising the wages of surface and underground workers. Not until *March* 1946, however, did employment in the mines reach a maximum within the limits of the housing facilities and mining equipment. The Government could not relax its drive to recruit workers because miners deserted their jobs whenever the delivery of food rations failed.[34]

As 1946 wore on, the government, under constant SCAP prodding, took care of the labor problem for the operators by the expedient of subsidizing their labor costs. The operators then began to complain that the price of coal was set too low for them to make a profit and that the radicalism of the coal miners' unions had unsettled management, thus causing continued low production. In reality production was higher than the official figures showed and much zaibatsu coal found its way to the black market, where considerable profits were made.[35] At any rate, one year after the occupation had begun, verifiable production of coal—the most critical raw material of all—had stagnated at half the 1935–37 average.

Sherwood Fine, director of Economics and Planning in Economic and Scientific Section, SCAP, throughout the occupation, later summed up the coal situation as the joint responsibility of the government and the operators.

Despite the coal mines being accorded top financial and material priority in meeting rehabilitation needs, monthly production for 1946 averaged only 1.78 million tons or a total of 21.3 million tons. Mine owners revealed only limited enthusiasm for increasing production and in the efficient direction of operations. Finite coal reserves were being exchanged for a rapidly depreciating yen. Mine operators were guilty of wasteful use of manpower and new equipment as well as unbusinesslike squandering of public loans and subsidies. The responsible Japanese ministries responding [sic] sympathetically to the operators' plight and abstained from undertaking any forceful measures to increase production.[36]

After pointing out that government subsidies were in fact a program of giveaways to the coal industry, Fine commented on profitability: ". . . The shockingly poor accounting systems maintained by the various coal producers completely defied disclosure of their actual financial condition. While it was strongly suspected that the mines were faring far better than claimed no satisfactory demonstration of this was ever possible."[37] In the end, there is no avoiding the conclusion that sabotage did indeed cripple industry and undercut SCAP attempts to speed economic recovery.

Worsening Social Distress

The general capitalist sit-down precipitated the social crisis that the big-business leaders of the Keidanren Committee had hoped to avert by a severe but short period of planned retrenchment intended to prepare the way for economic recovery on the old laissez-faire basis. Mass unemployment, spiraling inflation, food shortages—these problems and others weighed heavily on the Japanese people. City dwellers suffered the worst in the winter following defeat, and soon gave vent to their anger by rallying behind popular movements opposing the old order. Even so, the apparatus of oppression might have served to contain the social consequences of defeat and economic reconversion for a time, had SCAP not swept much of it away in October.

Bearing the Cost of Inflation and Unemployment

Particularly vicious in its effects on urban wage earners and the unemployed was the inflation that the government's huge disbursements in August and September had triggered. A continuous note expansion from the 28.5 billion yen in circulation on 1 August to the 55.5 billion yen at the end of 1945 fueled the inflation. Table 3.4 shows that two-thirds of the threefold expansion of note issue in 1945 took place after the surrender. By December 1947, note issue had risen to 219.1 billion yen, despite the currency conversion of early 1946.

Table 3.4 also shows the relative success the government had with its wartime price and wage controls until the combination of U.S. bombing attacks, increased note issue, falling production, and general disruption in 1944 greatly stimulated the black market. Although the wage index lagged behind the wholesale price index from 1937, the

TABLE 3.4
Index of Economic Indicators, 1935–47 (1935–37 = 100)

Year	Bank of Japan note issue (million ¥)	Industrial Production (mining and manufacturing) Index	Official Tokyo Wholesale Price Index	Tokyo Black Market Prices (Consumer Goods) Index	National Wage Index
1935	1,767	79	91	—	100
1936	1,866	96	95	—	98
1937	2,305	119	115	—	101
1938	2,755	131	121	—	102
1939[a]	3,679	164	134	—	105
1940	4,777	162	150	—	113
1941	5,979	169	159	—	124
1942	7,149	143	171	—	135
1943	10,266	114	181	—	153
1944[b]	17,746	86	202	—	191
1945	55,441	29	287	—	227
1946	93,398	25	1,387	17,482	978
1947	219,142	32	4,430	34,925	3,213

Sources: Japan Prime Minister's Office, Cabinet Bureau of Statistics, *Japan Statistical Year-book* (Tokyo: Cabinet Bureau of Statistics, 1949), p. 526; Bank of Japan, Statistics Department, *Economic Statistics of Japan (Annual), 1948* (Tokyo: Bank of Japan), p. 1.

[a]Year the black market begins to develop on a significant scale: Jerome B. Cohen, *Japan's Economy in War and Reconstruction* (Minneapolis: University of Minnesota Press, 1949), p. 362.

[b]Air raids begin and black market prices jump sharply: Ibid., p. 364.

deterioration in real wages was not so rapid until 1945—when wage earners had to turn increasingly to black market purchases to supplement the dwindling rations available at official prices.

Surrender saw a radical turn for the worse in every respect, as can be seen in table 3.5. Prices doubled in the four months from October 1945 to February 1946, and the cost of living increased twelvefold between June 1945 and January 1946, mainly because of the tremendous price increases in the black market—the ratio of black-market to official prices of consumer goods in January–February 1946 was forty to one. During the same period, the average daily wage in manufacturing increased only five times, revealing a drastic cut in real wages from surrender to midwinter.

By late 1945 real wages for workers lucky enough to have jobs fell below 10 percent of prewar levels. The gains that workers made beginning around spring 1946 were small, and for the first three years of occupation real wages never reached 30 percent of the 1937 base and

TABLE 3.5
Index of Economic Indicators, June 1945–July 1946

Year	Month	Bank of Japan note issue (million ¥)[a]	Tokyo Black Market Price (Consumer Goods) Index (Sept. 1945 = 100)[b]	Average Multiple of Official Price Level (Sept. 1945 = 100)[c]	Industrial Production (1935–37 = 100)[c]	Wage Index (1937 = 100)[d]	Cost of Living Index (1937 = 100)[d]	Real Wage Index (1937 = 100)[d]
1945	Jun	26,181	—	—	18.1	—	—	—
	Jul	28,456	—	—	12.8	—	—	—
	Aug	42,300	100	—	8.5	229	2,540	9
	Sep	41,426	92	28.7	9.0	218	2,330	9
	Oct	43,188	112	31.8	13.0	231	2,740	8
	Nov	47,749	128	29.7	13.6	313	3,080	10
	Dec	55,441	170	40.1	13.4	452	4,000	11
1946	Jan	58,566	200	39.8	13.4	606	4,470	14
	Feb	54,342	196	23.7	15.6	740	4,790	15
	Mar	23,323[e]	187	21.3	18.8	827	4,510	18
	Apr	28,173	191	15.1	21.8	888	4,820	18
	May	36,316	201	20.6	25.2	986	5,310	19
	Jun	42,759	200	14.7	25.7	1,060	5,330	20
	Jul	49,731			27.6			

[a] Japan Prime Minister's Office, Cabinet Bureau of Statistics, *Japan Statistical Year-book* (Tokyo: Cabinet Bureau of Statistics, 1949), p. 528.

[b] Bank of Japan, Statistics Department, *Economic Statistics of Japan (Annual), 1948* (Tokyo: Bank of Japan), p. 134.

[c] Japan Ministry of Finance and Bank of Japan, *Statistical Year-Book of Finance and Economy of Japan, 1948* (Tokyo: Ministry of Finance Printing Office), p. 558.

[d] Ōhara Shakai Mondai Kenkyūjo, *Saitei Chinginsei no Igi* (Tokyo: Daiichi Pub., 1949), p. 37.

[e] Currency conversion.

frequently lagged behind increases in prices of commodities.[38] According to budget surveys, in January 1946, " . . . current earnings accounted for only 35 to 60 percent of the cost of living while withdrawals from savings, sales of household articles, separation allowances and loans accounted for 30 to 55 percent of the current cost of living expenses.[39] Many turned to black marketing to make up the difference.

A few basic statistics can sum up the housing situation. Nearly 25 percent of Japan's housing units were destroyed in 1944–45, primarily in the cities, where destruction came to approximately 50 percent. Some twenty-two million people were made homeless and had to move in with friends or family, seek refuge in the countryside, or squat in the shanty towns that sprung up in the ashes.[40] Consequently, the distribution of population changed. In February 1944 the distribution was 30.3 million urban and 42 million rural; in November 1945 it was 19.5 million urban and 52.5 million rural. Tokyo's population alone fell by about 4 million, from 6.8 to 2.8 million as of 1 November 1945.[41] War destruction, unemployment, and hunger had created an exodus to the countryside.

The millions of overseas Japanese civilians and soldiers being repatriated in 1945–46 did not have a cheerful prospect before them. From surrender to June 1946 Japan's population increased from a little over 72 million to about 74.68 million, almost all of which was the net effect of the movement of over 4.2 million people to and from Japan. Of the 6.6 million soldiers outside the country, about half had been repatriated by June. At the same time, only 972,000 of the 1.8 million foreigners in the country, over 90 percent of whom were Koreans, had been sent back to their homeland.[42]

The Japanese returning from China, Korea, and elsewhere needed jobs, but jobs were not to be had. The wholesale closing of enterprises had put approximately 5.5 million workers out in the street. In the major industrial prefectures, perhaps two-thirds of the industrial work force had been discharged in the early fall of 1945. Despite the frequent replacement of female workers with males, the number of males unemployed shot up. For the first six months after surrender, the jobless rate probably fluctuated at around 10 million,[43] a tremendous number considering a total Japanese labor force of 30–32 million.[44] In the absence of any effective measures for public relief, many of these people had no choice but to turn to degrading and illegal pursuits like black marketeering and prostitution for sheer survival.

Some of the most unfortunate victims of the cynical and disastrous policies of big-business and government leaders were women. Nothing reveals the cynicism of the men in power better than the 15 August inauguration of the "recreation center" program, when "the central government authorities directed police chiefs of all prefectures across the nation to permit the establishment of special facilities of 'organized prostitutes' for members of the Occupation forces."[45] The government both initiated and capitalized the program with loan of thirty million yen. The Recreation and Amusement Association was ready for business by 23 August, attesting once again to the efficiency of the Japanese leadership in matters of self-interest. "The government theorized at the time that such facilities would serve as a sort of 'breakwater' to 'protect daughters of good families.'"[46] Most of the tens of thousands of women involved were not professionals at all, but girls and young women from both the country and the cities who had lost their families or their jobs.[47] In short, the daughters of Japan's privileged and powerful bourgeoisie were to be protected by selling poverty-stricken working-class women to the foreign occupiers.

Government and business cooperation extended to "non-official" brothels as well, as Mark Gayn's description of the International Palace, "the world's largest brothel," indicates:

The building now occupied by the brothel used to be part of a huge munitions plant. When the emperor proclaimed Japan's surrender, the management of the plant held a conference. Obviously there would be no more demand for war material. Yet, there was the idle plant, money, and managerial talent, all waiting to be reconverted. What would be the commodity most likely to be in demand when the Americans came?

The Tokyo Police supplied the answer. Accordingly, five of the workers' dormitories were converted into brothels. Some of the managers stayed on to provide the benefit of their experience. Some of the prettier workers stayed on as prostitutes.[48]

A much worse fate overtook some of the homeless and jobless in Japan's cities in 1945–46. For many there was no way out.

Food Shortages

Indeed, food was in extreme shortage, and many people were literally starving. In the days immediately after the war, it was not uncommon at all to see hungry and malnourished people collapse and die on the streets. On 18 November, 1945, the major Tokyo dailies reported that since the end of the war, a total of 300 people had starved to death in Kyoto, 148 in Kobe, 100 in Fukuoka, 72 in Nagoya and 42 in Osaka. "In Tokyo, an average of six persons were dying of starvation every day and an average of three in Yokohama," the newspapers added.

Most of them were homeless and jobless people who had become extremely weak and infirm; in the daytime they wandered around towns in search of left-over food, and at night they slept on the bare concrete floor or railway stations or underground tunnels with only a thin blanket to keep warm. Even if there was a job for them, the result was much the same. As a day laborer, a man could not get paid more than ¥1 or ¥2 a day—but a small rice ball cost ¥10 and a bun ¥15.[49]

When William McMahon Ball, the British Commonwealth representative on the Allied Council for Japan, arrived in Tokyo in spring 1946, the food situation was still grave. Ball recalled people congregating around Shinagawa railway station, where they were dying. Some were lying around the footpaths dead, and twice daily a cart came round to pick up the bodies.[50]

The actual food shortage in 1945–46 is nearly impossible to judge, but to attempt to live on the official ration quite literally meant starvation. Large quantities of staple foods escaped rationing, and only about 20 percent of agricultural perishables were sold through official rationing channels. The worst time was the first nine months, when the ration deteriorated swiftly in quantity and quality, and in many locations was not being issued at all on some days. Distribution of rations in parts of Hokkaidō, the worst-affected area, fell more than two months behind schedule by May 1946.[51]

The shortages led to the phenomenon of daily mass migrations of city people to the countryside for the purpose of bartering for or buying food for household consumption or resale on the black market. The "hunger" trains were jammed with people bringing back potatoes, vegetables, and fruits. Nearly a million people were making such expeditions from Tokyo to the country on a single Sunday.[52] There is no question about the reality of the ration shortages or about the inequality of the distribution. The families of wage and salary workers and the unemployed in the cities suffered most. Chronic malnutrition stunted the growth of children living through the early postwar years.[53] Almost anything could be bought for a price on the black market, but it was always a price much too high for the ordinary urban family to pay, without rapidly exhausting what little resources it might have. In the end everything went.[54]

It is difficult to get an accurate picture of the degree to which the 1945 rice crop fell short of the pre-surrender average, but it seems that yields were under 75 percent of the lower wartime averages. Collection quotas and actual collections were unaccountably low, and what has been referred to as the "marked loss of efficiency" displayed by the authorities is well documented.[55] At any rate, the ration shortages convinced SCAP of the need for large-scale importation of food. In

spring 1946, SCAP informed Herbert Hoover, chairman of the Fa-
mine Emergency Fund, that "mass starvation [is] in prospect for Japan
in the event that adequate imports are not secured." SCAP's explanation cited bad weather and lack of fertilizers, but also recognized the
role of business and government in creating the situation:

> The Japanese food position is further aggravated by: (1) the disrupted Japa-
> nese economy with attendant hyperinflation which has encouraged farmers
> to withhold crops for higher future prices and diversions to black market
> channels; (2) breakdown of the war-time system of ruthless enforcement of
> crop quota collections: (3) absence of consumers' goods as an incentive for
> farmers to market their crops; (4) great uncertainty concerning future Japa-
> nese business; (5) enormous devastation caused by war with consequent
> shortage in building materials, fabricated products and transportation; and (6)
> growth in population, including repatriation.[56]

Although the U.S. did begin sending food in increasing quantities from
May 1946, it might not have been needed if existing food supplies had
been distributed equitably.

Eric Ward, William McMahon Ball's economic adviser and an important figure in the Allied land reform, viewed the ration shortages
as a problem of distribution. He later recalled that the overall food
balance was quite satisfactory but food did not get distributed evenly,
largely because the farmers were not prepared to sell it at the fixed
price. They wanted to sell it on the black market in order to get enough
money to buy scarce consumer goods.[57] Ward also recalled that the
postwar governments felt that quota collection required more force
than they had at their disposal and would not be easy to enforce in
peacetime without calling on the military government.[58]

The "Scissors Crisis"

As both of the above explanations suggest, the Japanese economy
was in the grips of a "scissors crisis"—a combination of low official
prices for foodstuffs, soaring inflation, and extreme shortages of manufactured goods leading to the withholding of food in the countryside
for increased local consumption, barter, black market sale, or speculation.[59] It was senseless to exchange food for increasingly worthless
paper money when even the most basic agricultural fertilizers and
tools were unavailable due to the production stoppage. Whether or
not the government had the ability to make collection and rationing
work is debatable, but it certainly lacked the will for evenhanded enforcement, given its traditional reliance upon the landlord stratum in
the village.[60]

A local elite of landlords, businessmen, and officials had always had the political task of maintaining order and stability in the countryside. Because any lessening of their authority had to be compensated for by an increase in that of the police and other administrative agents responsible to the central authorities, the government could not afford to ignore their needs. In the moment of defeat the government was no longer as interested in regulating production and distribution as it was in bolstering the landlords' economic position vis-à-vis the poorer farmers. The government did two things to shore up the local elite. It left collection of crop requisitions in the hands of the landlord-dominated local agricultural associations—which pressed the poorer farmers harder for quota fulfillment—and turned a blind eye to the use of the agricultural associations to divert food into the black market with police connivance.[61]

The slackening of central administrative control over the villages and hamlets that was typified by the government's inefficiency in collecting food quotas did not signify so much a diminution of authority over the average tenant or middle farmer as it did a devolution of authority from the center back to the local elite.[62] Whatever minor differences this group had with the central government and big business, it could be counted on to hold the line in the countryside and defend establishment interests. It had no choice. The rural elite's power ultimately depended on administrative and police support from the outside, as it always had from the Tokugawa period forward.

The effects of sabotage spread in ever-widening circles, far beyond the narrow confines of coal or iron and steel production. Complete chaos lay ahead if someone did not take matters in hand. That worry animated the working class as well as SCAP officials and the leaders of big business and government. The workers made the first fumbling moves toward a reconstruction on their own in the midst of that first winter.

4

Workers' Control, Unions, and the Left

In January production control increased dramatically and directly involved nearly 30,000 workers. The spread of production control posed difficult problems for the old guard and for the leaders of the unions and the left-wing parties. Production control was apparently something quite new, and each of the different camps sought to confine it or direct it along the lines most favorable to itself.

Three struggles in the industrial heartland highlighted the potential production control had for further expansion and radicalization. These were the workers' transformation of the *Yomiuri* into an outspoken opponent of the old regime, the mass mobilization of Tōshiba workers against the company, and the readiness of the workers at Japan Steel Tube to take direct action to achieve their ends.

The first response of the old guard to production control was a straightforward attempt to combat it, both within the enterprise and by official means. Labor and the left-wing parties had the harder task, the crux of which was to determine the relationship of production control to the union on the one hand and to the revolutionary soviet on the other. That is, they had to decide if it was just another dispute tactic of unions or if it was the germ of a revolutionary movement.

Production Control on the Advance

An Organ of the People

An editorial in the *Yomiuri* on 12 December 1945—the day after Shōriki had signed the arbitration agreement—celebrated the "settlement of the *Yomiuri* dispute" and proclaimed a new policy: "Heretofore the newspaper has been the organ of capitalists, it has oppressed the people, it has published articles that deceived, and has suffocated the voice of the people. Now the *Yomiuri Shinbun* has been freed from this *yoke* of capital. . . . We proclaim that from this day the *Yomiuri Shinbun* will become truly a friend to the people and an organ of the people for eternity."[1] This was possible, the editorial said, because the employees of the *Yomiuri* had seized the opportunity of the freedom given by the Allies to fight for their demands: 1) for clarification of war responsibility, and 2) for democratization of the paper through the separation of capital from management and through worker participation in management.[2]

The editorial argued that political democratization was meaningless in the absence of economic reform. An economic liberation from below through the struggles of the people to stabilize their livelihood was essential for the realization of a true democratic revolution. The *Yomiuri* now stood ready to support the people in their fight for economic sovereignty. The editorial cited the success of the *Yomiuri* workers in running the paper on their own, despite having to overcome "sabotage" by the company.

After the arbitrated settlement, Suzuki Tōmin and the other members of the supreme struggle committee disbanded the production control committees and established a similar system based on the management councils that the agreement had provided for. The company was democratized and the employees gained unprecedented rights over what was to go into the paper and how the actual process of production was conducted. In effect, the reporters and writers were turned loose to dig up their own stories, regardless of how derogatory they were of the government and big business. And the typesetters and printers threw out the oppressive system of labor control that Shōriki had introduced in the twenties and took over the printing of the paper. Thus, workers' control became a reality at the *Yomiuri* to a great extent, with the enthusiastic participation of the mass of the employees, who went the old management one better by expanding the paper, getting it out on time once again, and increasing circulation.[3]

The "democratic" *Yomiuri* championed a radical, populist reconstruction. The paper called for the sweeping away of the landlords and monopoly capitalists in favor of the proprietors of medium- and small-scale business, and for the democratization of the workplace and enterprise through worker participation. Articles and editorials argued that the subsequent rise in productivity and in the workers' standard of living would produce an expansion of the nation's internal market and the attainment of economic prosperity.[4] Politically, the paper advocated the completion of Japan's postwar democratic revolution through the popular front capable of leading a mass mobilization powerful enough to throw out the old guard. Such a mobilization would be irresistible if it were based on an expansion of production control designed to place not only production but also distribution in the hands of the people.[5] Events at Tōshiba and Japan Steel Tube in January demonstrated the potential behind the democratic *Yomiuri's* insistence upon a popular reconstruction of the Japanese economy.

Mass Mobilization at Tōshiba Rolling Stock

In early December the workers at Tōshiba Rolling Stock (Tōshiba Sharyō) organized a union which became the nucleus of a joint struggle committee formed on 27 December to coordinate the demands of Tōshiba companies in Kantō.[6] The struggle committee presented a joint package of demands for the six Tōshiba companies in the locality, demands extending to employer control over the labor force and the means of production. The unions demanded participation in personnel administration, immediate suspension of the illegal activities of the company's private secret police, the right to make proposals for improving productivity and efficiency, retention of the existing system of working hours, and participation in all matters connected with worker welfare such as the distribution of rations and commodities.

Tōshiba flatly rejected the demands on 5 January, and two days later about 1,000 workers forced their way into the Tōshiba main office in Horikawa-chō, demanding a meeting with the company authorities. The meeting accomplished nothing and talks broke down completely on 12 January, after which the Tōshiba unions entered jointly into production control. By this time there were twelve Tōshiba unions participating in the joint struggle committee representing 30,000 workers, making this by far the largest worker action to date. A combined mass meeting on 17 January turned out about 3,000 workers who, after listening to militant speeches including a rousing one by Tokuda Kyūichi, mounted a street demonstration in Kawasaki city.

Among the organizations represented at the mass meeting were the Kanagawa Prefecture Labor Union Council (Kanagawa Ken Rōdō Kumiai Kyōgikai) and the South Kantō Labor Union Council (Jōnan Rōdō Kumiai Kyōgikai), two of the powerful regional councils of factory representatives that the unions had set up in December in response to the need for uniting the labor movement. The several Kantō councils soon united into a single council of factory representatives for the region which on 20 February joined with a number of militant national union federations to establish the Preparatory Council for the National Congress of Industrial Unions (Zenkoku Sangyō-betsu Rōdō Kumiai Kaigi Junbikai), the direct forerunner of Sanbetsu. The meaning of the support of the Labor Union Councils was not lost on Tōshiba.

The meeting on 17 January had demonstrated that a mass mobilization transcending both factory and enterprise lines was likely. Twelve of the Tōshiba unions in Kantō had joined together in the dispute already, and it seemed that if the struggle was lengthy, production control would spread throughout all the Kantō plants of Tōshiba, and militant unions on the outside would join in. Under pressure, Tōshiba settled on 29 January, accepting almost all the union demands. In partial confirmation of the company's fears, soon thereafter three regional federations organized within Tōshiba, one in Kantō of thirty unions, one in Kansai of fifteen, and another in Tōhoku of nine.

One worker demand had centered on participation in management, and the settlement provided for the establishment of a joint council of labor and management similar to the one at the *Yomiuri*. But the company dragged out the negotiations until early April. When the council was finally constituted, it had only powers of consultation, not decision-making, and its purview did not extend to production. Matters for consultation were to be the betterment and democratization of personnel administration, company organization, working conditions, operation of agencies for the workers' welfare, and standards of compensation. The council was to be made up of ten members from each side, and to be chaired by the company manager. In what would become a common maneuver, Tōshiba had used the time spent in negotiations most effectively to evade the demand for a voice in management by conceding in "participation" the shadow but not the substance of power.

The change in tactics Tōshiba made in the course of its struggle to maintain control is noteworthy in that it foreshadowed a general change for big business. Tōshiba had begun with hard-line rejection of the workers' demands and a refusal to engage in real negotiations. The company was ready to accept unionization as a necessary evil, but intended to make sure the union was a pliable one. The result was an unlooked-for escalation of the dispute until it involved a formidable combination of Tōshiba unions and outside organizations. When threatened with an even greater escalation in late January, Tōshiba decided to settle and negotiate, in the end regaining much of the ground it had apparently lost in the January settlement. The Tōshiba about-face from hard-line rejection to a show of conciliation and cooperation

with the workers through management councils was an early instance
of the course big business charted for labor relations as the workers'
movement gained in strength. The next major struggle in the Tokyo-
Yokohama industrial belt brought out even more forcefully the dangers to management of provoking head-on confrontations.

Direct Action at Japan Steel Tube

In late 1945 the management of the Tsurumi Steel Works of Japan
Steel Tube (Nippon Kōkan Tsurumi Seitetsu-jo), in an attempt to head
off incipient labor organization, tried to foster a company union, but
failed. Instead, 2,000 staff and production workers formed an independent union which promptly sent demands to the company for recognition and large pay increases. Moreover, the workers objected to
unilateral company dismissals and demanded union inspection of such
things as food rationing and distribution of commodities. As at Tōshiba, the company was willing to recognize a real union, but unwilling to concede to other demands except to say that it would not dismiss employees because of union membership and to propose a joint
labor-management committee to deal with employee welfare. The union
rejected the company's reply on the same day it was received, 10 January, and informed Japan Steel Tube that it was entering into production control.[7]

Negotiations continued until the company sent a second reply on
18 January which once again rejected the union demands, but went
on to say that "we are giving careful consideration to the hard circumstances of the employees" and proposed submission of the dispute to
third party mediation. The union interpreted the proposal as a meaningless diversion intended to cloak the company's refusal to negotiate.
Accordingly, it broke off the talks on that same day and set up a comprehensive organization that paralleled the company structure to take
control of production (see figure 4.1).

To begin with, the workers ejected all management personnel from
section heads (kachō) up and elected in their place nominees from
each shop and workplace committee. These nominees conferred together in a council for coordinating production and marketing and
were responsible for daily operations. Above the shop and workplace
committees that had elected the operations nominees was a control
committee, and at the very top a joint body uniting the new committee structure with the existing union. The control committee and the
union executive committee elected this six-member "brain trust." The
union was superseded by the new structure and fell into relative un-
importance.

Despite these changes, the workers were not able to grasp total

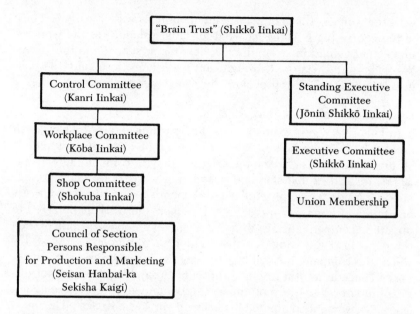

Figure 4.1. Struggle-Committee Structure at Japan Steel Tube. Source: Rōdōshō, ed., *Shiryō: Rōdō Undō Shi—Shōwa 20–21-nen* (Tokyo: Rōmu Gyōsei Kenkyū-jo, 1951), p. 30.

control over production at the Tsurumi Steel Works, since it was but one link in the integrated operations of Japan Steel Tube. The Tsurumi plant received materials produced at other plants of Japan Steel Tube, processed them into steel plate, sheet, and so forth, then generally sold them to the company shipyards. Worse yet, the company main office in Nihonbashi continued as always to control plant finances and wage payments.

The Tsurumi workers tried to overcome these weaknesses by concentrating on the production of steel products for the consumer market—for example, corrugated steel sheeting much in demand for building construction—at the expense of heavy steel plate for shipbuilding. In order to do so, the committees unilaterally changed rolling mill specifications and transferred workers. This attempt to produce and sell goods through channels outside of the enterprise family of Japan Steel Tube did not succeed in undermining the company's control. Conditions at Tsurumi were becoming grim by the last part of January due to shortages of raw materials and funds.

Feeling that their struggle was coming to a dead end, the workers began to think of direct action—that is, coercive action aimed at directly and immediately achieving their goals—as a last resort. One proposal was to "break into the directors' mansions": squads of four or five workers would force their way into the houses of the company executives and make them accept the workers' demands. Only a few ineffectual attempts at this were made, but the fact that such a confrontation was even briefly countenanced among workers whose society sanctioned only the most circumspect and formal expression of opposition to authority reveals how serious they felt their grievances to be.

The move toward direct action was the more surprising since the Tsurumi production control had been notable for its orderliness and the leaders' care to keep within the bounds of legality. The struggle organization never denied the rights of the company managers and owners to resume control over the plant. They kept accounts in order and proceeded as much as possible in accordance with the production plan that company executives had formulated before the dispute, as the later investigation by the Central Labor Relations Committee confirmed.

It soon became clear to the workers that scrupulous adherence to capitalist legality offered no way out of their difficulties, and frustration mounted. In desperation, the workers organized a demonstration for 26 January to put pressure on the company to settle. On that morning some 1,600 workers gathered before the Kanda railway station for a march on the Nihonbashi main office of Japan Steel Tube. The marchers arrived with red flags flying and demanded a meeting with the company president who, they had learned earlier, was there to attend an executives' meeting. After besieging the office for two and a half hours, the workers broke into the building and subjected the president to mass negotiations. In the course of the extremely hostile confrontation, arrogant company executives were threatened with violence by the workers. The workers forced unconditional company recognition of their demands, but shortly thereafter Japan Steel Tube repudiated the agreement as having been extorted under duress. Nevertheless, the main office demonstration gained fame as a show of the readiness of Japan's working class to resort to industrial violence.

One consequence of the events of the *Yomiuri*, Tōshiba, and Japan Steel Tube was to build up pressure among big-business and government leaders for taking steps before the situation got truly out of hand. All big-business and government leaders opposed production control and abhorred the direct action that frequently accompanied it, but there were differences of opinion concerning the proper strategy for putting an end to this challenge to their authority. There were but two alternatives—suppression or co-optation—and they tried both in that order. In February the old guard made an abortive attempt to prohibit production control by law and make it possible to put it down, by use of police force if necessary. When SCAP temporarily blocked that attempt, the more progressive leaders in big business and government turned toward the second alternative, co-optation, and began to speak of labor-capital cooperation.

Workers' Control and Capitalist Labor Relations

Business Unionism versus Workers' Control

The tendency of industrial management, especially since the advent of Taylorism, to extend its control into finer and finer reaches of the production process, had its counterpart in Japan. It would be unreasonable to believe that Japanese workers' response to their systematic exclusion from control over the work process, and to the consequent degradation of work, was different from workers' response elsewhere, as described so tellingly by Harry Braverman:

The apparent acclimatization of the worker to the new modes of production grows out of the destruction of all other ways of living, the striking of wage bargains that permit a certain enlargement of the customary bounds of subsistence for the working class, the weaving of the net of modern capitalist life that finally makes all other modes of living impossible. But beneath this apparent habituation, the hostility of workers to the degenerated forms of work which are forced upon them continues as a subterranean stream that makes its way to the surface when employment conditions permit, or when the capitalist drive for a greater intensity of labor overstrips the bounds of physical and mental capacity.[8]

Japan was no exception. The subterranean drive for workers' control—understood here in the common-sense meaning of control over policy making as well as the processes of production—surfaced after the war in the form of demands for the democratization of the enterprise and for participation in management. The Japanese working class did not come up with production control—their version of workers' control—overnight; instead it set out on the more orthodox path of trade unionism.[9] As they organized, workers put forth three basic types of demands: for recognition of their economic interest, for democratization of personal relationships in the work place, and for democratization of the processes of production.[10] The economic demands usually constituted a package—recognition of the workers' right to organize, strike, and bargain collectively over wages, hours, and working conditions. Goals like these represented an attempt to overcome personal catastrophe by collective action within the framework given by the capitalist enterprise.

Demands for democratization within the workplace focused primarily on putting an end to cruel and dictatorial treatment by employers and supervisors and the abolition of the status system in the plant, which discriminated sharply between white-collar staff and production workers. They also encompassed attacks on those employers and managers who had been supporters of Japan's imperialist policies. Important as they were, such demands were not in themselves much more radical than economic demands centered on wages, for they could be met by more employer attention to "human relations" in industry.

Workers' demands for democratization of the processes of production, which most often were summed up in the general demand for participation in management, could not be satisfied by half-measures as easily as could the other demands.[11] Whether they concerned the setting of company goals, organizing production, or personnel policies, demands of this type impinged on the rights of private property, and no employer was ready to concede more than symbolic participation in management.

These demands, which correspond to those of workers in all industrialized societies, took on a heightened meaning in a country on the edge of economic chaos. Japan's working class somehow had to protect itself against the wave of dismissals and to increase production of essentials, but neither could be achieved by tactics like strikes or slowdowns when there was widespread business retrenchment and mass unemployment. Employers could defeat a strike simply by locking out strikers, hiring strikebreakers, or closing down altogether. A strike might hurt employers in certain essential industries and services like fuel and transportation where employers had some stake in continued operation, but even in such cases striking would worsen the economic situation, victimize the public, and earn SCAP's displeasure. Sabotage had created conditions under which worker occupation of enterprises was the sole means available for attaining the mutually supportive goals of jobs and production.[12]

Had economic goals, even the key ones of saving jobs and resuming production, been all that there was to production control, it might well be dismissed as nothing more than a dispute tactic of unions, one suited to exceptional times when strikes did not pay. Many have argued in this way, discounting the seizure and operation of factories as the excesses of an immature union movement. Once production resumed, according to this view, there was no further use for such tactics and they faded away, to be replaced by collective bargaining as unions assumed their rightful place as the protectors of the economic interests of the working class.

The evolution of production control presents a picture contrary to this assumption that the basic demands of workers after the war were economic in detail and reformist in trajectory. Indeed, in the unresolvable economic crisis of early 1946, the desperate needs of workers and their families and the fundamental drive toward workers' control guaranteed that production control would not remain a mere dispute tactic of unions aiming at a better contractual bargain for labor.[13]

"Legal" Production Control

At the beginning, workers viewed production control as an effective if unorthodox dispute tactic of labor unions, not as a revolutionary act. Participants in the early production control struggles took care to stay within the law by keeping the locked-out management informed and by adhering to the existing production plan, often allowing company officials to continue making policy and operating decisions subject to worker review. Since they conceded tbe fundamental legitimacy of managerial prerogatives based on the rights of private property and kept accurate records and accounts in anticipation of turning the enterprise back over to the employer, the settling of a dispute easily enabled the temporarily dispossessed managers to resume control over the enterprise.

Even a "legal" production control struggle of this sort was indisputably an anti-capitalist act, because the workers, against the will of owners and managers, denied the rights of private property in the means of production. They had to. Once embarked on production control, the workers in the enterprise found it immediately necessary to set up machinery accountable to themselves in order to continue production. This commonly took the form of the "struggle committee" (tōsō iinkai).

The struggle committee system echoed the enterprise organization, but differed in that at the workshop, section, or department level the workers elected committees which became the building blocks for a three- or four-tiered pyramid culminating in an executive committee at the top. The committees might assume control over production by taking on the tasks of management directly, by election of responsible supervisors, or by holding existing supervisors accountable. The highest authority resided in the general enterprise conference (taikai), which often played an extraordinarily active role, making decisions as the need arose and implementing them at once through collective action. There was, consequently, no sharp organizational separation of policy making and execution. The workers ran their own enterprise through the production control struggle committee. Furthermore, the struggle committee either hollowed out or displaced the union, because it provided a more effective means for realizing the workers' interests than the union with its narrow bureaucratic channels designed for gaining economic rewards for its members.

The Radicalization of Production Control

The central issue of the emerging workers' movement in Japan, where the demand was for democratization and participation, was not unionization but workers' control, and the attack on the prerogatives of employers which had long been virtually total and absolute. Production control called into question the capitalist system in its most fundamental aspect, private property, however legalistic and temporary the early struggles were. It pointed toward a sweeping reorganization of the internal order of business enterprise and a rapid erosion of the rights of management in hiring and firing, in supervision of the work force, even in making policy decisions on what to produce, to whom to sell, and where to allocate the firm's resources. This aspect of production control—toward appropriation of always greater powers over the enterprise—is unmistakable in even the earliest struggles.[14] The workers' steady encroachment on management rights after the settlement of the dispute at the *Yomiuri* newspaper is a case in point.

Production control represented the disintegration of capitalist relations of production, not their modification. As such it was a transitory phenomenon which business and government leaders would not tolerate a minute longer than they had to. In constant contradiction with the imperative of modern capitalism to appropriate all matters of choice and of decision making as the exclusive preserve of management, production control could end in only two ways—in soviets and a revolutionary struggle for power or in the total defeat of workers' control and the reimposition of unquestioned employer authority over the processes of production.

Production control increased dramatically in January, when thirteen incidents of production control involving 29,000 workers took place. As table 4.1 shows, during the first ten months of the occupation, production control was by far the most important type of worker action. The total number of workers who engaged in production control struggles when they were at their height from January through May 1946 came to 139,148—as compared to 109,410 participants in strikes and slowdowns combined. April and May alone accounted for over half the total. Considering the phenomenal pace of unionization, the

TABLE 4.1
Labor Actions and Workers Involved, August 1945–February 1947

Year	Month	Total		Strikes		Slowdowns		Production Control		Production Control as Percentage of Total	
		Actions	Workers	Actions	Workers	Actions	Workers	Actions	Workers	Actions	Workers
1945	Aug	0	0	0	0	0	0	0	0	0	0
	Sep	2	—	2	—	0	—	0	—	0	0
	Oct	20	—	16	—	3	—	1	—	5	—
	Nov	27	—	21	—	2	—	4	—	15	—
	Dec	39	—	33	—	3	—	3	—	9	—
1946	Jan	49	37,720	27	6,142	9	2,549	13	29,029	26	77
	Feb	53	29,176	23	6,532	10	6,847	20	15,806	38	54
	Mar	80	79,950	32	48,527	9	10,722	39	20,651	50	26
	Apr	89	50,417	30	14,726	6	840	53	34,815	60	69
	May	106	51,295	42	9,047	8	3,401	56	38,847	53	76
	Jun	80	26,707	29	6,735	7	1,916	44	18,056	55	70
	Jul	90	27,346	48	14,721	17	10,147	25	2,478	28	9
	Aug	107	52,282	61	24,054	18	4,983	28	23,245	26	44
	Sep	124	118,242	59	81,368	28	14,484	37	22,290	30	19
	Oct	156	200,729	104	188,958	17	2,633	35	9,138	22	5
	Nov	127	87,488	89	76,563	14	3,262	24	7,663	19	9
	Dec	108	93,496	65	61,361	17	23,569	26	8,566	24	9
1947	Jan	65	26,050	30	17,491	9	2,316	26	6,243	40	24
	Feb	90	34,600	52	28,101	14	1,462	24	5,037	27	14

Sources: Japan Prime Minister's Office, Cabinet Bureau of statistics, *Japan Statistical Year-book* (Tokyo: Cabinet Bureau of Statistics, 1949), pp. 730–31; SCAP, Economic and Scientific Section, Advisory Committee on labor, *Final Report: Labor Policies and Programs in Japan* (Tokyo: 1946). p. 35; Miriam S. Farley, *Aspects of Japan's Labor Problems* (New York: The John Day Company, 1950), pp. 83–84.

table also reveals a surprisingly low number of actual disputes, suggesting that in the majority of cases employers did not have the stomach for confrontation.

Nonetheless, big business and government opposition to production control from January onward can be accounted one of the major factors conducive to its radicalization. Unable to prohibit production control by law and suppress it with the police due to SCAP opposition, the old guard sought to confine the duration and scope of production control by denying the participants access to funds, supplies, and markets, hoping thus to bring the workers to terms.[15] This policy of containment generated intense pressures among workers engaged in production control as they ran out of money and materials, watched operations grind to a halt, and saw the possibility of getting a breakthrough on their demands steadily recede. Rather than forcing the workers to settle, this often resulted in a rapid radicalization of the workers' struggle and a bursting of the framework of legalism that had constrained the workers theretofore. (See figure 4.2 for a schematic presentation.)

Two characteristics distinguished "illegal" production control from legal: a conscious repudiation of capitalist legal limitations and other obligations that the workers had previously accepted as legitimate in disputes between capital and labor, and the workers' resort to allies and resources outside the enterprise to continue the fight. Once having taken the step into illegality, it was but a short step further to the position that the enterprise need not ever be returned to the control of the owners. Workers who crossed this line were tying their own fate to the fate of their collectively operated enterprise. The cost of failure would be high, certainly the loss of their livelihood and perhaps worse, and men with families did not undertake such an effort lightly. Behind their decision lay a basic confidence that they as workers could not only run an enterprise successfully, but also do it better than the capitalist owners.[16]

Workers came by that confidence both by the example of others and by their own experience. For example, the workers at the Keisei Electric Railway gained tremendously in self-confidence as their struggle developed. Their successful operation of the railway gave credence to their threat to continue the fight indefinitely, if need be by illegally requisitioning fares in order to pay wages. This, more than the mass negotiations, can be credited with bringing the owners around. Similarly, the Yomiuri employees provided daily proof of their ability to operate a business every time the paper came out.

Production control was bound to fail if big-business and government

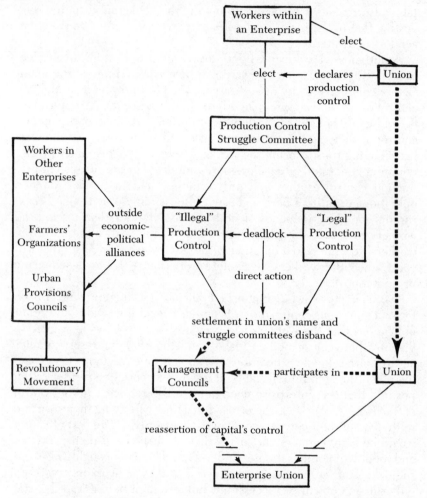

Figure 4.2. Evolution of Production Control. Dotted lines represent formal lines of control, but actual lack of power.

opposition confined it within the narrow legal bounds of a dispute tactic of labor within the capitalist order, because the workers under such terms were unable to secure raw materials and had difficulty selling the finished commodities. Used strictly as a dispute tactic, production control came closer in practice to the sit-down strike than is at first apparent. When workers began making a frontal attack on the legitimacy of management rights based on private property, as they soon did in heavy industry and mining, production control stood forth as a revolutionary act animated by the will to dispossess the capitalist owners and institute permanent workers' control.

The Views of the Left-Wing Parties

The Japan Socialist Party

The right-wing socialists did not trouble themselves about the relationship between workers' control and labor unions. They opposed the first and hoped to build an empire of conservative business unions from the second. In this they succeeded rather well. One reason was that the government had not persecuted the right-wing socialists nearly as much as it had their communist and left-wing socialist opponents. Consequently, they got an early start and quickly established their hold on the JSP and Sōdōmei from their postwar beginnings, notwithstanding a serious rebellion among the rank and file during 1946.[17]

The key leaders of the socialist right wing were Nishio Suehiro and Matsuoka Komakichi, who, while communist and left-wing socialist leaders were in jail or under detention, had been active as members of the wartime Diet. Both had been, at the very least, tacit supporters of imperialism abroad and corporate authoritarianism at home.[18] Furthermore, both had maintained close contacts with zaibatsu executives—Nishio being particularly close to Sumitomo, one of the big-four zaibatsu[19]—and both were vehement anti-communists. The freedom of action they enjoyed after the surrender is not surprising.

As early as 15 August Nishio was conferring in Kyōto with another member of the Diet, Mizutani Chōzaburō, about resurrection of a socialist party and the organization of peasant and labor unions. Next he went to Tokyo on the 18th to see Matsuoka and urged him to undertake the reconstruction of the labor union movement while he, Nishio, reorganized the socialist party.[20] Three days later Mizutani came to Tokyo and made contact with Hirano Rikizō, the prewar head of the right wing of the peasant union movement who was closely linked with ultra-nationalists during the war.[21] Soon, all four were hard at work.

Nishio, Mizutani, and Hirano met on 25 August in Tokyo's stylish Ginza area with a group of conservative politicians including Hatoyama Ichirō and Ashida Hitoshi. Hatoyama repeatedly urged that the two groups cooperate and form a single political party. Nishio reportedly replied, "We are like-minded and might possibly be able to cooperate, but we probably cannot vouch for the great number of people who are behind each of us respectively."[22] Finally Hatoyama gave up and so ended the first of many flirtations by the right-wing socialist leaders with the conservative politicians.

After a period of intense maneuvering to bring together all factions left to right in one party, Nishio, Matsuoka, and their supporters succeeded in organizing a new Japan Socialist party on 2 November with Nishio as secretary general and Katayama Tetsu as chairman. The right wing had undisputed control, and the JSP adopted a cautious platform having this section on labor:

V. Labor

1. Establishment of a labor ministry.
2. Official recognition of labor unions, enactment of a collective bargaining law, and revision of the dispute-arbitration law.
3. Participation by workers and employees in the management of industry.
4. Establishment of a minimum wage system.
5. Enforcement of a forty-eight-hour week.
6. Enforcement of an unemployment policy having full employment as its goal.[23]

The JSP proposals on labor anticipated the stand soon to be taken by the more progressive leaders of big business and government, namely recognition of the legitimacy of business unionism and of worker participation in management. Worker participation in management implied nothing more controversial for the JSP than the obvious point that big business was coming around to accepting anyway, that labor and capital both have rights within the enterprise, though the rights of ownership have precedence. The essential moderation of this notion would become evident by spring when the right-wing socialists agreed with the progressives that worker participation in management was best achieved through a system of joint labor-management councils stressing the workers' responsibility for increasing production but denying them any control over the processes of production or the profits derived therefrom.[24]

Matsuoka took a more roundabout course in setting up a new, national organization of labor. Rather than establishing a labor federation at once, which he said would look bad since it would give the impression that the old Sōdōmei leaders had been sitting around expectantly waiting for Japan to lose the war,[25] he insisted that Sanpō be dissolved first.[26] Accordingly, he began making the rounds of conservative politicans, government officials, and zaibatsu executives after the surrender, seeking to promote the dissolution of Sanpō in coordination with the formation of a cooperative labor federation. The attempt failed, but his means—private understandings with key members of big business and government— were typical of the socialist right wing.[27] Matsuoka became well known for these visits, about which Takano

Minoru, a left-wing socialist engaged at that very time in shop-floor union organizing, later had this to say:

> However, what surprised us at that time was Matsuoka turning toward the gang of big zaibatsu leaders including Isaka Takashi [head of the Japan Economic League, one of the big-four business federations consulted by Nakajima, and subsequently first chairman of the Keidanren Committee] . . . vigorously making rounds of calls trying to obtain approval for the organization of a national labor union congress as the main pillar for the construction of a new Japan.[28]

The right-wing socialists' strongest argument was that if the zaibatsu leaders did not help them to organize a plant, union militants or communists would surely get established. But in spite of such arguments, the attempt to supplant Sanpō failed.

Sanpō dissolved on 30 September, and Matsuoka extended invitations on 2 October to a conference to be held 10 October for the reconstruction of the labor movement. SCAP gave them added incentive to act by ordering on 4 October the release of all political prisoners including communists by 10 October, thus making conceivable an alliance between the left-wing socialists and the communists. The right wing's aim at the conference was to get an immediate commitment from the left wing to join in their plans for a unified national labor federation.

Matsuoka's task was made easier by the fear among the left-wing socialists of repeating the sorry story of splits and infighting that had plagued the prewar unions and parties. The left wing's position on the reconstruction of the labor movement, as represented by such people as Takano, stressed organizational unity behind three union goals: the betterment of working conditions and wages and the reconstruction of industry, the building of a national federation of industrial unions, and freedom to join political parties. In mid-September, Matsuoka told Takano he agreed to these goals.[29]

The conference endorsed the idea of a nationally unified federation and set up an organizing committee which was chaired by Matsuoka and included Nishio and other right-wing labor leaders. The conference affirmed three principles for the nascent federation: formation of a single national federation, perfection of industrial unionism, and freedom of political party affiliation for union members. It also unanimously approved a declaration committed to revival of the economy, democratization of industry, and realization of "high productivity and high wages."[30] The official history of Sōdōmei stated the goals as follows:

1. We will struggle for the continual betterment of working conditions for the working class as our labor unions' fundamental duty. Moreover, the working class, which bears the burden of production, must become the core of the reconstruction of our nation which has come to complete destruction.
2. Taking industrial labor unions and their national alliance as our goals, we will promote organization in locals in the present prefectures and gradually consolidate industrially.
3. As our political policy we will follow political party neutralism.[31]

Takano and the other leaders on the left accepted a minority position within the federation as soon as the conference had endorsed the left-wing socialist points. That it was an endorsement in words but not in spirit would soon become clear.

In early November 1945 the organizing committee made the decision to go ahead and establish Sōdōmei. At a conference on 17 January the Sōdōmei Preparatory Committee was formed and a program, policy, and bylaws adopted. Matsuoka was elected president, and Sōdōmei was as good as established.[32] All that remained was to make it formal in August.

By paying lip service to the principles of industrial unionism and freedom of political choice, the right-wing socialists gained the cooperation of the left wing at a critical moment. The right-wing leaders violated both principles from the start. They set up prefectural—not industrial—union federations which they used to secure their own electoral constituencies by compelling the affiliated unions to support the JSP and to combat the militant union movement supported by the JCP.[33]

The notorious Shirahige incident of February 1946 epitomized the technique of the JSP right wing in organizing labor unions. The personnel section chief of Kurashiki Spinning, Shirahige Katsuzen, in April publicly exposed the maneuverings of the right-wing labor leaders in the textile industry through an open letter that was published in the *Asahi* newspaper.[34]

Matsuoka, Nishio, and another right-wing socialist met on 13 February with representatives of four of the companies belonging to the management association for cotton spinning to consider a proposal put forward by the wartime labor section chief of the Ōsaka War Management Division, Kawagushi Yoshiaki. The cotton industry executives believed a militant labor movement would be "a mortal blow for us," but decided to meet with the right-wing socialists because the new conditions had made it necessary to "fight poison with poison." Matsuoka and the others accepted Kawagushi's proposal that they all join forces with the Sōdōmei leaders to organize the cotton textile workers of Japan into one union which would become a part of the Sōdōmei Preparatory Committee. General agreement was reached at a secret meeting on 13 February, and at the lavish banquet that followed both support and money were forthcoming for the political candidacy of the night's guests of honor, Matsuoka and Nishio, who were running for reelection to the Diet. Shirahige exposed this sordid deal at the time of the 2 April founding conference of the Kurashiki Cotton Spinning Labor Federation, embarrassing Matsuoka, who had to repeatedly explain that "there was no intention to make the union into a company union." In spite of the ensuing uproar, the textile union fell under the control of the right-wing socialists. Matsuoka became president of the federation, but Shirahige got fired for his pains. And Matsuoka and Nishio were reelected to the Diet.[35]

The Japan Communist Party

Theory of the Two-Stage Revolution

One difficult theoretical question for the Japan Communist party after the war was the proper characterization of Japan's postwar stage of development. If Japan was still to a significant degree feudal, then the proper policy would be completion of the bourgeois-democratic revolution. If Japan was now on balance a mature capitalist society— not to mention monopoly capitalist—then a socialist revolution was the objective.

Some fifteen years earlier, the promulgators of the 1932 theses of the JCP had resolved this debate by positing a rapid transformation of the bourgeois-democratic revolution into a socialist one through a two-stage revolution to be carried out by a soviet government of workers, peasants, and soldiers under the hegemony of the proletariat. The early formation of soviets and the rapid transition from the bourgeois-democratic to the socialist revolution could take place because "objective conditions for socialism exist and the necessity for the destruction of the capitalist system of exploitation has become fully developed."[36]

Only at first would the revolutionary forces—workers, peasants, and the urban poor—need to work with liberals and social democrats for the overthrow of the imperial institution in the name of the formation of a bourgeois-democratic republic. Once the republican form of government was in place, according to this program, the soviets born of the revolutionary process must immediately seize power and force the completion of the bourgeois-democratic revolution, lest the bourgeoisie make common cause with the landlords in order to maintain the pillars of the old system of power—the bureaucracy, the landlord-tenant system, and the zaibatsu. The task of the soviets would be to establish a new regime which would consolidate the dictatorship of the proletariat by abolishing feudal remnants and expropriating monopoly capitalism.

The two-stage revolution in the 1932 theses was telescoped to the extreme, coming down to a rapid and violent seizure of power by soviets under the leadership of the JCP. Far from envisaging a lengthy period of tactical common fronts with progressive petit-bourgeois or social democratic groups, the Theses treated only the workers, peasants, and urban poor as revolutionary, and castigated the others as false liberals and social fascists. The rallying cry for mobilizing the "revolutionary-democratic forces" was to be the people's revolution "for rice, land, freedom, and the workers' and peasants' government." The JCP intended to bypass the opportunistic leaders of the labor and peasant unions and forge a "close alliance of workers and peasants" in a "united front from below" which would bring together the hitherto fragmented working class.[37]

The thirteen years since 1932 had seen great economic and social change. The war had quickened the pace of industrialization, and heavy industry had displaced light industry to become the overwhelmingly dominant sector of the economy. By 1945 the numerically enlarged non-agricultural work force could justifiably be characterized, considering its largest component, as an industrial working class. Although "feudal remnants" like the landlord and labor boss systems did still exist, in Marxist terms Japan was indisputably a thoroughly capitalist society at the war's end.[38]

Even while tacitly acknowledging Japan's capitalist maturity in party policies and pronouncements, the JCP leaders also cited the facts of defeat and foreign occupation as preventing the use of tactics appropriate to normal times. That is, they did not believe it possible to take the theoretically logical next step of dedicating the party to leading the socialist revolution at once. Instead, the new policies lauded the Allied Forces as an army of liberation and declared the Communist party's readiness to cooperate with the occupiers for the completion of the democratic revolution according to the terms of the Potsdam Declaration.[39]

Democratic was the key word and meant economic as well as political democracy. If SCAP, in addition to erecting the political institutions of democratic government, was to undertake the dismantling of the economic props of the emperor system, so much the better. Such a democratic revolution would clear away two types of obstacles blocking the road to the socialist revolution—the landlords and the imperial institution which represented the dead hand of the feudal past, and the zaibatsu firms which represented the precocious advance of monopoly capitalism—and the Communist party would be well advised to cooperate.

At a time when the feudal legacy was still very strong, the 1932 theses had papered over the gap between those calling for socialist revolution and those arguing for a prior bourgeois-democratic revolution by asserting that the forthcoming revolution would be bourgeois democratic but with a strong tendency toward progression into the socialist revolution.[40] Now at a point when capitalist maturity had largely been reached, the JCP (under the lead of Tokuda Kyūichi and Shiga Yoshio) still felt it necessary to fall back on a variant of the old two-stage line. Only this time the two stages would be more clearly separated by an indeterminate period of progressive bourgeois democracy dictated by the length of the occupation.

The two-stage line created a series of contradictions that plagued the JCP for some time to come, and which would prove especially costly during the first nine months when the revolutionary tide was rising. This compromise formulation allowed the party to avoid a direct confrontation with SCAP, but the resulting ambiguity in party policies and formulations produced confusion among party ranks and softened the resolve of the party's Leninists to mobilize the working class for the cause of the revolution.

People's Republic and Popular Fronts

A prime example of the ambiguous analysis was the concept of the "people's republic" (jinmin kyōwa seifu).[41] The 1932 theses had not used this term, but had spoken of a soviet government to be followed by the dictatorship of the proletariat. Postwar party policy also called for the establishment of a people's republic, but this was not to be one composed of workers' and peasants' soviets. Rather, the term signified a parliamentary form of government in which a broad united front of democratic forces would hold power.[42]

It cannot be forgotten that political democratization was an immensely important end for communist and non-communist alike. Completion of the bourgeois-democratic revolution was in truth a primary goal for the JCP and partially separable from the longer-term goal of social revolution, and there is no reason to doubt the sincerity of the JCP policy of assisting SCAP in whatever way possible to accomplish it.[43] Yet there were significant differences between the Communist party's and SCAP's conceptions of political democracy.

The term *people's republic* meant a progressive bourgeois democracy in which the unions and parties of the workers and peasants would not only sharply circumscribe the powers of the big bourgeoisie and their feudalistic allies, but also outweigh and increasingly dominate other bourgeois elements that SCAP favored.[44] The U.S. occupiers were amenable at that time to a partial dismantling of the emperor system[45]—notably the power of the zaibatsu and the landlords—but Tokuda and the other leaders of the JCP were deluding themselves if they thought that SCAP would countenance anything approaching a quasi-revolutionary people's republic in which the working class would hold the major share of economic and political power.

It is clear that the strategic line of establishing a people's republic and completing the bourgeois-democratic revolution was an exceedingly elastic concept which could be used equally well to justify either an early drive onward to socialism or an extended democratic transition. The people's republic was an uneasy way station between the liberal capitalist order and socialism. Intentionally or not, these early Tokuda-Shiga formulations masked considerable theoretical vacillation about the speed with which the JCP could proceed to the main task of social revolution. It was one thing to talk about the present revolution being bourgeois-democratic with a strong tendency toward progression into a socialist one—as did the 1932 theses and, less precisely, postwar party policy—but it was quite another to put practical content into that ambiguous phrase.

A people's republic worthy of the program enunciated in the 1932 theses would have to be built not on parties and unions but on soviets, the very existence of which would compromise the viability of Japanese capitalism and arouse the wrath of SCAP. Pursuing the people's republic through parliamentary parties and interest groups like labor unions would serve Japan's democratization and avoid SCAP's hostility. But along that path lay the danger that the working class might be hemmed in and co-opted by the liberal capitalist order under construction.

The Tokuda-Shiga answer to this conundrum was to commit the Communist party to both policies at once by following a strategy of peaceful gradualism and pursuing the radical tactics of building revolutionary soviets, but the combination was too unstable to last. Nonetheless, it ran like a consistent thread through the early months of the JCP's activities, and echoes of it even survived Nosaka Sanzō's return and the Fifth Party Congress in February 1946 when the JCP decisively affirmed its commitment to gradualism in tactics as well as theory. The contradictions of simultaneously trying to complete the bourgeois-democratic revolution and to organize for the socialist one were most damaging to efforts to construct a popular front and to lead the workers' movement.

Tokuda proposed a popular front to the JSP leaders as early as 19 October, but they refused on the next day on the grounds that the JCP program was not yet clear. Tokuda also proposed to Matsuoka personally that they forget their differences so far as labor was concerned and form a single, united labor movement. In effect, Tokuda was proposing a popular front from above committed to the liberal program for betterment of the workers' lot through strong labor unions. Even while pressing for a popular front, the JCP leaders began attacking the JSP as a pseudo-socialist party, and stigmatized Nishio and Matsuoka as war criminals who had collaborated with the fascists and the zaibatsu. At the same time, the JCP was also working to establish a united front from below, in an obvious attempt to bypass the right-wing socialists by appealing directly to their bases of support.[46]

The Fourth Party Congress of the JCP on 1–2 December adopted an action program, a popular front program, and party regulations. Tokuda was elected party chairman and on 6 December—with the JCP program now published—he again proposed a popular front to the JSP, which again was promptly rejected, this time on the grounds that lack of mutual trust now made cooperation impossible. Both parties, the JSP declared, should work on consolidating their own organizations. After this rejection, some JSP leaders and local organizations denounced the decision and began cooperating with the popular front anyhow.[47]

The JCP made its third proposal for a popular front on 26 December, emphasizing common action to solve the food crisis. After the JSP rejected this on the 27th, the JCP published a vituperative attack on 7 January on the right-wing "social-fascist militarists," and appealed to the JSP rank and file to oppose their reactionary leaders and make common cause with the genuinely democratic program of the JCP.[48]

The JCP front attempts did succeed to the limited extent of putting the right wing on the defensive and eliciting cooperation from the local organizations of the JSP. But the overall purpose of the popular front proposal remained confused. If it was indeed intended to create effective grounds for coordination from above between the JCP and the JSP left wing for a gradualist program for Japan's socialization, it would quickly run afoul of Tokuda's Leninist tactic of mobilizing workers, farmers, and the city poor in a united front from below. In fact, so long as the JCP was trying to undermine the JSP at the grass roots, it could hardly expect to gain the broad support it needed among the

JSP national leadership, regardless of the merit of the proposals for joint action.

Combining Unions and Soviets

The first postwar edition of the JCP newspaper *Akahata* (*Red Flag*) on 20 October carried an unsigned article on party policies. The article said that Japan's democratization under the Potsdam terms would provide a "shield" protecting JCP activists from attack by the right, but the party must not lean on SCAP or forget that the people must be the ones to realize the democratic revolution. The discussion of the need for worker-farmer solidarity avoided use of the word "soviet," but sounded much the same theme in urging that labor unions and farmers' committees must link up in "people's liberation committees" led by the working class. Out of such organizations of workers, farmers, and city poor exercising substantial control over production and distribution, the JCP hoped to consolidate a united front from below which would encompass the whole working class and become the proletarian striking force in the eventual socialist revolution. In anticipation of that event, the popular organizations were to have two tasks: to prevent backsliding by the liberals and social democrats and to solve the crisis of production and distribution.[49] Tokuda's hand in this was obvious.[50]

How Tokuda and the other party leaders[51] expected to sustain a revolutionary workers' movement through the transition period of bourgeois democracy without seeing it succumb to parliamentary reformism was suggested in a policy paper on the relationship of the labor union movement to the coming general election that was published in *Akahata* no. 5 on 1 January 1946.[52] The key was to form a broad "factory representatives council movement" (kōba daihyōsha kaigi undō) through which the party could maintain contact with the workers, keep their revolutionary fervor alive, and guide them. At the same time, the party intended the inter-factory councils to be the mechanism enabling the workers to organize unions and federations above the factory or enterprise level, and to overcome the limitations of local actions, whether it be union activity or production control.

In respect to maintaining contact with the workers, the inter-factory councils were more union than soviet in spirit, for the ultimate goal was the creation of one solidary federation of labor at the national level, one big union. As for overcoming the limitations of local worker actions, the councils were to provide the organizational heart for the united front from below which was to coordinate joint struggles drawing together all segments of the working class. The inter-factory councils were to lead workers, farmers, and poor city people in a national movement contesting control over production and distribution, and to demonstrate that the people's daily struggle for existence was synonymous with the struggle to take power from the zaibatsu, bureaucrats, and landlords. Thus, the JCP thought it could both construct a national union movement and forge a revolutionary solidarity that would outlast the occupation.

Without doubt, the inter-factory councils had the potential for coordinating an anti-capitalist movement for workers' control, but unions are not revolutionary bodies, and the emphasis upon them is clear evidence of the underlying equivocation between reformist and revolutionary policies. The JCP leaders had yet to decide whether they were committed to turning the inter-factory councils into revolutionary bodies uniting the individual production control struggles in the enterprise into a national movement, or whether they were going to promote them as the framework for a national federation of labor unions.

In short, though the JCP leaders considered the production control struggle committee to be Japan's postwar analogue to the workers' soviet, it did not have a well-thought-out policy on production control, much less the conscious intent to use it solely for furthering social revolution. In reality the organizational connection between actual production control struggles and the JCP was tenuous at best, although communist workers participated wholeheartedly and the national party organization supported them. It was more a case of the workers' actions and the party's program coinciding than a relationship of cause and effect. JCP leaders like Tokuda sought to encourage and guide production control, but found it difficult to do so in practice.

The JCP "action program" adopted by the Fourth Party Congress reflected this confusion. It called for:

10. Formation of a popular front by the massing of all democratic forces.
11. The drastic shortening of working hours (a seven-hour day as the usual, not exceeding an eight-hour maximum, within a forty-four-hour weekly limit). The fundamental improvement of the workers' condition. Unemployment relief. The realization of full employment by the shortening of work hours. Freedom of organization and activity for labor unions. Establishment of collective bargaining rights.
12. Opposition to the semi-feudalistic employment system and semi-slave working conditions. Prohibition of heavy, injurious, and dangerous labor for women, youth, and juveniles. Abolition of the apprentice system. The same pay for the same work.
13. A general increase of wages. Establishment of a compulsory minimum wage. Opposition to capitalistic rationalization. Prohibition of juvenile

labor under fourteen years of age. One fully paid holiday per week, a fully paid vacation of two weeks or more per year.

. . . .

20. Putting into effect of workers' control over essential enterprise and regulation by the people's republican government. The elimination of enterprise management by the military clique, the bureaucracy, and monopoly capital. Freedom of small- and medium-scale commerce and industry.[53]

The action program also spoke of the need "to consolidate a class-based, single, industrial labor union movement" as a major goal.

The import of this program and such policy statements on the labor union movement as those printed in *Akahata* no. 4 on 29 November was that the JCP should promote both unions and workers' control.[54] Party leaders found a facile answer to one of the difficulties involved in extending the bourgeois-democratic phase by having labor unions assume contradictory tasks: 1) bargaining with employers over economic issues like wages and hours, and 2) progressively taking basic control over production, in order, first, to overcome the economic breakdown, and second, to pave the way for socialist revolution. They just as facilely regarded production control as a tactic appropriate for either task. Based as it was on worker direct action and posing a fundamental challenge to the rights of private property, production control was not a dispute tactic of unions but an early form of a worker soviet or council type of factory organization. And in fact soviet-like committees, organizationally distinct from and superior to the existing unions, invariably conducted production control struggles—unions did not.

The tactical merger of the tasks of union and soviet was perhaps the most troublesome contradiction inherent in the two-stage theory of revolution. Tokuda simply assumed that production control could coexist in the interim with unions exercising conventional labor tactics of strikes and collective bargaining, and could preserve within the capitalist order the germ of the revolutionary factory council through times of relative labor stability. Yet at least this much can be said in retrospect: production control challenged not only the capitalist organization of industry and society, but also the authority of the conventional union movement. In the final analysis, production control could no more coexist with unions bent on exercising maximum authority over labor's rank and file than it could with employers determined to safeguard property rights and their control over labor.[55]

Even though the postwar leaders of the JCP had returned to the idea of a distinct first stage of progressive bourgeois democracy, some,

like Tokuda, believed the socialist revolution was not a distant goal
but near enough at hand to require the systematic promotion of popular control over the means of production.[56] If so, the production control struggle committee would not so much coexist with unions as progressively engulf them. So, too, the theoretical and practical confusion
resulting from using production control as a dispute tactic to gain economic concessions from capitalists while at the same time strengthening its anti-capitalist claims on social and political power would presumably be solved by the continuous enlargement of its revolutionary role.

Conversely, of course, the longer and more difficult the progression
from bourgeois democracy to socialism, the more resolute would be
business and government resistance, thus raising the question of the
survival of production control in any guise. The JCP under Tokuda's
lead did not confront that problem, and by and large the business and
government foes of production control saw more clearly than did its
supporters the fundamental contradiction in preserving it within a re-
vivified capitalism. Production control, even if conceived of strictly as
a dispute tactic of unions, still amounted in practice to using revolutionary means for non-revolutionary ends. Sooner or later the JCP
would have to choose: either support of a strong labor union movement within the confines of a democratized but capitalist Japan, or
support of workers' soviets dedicated to the immediate overthrow of
the capitalist system. Under Tokuda's lead the JCP chose neither position but tried to pursue both at once.

5

"Modified" Capitalism and the
Co-optation of Workers' Control

New Moves against Labor

The main office demonstration that had ended the production control struggle at Japan Steel Tube made Japan's leaders disturbingly aware of the social consequences of a continuing stagnation of production.[1] The workers' defiance of authority and the connections being forged with the JCP shocked them into action against what they saw as a communist-directed attack against the rights of private property.[2] The government responded on 1 February 1946 when the Home, Justice, Commerce and Industry, and Welfare Ministries issued a joint policy declaration (the "Four Ministers' Declaration") at the request of the president of Japan Steel Tube[3] which branded production control an illegal act in violation of property rights.

While the Government has from the outset anticipated the development and activity of labor unions, the outbreak of acts of violence, coercion, and, what is more, violations of the rights of property that we are seeing in recent labor disputes is intolerable. Labor conscious of its responsibility for the reconstruction of a new Japan must not engage in acts like these. The Government, far from letting them go without challenge, will be compelled to deal summarily with such illegal and excessive actions. Accordingly, it is to be hoped that workers will take sufficient care not to fall into such errors from this time on.[4]

The intent of the declaration could not have been clearer. Henceforth the government would regard production control as an illegal act to be dealt with summarily by the police. The government acknowledged, in principle, labor's right to engage in dispute acts like strikes, but its declaration was a fundamental negation of that right. It prohibited the sole effective means of dispute available at the time—production control—as "illegal and excessive," a phrase flexible enough to permit application of the declaration much more broadly should the necessity arise.[5]

The day after the government published the declaration, Anthony Constantino, a Labor Division official, held a press conference at which he expressed SCAP's displeasure. SCAP would not take a stand on the issue, said Constantino, but the government was not to prohibit production control unilaterally. The question must be settled in the courts.[6] The left-wing unions and federations attacked the declaration as well, openly declaring their intention to defy it. After several cabinet meetings on the emergency, the Home Ministry instructed prefectural governors on 8 February to restrict the use of police in settling labor disputes, in effect directing the police to cease intervention in labor affairs. Soon after, the government further "clarified" the declaration by saying that it had not been intended to prohibit production control, only the illegal acts associated with it.[7]

While the government was engaged in this abortive effort to discipline the working class, big business was organizing itself for the same purpose. On 22 February, the Keidanren Committee sponsored a symposium on labor problems at which the participants ratified a plan to form a new national business federation with the sole task of dealing with labor.[8] The members wanted it to be strong enough to combat the workers' movement by preventing production control and checking the militant unions. Although business had begun research and consultation on production control and other labor problems earlier, the struggle at Japan Steel Tube and the February symposium coincided with the recovery of their will to confront the workers' movement. Translating that will into action was not easy in early 1946. One of the participants in the February symposium recalled that in the anti-business atmosphere of the time, they had to do their planning for regaining control over labor in private, because speaking out openly invited fierce attack, especially in the press, and risked the displeasure of SCAP.[9]

When SCAP was informed in March of the plans for a new national business federation to deal with labor problems, it intervened. The Anti-Trust and Cartels Division in ESS indicated that it could not grant its approval, because the federation might lend itself to the survival of the zaibatsu. Paul Stanchfield, chairman of the Labor Advisory Committee to SCAP, objected that a powerful, centralized management federation might well suppress the fledgling labor unions before they reached maturity.[10] SCAP did approve the founding in June 1946 of the Kantō Management Association (Kantō Keieisha Kyōkai, or Kankeikyō)—the parent organization of Nikkeiren. Since Kankeikyō operated from the beginning as the national combat arm of big business against the workers' movement, SCAP's opposition had little effect after all, aside from delaying the formal inauguration of Nikkeiren until 1948.[11]

The Workers Move Ahead of Their Vanguard

The JCP's Rejection of Workers' Control

The attitude of the JSP and Sōdōmei to the Four Ministers' Declaration was no more than mildly disapproving.[12] In an informal interview after issue of the declaration Matsuoka said: "The JSP does not believe that the government has embarked on trying to suppress [production control] unnecessarily. In short, employees must take a more sensible attitude; and indeed, through recognizing the standpoint of the capitalists we anticipate a raising of the position of employees."[13] Matsuoka and the right-wing socialist leaders—later characterized by the left-wing leader Takano Minoru as "endless labor-capital collaborators"[14]—agreed with the government's proscription of production control. Labor should eschew anti-capitalist radicalism and, placing the interests of the nation first, cooperate willingly with the big-business and government program for reconstruction. More than a hint of the old Sanpō ideology was apparent in this "national policy viewpoint" that assumed that labor should bear the burden of reconstruction without complaint and without question.[15]

Setting aside the ideological predilections of the socialist right wing, the union and party leaders had a quite practical reason for wanting to squelch production control. It immeasurably antagonized the very zaibatsu and government leaders whom they were quietly approaching in a spirit of compromise for aid in promoting their type of business unionism. They could hardly defend production control and in the same breath present themselves to big business as the moderate and dependable counter to the organization of labor by the radical left.[16]

Production control educated workers in direct democracy. The experience of collectively operating the enterprise engendered in them a spirit of radicalism and self-confidence that was no more reconcilable with the hierarchical and authoritarian business union than it was with the hierarchical and authoritarian factory. Production control inevitably stimulated worker antagonism both against employers and against those labor leaders who would collaborate with them. For right-wing socialists to encourage it was tantamount to encouraging rank-and-file rebellion. Accordingly, they obstructed it to the limit of their ability, in spite of the sharp reaction that policy called forth from left-wing socialists like Takano.

After Nosaka Sanzō returned to Japan on 10 January, he and the JCP Central Committee issued a joint declaration softening the party stand on many issues. The 14 January declaration stressed that the JCP "truly feared for the country, loved the country," and far from intending to plunge it into violence, would work to improve and stabilize the people's livelihood. The authors insisted that "it is essential that all democrats who have the same aims form a democratic popular front." The declaration closed with a call for cooperation in formulating a common program, and rejected the idea that the front would adhere to the program of any one party.[17]

On 16 January the JSP Executive Committee responded by making the decision to postpone cooperation with the JCP in a popular front or in joint struggles at any level until the election was over. The JCP reply in *Akahata* on 22 January once more argued the case for joint struggles by the parties, labor unions, and farmer organizations at every level in order to solve the food crisis and to win the coming election. It explicitly endorsed the popular front proposal which the left-wing socialist Yamakawa Hitoshi had been advocating independently of both parties since early January. Furthermore, Nosaka and the Central Committee stated explicitly that "the party is demanding a people's republic but this does not at all mean the formation of a soviet government."[18]

The changes Nosaka's return was working on party policy are already visible here, changes that the JCP would formalize at its Fifth Congress on 24–26 February. The new emphasis is evident in two slogans—the "loveable Communist party" and "peaceful democratic revolution." The contradiction between reformist strategy and revolutionary tactics disappeared in a new Nosaka line that emphasized completion of the bourgeois-democratic revolution as the Communist party's primary task. Nosaka visualized a form of bourgeois democracy in which a coalition of the JCP, JSP, and liberal elements from other parties representing the workers and peasants but also the petit bourgeoisie of medium-small businessmen and white-collar workers would hold political power. This he counterposed to formal bourgeois democracy under which a coalition of bureaucrats, zaibatsu leaders, and landlords excluded these groups from effective power despite nominally democratic institutions.[19]

Nosaka's version of the bourgeois-democratic revolution resembled earlier formulations in that it continued to point two ways at once: toward eliminating feudal remnants like the landlord system and toward checking monopoly capital. Japan could in this way follow the peaceful road to socialism because the Allied policy of democratization permitted the accomplishment of both tasks at the same time. The existence of SCAP and an army of occupation made it all the more necessary to take the parliamentary path, with the party solidly grounding itself in the popular movement. A greatly lengthened two-stage revolution became the orthodox line, and committed the party to the gradual attainment of socialism by parliamentary means. The new policy foreclosed the possibilities implicit in the Tokuda-Shiga approach, which had left the way open for an early and to some extent violent socialist revolution.[20]

The new policy appeared in the declaration of the JCP Fifth Congress on 25 February 1946:

Part I
The Japan Communist Party has as its present goal the completion of our country's bourgeois-democratic revolution, which is progressing at present by peaceful and democratic methods. Therefore, it is not the case that the party is insisting on abolishing the capitalist system in its entirety and on realizing the socialist system at once. The party will try to realize the following:

. . . .

4. Nationalization of the property of war criminals and the dissolution of monopoly capital. Strong control over big capital by a people's republic, management of industry by a management council system in which workers will participate, the complete unification of financial institutions, and transfer of these to the control of the people's republic. Freeing medium- and small-scale businessmen from the unjust interference of monopoly capital and the bureaucracy, and securing of freedom of business operations for them.

We anticipate the heightening of the general efficiency of industry by employing a system of management councils. We will check the collapse in all branches of industry by readjusting the entire system of production and giving it balance, and by assimilating the products of industry through improving the life of the popular masses.

. . . .

6. Establishment of a minimum-wage system for salaried people and workers sufficient to stabilize their livelihood. Equal pay for equal work. The seven-hour-day work system (maximum of eight hours). Protection of working women and youth. Institution of social insurance including the perfecting of the factory law, unemployment insurance, and old-age pensions. Control by labor unions of the rationing of foodstuffs and other essentials for living. The

strengthening of the management-council system. Establishment by the constitution and labor law of the workers' rights.[21]

The JCP had decided the national organizations for the working class ought to be the unions and the parties. The workers' council in the form of the production-control struggle committee no longer had a place; in its stead, the party endorsed the formation of a management council system through which workers would "participate" in management but not control it. The distinction is vital since it revealed the JCP's genuine rejection of the revolutionary tactics of building a soviet system capable of seizing political-economic power. The contradiction inherent in the merger of union and soviet in the action program of the Fourth Party Congress was now resolved in a pronounced shift to the right—from workers' control to workers' participation, from production control struggle committees to joint labor-management councils and industrial unions.[22] Moreover, the party now regarded the unions and the labor-management councils more as a means to stabilize and increase industrial production and bring efficiency to the existing system than they did as arenas for the class struggle.[23] The workers were to shoulder the burden of a capitalist reconstruction but were not to challenge the capitalist managers for control of industry.

SCAP interrogated Nosaka on 11 February about the new policy and reported his views on party strategy as follows:

"The old party strategy was 'infantile sickness,' but that period has passed." Immediately after the surrender and especially after the release of political prisoners, communist strategy was not efficient. SHIGA and TOKUDA were over critical of the Socialist leaders and others doubtless as a result of their long imprisonment but they are `. . . [now] convinced of the necessity for working with other people. (NOSAKA doubts if they have changed their opinions, but says they have learned tact)—communist ideology hereafter will remain grounded on Marx.[24]

The document also noted that "NOSAKA objects to the Social Democratic program as being too far in advance of Japanese conditions."

With tactics now accommodated to strategy, the JCP embarked on a course so parliamentary and moderate that by late July a conservative SCAP official, Harry Emerson Wildes, could write in a confidential study of the JCP forwarded to the U.S. State Department,

It is evident that the Communist Party is seeking to build a reputation as a party of effective force applied in a lawful and even conventional fashion. It is also evident, however, that unless the Communist Party holds private convictions at sharp variance from the published aims, its program is not as revolutionary, nor even as advanced, as that of certain of its rivals.[25]

Wildes mistakenly concluded that the JCP was concealing its revolutionary program. That was hardly the case, for with one brief exception following the outbreak of the Korean War, the party has followed Nosaka's lead and held to a parliamentary course ever since.

The relegation of production control to the role of a dispute tactic of labor unions or a mechanism for labor-capital cooperation in the form of the enterprise-level council blinded the party to the meaning of the quickening of the workers' movement in the spring of 1946. Just when the production control struggles were becoming militantly anti-capitalist and beginning to reach out and forge alliances with the city poor and needy farmers, the JCP fell behind the popular movement. As the party became more and more deeply involved in parliamentary politics and the formation of popular electoral fronts, a dangerous gap opened between the national leadership and the workers' movement.[26]

The Miners at Mitsubishi Bibai Hold a "People's Court"

Almost as if purposefully contradicting the plans of the right and the left to chart the workers' course for them, the miners at Mitsubishi Bibai in Hokkaidō seized their mines in February, put their employers before a "people's court" (jinmin saiban), and made them answer for their past crimes. Far from following any party line, the miners at Mitsubishi Bibai seem to have heeded the example of successful production control of their counterparts at Mitsui Bibai.[27]

The bare facts of the Mitsubishi Bibai situation were simple enough. The coal miners' union that was set up on 4 November organized the workers of the Mitsubishi Bibai mines, all told about 5,000 strong. On 10 November the union sent a package of largely economic demands to the company that were not completely satisfied by the company's reply on 12 November. As a result of a successful strike in mid-November, the miners gained a very substantial increase in total pay, in the form of a basic wage plus allowances. When the government published its new, upwardly revised standards for total pay per worker recommended for the coal industry in mid-December, the company discovered that it had been paying the miners a rate higher than the new standard. Thereupon the company proceeded unilaterally to deduct the "overpayment" from the workers' December pay and on the same grounds also abolished the special allowance for daily attendance at the mines.

Since the company's action threatened the miners' livelihood, the union hardened its position. It submitted a list of eight demands on 7 January. The most important of these were: 1) maintenance of the wage standard previously negotiated, paid according to the government's new system; 2) abolition of the contract system (under the contract system, a type of piecework, the "efficiency wage" productivity requirement was high); 3) continuation of the attendance allowance separately from the standard wage, contrary to the government's intention to combine all allowances into one payment; and 4) opposition to the transfer to Tokyo of the refining section head, who had been popular among the production and staff workers and had aided their efforts to organize unions. In addition there were demands for vacations and time off, including menstrual leave for women workers.

Assistant General Manager Noda Tōichi and union chairman Mizutani Takashi subsequently negotiated in Sapporo and came to a compromise agreement that conceded a great deal to the company. When the news reached the union, the miners' union repudiated the agreement on the grounds that Mizutani had conducted the negotiations entirely alone and did not have the authority to make an agreement in the first place. The company took an unbending stand on the wage issue, arguing that the matter had been settled and that in any case it could not exceed the new standard for wages for coal miners since this would cause difficulties at the company's other mines. The union reaffirmed its demands on 2 February and added three more, including one for participation in management. No progess was made, and a confrontation became unavoidable.

The union called an extraordinary meeting for 7 February at which the miners agreed by vote on a list of three key demands. They were 1) abolition of the contract system for surface and pit workers, 2) inclusion in the basic wage of all existing allowances, and 3) continuation of the attendance allowance in goods "to the bitter end." The company categorically rejected the demands and refused to retreat one inch from the Sapporo agreement. After this exchange, the union reconvened the meeting to consider what actions to take. After some discussion the members present voted to institute production control on the 8th if their demands were not met, and so notified the company. The company refused to recognize the union decision, terming it illegal, and declared it would continue operations as usual. It insisted it would defend its management rights "to the bitter end."

Sumiya Mikio's comment on the reasoning behind the coal company's hard-line stance is most interesting:

As for the company, there were rumors at that time that the Soviet Army would occupy Hokkaidō and so forth, and the company, fearing that private property rights would be infringed in the chaos of the lost war, hardened its resolve not to follow in the tracks of Mitsui Bibai. It seems they even thought that if they were beaten here they would be trampled down in the Hokkaidō coal mines one by one by "the planned actions of the Communist party." In this sense, the Bibai dispute was the first counterattack by monopoly capital against the labor movement.[28]

The example of Mitsui Bibai had certainly not been lost on Mitsubishi. The miners next set up a dispute organ (sōgi dan). The four union executives who had been acting as the miners' negotiating committee became the leaders of the dispute organ. They were, by occupation, an outside-the-pit railway worker, a clerk-in-charge in the labor section, a construction section assistant, and a coal miner. On the 8th the union entered production control at 7:00 A.M. and dispatched a control committee to the offices and to every workplace. The miners worked as they normally did under the direction of the responsible staff personnel, and overall nothing really changed aside from the nominal severing of the company's control. The union at this time also gained the backing of the Hokkaidō-based federation of coal mine unions.[29]

Despite its different name, the organization for carrying out production control at Mitsubishi Bibai did not differ in essence from the struggle committee system seen at the *Yomiuri*, as figure 5.1 makes clear. The similarity underscores the point that the usual union structure was simply too constricted to deal with running an enterprise. Only a comprehensive council type of organization could hope to measure up to that task.

Production control put the white-collar staff on the spot. The miners' union asked the staff union for its cooperation, but the latter was unable to take a stand because of its ambiguous position between the production workers and the company officials. It simply adopted a neutral stance and, without referring to the propriety of production control, stated that it would strive for a continuation of production as usual and for the preservation of peace at the mine. For the time being all went on much as before, with the staff taking orders from the company and the workers digging coal under the supervision of the staff. As at Mitsui Bibai, labor productivity and total output increased dramatically. Even when the miners' union extended the scope of its control to include the company offices at the mine and took control of management on 11 February, the staff union merely indicated it would exert its efforts toward a harmonious settlement.[30]

As elsewhere, the staff had been the uneasy point of contact between management and labor, and had been responsible for implementing harsh management policies, for which the company re-

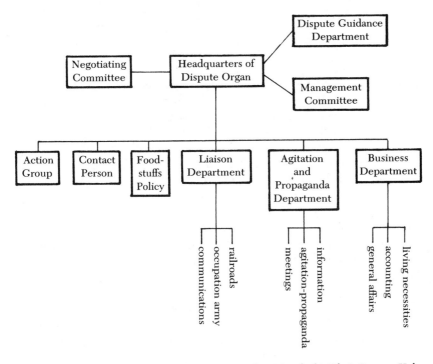

Figure 5.1. Organization of Production Control at Mitsubishi Bibai. Source: Hokkaidō Rōdō-bu, *Shiryō Hokkaidō Rōdō Undō Shi (Shūsen—Kōwa)* (Hokkaido: Hokkaidō Rōdō-bu, 1953), in *Seisan Kanri Tōsō: Shiryō Sengo Kakumei*, edited by Sengo Kakumei Shiryō Hensan Iinkai (Tokyo: Jōkyō Shuppan, 1 Oct. 1974), Rinji Zōkan, *Jōkyō*, p. 171.

warded it with a certain degree of status and privilege. After surrender, therefore, the staff workers had much less interest in organizing, but as inflation and general want steadily brought them down closer to the production workers' desperate position, they realized the necessity of banding together. On 6 December the office workers organized a staff association, which on 5 February became a staff union. Its goals were harmony between labor and management and the rehabilitation of Bibai. Within the staff, distinct differences did exist between lower and upper ranks, and as time went on and the production control struggle intensified, the lower-ranking staff shifted its support behind the miners' union. The staff union even began cooperating in getting rid of those staff employees who were obstructing the miners' control of production.[31] The sympathy of the lower-level staff employees no doubt accounts for the ease with which the miners' dispute organ was able to extend its supervision to the area of business management starting 11 February.

In addition, the miners' struggle was aided by the fact that the JCP sent a number of people to help, that it had the support of public opinion, and that the chief of the local labor section of SCAP in Sapporo was sympathetic. During the dispute this SCAP officer stated forthrightly that according to his view unions were free to conduct production control if they wished and that, accordingly, the U.S. Army units stationed in Hokkaidō would certainly not interfere.[32]

During this time, owing to the company's intransigence, no negotiations whatever had been going on, so on 17 February the union called an extraordinary meeting to discuss the situation. It ended with a resolution to push onward to victory. Afterwards a group of several hundred union members gathered together to go to the general manager's home to force a meeting to discuss the union's demands. They eventually caught up with General Manager Gotō Tarō and Assistant General Manager Noda at an executives' clubhouse where they were in conference with other high officials of Mitsubishi enterprises in Hokkaidō. They then forcibly marched the two through the bitter cold and snow to a meeting hall nearly two kilometers away, and sat them down on the stage across the table from the union officials. The workers and their families jammed into the hall, and thus began thirty-six hours of nonstop mass negotiations, the famous "people's court" incident.

Soon after the mass negotiations began, the persistent questioning of the union officials on why the company could not pay the workers' wage demands backed Noda into a corner from which he tried to extricate himself by an evasive and flippant, "Anyhow, we can't pay it," which provoked a torrent of abuse from the assembly. The deep anger of the miners and their families, and their reasons for it, are revealed in an account of the beginnings of the people's court by one of the main participants, Nishimura Takeo.

"What's this, you can't pay it?"

"We workers are never going to be silenced!"

"Hey! You managers, you came here to cheat us, didn't you? What about it? Answer!"

General Manager: "That is not the case."

"Liar! What about today's tempura?"

"You feed your dogs on white rice, where did you get that rice?"

"You are always cheating us of our sake and drinking it, aren't you? Just look at those red noses!"

In the midst of this twenty-some police poured into the hall with their boots on.

"What's this? Get those cops out of here! They're the capitalists' watch-dogs!"

"What kind of thing is this, coming into our hall with your shoes on? Take them off!"

"Take off your hats!"

The crowd of people knows the ugly side of the police, who were in collusion with the capitalists.[33]

SCAP took a hands-off attitude even during the people's court, and the Japanese authorities were unable to take action on their own. Nearly thirty police had come out to the mine at the outset of the incident, but were uncertain what to do and asked their superiors for instructions. All that was said, however, was "Take appropriate measures." The continuing abuse was too much for the police in the hall to take for long, and they left in pairs without doing anything. In the face of the extreme hostility of the miners and their families, and the lack of direction or support from the authorities, the police in the end felt compelled to cease their observations at the mine. The company's appeal to SCAP was equally fruitless since the local occupation authorities who came to see what was going on were not inclined to intervene, merely giving the company the indifferent reply, "Should the situation lead to acts of violence inform us immediately."[34]

The company officials were forced to respond time and again, point by point, to the union leaders' questions. They had to listen to the acrimonious personal attacks of the miners and their wives for treating the workers brutally in the mines, for callously feeding pet animals good food from their own excess stocks while the workers and their families ate scraps little better than garbage in order simply to survive. At one point, according to Nishimura's account,

A lone woman stood and rushed up onto the stage. Composing her white face, she took a handful of something from her pocket. Wanting to say something, lip quivering, boiling with agitation, she began to cry in mortification.

"Managers, please look at this. It's the guts of a pumpkin. While you were eating rice every, every day and drinking sake, there was no rice ration for us. We were told it was in order to win the war. The sweet potatoes ran out, and we came to the point of eating this, every day, every day (choking sob). Our family was patient with this, even though I couldn't even give my husband something to take when he went to work (cries). And what of the feelings of a mother when her child says again and again, 'rice, I want to eat rice' (voice rising and crying). If you are human, you ought to understand a parent's feelings. And recently, when we thought that, thanks to the unions, wages had been raised a little, now they say that you will take back the sardines that we have been living on. After all that, are you human? If that were all, it might be endured, but what kind of a thing is it that you are snatching away the things we eat, that you are raising pet horses and dogs and letting them eat white rice? The coal mine pit-workers are leading more miserable lives than dogs. We worry about something to eat every day, every day, and it feels like we will go crazy over getting something to eat. While I'm standing here right now I'm thinking about what we will eat this evening."

Unable to go on she broke down in tears. Her heaving shoulders touched the hearts of those present. It was probably the first time in her life she had spoken in front of people. Deeply moved by her own words, she finally broke down completely on the stage. The women in the hall raised their voices in a wail at the sad memories she had called up.[35]

The attitude of the gathered workers and their families was menacing. Periodically the hatred bred of years, even decades, burst out in words such as these. Yet in the end the company officials escaped without injury, a remarkable outcome considering the baring of the workers' emotions as they contrasted their own fight for survival to the comfortable lives the officials had lived. Assuredly, the people's court left the company officials with emotional scars, if not from the personal abuse they had to endure then from the fear they must have felt that the miners' anger would burst into violence against them.

The Mitsubishi Bibai miners were, nonetheless, several steps away from conscious, anti-capitalist class solidarity of the kind that would be needed to bring their single-minded concentration on production and obtaining life's necessities into focus in a coherent revolutionary program. A large step closer would be taken in subsequent production control struggles when, in complete disregard of legality, the struggle committees would reach out to other organizations to make the breakthrough into a self-sustaining form of production control. At Mitsubishi Bibai the struggle organization made faltering, and finally unsuccessful, efforts in this direction when it appealed to the farmers' unions for a joint struggle to secure foodstuffs for the miners.[36]

However radical the people's court incident was in some respects, it was settled within the framework of the existing system. The struggle did not go all the way. When the company officials finally broke under the pressure and gave in to the union demands, the result was the same type of settlement that had come at the conclusion of previous production control struggles—large pay hikes, democratic reforms of the enterprise, recognition of labor rights, and formation of a management council. The conscious intent to go on to break with the capitalist order was yet to come. When it did come, the left-wing parties had little to do with producing it.

Confrontation or Collaboration?

The Conservative Mainstream Proposes More of the Same

On 12 February 1946 while the struggle at Mitsubishi was building to its climax, a high official in the Office of the U.S. Political Adviser to SCAP, William J. Sebald, attended an informal luncheon with a group of Mitsui executives. The group included a partner of Mitsui Holding Company, Mitsui Takaatsu, the president of Mitsui Trading Company, and the managing director of the Mitsui Head Office. In his report afterwards, Sebald stated that he thought their ideas "probably typical of most successful Japanese industrialists and businessmen," and that he "found the Japanese so eager to present their views that it was generally unnecessary for him to offer direct comment or actively to enter the discussion."[37]

The executives explicitly linked a punitive U.S. policy toward the zaibatsu with a communist takeover, their transparent purpose being to persuade the U.S. government that the zaibatsu were the essential ingredient if Japan was to have both social stability and economic recovery. They predicted "an increase by leaps and bounds of social unsettlement and unrest" if SCAP did not permit them to rehabilitate industry quickly, for "time is of the essence, and the situation continues to deteriorate."

Either the Government must "grab the ball" and start the wheels of industry, or industry itself must do it. However, industry cannot, because it is frozen by lack of capital, refusal to allow new undertakings, and general uncertainty and bewilderment. In consequence, the general atmosphere is one of frustration at every turn. The very people who can most help the General Headquarters in carrying out its policies, and they are only too willing so to help, are barred by Governmental red tape, refusal to clarify policies except in vague, general terms, and the propensity for giving negative decisions with no alternatives offered.

The large business interests in Japan have always been pro-American in their sentiments, but the present seemingly destructive trend of American policy, without encouragement or assistance in reconstruction, is rapidly alienating previous ties of good will. As a result, business leaders in Japan are beginning to think about the possibilities of help from non-American quarters. This would be most unfortunate, but desperation makes for strange bedfellows.

The so-called *Zaibatsu* cannot understand why there is so much commotion to "break up" the big combines. As a matter of fact, with the present tax structure in Japan, it is practically impossible for any large organization to continue in existence and also make a profit. After all, even Americans must admit that profit is one of the impelling motives of business; without profit, any organization will eventually fall apart. This is well illustrated by the fact that many of the "Mitsui" companies competed among themselves. Furthermore, Mitsui enterprises were not solely financed by the Mitsui Bank. On the contrary, Mitsui companies placed their business with those banks which advanced loans at the lowest rate of interest.

Mere "bigness" should not necessarily be taken as "badness." American Telephone and Telegraph Company, General Motors, United States Steel, Du Pont, Ford, and other large American corporations were cited as precedents for "bigness" which yet had the blessing of the American people. As Japanese companies, under the lash of the military, it is hardly reasonable to expect the large Japanese combines to do otherwise than carry out the instructions of the Government during the war.

Too rapid a disintegration of the large combines can only result in economic chaos in Japan. Once such chaos does result, Japan will be ripe for Communism, already growing as a result of the clever infiltration of Communists among the workers in all branches of industry. Is it believed that a Communistic Japan is in the best interests of the United States?[38]

All SCAP needed to do was to give the zaibatsu a blank check. The pro-American zaibatsu executives could be trusted to put their know-how to use to see to it that the communists would be kept at bay, that industry would be rehabilitated, that competition and profits would be preserved, and that more food would be produced, that the workers would be guaranteed a livelihood—just as they had done in the past. It would be hard to exceed the fatuousness of the Mitsui executives' protestations, but all members of the Japanese leadership shared their fear of the consequences of economic and social chaos.

The zaibatsu leaders understood full well that the only way to scotch the charge of sabotage once and for all and to disarm production control was to recommence industrial production. How to do this and yet retain control over the course of economic revival was the crux of their problem. Zaibatsu leaders had been conferring among themselves in January in search of a way out of the impasse, and the Keidanren Committee set up a Policy Committee on Industrial Reconstruction (Kigyō Saikai Taisaku Iinkai) on 17 January. This committee concluded that it was of the utmost importance to hasten the consolidation and centralization of the private business associations behind the lead of the Keidanren Committee in order more effectively to coordinate and communicate business policy for government implementation.[39]

Revival of the economy clearly required close policy coordination if big-business and government leaders were to keep control of the process, but that too would be difficult while they were under the constant scrutiny of SCAP as it carried out its policy of economic democratization. As expected, SCAP took action against the major business federations, forcing dissolution of the Essential Industry Council and the Japan Economic League in May, two of the founding organizations of the Keidanren Committee. This posed major organizational problems for big-business leaders, since it came on top of the dismantling of the wartime mechanisms for economic control, such as the National General Mobilization Act and the Munitions Ministry. As already noted, SCAP did not dissolve the control associations, and big business partly overcame its problem of control and coordination by the expedient of reorganizing the associations one after another into private "autonomous control organizations" (jishuteki tōsei dantai). These remained under the Essential Industry Council—which had long been the leading zaibatsu business association—until its dissolution on 27 February. Thereafter, they came under the direction of the Japan Industry Council (Nihon Sangyō Kyōgikai), which had been sponsored by the Keidanren Committee.[40]

Between the enterprise and the "autonomous control organizations" a host of other business associations existed on an industrial or regional level, such as the Hokkaidō Coal Industry Federation. These mid-level associations were the building blocks of both the "autonomous control organizations" and the two most powerful big business federations which arose after the war, Keidanren and Nikkeiren. The Keidanren Committee had been wrestling with just this problem of coordinating the associations under its own auspices in order to live up to its aspiration of becoming the new "control tower" of the business world.[41]

Despite the success of the conservatives in big business in consolidating the Keidanren Committee and establishing Kankeikyō in the first half of 1946 in order to strengthen their grip on the economy and maintain the upper hand over the workers' movement, they could not overcome the contradictions brought on by the prevailing ideology of laissez-faire. Their only solution was more of the same, and that prescription had demonstrably failed to end either sabotage or production control. Even so, perhaps they could make SCAP see the light if they pointed out the dangers of economic democratization assiduously enough. A start had been made.

Many among the leaders of big business did not accept the simplistic solutions of the conservatives, and feared they would bring social upheaval. Indeed, their fear compelled them to question the laissez-faire approach to the postwar reconstruction.

Shidehara and the Controlled Economy

Even while the government was trying to bring the workers' movement to heel by means of the Four Ministers' Declaration, the Minister of Commerce and Industry declared a shift in economic policies on 6 February in a paper entitled "Fundamental Principles for a Policy for Increase of Production to Deal with the Emergency Situation" (Kinkyū Jittai ni taisuru Seisan Zōkyō Hōsaku Tairyō). According to the official history of Keidanren, "these fundamental principles saw cabinet ratification on the 8th and became the starting point for an important policy change from laissez-faire toward the strengthening of controls."[42]

According to the fundamental principles, the relaxation of wartime controls was the most important cause of the paralysis of production, and serious social disorder would be the result if the government left private industry to effect industrial recovery on its own. Furthermore, a system of integrated controls would be needed in order to facilitate an orderly rehabilitation of key industries, starting first of all with an increase of production in coal and foodstuffs. A small number of designated priority industries would receive preferential treatment in the controlled distribution of critical commodities, from raw materials to food for the work force. Government authorities would administer and enforce production, distribution, and price controls for key commodities and in general supervise the completion of the plan.[43]

The government assigned priority to industries whose revival would stimulate production of consumer goods and foodstuffs. In practice, that meant coal and chemicals but not iron and steel, because increased food production depended on more fertilizers, and fertilizer production could only be expanded if the chemical industry had more coal. Coal was desperately needed for transportation, textile manufacturing, and power generation as well.

Another aspect of the fundamental principles, the setting up of joint deliberative bodies composed of labor and management (kyōgi kikan) in priority enterprises, had almost nothing to do with production but everything to do with defusing the social crisis the authorities feared was close at hand. Unable to outlaw production control, the government was implementing the one alternative countermeasure at its disposal: a carefully restricted official endorsement of labor-management councils springing up in the wake of the *Yomiuri* workers' success. The intent was to smother workers' control within the enterprise by timely and minor concessions rather than fighting it.

The principles enunciated in the Commerce and Industry paper were applied in a series of ordinances made public on 17 February. The eight key ordinances may be grouped under six major headings corresponding to their intent: currency and finance controls, wage and price controls, foodstuffs policy, concealed goods policy, coal production increase, and employment policy.

The currency and finance controls aimed at halting inflation by blocking bank account withdrawals and by exchanging the old yen for new at a rate that would drastically contract the money supply. Coupled with this was an ordinance providing for a survey of business assets for the purpose of making a tax levy against the war profits of big business. Wage control limited pay theoretically to a ¥500 monthly limit. The price policy amounted to a reimposition of a system of price controls which would take the prices of rice and coal as the standards for setting the value of other commodities, agricultural and industrial. The intent was to rectify the gross distortions in the price structure arising from the postwar food shortages, stoppage of industrial production, and hoarding. The foodstuffs policy was intended to enforce fulfillment of delivery quotas of staple goods, especially rice, by a combination of coercion and incentives. It threatened to use force to collect compulsory delivery quotas and at the same time would allow an increase in the price of rice and preferential distribution of fertilizers, textiles, and other essentials to those who complied. The concealed goods policy aimed at recovery of the commodities released by the military and the government at the end of the war, and their distribution through regular channels instead of the black market. The coal policy boiled down to recognition that increased coal output was the key to recovery in food production and distribution and also to recovery in textiles and consumer industries in general. The employment policy proposed a revitalized consumer industry which would at one and the same time provide employment and produce more of the critically short daily necessities. [44]

This emergency economic stabilization program failed miserably in almost every respect, its most noticeable effect being to depress real wages. Inflation, black marketing, and speculation all flourished as before, while unemployment and shortages of coal and food worsened. Production did not recover, and in every direction the economic crisis deepened. The crux of the problem was that the individual zaibatsu enterprise had nothing to gain from increasing production at that time and much to lose. Even though social unrest was endemic and overt revolutionary activity seemed imminent, the fact remained that no government could protect big business from the consequences of economic democratization as well as private business retrenchment could. It was a situation in which the rational pursuit of profits by the individual enterprise was in clear contradiction with a rational economic policy for the nation. Sabotage was not the result of a conspiracy among zaibatsu leaders. They knew without conspiring that it was virtually impossible to replenish stockpiles that would be consumed by increased production and that it was worse than senseless to exchange finite reserves of intrinsically valuable resources for rapidly depreciating paper money. Then there was SCAP, ready to take advantage of an improving situation to further its policy of economic democratization and cut the zaibatsu down to size.

A Special Research Committee under the Research Bureau of the Foreign Office, first organized in August 1945, attacked these same problems from a yet more liberal perspective in a book-length report submitted in March 1946 entitled "Basic Problems for the Reconstruction of Japan's Economy" (Nihon Keizai Saiken no Kihon Mondai). Among the eleven academics on the nineteen-member committee that wrote it were two "progressive" Tokyo Imperial University Professors of Economics who exerted great influence upon the postwar economic reconstruction, Arisawa Hiromi and Ōuchi Hyōe.[45] When Arisawa later in the year formulated a plan for reviving production which the government adopted in December 1946, he based many of his recommendations upon the analysis in this report.

The plan accepted economic democratization and comprehensive planning without qualification, and advanced as its goal the guaranteeing of the people's livelihood and the raising of the standard of living. The writers began by linking economic democratization and the development of technical know-how in the following manner. Past attempts to compensate for Japan's inherent weakness in foreign trade had led to the "chronic illness of Japan's economy and society," and the committee did not believe the postwar trade and employment problems to be resolvable by the old solutions. The departure point for the postwar period had to be in agriculture—specifically, in the rationalization of agriculture as an industry. The tenant system had to be overthrown and the scale of operations expanded sufficiently to admit of efficient use of fertilizers, machines, and tools. This would increase food production enough in the future to make it possible to maintain the postwar population and at the same time allow the farmer to prosper, thereby creating a strong and continuing internal demand for the products of industry, which would then contribute to stimulating economic growth still further. The excess labor thrown out of rural communities by agricultural consolidation and mechanization would be absorbed as industry recovered and began to expand. Furthermore, this would put an end to the "semi-feudal 'cheap labor'" condition of the surplus agricultural labor force, and transform it into a modern industrial labor force, skilled and productive. "And this will become the economic and technical basis for rational participation in world trade."[46] The continued starving of agriculture and medium- and small-scale commerce and industry as under the previous laissez-faire policies could only severely damage Japan's economy and lead to a drastic lowering of the standard of living for all ordinary Japanese.

The labor force must, of course, be spared the shock of dislocation by relief measures like unemployment compensation until it could be reabsorbed into recovering industry. But the solution of the labor problem was integral to the general plan:

Thus the industrialization of Japan's economy is vital since it provides the concrete foundation for economic democratization.

On the other hand, due to the annual import of foodstuffs, clothing, and other essential goods in large quantities, it will be necessary to promote exports to compensate for this. However, internal resources are exceedingly meager and only labor power is abundant. Moreover, since the direct export of labor power is not permitted, we must place priority on the export of industrial goods which change labor power into the form of commodities. . . .

Industry must exploit the internal market to its maximum extent . . . in order to give birth to the desirable cycle of advancing technical skill and economic democratization. Thus, both industrial production and external trade must concentrate on this one point, that is, the goal of qualitatively improving the people's life. . . .[47]

The committee saw the dangers and difficulties in too great a dependence on world trade that the indirect export of labor power would entail. Thus, while supporting "positive participation in the international division of labor" they also warned that a policy of internal economic development involving the worker and farmer as consumers of industrial goods must accompany it.

The highly motivated, highly efficient industrial labor force needed to ensure the attainment of these goals could not be treated callously, as workers had been before the war. The concomitant to the prosperous farmer had to be the prosperous worker if both sectors were to advance technically and generate an internal market for Japan's production. The most suitable workers' organization would, accordingly, be one capable of securing and defending economic gains. Thus, the machinery of trade unions and collective bargaining being erected under SCAP prodding was a hidden blessing, but production control was not.

The Theory behind the Joint Labor-Management Councils

One of the most influential of those anxious to persuade the government to cooperate with private industry in the taming of production control through the system of joint labor-management bodies postulated in the fundamental principles of 8 February was Suehiro Izutarō. Suehiro, a distinguished professor of law at Tokyo Imperial University and one of the best-known legal scholars in Japan, held various government posts during the early occupation. He was a key figure in the construction of a new system of labor relations for postwar Japan, and became chairman of the Central Labor Relations Committee, which was established in March 1946.[48] As has been noted, he took part in the compromise settlement of the *Yomiuri* production control dispute that resulted in the formation of the first postwar joint labor-management council. That experience without doubt prompted Suehiro to view such councils as the panacea for the ills of postwar industrial relations.

In his book on the Japanese labor union movement, Suehiro found the stimulus behind the councils to have been labor's desire for economic democratization.

The labor-management councils was [sic] established during the period immediately after the termination of the war at the strong request of the labor union. This was the result of one of the main slogans of "industrial Democratization" that had been propagated by the labor union movement. As far as this writer knows, this movement was initiated by the advocacy of leaders of leftist labor organizations, who insisted on divorcing capital from management which the union wanted to control for the purpose of realizing a thoroughgoing industrial democratization. In reality, however, the labor-management council became an organ to exchange views and consult on various matters concerning managerial operations between the representatives of the management and the labor union on an equal basis.[49]

By spring 1946 the strongest supporters of the labor-management council system were in fact in big business and government, and their intent diverged greatly from the workers' demand for democratization. In their hands the council soon degenerated from an organ for union participation in management into, in Suehiro's words, "a merely consultative" joint body.[50]

Suehiro's outspoken and persistent advocacy of the labor-management council after the issuance of the Four Ministers' Declaration amounted to a valiant but desperate attempt to carry out nationwide the same compromise he had been instrumental in effecting at the *Yomiuri*. His goal was to prevent an explosive polarization between, on the one hand, workers moving to seize all authority over the enterprise, and, on the other, employers bent upon restoring unquestioned managerial authority by the breaking or co-optation of the workers' movement.

Suehiro responded to the Four Ministers' Declaration in consecutive articles published in the *Mainichi* on 7 and 8 February, entitled "The Legality and the Limitations of Labor's Exercise of Management Controls." Suehiro began by denouncing the declaration since it "not only obscured the issues, but fostered public hostility to labor through its misrepresentations." Suehiro denied outright the government's allegation that violence, coercion, damage to property, and similar acts had taken place. Such acts were already subject to prosecution under existing law; but "they were not present at all in the recent labor disputes which led to labor's assumption of control over management." Attempts to deny to labor the right of dispute on these or any other grounds were simply wrong. The point was to define the limits of legality in exercising a specific dispute tactic. By law, labor organizations may only engage in "proper acts" during a dispute. As to what that might mean:

Opinions naturally will vary as to the propriety of acts. Certain categories—such as acts of violence, property theft, destruction, and intimidation—are clearly illegal and should be punished as crimes. On the other hand, a general strike which interferes with the operation of a factory and likewise damages the owner, is not a crime. Nor is a demand on the part of labor representatives to confer with company officials, which is recognized under article 10 of the labor union law as a valid exercise of the power of negotiation. There is no such crime as that of "forcing an interview."

The issue of the legality or illegality of labor's exercise of managerial powers is completely different from that of the legality or illegality of acts which are incidental to the exercise of managerial controls. Examples of illegal means of obtaining management control would be the locking out of company officials, or the disposition of company property. Quite rightly, acts of this nature are crimes, and could be prosecuted as false arrest, embezzlement, or theft.

However, such acts did not occur in the recent Yomiuri Press and Keisei Electric Railroad disputes. Throughout the difficulty, good order was preserved and advice was taken from managers as to things which had to be done. No acts occurred which can be regarded as illegal.[51]

The standard for judging the propriety of acts committed incidental to the assertion of managerial powers by unions was relatively clearcut, then, and boiled down to application of existing law.

The legality of production control itself was a more difficult question; Suehiro held that the conventional view was outmoded in holding that ownership of property conveyed absolute powers of management which could not be abridged by a labor dispute. Labor had been granted the right to strike, a weapon capable of inflicting great damage on an employer—an abridgement of property rights in effect—and yet strikes were legal. It was therefore logical to argue by extension that "assertion [sic] of management powers are far less injurious than strikes, and in public utilities are preferable. If the stronger solution is legal, the lesser should be acknowledged as legal also." Suehiro concluded that production control defined as "the temporary control over management as a method of prevailing in disputes" was legal.

> But also labor must use great care not to use improper measures in pressing claims.
>   A permanent participation of labor in management, or a permanent exercise of rights of management is quite another matter. The scope of labor's rights of participation in management, even if secured through labor contract, is exceedingly circumscribed under existing law. Managerial powers stem from stockholders' assemblies, and to provide for labor participation a revision of Company law would be necessary.[52]

On the basis of the *Mainichi* articles and a discussion with Suehiro on them, the SCAP official concerned with this matter, Thomas L. Blakemore, stated the distinction between legal and illegal production control as follows: "Whenever labor finds it necessary to engage in financial transactions on behalf of the plant or company or to contract for services of supplies, it is getting into the realm of permanent management. As a practical matter, temporary management usually would consist of continuing plant operations with existing stocks of raw materials."[53]

Suehiro returned to the subject in another article in the *Mainichi* on 15 April on the state's policy in respect to production control,[54] in which he expanded his argument to take in the production aspect of production control. The occasion for the article was what Suehiro considered to be the government's unwise and illegal decision to prohibit direct payment by the government coal control board to miners for coal delivered and produced during production control. The problem had serious ramifications, as Suehiro saw it, since the government's attitude was not only useless for settling labor disputes but also provocative. "Labor will retaliate, if necessary, and the disputes and antagonism will grow more and more bitter." He repeated that he only supported the use of production control as a proper dispute tactic, but went on to add that "there undoubtedly is a tendency on the part of labor to regard this as the sole method of settling disputes." More unsettling was the fact that workers engaging in production control struggles since the Four Ministers' Declaration were reaching out to labor unions and other outside organizations to overcome the limitations inherent in production control as a dispute tactic—shortages of capital and materials, and difficulties in marketing products. If such efforts proved successful, the owners would be in a fix.

Although he considered production control less harmful to the public good than a strike, Suehiro believed that unfortunately labor was now using capitalist sabotage of production as an excuse for assuming production control, insisting that its sole objective was to regain normal levels of production. Suehiro clearly disapproved of such a worker-led recovery of production.

> Of course, production can be revived only through the joint efforts of Government, Labor, and Ownership. Arbitrary use by labor of production management techniques results in a disorderly revival of production. It may increase the productive rate, since when the workers do take over they work as best they can. Actually, therefore, the employers come out with more profit than if production management had not taken place. Some participation of labor in management is desirable therefore,
> A. From owners' standpoint in that they make more profits.
> B. From Workers, in that there is more incentive.
> C. From the Government's, in that production is upped.
> But production must be orderly.[55]

Suehiro could not have made it more explicit—the production aspect of production control must be singled out for encouragement and tightly integrated with the capitalist order. Business and government would have to concede labor's right to participate in management in any case. Far better to grant it now and promote harmonious cooperation between labor and capital in labor-management councils than to provoke hostile confrontations and production control struggles that would only radicalize the workers further: "The great mass of workers are convinced that a democratization of industry is an essential element in economic recovery. No longer will workers accept as heretofore a labor control which is imposed from outside: they demand a measure of self-determination—self-discipline."[56]

Suehiro felt that a means lay ready at hand for use in resolving this volatile situation, yet the government would not use it.

Although it confers with businessmen, capitalists, and specialists, the government never thinks of talking with the representatives of labor. It never occurs to them to use positively the new labor committee (established under the labor law)—rather they think in terms of its effect on the new social system, or its economic effect.

If the government really wants to speed production, it should without a day's delay convene an economic conference with representatives of labor and capital.

This committee, composed of labor and managerial representatives both from localities and national organizations, could sit down and thrash out some of the problems and construct a sound policy.[57]

Suehiro obviously had in mind the use of the Central and Local Labor Relations Committee to bring about settlements of production control disputes through their sponsorship of the formation of joint labor-management councils on the model of those pioneered at the *Yomiuri* and other early struggles. The web of rules would have to be spun of strong stuff if it was to fulfill its purpose of reconciling labor to capital's view of reconstruction. The good offices of the state must be used to bind a moderate labor union movement to a democratized version of business through aiding in the building of a national system of joint labor-management councils.

Dōyūkai, "Modified" Capitalism, and Labor-Capital Cooperation

The official five-year history of Keizai Dōyūkai, (the Japan Committee for Economic Development) states that from the fall of 1945 to the spring of 1946 the business world faced "an unprecedented period of revolution,"[58] and the ten-year history credits the revolutionary upsurge with giving rise to "a half-anarchic state of affairs" and "an unparalleled political crisis" in April and May.[59] What had produced the crisis was above all the expanding workers' movement with its readiness to take to direct action in the form of production control, a movement that the conservative mainstream in the Keidanren Committee showed no signs of being able to handle.

Progressive business leaders from the middle strata of professional managers and technicians became alarmed enough to come together in early 1946 with the plan in mind of creating their own business association, which they did on 30 April. In contrast to the Keidanren Committee's policy of a return to unfettered laissez-faire, the Dōyūkai members raised the twin flags of economic democratization and planning.[60] The Dōyūkai program for revitalizing big business and stimulating reconstruction came to be known as "modified capitalism" (shūsei shihonshugi), the essence of which has been summed up as the implementation of economic controls and planning, the ascendance of professional management over capital, and the ideological mobilization of the working class.[61]

One of the speakers at the founding conference of Dōyūkai made a telling indictment of the reactionary character of the earliest policies of business towards reconstruction and labor:

> Not only in the government but in the business world too, the leaders are constructing the formal but superficial appearance of democratization, and are trying to preserve old-style capitalism as it is. It is to be regretted, moreover, that they do not happen to have an up-to-date sense about what a new industrial economy should be. In this, the labor movement alone is the vigorous one. It seems as if the motive power for the construction of a new Japan is being generated from within this movement. Even so, because it is impulsive, we must take heed henceforth to progress in the correct direction.[62]

Dōyūkai leaders understood only too well what had impelled the workers' movement to progress in the "wrong" direction. They recognized that production control was a rational response for labor at a time of capitalist breakdown. They could not but agree when an employers' representative on the Central Labor Relations Committee, Okada Genjirō, made the point to them concerning business leaders that "although there was no intention to sabotage, they could not help but sabotage." Dōyūkai's own assessment was that "perhaps there was no sabotage by individual intention, but indeed there was sabotage socially [i.e. as a social class]."[63]

If sabotage arose from the single-minded concern of the owners of industry with the short-term profits of the individual enterprise—as exemplified in the kind of thinking that dominated the zaibatsu creators of the Keidanren Committee—then a changing of the guard was in order. Dōyūkai believed that the long-term survival of capitalism in Japan depended upon allowing expert, professional managers to carry out a liberal reform from within. It strongly advocated the separation of management from capital and the assumption of leadership by the former. In line with its principles, Dōyūkai organized on the basis of individual membership, not zaibatsu enterprise, and presented itself as an association representing the interests of the entire business world in the fight for capitalism's preservation through its timely modernization.[64]

Dōyūkai charged that the conservative, even feudalistic, owners of industry lacked the broad perspective, technical expertise, and practical experience that would be needed to check the government bureaucracy in its inevitable encroachments on private enterprise in the area of economic planning, no matter how much they opposed it. Dōyūkai leaders did not view the controlled economy and government regulation with the same antipathy as did the conservatives. They believed government involvement in the economy to be indispensable, but maintained it was necessary to prevent the bureaucracy from getting the upper hand in economic planning and administration.[65] Only the enlightened manager-technician stratum possessed the knowledge and experience to ensure that ultimate control over the economy would remain in private hands despite a growing governmental role.

Dōyūkai foresaw that in order to do this under the new postwar order, the conservative parties must serve as the mechanism through which business leaders could guide and coordinate public economic policy. Dōyūkai's inauguration would, according to the *Asahi*, strengthen the ability of the parties to represent business interests effectively to the bureaucracy in that it would supply the professional politicians with the solid organizational and technical backing in economic matters that they had been lacking.[66]

In early 1946 proof of the bankruptcy of the traditional labor policies of big business was distressingly visible in the failure of the Four Ministers' Declaration and the confrontation tactics of the conservatives in coping with the workers' movement. The feeling of those associated with Dōyūkai was that although labor was usurping management rights through the use of production control, it was senseless to confront the workers' offensive head-on. It would only drive the workers to greater excesses. Labor was not the "enemy." Labor and capital must combine their strength to rebuild Japan.[67]

There was no need to proscribe production control, argued Dōyūkai in an early study of it. It could be justified when production was so desperately needed and employers reluctant to provide it, and when striking would either be ineffective or damaging to the economy. What must be done was to bring out the *production* side of production control, and purge it of its spirit of workers' *control*. As the study argued:

If operations and production are carried out temporarily by the employees, to the extent that they continue normal operations by methods which the regular managers employ, the authorities may refrain from interference.

In cases of production control which are accompanied by wrongful disposition of assets, intimidation, and acts of violence, the government must maintain strict control over these actions.

When production control is carried out, the employers and workers will report to the labor relations board.[68]

Dōyūkai continually stressed the theme of labor-capital cooperation. Business must listen to what labor was saying, and realize that
there were "two roads to the labor union," the destructive and the
constructive. It was incumbent upon Dōyūkai "to cooperate with constructive labor unions" and enlist the workers in a capitalist reconstruction. Even production control had its positive side, if business
leaders would only recognize it and make use of it.[69]
There was danger in allowing the workers to seize the initiative in
reconstruction through the capitalists' default, for they might come to
conceive of their movement in a broad, anti-capitalist framework. Labor must be kept from doing what it seemed about to do—expanding
the production control struggle to unite the interests of many classes
including farmers and city people, thereby enabling a popular movement to arise that might be capable of striking a deadly blow at the
capitalist system.[70] The business world must at all costs combat this
mistaken objective. Gōshi Kōhei, a high executive of the Essential
Industry Council and a key figure in the movement for the formation
of Dōyūkai, expressed the viewpoint of "modified" capitalism most
clearly in an article published on 1 May.[71]
Gōshi began by noting that production control had received social
approbation and must be accorded a certain recognition, especially
since government and business had failed to suppress it due to worker
resistance and SCAP disapproval. Recognition, but within what limits?—that was the problem.
Gōshi insisted that production control could be justified only under
the specific conditions peculiar to postwar Japan when the economic
situation was critical and strikes could not be permitted to stop production, however momentarily. Production control could be approved
only to the extent that it coincided with "national economic requirements" and "the viewpoint of production itself." If it operated from
"dispute-first-ism" and took a "class standpoint toward labor-capital
relations" it could not be tolerated. Workers contemplating production control must truly adopt a production-first standpoint and be willing to sacrifice themselves for the greater good by continuing production during labor disputes. Gōshi insisted that production control be
based on "the usual order of enterprise management." Accordingly, he
specifically disallowed what he called a union dictatorship over the
enterprise or inappropriate workers' control over the processes of production. Gōshi claimed that waste, destruction of property, and slip-
shod and hasty work resulted when workers took a class standpoint.
Gōshi called for the setting up of investigative machinery to monitor
production control and check its excesses. A tripartite labor-capital-
government committee was to be charged with determining whether

a given production control struggle was being carried out from a production or a class viewpoint, and was to have enforcement powers to bring illegal, class-based struggles back into line. It is impossible to miss Gōshi's intent. He wanted to enlist the state in spinning a web of rules to contain the unwanted class content of production control and to capture the production-first aspect of the workers' movement for the purposes of a capitalist reconstruction.

6

The Working Class Crosses the Line

The Challenge to the Government's Economic Control

Production Workers and Government Employees in Joint Struggle

The production control struggles in coal had raised the question to whom payment should be made for the coal mined and delivered. SCAP had pressured the government to set up a Coal Board in the Ministry of Commerce and Industry in December 1945 in order to overcome the bottleneck of coal production, but the government still allocated and distributed coal through the wartime coal control association, now renamed the Japan Coal Company. Since early 1946, the employees of the main office of the Japan Coal Company in Tokyo had been studying the problem of whether or not to pay the fee for the coal it received to unions engaged in production control.[1]

Miike

When on 9 March 1946 the Miike miners went out on strike, the union of the Japan Coal Company workers warned the Miike union against crippling production through strikes. The Miike union replied that it would switch to production control if the government paid for the coal produced. The Japan Coal Company union notified the branch offices of the company to pay for the coal produced by unions carrying out production control, but on 25 March the head of the Coal Board overruled them and prohibited payment. The Japan Coal Company employees convened an extraordinary general meeting of their union two days later and by mobilizing outside labor support and holding a large demonstration at the Coal Board got the order countermanded. On 30 March the Coal Board head once again ordered payment to the holders of the mining right as a matter of principle, and said "The problem of the legality or illegality of production control when there is a coal mine dispute is at present under investigation by the government."[2] The Japan Coal Company union issued a declaration accusing the government of taking the occasion to initiate an attack on production control. The fight soon spread to other unions, eclipsing the Miike dispute that had precipitated the conflict.

Tōshiba

The dispute at Tōshiba, which had begun at Tōshiba Rolling Stock and had seen an interim settlement in late January, now flared up again. The company had dragged out negotiations until it became only too clear that the company and the union were poles apart on the central issues of worker participation in management through a council system, of obtaining prior union consent to discharge or transfer union members, and of retirement of all anti-democratic company officials. The company objected to the union proposal on labor-management councils as an encroachment on managerial prerogatives, but the sticking point was the issue of prior union consent for transfers and discharges. After receiving yet another unsatisfactory reply on 28 March, the Tōshiba union called an extraordinary general meeting which resolved to commence production control. A meeting on 1 April set up a struggle committee and production control began.

At the same time, the Tōshiba union had been negotiating with the Ministry of Transportation over whether or not it would receive payment if it delivered some locomotives that the Ministry had ordered. On the 31st the officials had said it would not. Predictably, the Tōshiba union reacted by becoming a central part of the anti-government movement which led to the formation on 14 April of the "Struggle Committee against Suppression of Production Control" (Seisan Kanri Danatsu Hantai Iinkai).

Takahagi

Yet another coal mine dispute had broken out at about the same time at the six Takahagi mines in the small Jōban-Ibaraki coal field northeast of Tokyo. The origins of the Takahagi production control struggle that began in early April dated back to midwinter when the 2,000 miners at Takahagi first unionized. The individual unions at each mine combined on 1 March with a total membership of 1,808, of which

157 were white-collar staff. The conditions at Takahagi were unusually bad, for the company president had run the mines as his personal fiefdom. In addition to the usual demands, the miners wanted participation in management. The company response was to set up an elaborate but impotent system of committees at each mine in which labor and capital had equal membership. Discontent was such that only a spark was needed to set off an explosive confrontation.

The miners at Takahagi had discovered hoarded rice in the company warehouses earlier and revealed it to the police, who confiscated it. The miners insisted that it was theirs by right, since it had been stolen from their wartime rations by the company for sale on the black market. Before this matter could be settled, the miners discovered that someone had stolen the blankets that the government had allocated to the mine for rationing to the workers. The miners believed the theft to have been a put-up job and that the company had sold the blankets on the black market. They demanded that the union be allowed to inspect all the warehouses at once, to which the company assented on 28 March. Most warehouses were inspected by 1 April, but the manager said he could not let them into certain ones because they held the president's personal goods and the president had the key.

That was the spark. Some 1,000 miners poured by foot and by truck out of the mines into the town of Takahagi, where they surrounded the coal company office and confronted the office manager. That night, about midnight, the union executive board paid a call at the president's house and forced him to negotiate while a group of miners gathered outside. The president would not budge, and negotiations broke off at dawn. Then the miners besieged the pit bosses, demanding their participation in production control. The pit bosses decided to cooperate, and production control began on 2 April. The workers set up a three-tiered organization: a supreme struggle committee composed of one member from each mine, a struggle committee of five or six members from each, and in each workplace a production control committee to undertake actual operations. One of the participants later recalled that the example of the Hokkaidō struggles had stimulated their efforts.[3]

Production control did not actually begin until 6 May, the day after a mass meeting that had renewed the miners' demand for worker participation in management through an effective council system. The bone of contention was what rules would govern the council's operations. The president rejected the workers' proposal that miners, staff employees, and management have equal representation on the council as nothing but a scheme for the union to seize control of the company. No doubt that would have been the result.[4]

Not only did the white-collar staff participate in production control, but the workers in the transportation department and from an affiliated oil and chemical plant joined in too. The workers occupied the company offices and continued working at the mines under the pit bosses. Theoretically, the general manager was barred from reporting to work, but he reported anyway, and the company president was allowed to keep the keys to the safe and the warehouses. During the seventy days the struggle lasted, the miners both raised their own wages and raised coal output by 15 percent. Despite the later charges of mismanagement, the mines clearly operated in good order.[5]

After the Takahagi miners' union had proclaimed production control on 2 April, it at once sent a demand to the local office of the Japan Coal Company for payment of the coal fee to the union. When the Japan Coal Company refused, the union contacted the Japan Coal Company union in the Tokyo main office—both the Takahagi union and the Tokyo union were affiliated with the leftist national miners' federation, Zentan—which replied that it would try to see to it that payment went to the Takahagi union. On the day that production control actually commenced, part of the production control committee traveled to Tokyo where they confronted the Japan Coal Board authorities with a choice: either pay the coal fee to the union, or the union would sell coal on the market at a price below that officially set by the Japan Coal Company. The union at the Japan Coal Company went further by declaring, "We will carry out business control and pay the coal fee directly."[6] The Takahagi and Japan Coal Company unions would not yield on this point in their negotiations with the Coal Board.

In the meantime, SCAP had become aware of the growing controversy over payment for goods delivered by unions conducting production control. It too interpreted the government's stand in late March and early April to mean that it was contemplating issuing an official statement declaring production control illegal. Chief of Labor Division Theodore Cohen on 4 April officially warned the Japanese government again to make no declaration of any kind without prior SCAP clearance.[7] The government refrained from issuing a declaration, but nevertheless resisted payment to anyone other than the owners or their appointed representatives for goods produced during production control.

On 11 April the Tōshiba, Takahagi, and Japan Coal Company unions joined thirty-five other unions and federations outside the Imperial Palace in a rally against suppression of production control. A demonstration followed, with contingents going to the Ministries of Transportation and of Commerce and Industry with demands for recognition of the legality of production control and cessation of attempts to suppress it. The demonstrators succeeded in forcing the Minister of

Commerce and Industry to negotiate with them on the Takahagi case. The thought of production control at the Japan Coal Company main office in Tokyo, concern that the Takahagi union would establish a precedent for other unions by selling coal at lower prices outside official channels, and the rising temper of the workers' movement were too much for the Minister to withstand. He gave in under the pressure, stating, "Until the government policy toward the legality or illegality of production control is decided, we will leave the decision concerning payment of the coal fee during production control to the parties concerned."[8] When officials of the Japan Coal Company subsequently decided to pay the owners, the employees' union began production control and paid the coal fee to the Takahagi union anyway.[9]

The Takahagi workers' threat to sell coal cheaply outside official channels greatly upset zaibatsu and government leaders because they saw that such tactics would strengthen the workers' hand in production control thereafter by giving them a measure of financial independence. Takahagi was not an isolated instance. Workers at Edogawa Manufacturing, a chemical company in Tokyo, were already selling goods through their union in preparation for a long fight.[10] Furthermore, one of the goals of the group that had gone to the Ministry of Transportation on 11 April had been to force the government to pay the Tōshiba union for the locomotives. It was hardly coincidental that Tōshiba, which had been standing firm against the workers' demands ever since production control had begun in March, abruptly softened its stance after the government backed down on the coal fee. Within a week, on 17 April, Tōshiba settled on terms favorable to the union.

The Struggle Committee against Suppression of Production Control, organized on 14 April, declared that the participating organizations intended to establish the legality of production control by mounting powerful joint struggles. Yet Tokuda's statement on that occasion subordinated production control to the political struggle for parliamentary power: "Besides production control, the emergency problems at this time are food and shelter. In order to solve these we must prevent the appearance of a reactionary cabinet. The workers must gather their strength to develop a joint struggle."[11]

Contrary to the rhetoric about extending production control everywhere and conducting powerful joint struggles to force its acceptance, the leaders of the left-wing parties and unions at the head of the national Struggle Committee against Suppression of Production Control did not aim at creating a mass base for a revolutionary seizure of power. Their purpose was to mobilize the labor unions in the political arena in order to pressure the national political leaders of the JSP right wing and the liberals in other parties into agreeing to the formation of a left-of-center coalition government. Unfortunately, the political maneu-verings among the left-wing leadership were going in a different di-rection from events in workshop, mine, and office. Whether in the form of the production-control struggle committee or the joint labor-management council, workers in the spring of 1946 were reaching out toward a council type of organization which would give them greater control over the enterprise.

It was one of the ironies of the time that even while workers at the enterprise level were moving toward a contest for power at the point of production, the leadership of the left was moving in the opposite direction. Especially in the coal mines the workers' move to the left was pronounced, threatening to reach such proportions that a nation-wide seizure of mines by the workers would become a possibility for the first time.

The Hokutan Miners Demand Control of the Labor-Management Council

The actions at Mitsubishi Bibai and Takahagi had been relatively small, but the next one was not. Hard on the heels of the Takahagi victory on the coal fee came the Hokkaidō Colliery and Steamship Company (Hokkaidō Tankō Kisen Kabushiki Kaisha, or Hokutan) pro-duction control in April and May, involving fifteen mines employing nearly 20,000 workers. The Hokutan struggle began when the unions of the mine workers and white-collar staff presented their separate demands at each of the mines in mid-April. The union federation cov-ering the Hokutan mines, the Hokkaidō Federation of Coal Miners' Unions, coordinated the local campaigns. Unsatisfactory replies by management led to production control, which extended beyond coal mining to the offices where the white-collar staff carried out "manage-ment control." After it became clear that the local struggles were ac-complishing nothing, the union pulled together all demands into one package and sent this to the Tokyo main office of the company on 11 May. The negotiations in Tokyo thus involved three parties; the min-ers' union, the staff union, and the company.[12]

The key demands were: establishment of a management council weighted two-to-one against the company, the permanent relocation of the company's highest decision-making bodies in Hokkaidō, resig-nation of undemocratic officials, reinstatement of those unfairly dis-missed after the war, abolition of the status system that discriminated against production workers, and dismantling of the despotic system of local government by neighborhood associations and its replacement by elective bodies of paid officials.

During the negotiations the company's main line of attack was to give way on secondary points but to insist on a collaborationist management council system in which the company would be the dominant party. In this the company was successful, although it had to make extensive concessions in other areas. The company reply to the package of demands stated: 1) that it could not relocate the main office to Hokkaidō but it would increase the authority of the Hokkaidō offices to make decisions; 2) that it would cooperate in getting rid of undemocratic officials; 3) that it would not hinder the reemployment of discharged workers; 4) that it would abolish the differential treatment of staff and mine workers as soon as possible; and 5) that a system of elective officials would replace the old apparatus of local government.

On the key point—the labor-management council—the company had several objections to the workers' proposal. It wanted no part of the council system in its Tokyo main office, nor would it agree to unequal representation on the councils to be set up at the mines. Furthermore, it objected to the wide scope and the extensive powers the miners wanted to give to the councils. And when the company and the union signed an agreement on 26 May in the midst of a SCAP-supported counterattack on the workers' movement by the old guard, the company had its way: "The company approves of the union's just and proper claims and actions, and in order to promote rational and democratic management of production, and simultaneously to maintain and improve working conditions, to increase efficiency, and to raise the workers' status, it has decided to establish a management council."[13]

The agreement stipulated that neither the company nor the union could enter into a dispute without submitting the problem to the management council, but the council had no power to effect a settlement. Its regulations defined its role as providing a forum for labor-capital *consultation*, not participation.

Toward this end, a system of subcommittees was to be set up to consult on "execution of the production plan, promotion of technology, improvement of facilities, efficiency of operations, and other necessary matters for the increase of production."[14] The company had indeed emasculated the workers' demand for participation in management. It had held out successfully for a labor-management council designed not only to create among company employees a strong feeling of belonging to the enterprise, but also to turn to company use the general consciousness of the postwar workers' movement of the need for production. Gōshi Kōhei of Dōyūkai must have been proud of the Hokutan negotiators.

The settlement at Takahagi, though reached some time after the Hokutan agreement, was very similar. The company conceded almost all of the workers' practical demands, but gutted the powers of the management council. The council was to have equal representation of labor and capital—not two-to-one in the workers' favor as originally demanded—and was to "cooperate" in management rather than participate. Matters for cooperation were to be such things as fixing the quantity of coal to be produced under the production plan, improvement of technique and of the repair and upgrading of facilities, democratization of the enterprise, and the acquisition and distribution of materials. The workers' original goal of participating in financial management and personnel organization was suppressed in this company version of "allowing workers to cooperate positively in management." Whenever such councils appeared they merely provided for the institutionalization of the principle of labor-capital collaboration and allowed the companies to profit from the workers' concern with production.

Perhaps the crucial factor in the miners' failure to attain their ends at Takahagi even after seventy days of production control was outside obstruction on the part of the capitalist enterprises upon which the miners had to depend for working capital and supplies. Whether at Takahagi or elsewhere, workers engaged in production control had to link up with outside organizations friendly to their cause. The Takahagi miners, for example, could have sold their coal or bartered it for food and mining supplies, or even exchanged it for something that could be exchanged in turn for needed items. But the leftist leadership, including the JCP, either did not recognize the miners' problem or chose not to commit themselves to aiding them.[15]

The Breakthrough to Revolutionary Workers' Control

What the Takahagi workers had the consciousness and will for, but not the means, the chemical workers, coal miners, and farmers in the Tōyō Gōsei production control struggle from 13 March to 27 August accomplished. Tōyō Gōsei was a small chemical factory in Niigata City that was part of the Mitsui combine. Mitsui ordered the factory to be closed around the end of January, but the employees defied the order, publicly declaring, "Despite the closure order of the authorities, we will not close." Mitsui caused production to be suspended anyway on 19 February by cutting off materials. The next day the employees gathered to organize a union of 190 members. Besides presenting the usual demands for union rights, the employees expressed their total opposition to dismissals and demanded a guarantee of a minimum living as well as the setting up of a labor-management council. The union also denounced and called for the ejection of the two top officials at the factory.[16]

In reply the company called in all the white-collar staff separately from the more radical production workers and put pressure on them. One company official said he was determined to either dismiss the union executives and close the factory or resign himself. The union held a third mass meeting on 27 February at which the production workers, over the objections of the staff, rejected the company's stand. At that, thirty-one staff workers withdrew from the union. The company dealt the union another blow two days later when the two company officials put out the following directive: closure of the factory no later than the 28th, retention of 108 people as interim employees for winding up business, and a 10:00 A.M. deadline on the 28th for those who wanted to accept a dismissal allowance. Fifty-three workers left the union at once to accept the offer of temporary employment.

On the day set for closure, the remaining union members convened an extraordinary meeting which demanded that those who had left the union for temporary employment be discharged, that the factory not be closed, and that all union members be retained as employees. The company agreed to the discharges, but rejected the rest. The situation remained in limbo until 13 March when a company official visited the factory and declared that it was closed and that the company would not retract the dismissal of all employees.

Once again the union convened a general meeting, at which the workers decided to reopen the factory that very day through instituting production control. Contact between the workers and management at Tōyō Gōsei was completely severed, and the workers unhesitatingly took whatever steps they deemed necessary to keep the factory in operation. They abolished the old hierarchy of managers and department and section chiefs and shouldered the burdens of management collectively, since most of the white-collar staff had already deserted the struggle.

The production workers took a long-range view and methodically set about reconverting the plant to the production of chemical fertilizer with the aim of attaining full operations on 16 June. The biggest hurdle was capital, and the first attempts to secure working funds failed. Then the Tōyō Gōsei workers learned about a Tokyo chemical factory, Edogawa Manufacturing, that was in the midst of production control and had solved its cash problems by selling formalin (a 40 percent solution of formaldehyde in water) in the union's name. The Tōyō Gōsei union decided to sell methanol (used in the manufacture of formaldehyde) to Edogawa and obtained ¥300,000 in cash.

In a related step, the Tōyō Gōsei workers worked out a mutually beneficial barter arrangement with the 15,000-member Niigata farmers' association whereby the factory got coal and coke and the farmers fertilizer. The farmers' association organized among its members a special cooperative to which the farmers subscribed ¥100 apiece. The association used the proceeds to buy coal and coke from coal mine workers, and bartered this in turn to Tōyō Gōsei for the fertilizer ammonium sulphate.

This arrangement, through which production of both industrial goods and foodstuffs rose, illustrates the capacity of ordinary working-class people to manage their own interests. The Tōyō Gōsei workers acquitted themselves well. They installed complicated equipment, changed over from one product to another, expanded the work force, increased wages, and raised production using machinery that the company said was so antiquated and out of repair as to be nearly useless. They did all this in cool disregard for property rights and capitalist managerial prerogatives. What is more, the company and the government seemed powerless to resist.

Equally significant was the struggle at Edogawa Manufacturing, a small Mitsubishi company of about 500 employees. The employees had organized a union in January encompassing both the staff and production workers and simultaneously set up a three-tiered system of elective workers' councils organized functionally according to the company's operating structure. The main decision-making body was the employees' general meeting, but there were also an elected central executive committee of twelve members, a small number of workshop committees, and a larger number of departmental committees staffed by workers which took over the formulation and implementation of a production plan.[17]

The Edogawa union presented demands on 12 February, but company officials arrogantly rejected them, the business manager going so far as to say, "I don't care if you employees die, I don't have to guarantee your right to live."[18] Until 1 March, when the workers instituted production control, the company and the union fought over which side was to receive payment for a large order of formalin that the national agricultural association had placed much earlier. The business manager, who controlled official allocations through his power over the chemical control association, had been quietly sabotaging shipment by obstructing the arrival of railroad cars. This he did because the price of methanol was rising at a dizzying rate, from ¥1,800 per ton in January to ¥8,600 in February and ¥13,500 in March, and he hoped to reap a speculator's profit. Now he suddenly rushed to complete the transaction with the national agricultural association in order to cripple the workers' position before production control commenced.

The Edogawa union frustrated his plans by itself negotiating with the agricultural association and obtaining promise of payment to the union. The shortage of formalin needed in the manufacture of fertilizers for use in the fields of Tōhoku and Hokkaidō was becoming critical at this time, and each day that passed without delivery would result in lower yields. The Edogawa workers' success was directly related to their ability to make early delivery, which it could do because of the support of the railroad workers' unions.

At this juncture the Edogawa workers received another hard-line rejection of their demands and decided in a general meeting on 1 March to begin production control. The employees organized for this by tight coordination of the union central executive committee vested with the highest authority with a production control committee to administer operations. Overall they made few changes and ran the plant much as before, though entirely without the old managers.

The Edogawa workers immediately sent off the available railroad cars for Tōhoku and Hokkaidō loaded with formalin and, over the obstructions put up by the Ministry of Transportation, managed within nine days to transport the whole amount that had been on order for two months. The cooperation of the transportation workers and their unions was important, as was the dispatching of two Edogawa union members to Hokkaidō for liaison work. Mitsubishi and the government tried to obstruct payment, too, by tying up funds through litigation. But the employees' union of the national agricultural association made common cause with the Edogawa workers and saw to it that payment was made.

Acquiring the raw materials for production posed a greater problem, one not entirely solved. To a small extent they were able to circumvent the monopoly control over coal supplies of the zaibatsu and the government by establishing tight liaison with the employees' union of the Japan Coal Board. Absolute shortages of coal and coke brought about the suspension of production of methanol in April, but, as related above, the workers managed to get it from Tōyō Gōsei. In this instance, the Edogawa and Tōyō Gōsei workers, through maintaining their internal solidarity and uniting in joint struggles with sympathetic outside organizations, overcame the limitations of workers' control conducted in a hostile, capitalist environment.[19] The relationships they developed are presented schematically in figure 6.1

Workers might have embarked on production control in these coal mines and chemical companies and elsewhere at the outset in order to achieve a set of concrete and not very radical goals having to do with wages and job security. But as their struggles lengthened and became more difficult, they tended to escalate to a new phase. This new phase was marked by a more or less conscious decision to seek

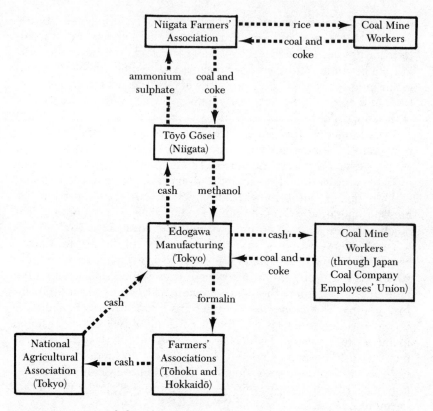

Figure 6.1. Expanded Production Control at Tōyō Gōsei and Edogawa Manufacturing. Source: Yamamoto Kiyoshi, ed., *Sengo Rōdō Undō Shiron* (Tokyo: O-Cha no Mizu Shobō, 1977), vol. 1, *Sengo Kiki ni okeru Rōdō Undō*, pp. 147–50.

outside cooperation in producing essential commodities in critically short supply, commodities that were vital to the revival of most people's livelihoods. Altruism was a factor, but what counted most was that different sectors of the working class were able to advance their mutual interest in the economic revival outside capitalist relations of production. In short, profits and wages ceased to be the sole object of operations, and social needs assumed first place.

Farmers and City People Stand Up

The inhabitants of rural villages and urban neighborhoods were creating popular organs of their own in a manner remarkably similar to the evolution of the production control struggle committee. That is, these movements took a literal approach to democratization, favored the council type of organization, and exhibited a readiness to take matters into their own hands to overcome economic breakdown. These movements contained the potential for uniting with the workers' movement and had begun doing so in the spring.[20]

The rural community had food, but needed manufactured agricultural and household goods, above all chemical fertilizers. The urban neighborhood needed food, was indeed coming ever closer to mass starvation, but had nothing to exchange except daily-more-worthless paper money and a limited quantity of household possessions. The government's response was in keeping with its pre-surrender attitudes. It proposed to confiscate food from the farmers at ridiculously low official prices, by force if need be, and to compel the urban resident to buy it through the old official rationing channels, by eliminating the petty black marketing that all city households had to depend on just to survive.

That the government's answer to the food crisis was useless became ever more apparent as spring approached. In the countryside, despite the new measures, crop deliveries remained far below expectations, and farmers were organizing to resist forced requisitions. In the city, rations could not provide enough calories, let alone a minimum standard of nourishment. Even this inadequate ration was days, in some places weeks, in arrears, and urban neighborhoods began to organize to take over the rationing system. The government failure to overcome the "scissors crisis" separating farmer and worker lent great urgency to the popular search for solutions. Somehow a mutually beneficial circulation of goods between town and country had to be achieved.

What the farmers needed only urban workers could supply—those factory and office workers engaged in production, transport, and distribution, workers whose own families were suffering from hunger. Hitherto the urban working class had presented only the face of the *consumer* to the countryside in the form of city people searching for food. With the commencement of production control struggles such as those at Takahagi and Tōyō Gōsei, the worker as *producer* began groping toward a way to supply the farmer with essential goods and services. The working-class answer to the "scissors crisis" produced by capitalist sabotage was to throw off the restraints of capitalist relations of production and to reintegrate production and consumption through workers' control.

Opposition to Forced Crop Deliveries

Much as had happened in the labor movement, the left and right wing currents of the prewar farmers' unions reappeared after the war, and the right-wing socialists took an early jump on the left because they enjoyed much more freedom of action at the time of surrender. Under the leadership of Hirano Rikizō, the right wing had taken the first steps toward reorganization of the farmers' unions before the communist political prisoners were released. Despite this early lead, by the time the Japan Farmers' Union (Nihon Nōmin Kumiai) held its founding conference on 9 February 1946, left-wing leaders sympathetic to the JCP like Kuroda Hisao had made substantial progress in bringing the union to a more radical point of view. At this time the union had perhaps 75,000 to 100,000 members, but other organizations were also appearing at the local level, council-type bodies that were often close to the Communist party. In early 1946 the farmers' movement was entering a period of rapid growth and radicalization, similar to that of the workers' movement.

Talk of a land reform had begun at an early date, but the government had no satisfactory program. The program it advanced in December under SCAP prodding was so pro-landlord that SCAP immediately repudiated it, as it did the second plan presented in March.[21] Rather than pinning their hopes on such unsubstantial indications of future reform, farmers during these months of early occupation were forming unions and other local bodies to further their interests. On 30 March there were around 300,000 farmers organized in about 3,000 unions, and by February 1947 union membership had grown to about 1,200,000.[22]

Unlike the right wing of organized labor, which was tightly controlled from the top, the local farmers' unions were free from the outset to act pretty much as they saw fit despite their theoretical subordination to the lead of the right-wing socialist majority on the central committee of the Japan Farmers' Union. Organizers from the national union were few and unable to maintain close supervision over the local unions' activities, so right-wing socialist influence waned as effective leadership developed in local unions.[23]

The new local organizations took on the traditional power holders, specifically the heads of the local agricultural associations and local government bodies. As early as December there were instances of farmers' mass meetings hauling such local power holders before the village equivalent of a "people's court," indicating that farmers too wanted democratization. It was no more true of them than it was of industrial workers that their vision of the world was a narrow and constricted concentration on immediate economic self-interest. Farmers were quite capable of understanding that a fundamental reordering of village society was one of the prerequisites for a truly democratic reconstruction of the nation.[24] Economic, social, and political power were even more closely linked in the hamlet and village than in the factory, and had been the monopoly of the local power holders. An attack on the local power structure of landlords-officials-businessmen united the majority of the rural community and helped to unite tenants and owner-cultivators in the potentially divisive question of land redistribution.

A more practical matter also helped the farmers' movement to unite tenants and owner-cultivators. Very simply, the farmers all had to sell their produce at artificially low prices to the state, but had to buy the means for agricultural production and their own consumer needs at highly inflated free market prices, to the extent that such goods were available at all. This necessity had never weighed as heavily on the local power holders, who had many opportunities to evade government regulations through their influence in the agricultural associations and on the government. Accordingly, when farmers demanded replacement of the existing system of compulsory crop deliveries by autonomous delivery of food and furthermore demanded the democratization of the rationing and distribution system, this constituted a direct challenge to the local power holders. These changes threatened to undermine the rural power structure, since it was the conjunction of landholding and local authority that had sustained the system.

Such was the situation in midwinter when the Shidehara cabinet tried to alleviate the pressing food shortages by strong measures aimed at forcing the farmers to fulfill their quotas for staple food delivery and at increasing the amount of food available for distribution at official prices through the rationing system. The Emergency Food Measures Ordinance of 16 February 1946 (Shokuryō Kinkyū Sochi Rei) allowed the government to expropriate staple foods not yet delivered by the responsible farmer and to pay for this expropriated food at the fixed government purchase price. In cases of resistance, the government could seek a special warrant for delivery at the public procurator's office, after which the police could search out and seize the food. In this event, the farmer would be arraigned and, if he were found guilty, the government would confiscate the food and appropriate the purchase price to the national treasury.[25]

The ordinance cast a net which ensnared more than just farmers, for it made a variety of common, everyday acts that were necessary for mere survival punishable by fines or penal servitude, such as:

(1) Making false reports concerning the rationing of staple foods or receiving or causing others to receive an illegal ration of food.

(2) Advising or assisting others to withhold staple foods from the government.

(3) Refusing, obstructing or evading the expropriation of staple food as provided in the ordinance.[26]

Certainly the government had every reason to want to increase the amount of food available for rationing in the hungry cities, but just as clearly the new ordinance, if strictly enforced, would bear most heavily upon the corrupt landlords, government and police officials, and other figures whose support was vital to the old guard in its fight for political survival. The government, therefore, applied the measures one-sidedly against the small-scale farmers and black marketeers, and the hordes of people who daily journeyed into the countryside to barter their few personal possessions for food. The government's actions did not attack the root cause of the food shortages—the "scissors crisis" resulting from economic sabotage and large-scale hoarding. Yet it was not surprising that, unable to attack either the root cause or the immediate malefactors, the government tried to shift the blame and the burden onto those least able to evade it.[27]

Farmers' demands at the time of the organization of the local farmers' unions had usually been for reduction and remission of tenant rents and their payment in cash, opposition to the food delivery system, resignation of local government and agricultural association officials, and the establishment of farmers' committees to take charge of ration distribution. As can be seen by these demands, the anti-landlord tenant struggle and the anti-government democratization struggle developed together; but the emphasis shifted after the government's ordinance on emergency food measures in February away from the tenant struggle and toward opposition to compulsory deliveries. Demonstrations in rural areas brought out large numbers of farmers in protest against local and prefectural authorities.[28] One such demonstration took place at Mito in Ibaraki prefecture in late March. SCAP's description is revealing.

PROTEST AGAINST FORCED RICE COLLECTIONS

On 29 March 1946, a mass meeting of some 1,200 farmers was held at Mito, capital of Ibaragi [sic] Prefecture. This meeting was sponsored by the NIPPON NOMIN KUMIAI (Japan Farmers Union). Arrangements were made for five representatives of the farmers to consult with the governor TOMUSUE [sic] Yogi on the question of the government's forced rice collection policy. The discussions lasted throughout the day and the following night. During this conference, approximately five hundred farmers awaited word from their representatives in the Prefectural assembly hall. Permission to remain in the hall had been granted by the Prefectural Chief of Home Affairs, but at 0930 on 30 March, the Farmers were ordered to leave the building by approximately three hundred policemen who, according to a representative of the Farmers Union, were directed by the Prefectural Chief of Police.

About 0800 on 30 March, negotiations between the Union's representatives and government officials finally reached an impasse and the conference adjourned.

The Military Government detachment of that area stated that the meeting of 29 March became disorderly and when the Nippon Nomin Kumiai's representative could not come to an agreement with the Governor, they had threatened to return with 5,000 farmers to force his compliance with their demands.[29]

In addition, throughout this early period, landlords had been carrying out repossessions of tenanted land in order to shore up their position against the perils of land reform and against the chaotic market for agricultural products. Landlord self-cultivation would bolster their claims for possession of land that, if left in tenant hands, might be liable to expropriation as surplus. Moreover, self-cultivation was more profitable, given the inflated prices of agricultural products and the cheapness of hired labor.[30]

Whatever incitements there were to action, there is no doubt that the farmers' movement lagged behind the workers' movement. This was to be expected, considering their very different relationship to the means of production. Workers were locked in common struggle to raise output and to democratize the social relations of production within large-scale, modern industry that was already socialized to a degree that made petit-bourgeois notions of private property anachronistic. Farmers, on the other hand, although themselves engaged in a struggle to produce and to democratize their communities, still tended to conceive of individual ownership of their minute holdings as the solution to exploitation.

Nonetheless, it is not necessary to prove that farmers were positively in favor of collectivized agriculture or socialism in order to maintain that the farmers' movement was a potential ally of the workers' movement. It need only be shown that farmers were not likely to stand in the way of a worker-led social revolution because they, too, stood to gain something concrete from it both as tenants and as cultivators. This is why a coming together of the workers' and farmers' movements was not only possible, but rational and probable; for the workers' movement held the key to solution of the "scissors crisis" that divided city and country. The Tōyō Gōsei/Edogawa Manufacturing struggle foreshadowed the breaking of the "scissors crisis" by the creation of non-capitalist channels for the circulation of commodities among city, mine, and country. One indication that the farmers were ready to follow the workers' lead in developing alternative modes of production and distribution was that in this struggle the agricultural association—the traditional organ of the government and the landlords—had cooperated so that the farmers could obtain the fertilizer they needed.

Although conditions were ripe for forging a joint worker-farmer solution to the problems of production and distribution, the national leadership of the left did not press ahead in this direction. Instead, they chose to concentrate on gaining power via parliamentary politics and united fronts, and turned the possibilities of workers' and farmers' control over the means of production and distribution into political slogans suitable primarily for arousing popular support in the arena of bourgeois-democratic politics. The leadership of the left similarly underestimated the importance of neighborhood groups arising in the cities during the same period and misjudged the significance of their opposition to the system of food rationing.

Popular Control of Food Rationing

An early instance of popular opposition to the food rationing authorities occurred on 26 September 1945 when a crowd of about 150 people converged on the local rice warehouse in a small town in Miyagi prefecture and requested a loan of rice for distribution to local farmers. The clerk of the local agricultural association, who was also the custodian of the government warehouse, refused the request, whereupon the crowd broke into the warehouse and took fifty-four bags of rice. The clerk reported them to the police, who arrested the spokesman of the group—a member of the local village assembly—and some sixty others. Although the spokesman was sentenced to four months' imprisonment, the others were released.[31] The details are sparse, but this action exhibited the same matter-of-fact defiance of authority that would later characterize the far more radical "Give us rice!" (kome yokose) demonstrations.

The rice rallies of spring went far beyond requesting the distribution of rice to the hungry by demanding people's control of all food distribution. The main goal of the rallies was the abolition of the irredeemably corrupt neighborhood associations which even then continued to be, alongside the police, a primary institutional prop for the old order. The main justification the government had made to SCAP for their retention was that they were essential to the rationing system, but that was the least of their services to the old guard. A popular seizure of rationing would deal a much heavier blow to the state's ability to enforce its will at the local level than might at first be realized. The kome yokose demonstrations were dangerous because they threatened to short-circuit government control at the vital point of contact, the local neighborhood. The forcible seizure of food stores in May by neighborhood food-control committees plunged state authority into momentary chaos precisely because the committees were potential organs of local government bent on displacing the neighborhood associations from that role.[32]

The participants in the "Give us rice!" demonstrations were quite aware of the complicity of big-business and government authorities in the hoarding and speculation that had created the food crisis. In fact, they originated out of the movement for "exposure of concealed goods" (intoku busshi tekihatsu) which erupted around the first of the year. This movement had its roots partly in reaction to the petty but extremely damaging peculation practiced by lesser authorities all the way down to the local business enterprises, neighborhood associations, and village power holders that had been going on for years. Diversions of goods at the local level increased tremendously with the end of the war, but what gave the popular movement its impetus and radical élan was the old guard's cynical and comprehensive looting of the economy after the surrender. Knowledge of the enormous quantities of stores that officials had handed over to big business spread rapidly in late 1945, and by the end of the year there had been several well-publicized cases of the exposure of concealed goods and popular seizure and distribution of food in the Tokyo region.[33]

The action program of the JCP as adopted by the Fourth Congress endorsed the movement for exposure of concealed goods and called for control of food and other essentials by urban people's committees. JCP involvement helped to spur the movement on and to give it a coherent purpose by encouraging the participants to take the next step of demanding popular control over the distribution of rations.

The evolution of the Itabashi ward incident which came to a head in January 1946 illustrates the manner in which local groups passed from the simple exposure of hidden goods to the demand for control over the ration system. This incident dated back to September 1945, when removals began of the enormous quantities of goods stockpiled at the former army arsenal in Itabashi ward. With the connivance of police authorities, the leaders of the neighborhood association were spiriting the goods away for disposal on the black market to business buyers, or to ordinary city people in the case of consumer goods. This was no isolated case of local corruption. It was common knowledge that police involvement in such activities reached as high as the chief of the Peace Preservation Division of the Metropolitan Police Board.

The Itabashi arsenal had employed 20,000 workers who were dismissed at the end of the war without payment of the expected severance allotment. On 14 December approximately 800 workers and their families still living in the Itabashi area convened their "Fourth Mass Meeting of Dismissed Employees," at which they decided to demonstrate at the Finance Ministry and if possible confront the minister in direct negotiations. The demonstration of 300 workers and wives succeeded. The minister signed a paper promising immediate payment of dismissal allowances, but only after the demonstrators had berated him with attacks on government incompetence and on the cold indifference of the arsenal and the crookedness of its officers.

Iwata Eiichi and two or three other JCP members who had led the dismissed employees' struggle afterwards helped reorganize it into a "Livelihood Protection League" (Seikatsu Yōgo Dōmei). It was this league which in January carried out the exposure of the concealed goods at the arsenal. Beyond that, the league sponsored a meeting on 20 January that came out in favor of the creation of a "goods-control committee" (shokuryō kanri iinkai). On the following day the league spearheaded a demonstration at the arsenal. The former employees and local residents forced the former army major general in charge of the arsenal to stand on the bed of a truck and take part in five hours of mass negotiations. Some of the demonstrators carried signs with slogans such as "Give us jobs, food, and housing," "Beat and drive out the military crooks, send them to the coal mines," and "Put control of the rationing of food into the people's hands." Despairing of being rescued by the police, the ex–major general gave way to the extent of not hindering the transfer of some bags of soybeans and other goods to the league for distribution.

The demonstrators were still not satisfied and gathered again on the two succeeding days. On the 23rd the situation became very tense, and violence seemed near. At this point a small number of national JCP leaders, including Shiga, came to the arsenal and convinced the assembled crowd of 3,000 to refrain from direct action. The JCP leaders persuaded them instead to strengthen their organization for the dual purpose of negotiations with the authorities over the supplies in the warehouse and the equitable distribution of those goods to the local residents. The demonstrators next turned to choosing representatives and organizing a "Preparatory Committee for City-People's Control of Food" (Shimin Shokuryō Junbi Iinkai).

Unquestionably the spontaneous mass movements of that first winter needed organization to give them a clearer purpose and staying power, and lower-level JCP activists helped provide this. Yet in this instance, the relenting of mass pressure played directly into the hands of the Tokyo authorities, who sent 300 armed police on 25 January to transfer the remaining stockpiles to a secure warehouse of the food-stuffs-control corporation. On that same day, the Metropolitan Police also arrested two of the leaders on suspicion of extortion. These two actions effectively checked the Itabashi movement.

Another attempt to deal with the breakdown of food rationing developed within the government bureaucracy at around this time. Toward the end of 1945 the employees of the Agriculture and Forestry Ministry were discussing among themselves in their employees' association the severity of the food problem and what might be done to alleviate it. They saw as the most pressing need the democratization of the bureaucracy, especially those sections with control over food. Accordingly, their association called for the democratization of government offices and for a joint struggle of all government employees to overcome the food crisis.[34]

This call fell on receptive ears, and on 7 January these employees, now joined by employees from other offices having to do with food distribution like the Ministry of Communications, the Ministry of Justice, and the national railways, formed a preparatory council for a joint struggle committee for resolving the food crisis. The preparatory committee took on the task of creating a common front of labor unions, farmers' organizations, and urban people's groups as the basis for a joint struggle. Their appeal for concerted action to these other groups charged that food was still being concealed in amounts adequate for meeting the current shortages and that "Almost all of [the abundant food on the black market] is from illegally concealed goods of the military or from goods illegally diverted into black market channels."[35] The conclusion was, "We cannot go on entrusting the distribution and control of food to government offices and bureaucratic foodstuffs-control corporations."

Two weeks later, on 21 January, a variety of organizations in the Kantō region encompassing government employees, farmers, workers, and war victims got together to form a regional council for resolving the food crisis. Concurrently, the Japan Farmers' Union, the Japan League of Cooperative Unions, the Sōdōmei Preparatory Council, and other organizations created their own council, which they inaugurated on 31 January. Perhaps the right-wing socialist organizers had intended their group to compete for leadership of the movement, but in any event the two councils united on 11 February as the Kantō Democratic Food Committee (Kantō Shokuryō Minshu Kyōgikai) under the chairmanship of Suzuki Tōmin.

The council represented over thirty participating groups with an astonishing estimated combined membership of 1,500,000. The unification conference agreed on a policy of: "discovery and control of hoarded goods; acquisition of control over food; setting up of urban people's food committees; a system of voluntary food deliveries by farmers; production of fertilizer and agricultural materials; and democratization of the control associations and government offices connected with foodstuffs.[36]

The Kantō Democratic Food Council put pressure on the authorities, local and national, over late rations and corruption in administration, but the food crisis worsened. As it did, the political side of the food struggle came to the fore; for the left-wing leaders used the considerable top-down control they had gained over the food-control movement to mobilize it behind the popular front they were mounting in opposition to the Shidehara cabinet. The neighborhood groups that had attempted to take control of food distribution fell quiet, but they would reemerge in April and May much more prepared than ever to use direct action to achieve their goals.[37]

The Movement to the Streets

The April Mass Demonstrations

On 7 April, just three days before Japan's first postwar election, tens of thousands of angry people marched on Premier Shidehara's residence with the intent of forcing his cabinet out of office that very day. The ensuing demonstration developed into a violent conflict with armed police. Yet on election day the two left parties did not receive even 100 of the 466 seats in the new Diet, and General MacArthur hailed the results as a rejection of the extremes of either left or right and as evidence of the healthy forward advance of democracy in Japan.[38] But on 1 and 19 May, millions of people turned out into the streets to protest the formation of a new conservative cabinet. And in July an Asahi opinion poll showed that a scant third of their respondents supported the Yoshida cabinet while 45 percent preferred the Socialist and Communist parties.[39]

What can be made of such contradictory events? One thing at least is certain: the election results were an exceedingly insecure basis for generalizing about the health of democracy in Japan. William McMahon Ball, the British Commonwealth member on the Allied Council for Japan, wrote to the Australian Secretary of External Affairs on May 16 that "The future of the Japanese Government machinery will largely depend on the kind of government that is formed as a result of the elections of April 10th." The lavish praise of Hatoyama and his party had embarrassed SCAP, but the underlying problem was more serious.

> I have talked to ten or twelve leading Japanese citizens who might be re-
> garded as representative of the business and financial classes and all of them
> would commonly be described as liberals. My impression of these people is
> that defeat has not changed them at all. They sincerely regret the war for the
> very good reason that they lost the war, but their disagreement with the
> militarists seems to have been a disagreement about tactics and timing and
> not a disagreement on anything more fundamental. There is a sort of sup-
> pressed insolence about most of these people, an assumption that they can
> take up their relations with the Allies exactly where they left off in 1941. They
> seem to believe that now that the war is over and the militarists purged,
> Japan can set to work to rebuild her national power and to win quick accep-
> tance into the family of nations. Meeting people of this kind impresses me
> with the gigantic sort of task the Allies have before them in Japan, a task that
> must take at least a generation.[40]

In approaching this question, the American occupiers assumed, as so many scholars have since, that democratization meant Japan's transformation into a society approximating the United States or the European democracies. They foresaw a period of tutelage before the inexperienced Japanese could put into practice such a sophisticated concept as political democracy, a concept not thought to be readily assimilable within the Japanese body politic. After all, what did workers and farmers only just freed from the "militarist yoke" know of such things? Clearly, the American occupiers misjudged the situation. In fact, the ordinary people were only too willing to pursue the ideal of democracy, and to apply it fully to all spheres of everyday life.

Democracy to a worker or farmer in 1946 was not at all abstract, to be practiced within the constricted sphere of voting booths, parliaments, and cabinets. It was both concrete and comprehensive; a world view, so to speak. The people trying to build a new Japan out of the ruins did not neatly categorize their concerns according to the pigeonholes of social science, and take painstaking care to isolate democracy as a political concept from democracy in economic and social life. If landlords or factory owners or government officials behaved "undemocratically" and resisted the extension of popular control into areas that had been traditionally their private preserve, then they must be "democratized," and the institutions they controlled remade in ways admitting of popular control. Hence the universal use of the word democracy and the demand for democratization that surfaced when conflict burst out between ordinary citizens and the privileged and powerful. There can be no doubt that the popular understanding of democracy was radical and egalitarian, though unsophisticated by Western standards.

This the left-wing parties seemed to have understood imperfectly at best, even though the evidence was plain to see in the various movements for remaking Japanese society. It may be embarrassing for a communist party to be surpassed in radicalism by parts of the mass movement it is supposedly leading, but the JCP was embarrassed twice by massive street demonstrations in April and May, at the very time when the old guard was skirmishing with the left over succession to the crumbling Shidehara cabinet.

The changes Nosaka made in JCP policy between his return in early January and the Fifth Party Congress in late February laid the groundwork for the party's plunge into parliamentary politics. The object of the new political program was to bring together all groups opposed to Shidehara—parties, unions, citizens' and farmers' organizations—into a broad popular front capable of propelling a left-of-center coalition government to power.

Other left-wing leaders shared this goal, and some had begun building a popular front movement in January quite independently of the JCP. Foremost among them was Yamakawa Hitoshi, a man highly respected for his political integrity by both socialists and communists but affiliated with neither group. The right-wing leadership of the JSP was still resisting cooperation with extra-party groups it could not control, and wanted no part of Yamakawa's front, fearing that they would be swallowed up, particularly if the JCP participated. They were finding it harder to resist because the JCP attacks had weakened their hold on the JSP. Then in February they sustained a hard blow from another direction, when the government unexpectedly applied the January SCAP purge directive against a number of notable right-wing socialists in the process of its screening of candidates for the coming election.[41] The communists, on the other hand, had gained in prestige and had decided to throw their support behind Yamakawa's proposal for a popular front.

The organization that grew out of Yamakawa's efforts, the Democratic People's League (Minshu Jinmin Renmei), was born in early March. The sponsors included not only the JCP and left-wing socialists like Arahata Kanson, but public and academic luminaries like Ōuchi Hyōe, Ishibashi Tanzan, Hani Setsuko, and Suehiro Izutarō. Among the political parties, only the JCP endorsed the league when it was formed, but the growing enthusiasm for the idea of a popular front soon forced the JSP leadership into grudging cooperation.[42]

The league's tentative program, announced on 27 March, was a veritable shopping list with something in it for everyone, but the political core was the demand for Shidehara's resignation. The other points included: "adoption of a new constitution by democratic methods, liquidation of bureaucracy, democratic planned economy, industrial democracy, democratization of farm villages, relief to small businessmen, democratization of food distribution, liberation of women, reform of education, and an international system based on peace and justice."[43] Though the immediate purpose of the league was vague, consisting only of the overthrow of the Shidehara cabinet and support for progressive candidates in the election, it did intend to put up its own candidates behind a specific political platform, once it had gained sufficient coherence and strength.[44]

As part of its campaign strategy, the league organized a People's Rally for the Overthrow of the Shidehara Cabinet (Shidehara Naikaku Datō Jinmin Taikai) for 7 April. This was the first concrete action taken by the league. It had had little time to get prepared for the election, since the government had announced 10 April as the date for the first postwar election at the very time that the league was taking its first steps to organize in early March.[45]

The sponsors of the People's Rally and the speakers on that occasion had little more in mind than the electoral goal of drumming up the maximum number of voters for progressive candidates, thereby putting the left-wing members of the Diet in a good position to contest with the Shidehara cabinet for control of the government. As another means of putting maximum pressure on the Shidehara cabinet to resign after the election, the sponsors hoped to rally public opinion against the government. It is unlikely that the left held any hopes of winning the election outright. Yet they did hope that the combination of a sizeable vote for the left-wing opposition plus mass rallies mobilizing public opinion against the policies of the conservative politicians might accelerate Japan's democratization, and get their policies through the Diet. Beyond that, they no doubt expected an electoral victory for the left to come in the not too distant future.

Many of those who attended the rally on 7 May proved to be less than enthralled with the slow legalism of constitutional reform, the ballot box, cabinet responsibility, and the other stocks in trade of liberal politics. The 70,000 who gathered at Hibiya Park in the early afternoon came as much in quest of a way out of the breakdown of their personal lives as anything. The popular demands were for food and production, for an immediate end to government corruption and coercion in food collection and distribution, and for an end to business and government efforts to suppress production control. To achieve these ends, they wanted Shidehara out at once, without waiting for the ambiguous judgment of the ballot box, and the installation of a government truly responsible to their needs.[46]

Ten of the unions officially attending presented a joint emergency resolution asking the rally to endorse a policy opposing the suppression of production control. The resolution was adopted, for the workers present had the idea of workers' control very much on their minds. Nosaka did not mention this in his speech, but urged the creation of one great national federation of industrial unions and mooted the idea of a nationwide general strike as a tactic for pressuring the government. He made no call to action, no call for more worker takeovers.[47] As might be expected, the crowd gave its approval to the program of the Kantō Democratic Food Council, which was demanding people's control of food.

Considering the temper of the workers and ordinary city people who made up the crowd on that day, a more fitting rallying cry for the JCP might have been for the creation of popular councils everywhere, in city and country, in neighborhood, office, and factory. Down that road lay the possibility of building popular institutions ready and able to respond to the specific needs of workers and farmers independently of big business and government. The JCP's moderation on 7 April was of a piece with its February rejection of the Leninist road to power in postwar Japan through the building of soviets and a system of dual power inside the shell of the old order. It almost seemed as if the JCP was retreating within the bounds of peaceful, bourgeois-democratic gradualism in contrast to the leftward-shifting popular movement. Tokuda was a partial exception. He retained a preference for more radical tactics than Nosaka, and during his speech he exhorted the crowd to besiege the prime minister's residence.

At about 3:00 P.M., after the speeches were over, some 50,000 people did march to the residence of the prime minister and mass in front of the grounds. Then they advanced up the hill to the barricaded compound of the residence. Some began pushing at the gates; others climbed the walls, and the crowd started throwing rocks at the police guarding the residence.[48] Mark Gayn, a correspondent for the *Chicago Sun*, has left an eyewitness account:

Then, with one great surge, the crowd broke through the gate. Skirmishes broke out all over the yard. Most of the policemen took to their heels. Others fought a rearguard battle. One policeman was caught inside a small hut under construction. The crowd closed in on him and beat him to the ground. A bespectacled demonstrant, struck by a policeman, turned around, calmly put his spectacles in an inside pocket, and began to punch the policeman in the face. They were separated by marshals.

Meanwhile, the bulk of the crowd threw itself against the wide front doors of the premier's building. The doors groaned, and glass came down with a crash. Men started throwing rocks into the windows. The fighting continued.

The building stands on a hill, and right behind it there is a sheer, stone-lined drop, with a narrow concrete stairway leading down. The police were now driven down to the canyon below, and we could see them standing there in indecision. Some of the demonstrants tried to follow them, but stopped when the policemen took pistols out of their holsters, and waved them menacingly. Soon a force of 150 police reinforcements came up on the double quick, and the reorganized force began to advance. One of the policemen opened fire, others followed. The shots sounded thin and sharp, like firecrackers. The crowd milled in one spot, and then began to run back into the compound.[49]

There was hostility toward the police from the outset, and cries of "beat the police, kill them" were heard.[50] If the demonstrators had succeeded in breaking into the residence and subjecting Shidehara to mass negotiations, that would have been a tremendous blow to the prime minister's prestige and to the foundations of the old order. The 300 police on hand, fifty of them armed, were no match for the tens of thousands of demonstrators. Firing into the crowd would be sure to inflame things, yet retreat threatened the police with a severe loss of face. Things did not look good for the police when they regained the top of the hill again and stopped firing. The only thing separating the infuriated crowd from the hesitant police were crowd marshals who tried to calm the situation. On the advice of the marshals, the police decided to go back down again.[51]

At this point American military policemen made a timely entrance and forcefully cleared the compound. Once it was cleared and the barricades replaced, a delegation of thirteen leaders from the rally was allowed inside to present their demands to the cabinet assistant secretary. When the secretary replied to the demand for resignation by saying he doubted that Shidehara would comply, Tokuda began to pound the table in anger.

"We want Shidehara here," he shouted. "We want a responsible answer."
"Shidehara has an appointment?" shouted Tokuda. "We can't tell the people outside Shidehara can't see us. You go out and tell them. We're not children's messengers. Is Shidehara on vacation? He must've known we were coming. Keeping that crowd outside in order is a terrible job."

Tokuda and Arahata read their statements, while from the outside came the roar of the assembled thousands. By then Tokuda knew the whole thing had fizzled out. But he tried to maneuver for an advantage, for anything that could be used against Shidehara in the future. They all looked like poker players, Tokuda betting on the crowd, the secretary on the American MPs. I did not know it yet, but six American armored cars and six jeeps armed with machineguns already had begun to patrol the street, slowly breaking up the demonstration.[52]

The delegates were promised a meeting with Shidehara the following afternoon, which Gayn also witnessed. Shidehara appeared, and:

the violent meeting began, a meeting of abuse and denunciation, of contrast between the old and the new, of politics in the raw. The delegates demanded to know if Shidehara thought the ¥500 limit on monthly income was fair, and whether he lived on it. "Look at you," said Tokuda scornfully. "You're so fat. One can't get far [fat?] on ¥500. You must be buying food in the black market."

One after another the delegates jumped up, to demand that Shidehara resign, that he repair the rationing machinery, that he end the black market. They were, most of them, earthy, untutored men with calluses on their hands and their speech. They called Shidehara a cheat and a liar. From time to time, the *Yomiuri* editor, Suzuki, cut in with a reasoned attack on the government's policies, or lack of them. But as soon as he ended, the trade union people burst in the speeches of denunciation.[53]

When a commotion broke out over the presence of armed secret service men guarding Shidehara, the premier fled the room in fright, at a half-run, and so ended what Gayn called "a bit of violent history." But Gayn knew it was more than that:

In the past two days, the leftists have demonstrated great strength. The streetcars are decorated with posters denouncing Shidehara. By courtesy of the railway workers' union, yesterday's demonstrants were brought to Tokyo from the suburbs free of charge. A truck drivers' union assigned fifty trucks— a large number in present-day Japan—for yesterday's march. A thousand farmers came into town for the demonstrations. As distress mounts, and the government continues to do nothing, the Communists [sic] strength in the unions and among the sharecroppers grows.[54]

The hitherto separate strands of the popular movement came together tentatively on 7 April for the express political goal of overthrowing the cabinet. The popular movement had appeared on the national political stage as a force to be reckoned with for the first time since the occupation began. It had fleetingly revealed the will to move into the streets and take direct action to topple the old order. In the end, the combination of a reluctant leadership on the left and the first SCAP show of force in defense of the old guard broke the momentum of this first mass confrontation with the state.[55] The next surge of the popular movement would come after the general election.

It is revealing that the left-wing leaders, in particular the JCP, did not grasp the chance to build on the energy of the mass movement when they met Shidehara on the following day. They did not gamble on another mass mobilization in the streets, no doubt believing SCAP to be opposed to another street demonstration that might develop into violent direct action. In short, the leaders of the left showed a certain distrust of the mass movement and a certain hesitation to commit the popular front to a course of action that might erupt into something far more radical than parliamentary reform.[56]

The election took place on time, and the returns gave the Liberal party the leading position with 24.4 percent of the popular vote, not enough to form a government on its own. On 19 April the four major opposition parties—the JSP, the JCP, the Cooperative party, and, ironically, the Liberal party still being led by the vehement anti-communist Hatoyama—inaugurated a four-party joint council for the overthrow of the Shidehara cabinet. Shidehara had been desperately trying to hold onto power, but the organization of the joint council tipped the balance. The cabinet tendered its resignation on 22 April, and on the 25th the four opposition parties opened negotiations to form a new cabinet. Because Shidehara's resignation had removed the main cause for their unity, the negotiations broke off the next day with no result, effectively ending the life of the four-party joint council. From then on, the activities of the five major parties degenerated into opportunistic maneuvering to enhance their own leverage in the formation of a coalition cabinet.[57]

The May Days

In the meantime the mass movement was building up to the first postwar May Day. The celebrations in 1946 were unprecedented for Japan and were perhaps the largest in the capitalist world, with about 2,000,000 people attending the parades and demonstrations taking place around the country. Estimates vary, but in the capital alone around 500,000 came out.[58] The Tokyo rally adopted familiar demands: "establishment of a democratic people's government, purge of war criminals, food for the working people, people's control of food supplies, a drive to uncover hoarded food, recognition of labor's right to strike and to bargain collectively and of workers' control of production."[59]

In contrast to the rally against Shidehara on 7 April, the mood on May Day was buoyant. Mark Gayn caught the sense of hopeful euphoria in describing it as "a day filled with a curious kind of joy—perhaps the kind of luminous joy a war prisoner feels on regaining freedom."[60] Gayn was also aware that something more stern underlay the euphoria. He reported an incident that came at the close of the rally in the Imperial Palace Plaza that showed something of the trend of the popular movement.

Tokuda was the last speaker. He stood surveying the cheering thousands with a stern face. He, too, spoke of the short rations, of rice hoarded by the rich and the speculators, of the workers' inability to make ends meet. The crowd yelled its agreement. But the loudest, the most prolonged cheers came when Tokuda, both arms in the air, shouted: "Down with the emperor!"

Behind Tokuda the audience could see the palace buildings towering over the thick, gray walls, and the American sentries standing on guard.[61]

Reverence for the emperor, the most important ideological buttress of the old order, was evidently giving way.

Several large demonstration marches followed the mass rally in the Imperial Palace Plaza. One group marched to the premier's official residence to present the May Day demands, but made no attempt to enter. Another streamed past SCAP headquarters where they delivered a "message" which the May Day Executive Committee had drafted in late April for adoption by the rally. SCAP denied the message was delivered at this time, but either on this day or soon afterwards all members of the Allied Council for Japan received the same document. It became the cause for the first overt confrontation between the U.S. and the U.S.S.R. on the Council. It read:

We express our sincerest appreciation for the measures taken by the Allied Powers to liberate the people, grant freedom, and extend the rights to labor and agricultural groups.

Inspired by this, we hope to uproot feudalistic and despotic oppression; establish a popular government, based on the true will of the people never to break the peace of the world again; realize political, economic and social conditions which will not jeopardize the livelihood of the people; and be recognized internationally as a peaceful and democratic nation.

However, it is true that by spreading false reports, the bureaucrats, capitalists, landowners, and other controlling interests are interfering with the correct judgement of the Allied Forces, hindering activities designed by farmers and laborers to achieve freedom and to protect their interest.

1. In IBARAKI-Ken a popular movement in protest of the unreasonable rice ration and to their forced quotas was suppressed.

2. In HYOGO-Ken control of production as a weapon in labor disputes is suppressed.

3. In the SHIKOKU Area gatherings and speech assemblies are rigidly controlled and activities and expressions of opinion restricted.

4. Rowdy reactionary groups interfered with the processes of the general election.

5. Execution of purge directives issued by the Allied Forces have [sic] been perverted.

6. Food and other daily necessities which were allotted to the Japanese government by the Allied Forces have not been equitably distributed to the general public; instead, they were diverted to certain influential groups.

Many such incidents can be indicated. We sincerely regret that the Allied Forces have not opposed such incidents with measures that will convince the people.

These facts, in short, prove that the present Japanese government lacks the sincerity to fulfill the requirements of the POTSDAM Agreement to administer the affairs of JAPAN.

They are in truth enemies of the democratic revolution. We of the Japanese labor class categorically oppose any element which retards the democratic revolution.

In consideration of the lofty mission of the liberating Allied Forces, we will continue to hope for the cooperation and assistance necessary for the democratic movement of laborers, farmers, and others of the general populace to attain full development.[62]

When the Soviet representative put the matter on the agenda of the Allied Council for 15 May, George Atcheson—the U.S. representative who was also chairman of the Council and the State Department Political Adviser to SCAP—took the occasion to deliver an anti-communist diatribe. This was directed against both the Soviet Union and the popular movement in Japan, which he linked by innuendo when he stated the document was nothing but communist propaganda, and bore all the earmarks of being a translation from a foreign language (implicitly Russian) into Japanese. (As Atcheson most likely knew, the authoritative Allied Translator and Interpreter Section had concluded that the document was not a translation, being written in good, idiomatic Japanese.)[63]

At the afternoon session of the Allied Council on 29 May Atcheson repeated that an investigation had revealed that "those allegations have no foundation in fact." It is difficult to reconcile this bald statement with an eight-page summary of twenty recent incidents involving violence or the threat of violence appended to Atcheson's own 10 June dispatch to the U.S. Secretary of State. Although this document was intended to justify the May crackdown by SCAP against the popular movement, the information included therein indicated there was a considerable measure of truth in the allegations.[64] Atcheson had other purposes in mind than a thorough and unbiased investigation of the charges made. His crude anti-communist diatribe at the Council sessions made clear that both Washington and SCAP had suddenly begun to take the true measure of the popular movement. And they did not like what they saw.

There is no doubt that the mass movement, with or without the JCP, was traveling in a radical direction and building toward a release of the pent-up frustrations of the preceding nine months of misery and thwarted hopes. Hard data for something as volatile as a change in public opinion are hard to come by, but some evidence does exist of growing anti-emperor feelings and of a greater receptiveness to leftist solutions. According to polls taken to determine the trend of opinion in selected industries employing over 500 in the Tokyo area in December 1945 and March 1946, both the JCP and JSP made resounding gains in popular support, while the emperor system slipped badly in worker esteem. Workers surveyed in March were opposed to the Shidehara cabinet (59 percent) and supportive of the popular front (68 percent), but not particularly supportive of the JCP and JSP (27 percent and 37 percent respectively). And they still favored the emperor system (55 percent) and approved of SCAP policy (46 percent). When asked where sovereignty ought to be located, however, their answer very clearly favored the people (75 percent) over the ruler (14 percent)—and revealed that one of the fundamental traits of the popular movement in spring 1946 was its leftward trend.[65] Much was to happen in the popular movement, of course, between March, when the latest of the polls was taken, and May. By the end of April the emperor was becoming the target of constant public abuse; and after the May Day rally the imperial palace became the scene of highly embarrassing "hunger" demonstrations.

The most well known of these occurred on 12 May when about 1,000 residents of Setagaya ward held a rice rally that brought together both local unions and the local food-control committee. Afterwards representatives from the rally went by truck to the imperial palace where 113 people forced their way through Sakashita gate into the palace grounds. They demanded an interview with the emperor and release by the imperial family of their stored food stocks for public distribution. They actually succeeded in breaking into the great refrigerator used to store food for the emperor's table. In the course of their investigations they found many food items not to be seen in those days of hunger, such as white rice. Not content with that, the demonstrators returned to Setagaya where they forced their way into the local food-stuffs-control corporation warehouse and took more food, which they then distributed to residents through the Setagaya food-control committee. This inspection of the imperial household kitchens rocked public opinion, and made the 12 May demonstration the most notorious of the many food demonstrations to break out in May that challenged state authority in the capital.[66]

While the popular movement was taking to the streets, the government was going through a dangerous political crisis. The discredited and fumbling Shidehara cabinet had continued as a caretaker government after tendering its resignation 22 April, but it lacked the will or the authority to take decisive measures to control the situation. The month-long period of political vacuum between Shidehara's resignation and the formation of the Yoshida cabinet could not be overcome by the usual means of political maneuverings among politicians, because the balance of forces in the Diet (the two conservative parties together held a clear majority) did not reflect the popular trend. The result was a stalemate in which the conservative parties used their majority to block formation of a left-of-center coalition cabinet, while popular mass action prevented the conservatives from establishing their own government. In the meantime initiative was passing not to the left-wing parties but to the mass movement.

After May Day the executive committee for the rally had reorganized at once, forming a committee for a workers' united front which took over the duties of organizing the next rally, the Food May Day mass meeting scheduled for 19 May. This organizational change reflected the changing character of the popular movement in that the position of the Kantō Democratic Food Committee and the left-wing labor unions was greatly strengthened at the expense of the right-wing socialist organizations.[67]

The spontaneous food demonstrations of workers and city people erupting in Tokyo in the second week of May—each drawing anywhere from a couple of hundred to a thousand or more participants—provided the backdrop to Food May Day. Participants in the rice rallies were not merely protesting, or petitioning the government authorities to heed the people's distress. Nor were their protests anarchic rice "riots." On the contrary, the local inhabitants responsible for them—eight such actions occurred in Tokyo on 17 May—organized themselves into bodies intended to *replace* the local foodstuffs-control corporations and the neighborhood associations through which they operated, thereby constituting themselves as de facto organs of local government. Insofar as workers intent upon replacing capitalist management in the enterprises through production control were a key part of the food demonstrations and the food-control committees, it is possible to see, for the first time, the rudimentary outlines of the local soviet. Now, if ever, was the time for the national left-wing leaders to call for the formation of soviets everywhere.[68]

Some of the left-wing leaders seemed to feel that the moment for decision had come. Suzuki Tōmin called upon the workers to demonstrate their real power and bury the reactionary Yoshida cabinet in his speech at the mass rally on 19 May: "A twenty-four-hour general strike will be enough to smash this tottering cabinet. Right now, from the struggle in the streets, the revolution has begun!" Tokuda spoke last on that day and received the greatest applause of all during his vehement attack on the emperor and his call for the establishment of a people's republic.[69] Tokuda, too, felt the same quickening of the popular pulse that Suzuki had, and understood the power of a general strike; but doubts remained—not about the strength of the movement to topple the Yoshida cabinet, but about the American attitude if the left called a general strike involving coal, utilities, and railroads. SCAP had, in fact, overruled the railway unions' decision to offer free rides to bring people to the rally, as it had done in April.[70] SCAP and Washington were indeed coming to the conclusion that things were getting out of hand, and that the labor movement and the JCP were the culprits.[71] SCAP had actually given Yoshida its blessing before he got imperial approval on 16 May to organize the next cabinet. Yoshida set about forming a coalition cabinet composed mainly of the Liberal and Progressive parties but allotting several seats to left-leaning people who might be useful in responding to the demands of the popular movement. Due to internal disputes over who would fill certain cabinet posts, a slate of portfolios had not been completed when Food May Day arrived, much to Yoshida's disadvantage.[72] In the meantime, despite the best that had been done by everyone—Shidehara, Hatoyama, Yoshida, and the right-wing socialists—the political situation had developed not necessarily to the old guard's advantage, while the general trends of the popular movement had all turned against its interests.

Events began early on the 19th, the day of the "People's Rally for Obtaining Food." By 10:00 A.M., about 250,000 people had gathered at the Imperial Palace Plaza, or the People's Plaza (Jinmin Hiroba), as it had come to be called. One of the speakers was an ordinary house-wife, who carried a crying child strapped to her back while she bitterly denounced the police and rationing officials. She was from Setagaya ward, where there had been no rice distribution for two weeks, and her milk had failed because of hunger. She also told how she had lost her father and her husband both "for the emperor."[73]

After the last speech around noon, the assembled people set out on demonstrations. One contingent went on a long march around the Metropolitan Police Board, the Diet, and the prime minister's official residence where a delegation including Tokuda demanded to see the premier designate. The delegation was let in while a guard of armed American military policemen stood by to prevent any attempt to oc-cupy the residence. When Tokuda and the delegation found out that Yoshida was in hiding elsewhere, and would not see them, they re-sponded by saying they would sit there until he resigned, for days if need be.[74]

Another demonstration occurred at the imperial palace, where a delegation went inside to demand that the emperor meet them and discuss the people's plight. This delegation was long in returning, and in the meantime—despite the presence of American armored cars[75]—some of the demonstrators tried unsuccessfully to cross the bridge and push through the cordon of Japanese police blocking the palace gate. At length the delegation returned to report that they had not even been able to talk to the minister of the imperial household, much less the emperor, but that they had promised that the emperor's reaction would be conveyed to them on the 21st.[76]

The delegation also reported what they had discovered in an inves-tigation of the palace kitchen—fresh milk, pork, eggs, butter—giving added impact to one of the banners that had been waving before the crowd on that day:

> The national polity has been saved,
> I am eating my fill,
> Subject people, starve and die.
> Imperial sign and seal.[77]

The climax to Food May Day came at the premier's residence, where Tokuda and the others were sitting in. Yoshida and his advisers were closeted with Hatoyama trying to find a way out of the threatening situation. Things did not look at all good, and around seven in the evening word came through one of Yoshida's followers that he had given up. The answer of Tokuda, Suzuki, and the rest was that they would continue the sit-in until Yoshida delivered the message personally. That never happened. The sit-in ended abruptly the next day when MacArthur made a strong statement warning against "demonstrations and disorders by mass mobs."[78]

I find it necessary to caution the Japanese people that the growing tendency towards mass violence and physical processes of intimidation, under organized leadership, present [sic] a grave menace to the future development of Japan. While every possible rational freedom of democratic method has been permitted and will be permitted in the evolution now proceeding in the transformation from a feudalistic and military state to one of democratic process, the physical violence which undisciplined elements are now beginning to practice will not be permitted to continue. They constitute a menace not only to orderly government but to the basic purposes and security of the occupation itself. If minor elements of Japanese society are unable to exercise such self-restraint and self-respect as the situation and conditions require, I shall be forced to take the necessary steps to control and remedy such a deplorable situation. I am sure the great mass of the people condemn such excesses by disorderly minorities, and it is my sincere hope that the sane views of this predominate public opinion will exert sufficient influence to make it unnecessary to intervene.[79]

Even though over 2,000 workers from several of the more radical unions behind Food May Day at once rushed to the premier's residence in a last-ditch try to force a meeting with Yoshida, the damage had been done. Yoshida was now assuming a superior attitude. Instead of becoming the second casualty of the mass movement in the streets, Yoshida recovered and organized his own Liberal party cabinet. He formally took power on 22 May.

7

The Conservative Reaction

Housebreaking Labor

Although it was obvious to Japanese workers that they needed strong industrial unions, the old guard was far from adopting an approach to economic reconstruction that recognized the unions' right to act in defense of workers' interests. The new Yoshida cabinet would, in fact, attack the unions as an obstacle to the re-creation of the "free economy" of the twenties which was largely built upon a cheap and weak labor force. The workers fought back, of course, in the second half of 1946. After months of strife and the threat of catastrophic economic collapse, it became clear that the working class had stymied the old guard. More moderate elements were then able to hammer out a consensus on a program for reconstruction that was at least minimally acceptable to labor and capital.

The struggle of labor and capital went through two phases before that consensus was reached. First was the conservative reaction of summer 1946 when the Yoshida cabinet did its utmost to reverse working-class gains and to implement a "laissez-faire" reconstruction of the Japanese economy. This was followed by a powerful union offensive in the fall that blocked the government's economic plans but failed to break through and win positive acceptance of labor's program. Out of the standoff in winter 1946–47 came a compromise approach premised on friendly cooperation between capital and unionized labor which turned out to be close to the actual course reconstruction would take in the postwar period.

Reverse Course in Labor Reform

With the climactic events of mid-May, the immediate danger was past. SCAP had come out against the mass movement, but the Yoshida government could not rest secure until the food crisis was overcome and production control was outlawed. The situation was still so dangerous that the extraordinary step was taken of calling upon the emperor to address the nation for a third time. The first time had been to announce surrender, the second to declare himself an ordinary mortal. The emperor's address on 24 May asked the Japanese people to trust their government and cooperate wholeheartedly, and called upon them to forget individual selfish desires and carry on Japan's time-honored tradition of the family state in reconstructing the country.[1] Yoshida's issuance on that same day of a preliminary cabinet statement condemning production control and calling for its elimination[2] provided an additional cause for conservative rejoicing.

SCAP's threat to act against the mass movement contributed immeasurably to the government's ability to reconsolidate state power at the point of contact with the people, that is, at the level of the neighborhood association, the food distribution point, the agricultural association, and the police box. Of course, a reassertion of state power alone could not solve the underlying breakdown of capitalist relations of production and state authority. Only a resumption of production could provide a lasting solution, but the most urgent needs, which had to be satisfied before economic reconstruction could even be attempted, were to supply the country with more food and to restore the rebellious workers' active respect for private property.

The U.S. acted quickly, importing enough foodstuffs in summer 1946 to make the difference between bare subsistence and slow starvation that had set in during the spring.[3] This saved the Yoshida government from having to wield naked force to obtain satisfactory deliveries from farmers and compliance with the rationing authorities from city dwellers. Since the symbol of anti-capitalist defiance and the core of the popular resistance movement had been production control, the breaking of that movement became a matter of high priority for Yoshida— and for SCAP.[4]

The Yoshida government took its first important step on 13 June when it issued its "Declaration on the Maintenance of Social Order." It stressed that it was "necessary above all things to stabilize the national economy by increased production and maintain the social order on a democratic basis," and cited a host of problems—food scarcity, increasing inflation, mounting unemployment, resistance to government grain collection, popular action against hoarding, mass demonstrations, labor-capital violence, contempt for law and order. Yoshida's declaration read like a catalogue of events preceding a revolution, and, indeed, the fortunes of the leaders of big business and government had never looked as bad as they had that spring. The crisis had been temporarily staved off by American food and the occupation army, but not solved. Everyone understood production was the key. How Yoshida proposed to overcome the obstacles to a capitalist reconstruction was as yet uncertain, but in singling out production control for harsh condemnation, he did make it clear that a reconstruction by the workers themselves was not going to be tolerated.[5] The declaration said:

A word may be added here regarding the so-called production control which has recently occurred. The Government finds it difficult to justify it as a recognized form of labor dispute. There may have been cases where "production control" seems to have actually increased production. But from the viewpoint of the national economy as a whole, not only has it brought forth numerous undesirable consequences but it is also likely to destroy the industrial structure of the country and plunge the national economy into chaos. Especially when it is carried out by violence and intimidation, it presents a grave menace to social order.

Echoing the ideas of the Dōyūkai and Suehiro Izutarō, Yoshida also proposed that joint labor-management councils be set up in enterprises for the purpose of providing a means for employers and workers to come to an understanding before the outbreak of labor disputes. A large number of such councils had appeared at the enterpise level already, but the government did not assume the lead in coordinating and rationalizing them in a nationwide system, as Suehiro wished. Yoshida's feeble moves in the direction of creating a semi-official system of management councils for adjusting labor management relations during the summer of 1946 were no more than a belated reaction to the radical phase of production control. When that crisis waned, so did the government's interest in the idea of a national system of councils, until the labor situation again began to look ominous in December 1946.[6]

The councils were of tremendous use to big business at the enterprise level, nonetheless. As Suehiro later pointed out, the councils suffered one of two fates. Were the union strong and militant, the employer would severely limit the matters it brought up and treat the council as a merely consultative body. Were the union cooperative, the employer would bring up "as many topics as possible in these council meetings to eliminate the trouble of discussing such topics in collective bargaining." In neither case did the unions benefit. But management and the right-wing socialist labor leaders did. The councils provided them with a useful forum for labor-capital collaboration that could avoid the antagonistic confrontations inherent in collective bargaining between management and truly independent unions.[7] Yoshida's initial promotion of joint labor-management councils therefore was perfectly in keeping with the direct assault he would soon wage on the labor movement.

Yoshida was able to get away with anti-labor measures where Shidehara had failed because SCAP, as a result of the events of May, had finally become aware of the potential for radical change in postwar Japan which the old guard had been trying to warn it against from the start. SCAP had become convinced of the necessity of putting limitations on the workers' freedom of action after coming face to face with the power and radicalism of the working-class movement in spring 1946 and having to make the decision that even the maintenance of an unpopular conservative government was greatly preferable to allowing the left-wing opposition to come to power. SCAP had been drawn into the month-long struggle for power following the resignation of the Shidehara cabinet in April and had quietly lent its weight to the attempts of the conservative parties to form a successor cabinet. The near frustration of those efforts by popular protests against the discredited old guard provoked the occupation authorities to issue their first public condemnations of communism and the mass movement.[8]

By these acts, SCAP for the first time openly endorsed the view of the Japanese leadership that communist agitators and organizers, taking advantage of the unprecedented freedoms granted by the Allied reforms, were stirring up worker unrest and mass demonstrations in the streets. Workers would have to be taught to respect the labor reforms as originally conceived, and to stick to business unionism pure and simple.[9] Thus, SCAP henceforth put its emphasis upon the building of a healthy labor movement that would avoid politics and radical actions such as production control, while encouraging business and government leaders to resist such worker excesses. A document produced at the end of the occupation by the "Community Countermeasures Committee" of Government Section in SCAP spelled out, in retrospect, the new American attitude. The committee's list of "countermeasures against the subversive potential in Japan" began with Atcheson's 15 May anti-communist speech before the Allied Council. Second came MacArthur's 20 May declaration. Next was cited the Yoshida 13 June declaration against production control, under the heading, "SCAP prohibited use of the Production Control Strike."

The production control strike, a device conceived in Italy, is very effective when government mechanisms are uncertain in action. Immediate postwar Japan was an ideal field for such techniques, which were first used in the Yomiuri Press Strike, 25 October 1945, and the Keisei Dentetsu Strike of 1 December 1945. It appeared that the communist leaders of Japan labor could gain control over any industry by this method.

To perfect the application of the production strike technique, the Communist Party decided to concentrate on single industry organization. Recognizing that control of public information media meant virtual control of public thinking under the existing chaotic conditions, the party concentrated first on organization of newspaper and communication workers' unions. Their gains were impressive here and in other industry-wide unions. On 10 March 1946 they set up a National Labor Unions' Liaison Council. May Day 1946, the Council directed a demonstration in which more than two million workers throughout Japan participated.

Political party purpose rather than the welfare of the worker was apparent. Demonstrations were directed at national and local government offices in a show of force to intimidate officials and soften their resistance to the demands of the Communist Party. SCAP pointed out the dangers of the situation. Thereafter the Japanese Government, on 13 June 1946, prohibited the Production Control Strike. The Japanese worker, glad of sane guidance, responded admirably and the first crisis was past.[10]

The change amounted to an abrupt reversal of the unofficial SCAP policy of benign toleration of almost any effort of workers to organize and resist their employers. The Yoshida cabinet was only too happy to return to the anti-labor policies of the past, and encourage union-busting tactics including use of the police to suppress disputes to a degree that would have been unimaginable even a few months before. As if to underscore SCAP's approval, on several notable occasions even U.S. military police participated.[11]

The new policy was called, in a cynical phrase current among SCAP officials, "housebreaking" the labor movement, and was the first benchmark in the "reverse course" in labor reform.[12] This is not to say that most SCAP officials in mid-1946 were anxious to bring about the destruction of independent trade unions, as the conservatives clearly intended, and superintend their transformation into company unions. They were not. Rather, for the next nine months up to the general strike movement, SCAP would try with notable lack of success to pursue two policies at once toward the workers' movement: one that was pro-labor—meaning supportive of responsible business unionism—and another that was anti-communist.[13] SCAP intended to instill into organized labor respect for the line between legitimate economic ends of labor unions and unacceptable political activism, and hoped to do this without formally restricting or reversing the stated Allied policy of democratization.

The *Yomiuri* newspaper became the main target in the reverse course in labor reform in summer 1946 because it had been in the vanguard of the radical workers' movement for the preceding six months. The *Yomiuri* workers pioneered the use of production control in late 1945 and went on to establish workers' control over the newspaper. Afterwards, editorial policy and daily production of the paper came under the direction of the editorial and printshop workers, although finance and business operations remained in the hands of supporters of management who remained in constant opposition to the policies of the democratized paper. The "democratic *Yomiuri*,"[14] as it was called, became the most fearless and radical of Japan's newspapers.

The democratic *Yomiuri* delighted in exposing big-business and government corruption. It encouraged workers and farmers to extend production control and take matters into their own hands locally, and acted in general as the organ of the political movements and demonstrations of spring that aimed at overthrowing conservative rule and establishing a left-wing government. At the same time, the *Yomiuri* union was the main agent in setting up the powerful national press union—the All Japan News and Radio Workers' Union (Zen Nihon Shinbun Tsūshin Hōsō Rōdō Kumiai), hereafter JNRU)—which, in turn, took the lead in drawing the most militant unions together in a national federation similar to the Congress of Industrial Organizations in the U.S.[15] The crowning outrage to the paper's conservative critics had been the paper's support of and its employees' participation in the mass actions on May Day and Food May Day which had shaken the foundations of the old order. These actions earned the enmity of both business and government leaders and SCAP, all of whom now viewed the democratic *Yomiuri* as both the symbol and the leading edge of a communist plot to use working-class unrest for party purposes.

It was logical that the reverse course in labor reform began within the Press Division of the Civil Information and Education Section (CIE), for CIE had been one of the first sections of SCAP to undergo a purge of liberal officers, and about the time Yoshida took office its orientation had taken an abrupt turn to the right. The relatively liberal Brigadier General Kermit R. Dyke was replaced in late June by Lieutenant Colonel Donald R. Nugent as chief of the section, shortly after Major Daniel C. Imboden had become chief of Press Division. Both men were ultra-conservatives by any definition.[16] The redirected section was goaded into action by the *Yomiuri*.[17]

One of the first steps CIE took was to tighten censorship. CIE censorship of leftist publications had been so lenient as to have been hardly operative through the June issues. Beginning with the July issues, which were under scrutiny at the time, the section applied censorship with a heavy hand. It suppressed whole issues of left-wing publications, and the censors riddled many others with their blue pencils.[18] Henceforth, left-wing writers could no longer count upon freedom of the press to ensure that unpopular opinions got into print.

On 18 May, Dyke had already seen General MacArthur and secured his consent to clamp down on the press unions. Two days after that, Imboden issued a strong warning to the press, threatening to close down "irresponsible" papers as General Hodge had done in Korea. He stated that "labor unions had no right and could not dictate the editorial policy of a newspaper" for "that was the right of the owners and men who are nominated by the owners."[19] In addition, in the week following MacArthur's consent, CIE twice told the publishers informally that they did not "have to stand for any union interference."[20]

General Dyke underscored the point again on 27 May at a meeting of presidents, directors, editors-in-chief, and managers of Japanese newspapers. He said that freedom of the press meant that only men directly responsible to the publisher could frame editorial policy. Although unions were essential, nevertheless "if an individual is out of sympathy with the editorial policy of a newspaper, he has the perfect right to resign and go somewhere else."[21]

The democratic Yomiuri turned out to have the courage of its convictions, and refused to toe the line as the other newspapers did. Its continued attacks on the conservative establishment gave SCAP, the Yoshida government, and its owners ample reason to cooperate in provoking another crisis at the paper.

Suppression of Workers' Control at the Yomiuri

Three separate issues were involved at the democratic Yomiuri: workers' control, freedom of the press, and political unionism. Only the first held revolutionary implications in and of itself, since it constituted a direct challenge to capitalist rights of private property. The others could be tolerated within the capitalist order with certain restrictions; but workers' control, never. Thus the breaking of the Yomiuri workers' control over the paper became a matter of first priority for the Yoshida government and for SCAP.[22]

In reality, high SCAP officials in General Headquarters and CIE did not sharply distinguish the problem of workers' control from the related but very different issues of freedom of the press and of labor's right to organize in defense of its interests. So the Yomiuri union and JNRU remained targets after the employees' control over the paper had ended because they were convenient and highly visible examples of so-called left-wing propaganda and political unionism.[23]

Over the opposition of Labor Division, General Headquarters and CIE set out in late May to illustrate in the case of the *Yomiuri* and the national press federation just what would happen to labor organizations that went beyond the acceptable limits of business unionism. The Yoshida cabinet of course pitched into the fray, delighted that SCAP was at last beginning to see the error of its liberal ways in regard to labor reform. The lesson of the *Yomiuri* struggle would be hard but clear: workers would have to organize to fight the government for the rights they had supposedly been granted by the Allies, or lose them.

The opponents of the democratic *Yomiuri* now virtually identified labor militance with communist influence, and needed only the barest excuse to attack the radicals who controlled the paper. CIE precipitated the second *Yomiuri* dispute over an article the newspaper printed on 4 June about a government plan for payment of subsidies for delivery of staple food quotas which denigrated the plan as a measure for protecting the landlords' interests.[24]

Major Imboden, new chief of the Press Division in CIE, told the *Yomiuri* on 5 June that this was a violation of the press code issued by SCAP in September 1945 in that it was an instance of inserting opinion into a news article. He issued a stern warning and demanded that measures be taken to establish responsibility for the article and to ensure that there be no more such violations.[25]

At the order of the publisher, Baba Tsunego, Suzuki and several other company supervisors drew up a proposal for Imboden. It punished Suzuki and the other two employees responsible with such penalties as reprimand, docking of salary, temporary suspension, and transfer. The proposal also included an informal system of pre-censorship whereby the copy for each edition would be rigorously checked for possible violations before going to press. This was communicated on the day of its drafting to Imboden, who indicated his satisfaction. Press Division responded to the effect that these measures were adequate, but if such a mistake were repeated, drastic measures would be taken against the *Yomiuri*.[26]

It is odd that Imboden agreed so readily to the proposal of the *Yomiuri* employees for dealing with their alleged violation of the press code, since he obviously had second thoughts overnight and decided to take advantage of this opportunity for bringing the democratic *Yomiuri* to heel. The next day, 6 June, he sent a memo to Baba "suggesting" that he put in a new editor, that all copy be inspected, and that the paper not print articles deviating from press regulations.[27]

It was up to Baba to make the next move. After failing to persuade Suzuki to accept responsibility and resign as chief of the editorial bureau, as Baba must have known he would, he stated that the measures proposed to CIE the day before were an inadequate response to a grave problem. Accordingly, he took responsibility himself and submitted his resignation to the Yomiuri directors and also in English to Imboden.[28]

After Imboden sent his memo to Baba on 6 June, a group of Baba's supporters began to cast about for a way to ensure that the impending crisis would be solved in the company's favor. Not all their efforts over the next few days are clear, but at least this much seems certain. Baba's people succeeded in getting in touch with Yoshida's private secretary and explaining their story. The secretary requested a list of the main communists at the paper, and six names were supplied, including Suzuki's.[29] Probably all but Suzuki were members of the JCP by that time.[30]

This list passed through Yoshida to MacArthur, and had reached Brigadier General Frayne Baker, public relations officer for SCAP, by the time Baba went to see him about his troubles on 12 June.[31] At one point during the meeting, "when Baba hesitated in reciting the six names, Baker picked up a slip of paper on his desk, read off the remaining names, and said, 'Aren't those the men?'"[32] Baba claimed later that Baker ordered him to return to the Yomiuri and dismiss the six men. After leaving Baker, Baba first met with Yoshida, then returned to the Yomiuri,[33] where he convened an emergency meeting of the directors and bureau chiefs and stated that the condition for his returning to the presidency of the paper was the resignation of the six and that this had to be done to establish his unquestioned authority over editorial policy. On the next day, 13 June, Baba called a meeting of approximately 100 people in positions of managerial responsibility and announced that he awaited submission of the resignations. The six employees said they would give their reply on the following day.[34]

Also on 13 June, Dyke's successor as chief of CIE, Lieutenant Colonel Nugent, issued a statement of SCAP policy concerning the press. The key parts of that statement read as follows:

Such freedom [of the press] means fundamentally, the right of free access to legitimate sources of news, and the right to present news and editorial opinion in the columns of a newspaper free from influence, domination, or any form of totalitarian control by any employees' association, by a labor union, or by any other pressure group. It means the freedom of the newspaper to determine its own editorial policy and to advocate that policy in its editorial columns . . . The custodians of responsibility on each newspaper are the owners or the management selected by them. It is they who determine and enforce the editorial policy of the newspaper and the manner in which its news is presented. Conscious of their responsibility to society and of the freedom with which they have been endowed to fulfil that responsibility, they must resist courageously not only all endeavours by private individuals or groups, even their own employees, to interfere with what they believe to be the proper policy and purpose of their newspaper. Employees who cannot work willingly under such a policy are at liberty to sever their connections with the newspaper and seek employment elsewhere.[35]

A report on the *Yomiuri* dispute prepared by the Office of Intelligence Research of the U.S. Department of State concluded that Nugent's statement, whereby he "went on record as strongly against production control by newspaper unions," served to give the stamp of official SCAP approval to Baba's actions. The report also concluded: "It is certain that President Baba did not take action without assuring himself of SCAP support."[36] Baba could be assured of the open support of the Japanese government, too, since the Yoshida cabinet issued its condemnation of production control, the "Declaration on the Maintenance of Social Order," on that same day.

The supporters of the democratic *Yomiuri* rallied behind Suzuki and the others. The 500 who attended the mass meeting of employees on 13 June to consider the dismissals resolved that the company must withdraw them as unfair and refer the problem to the management council. Suzuki proclaimed the beginning of a union struggle, saying "This isn't a problem of editorial authority, but of our right to live".[37] Baba responded the next day by posting a dismissal order for the six and prohibiting their entering the company. The fired men defied Baba's orders and continued to come to work, backed up at the entrance by the printing and publishing workers.[38]

Establishing a dispute headquarters in the editorial offices, Suzuki and the others took the leading part in the ensuing struggle for the allegiance of the employees. The pro-union workers held mass meetings daily and threw the company into a turmoil, but the paper kept coming out. Another employees' mass meeting on 17 June drew up a full set of demands and presented them to Baba. They were: 1) retract the dismissals; 2) nullify the personnel changes; 3) submit the entire problem to the management council; 4) punish the betrayers of the union; 5) suspend provocative acts; 6) provide a sum of money to the employees for overcoming the food crisis; 7) open the company accounts to the public; 8) assume financial responsibility for a consumers' union; and 9) observe the December arbitration agreement completely. Baba rejected the first five out of hand, agreed to item nine, and said the others were under study.[39]

Already on 14 June, Baba's supporters had set up an "inter-bureau liaison committee" in opposition to the union. This committee presented a "statement of resolution" to Baba on the 19th in the name of 1,200 of the 2,028 employees of the *Yomiuri*. It said that they intended to establish a healthy union which would not interfere with editorial authority. They accepted the firings as "an extraordinary measure," but asked that it not become a precedent for carrying out unjust dismissals.[40]

Upon arrival at the *Yomiuri* on that same day, the fired men found thirty or forty "guards"—toughs hired as company agents—blocking their way. Furthermore, the workers discovered two police investigators who had slipped unnoticed into the printshop.[41] In response, the union side organized an "action squad" of about 100 of its members. On the next day they battled about 100 guards and once again succeeded in bringing the fired men into the building. On the day following, there were 150 guards and it took 200 union members to get the job done. The same happened the next morning, 21 June.[42]

Then at around 2:30 P.M. a detachment of armed police from the Marunouchi station—later stated by authorities to be 150 strong but probably numbering three times that—surrounded the building. In short order they forced their way inside and attacked the union supporters. This was the government's first use of armed force to suppress a labor dispute since the war. The police had raided the *Yomiuri* to arrest the six leaders, four of whom (not including Suzuki) were among the fifty-odd people arrested.[43] The government's intention was to cripple the union by putting its leaders out of action, so all but the four leaders were released that evening. The four were charged with violent acts, breaking into premises, intimidation, and interference with business operations, and were jailed.[44] They were never tried, probably because the prosecution's case would not have held up in court. After the strike was broken, the charges were dropped, and the four were freed on 4 July.[45]

The police raid on the *Yomiuri* and the arrests ended the union tactics of ensuring attendance at work of the fired leaders and of occupying the editorial offices. The union protested to the police the next day and reorganized the negotiating committee that had been leading the dispute up to that point into a "struggle committee" on the model of the organ through which production control had been carried out the preceding fall. This made it clear to Baba that the Suzuki faction was determined to fight on, perhaps by reinstituting production control.[46]

Baba countered by making a special announcement over the company loudspeaker system at 5:30 P.M. on 24 June that if the dispute were not settled with forty-eight hours, he would shut down the paper.[47] Closure was a powerful threat in times like those, when there were literally no other jobs to be had, and such pressure tactics undoubtedly had brought a good many around even though their sympathies might have been with the dispute factions. The *Yomiuri* management and the liaison committee had been conducting their campaign against the employees' support of the dissidents under such cynical slogans as "Why sacrifice the lives of 2,000 for the necks of six?"[48]

The newly formed struggle committee stood up to Baba's ultimatum, however, and on 25 June came out in favor of a strike. It completed plans for the strike by noon of the 26th. When Imboden suddenly showed up ready to give an address to the employees at 2:00 P.M., the struggle committee urged everyone not to go to the lecture hall to hear him. But most went, no doubt in expectation of some kind of statement of support for Baba and the pro-management faction.[49]

Imboden began by saying that on this occasion he would explain to them all what henceforth was to be considered the work of a democratic newspaper. He rambled on at great length, interposing platitudes about reporting the news accurately and about freedom of the press with threats to close the *Yomiuri*. His main message was, once again, that no one but the owners or their delegated representatives had any rights over the operation of the paper, most especially over editorial policy. In no case would control by unions or workers be acceptable. He accused the paper of printing lies while under the control of Suzuki, and likened the "union despotism" over the *Yomiuri* to Tōjō's control over the press when the secret police simply murdered dissident editors.[50]

Imboden's direct intervention at this critical stage broke the back of the struggle. The great majority of the union members lost the will to fight, with one exception—the blue-collar workers who actually printed the paper, and who all the way through had been the staunchest supporters of the struggle to democratize the *Yomiuri*. After Imboden finished, Baba's supporters proposed that the audience be constituted as a general meeting of employees. That was done and the employees unconditionally approved Baba's measures. In defeat, the union held an executive committee meeting on 28 June at which it recognized the firings and made a promise to hold a general union meeting on 14 July in order to reconstruct the union and elect new officers.[51]

Ishibashi Finance

Alternative Views on Japan's Revival

Three distinct models for a capitalist reconstruction were being offered at the time of the government counterattack upon labor and the
Yomiuri. SCAP was sponsoring an American approach that extolled
small-scale, competitive capitalism, strong labor unions, and a weak
state distinguished by a decentralization of political and economic power,
all to be attained within the boundaries of a much-reduced level of
industrial production.[52] Because the Japanese leadership opposed this
alternative almost unanimously and were prepared to go to great lengths
to prevent its implementation, the actual choice was between the
"laissez-faire" capitalism expounded by the Yoshida government and
the "modified" (shūsei) capitalism espoused by the more progressive
elements in business and government.

In that first winter of occupation the old guard had advanced a reactionary but coherent policy which largely coincided with the thinking of the "Japan crowd" among U.S. policy makers and aimed at con-
fining the reforms to demilitarization and a narrow political
democratization that would allow a return to business much as it had
been before Japan went to war. Yoshida hewed closely to this line. The
combination of a zaibatsu-controlled economy and an elite-dominated
political system had proven highly effective in promoting growth in
the past and presumably would do so once again, albeit through continuing the reliance upon cheap and repressed labor.[53] By the time
Yoshida formed his cabinet the conservative approach had been tem-
pered slightly by a grudging recognition of the inevitability of certain
of the basic measures of political and economic democratization that
SCAP was carrying out, but the old insistence upon big-business leadership of the economy, heavy industry, textile exports, cheap labor,
and a minimally interventionist state remained.

Not all big-business and government leaders thought it self-evident
that the conservative program was a correct response either to the
long-run needs of the economy or to the immediate problems of inflation and stagnating production. The preceding months had convinced
the progressives of the need for economic planning to make the most
of Japan's scarce resources and for a conciliatory policy toward labor
built upon recognition of the hard facts of unionization and higher
wages. They feared that the conservative program would bring about
an economic collapse and a labor revolt.[54]

The essentials of the progressive program were the planned development of the economy by professional managers with the positive aid

of the state bureaucracy, recognition of healthy labor unions, and increased reliance upon a strong internal market for the products of industry. They argued that if big business was to be competitive in world markets in the future, henceforth it must rely on capital-intensive technology in order to secure the productivity from its work force needed to offset the higher wages organized labor was going to bring. Higher wages would mean, moreover, creation of an internal market capable of absorbing a substantial part of Japan's output, and the resulting economic prosperity for the Japanese people would create a solid base for attaining the Allied goal of a democratized but capitalist Japan.[55]

The Yoshida cabinet rejected the progressive solution and attempted to turn back the clock in the summer of 1946. Though the conservatives loudly proclaimed their adherence to laissez-faire and believed that, in principle, abolition of bureaucratic controls and noninterference in business affairs were sufficient for the resurrection of the "free" economy of the twenties, even they understood that some kind of government action would be needed to overcome the stagnation of production.[56] Accordingly, the cabinet's first recourse was to "Keynesian" deficit finance in order to stimulate industrial recovery. Shorn of all the rhetoric, the Yoshida policy consisted of inflationary handouts to big business and a counteroffensive against labor intended to accomplish the recapitalization of the zaibatsu and the provision of an abundant supply of cheap labor.

Financing a Laissez-Faire Capitalist Reconstruction

The earliest measures taken by the Yoshida government against the working class had been overtly counterrevolutionary in that they aimed at stopping anti-capitalist direct action in its tracks. Once the immediate threat of production control had been contained, the government's attitude toward labor was governed by its policy on economic reconstruction.

Yoshida owed his allegiance to the old guard and endorsed their conservative prescription of a return to prewar "laissez-faire." Wishing to avoid the active intervention through economic planning that SCAP was pressing for,[57] and to erase the steps in this direction that the Shidehara cabinet had already taken, Yoshida turned to the panaceas being offered by Ishibashi Tanzan, publisher of *The Oriental Economist*. Big business welcomed Ishibashi's appointment to Finance Minister as a sign that the economic controls instituted by Shidehara would be withdrawn and restrictions on capital supply would be lifted.[58]

The new Finance Minister outlined his economic policies in a speech before the Diet on 26 July 1946.[59] His speech made it clear that he had no quarrel with the conservatives' goal of participation in international trade after the war on the old basis; that is, by supplying light industrial exports underwritten by cheap labor at home in exchange for the wherewithal to rebuild heavy industry. He described his policies as laying the groundwork for Japan's eventual reemergence in the international economy.

The speech began with the "Keynesian" argument that, in times when there were both idle productive capacity and mass unemployment, a positive financial policy of supplying public funds to private business to promote production was the best way to overcome both inflation and economic stagnation. He argued that in such times sound finance in its true meaning was red-ink finance,[60] and that Japan was not experiencing inflation in the usual sense, but a kind of panic attendant upon the postwar scarcity of goods. High scarcity prices—the essence of the postwar "inflation"—would quickly be overcome, he said, by the increased production and marketing of goods which would be stimulated by the government's policy of supplying funds to business through deficit finance.[61]

Ishibashi next outlined a "negative" policy of removing barriers to recovery, such as the financial and economic controls which circumstances had forced the Shidehara cabinet to put into effect. He also indicated that he would carry out SCAP's long-standing demands for cancellation of wartime indemnities to business through a confiscatory tax and for imposition of a steeply graduated capital levy.[62] Despite their likely bad effect upon the capital structure of big business and banking, these actions had to be taken quickly in order to restore business prospects, even at the cost of necessitating a drastic financial readjustment and retrenchment of operations. Alongside this negative policy, Ishibashi said the government would take positive measures to soften the blow and make it possible to repay debts and continue operations.

First and most important of the five "positive" policies Ishibashi then sketched was one of providing a special stimulus to "pivotal industries" based on a temporary system of subsidies for production of producer goods (especially coal—which he saw as the key to revival of every kind of production) and also for chemical fertilizers and foodstuffs. Subsidy was essential in order to make up the difference between production costs and the low, controlled prices which would temporarily be kept in effect. The ultimate goal was a large increase in prices for producer goods that would obviate the need for subsidy.

The second policy was for the government to provide large sums to finance reconstruction, in part through existing channels but primarily through setting up a special organ for that purpose. This was accomplished in October when the Reconstruction Finance Bank was organized. Coupled with this, Ishibashi made the pledge not to revalue money again or to block accounts as Shidehara had done.

Third was encouragement of industry's rationalization, that is, the carrying out of technological improvements for the purpose of increasing productivity per employee. Fourth was to be government preparations for coping with the substantial increase in those unemployed "of necessity" that was anticipated as a result of the financial readjustment and subsequent industrial rationalization. Government officials—prone to professional optimism in situations like this—estimated that the readjustment would occasion the unemployment of about 750,000 workers. Others have cited figures as high as 2,000,000 for those who would have become unemployed had dismissals taken place as contemplated.[63] Presumably the increase would have been taken care of by a combination of temporary unemployment benefits and a rapid expansion of employment in other areas as economic activity revived. The last proposed policy, a sop to the ordinary citizen who was going to have to pay the bill for Ishibashi's financial program through an erosion of real income by inflation, was an increase in "educational and cultural expenditures" by the government.

Ishibashi finance, as these policies came to be called, was obviously predicated on the unstated assumption that the task of economic recovery could only be accomplished by government backing for the great enterprises in control of heavy industry, that is the zaibatsu firms then undergoing the first phases of what was to be an incomplete dissolution.[64] It was just the kind of hands-off, unplanned approach to economic reconstruction guaranteed to find favor with the advocates of the free economy, for it tapped the conservative belief that all the government really needed to do was create a positive climate for business confidence, whereupon business leaders would naturally rise to the occasion, their will to produce revitalized by the prospect of future profits.

Just as obviously, Ishibashi finance pointed toward increased conflict with labor, since the recapitalization of big business was to be accomplished by the provocative combination of inflationary government subsidies and savings on labor costs. The latter depended upon the reductions in work force and increases in worker productivity singled out in Ishibashi's speech, but also upon the (unmentioned) technique of holding the line on wage increases.[65] In essence, Ishibashi finance depended upon recreating the conditions for the "free" labor of the past, and would require extraordinary measures if working-class demands for better wages and job security were to be contained while inflation took off again.

As publisher of *The Oriental Economist* and self-proclaimed economist, Ishibashi had long argued that the government ought to assume as much responsibility as possible to help the business world through financial readjustment and to increase output, even proposing in early 1946 a temporary nationalization of industry to do so. Yet his attitude toward workers, as candidly revealed in a speech in February 1946 ("Inflation or Deflation?") that was published in pamphlet form in July while he was Finance Minister, was based on the harsh axiom that those who do not work shall not eat.[66] Productivity was low and unemployment high in large part because workers were shirking, he argued, and the way to deal with such base and lazy fellows was to have the government find them and draft them for work in coal mines, government-managed enterprises, and agriculture.[67]

Despite Ishibashi's predilection for extreme measures like labor conscription, it was impossible to revive the government surveillance and police suppression that had underlain the "free" labor markets of the past. In the end, government and business leaders attempted to make the new policies work by a combination of maximum resistance to the organization of powerful industrial unions and maximum support to cooperative company unions organized at the enterprise level. Both were prepared, in pursuit of their goals, to use the scourges of unemployment and economic deprivation to stimulate the working class to a healthy respect for the virtues of hard work and self-denial.

The Yoshida cabinet encouraged private industry in its new-found resolve to limit and undermine the workers' new rights to organize and to take collective action in defense of their interests, regardless of guarantees in the Trade Union Law and other SCAP-sponsored labor reforms. Further, as a major employer in its own right, the government repeatedly confronted public employees over the same issues in the months to come. SCAP's support for the government, though qualified by the goal of seeing American-style business unionism implanted, would nevertheless be forthcoming at the critical times; for SCAP increasingly felt it had to choose the lesser evil of countenancing capitalist anti-union activities to avoid the greater evil of the growth of left-wing militance within the working class.

Already pressed to the wall by inflation, food shortages, and mass unemployment, Japan's working class could not be expected to go along willingly with this one-sided distribution of the burden of reconstruction.[68] They were ready to fight, indeed had to fight, to preserve their unions and protect themselves. As events were to prove, nothing short of the breaking of a union could compel workers to acquiesce in the wholesale dismissals and cuts in real wages in store for them.

The government's financial largesse flowed into the coffers of big business, which, no longer fettered by effective controls, proved only slightly more willing than it had been under the Higashikuni and Shidehara cabinets to engage in new productive ventures. The zaibatsu preferred to use the government funds for such non-productive purposes as speculation and debt repayment, or to buy labor peace by granting wage demands. The government policy was highly inflationary given the extreme scarcity of commodities of any kind, causing even large wage increases to lag behind price rises. Moreover, it was dangerous in that it did little to overcome the stagnation in output of producer goods that lay at the center of the economic crisis.

Economic revival could only begin when labor and capital arrived at some consensus on a program for postwar reconstruction, for the working class was hardly likely to permit the conservatives to undermine the Allied labor reforms without a fight. Sooner or later the conservatives would have to move substantially toward the position of the progressives, and at a minimum give up their antipathy to unions and their insistence upon cheap labor as a prerequisite for Japan's economic recovery. The reactionary labor policies of the past were no longer possible; but the nature of the necessary accommodation between labor and capital would not be decided for some months to come.

Union Busting Begins

The crackdown on the labor union movement intended by the Yoshida cabinet began even before Ishibashi made his speech to the Diet. The government fired the first shot in its anti-union campaign at the *Yomiuri*, where the workers had continued to defend their union rights after the final destruction of workers' control over the newspaper. Just as the democratic *Yomiuri* had been the target in the drive to crush production control, which was at the heart of working-class radicalism, so now it became the first object of the tactics business and government leaders would use against industrial unionism. These tactics amounted to the breaking of militant local branches by refusing to recognize their legitimacy and forcibly replacing them with "second unions," that is, company unions. Management would then write a collective bargaining agreement with the new union, thereby undermining the power of the national federation which had failed in its task of defending local workers.

The resumption of the conflict between labor and employer at the *Yomiuri* arose over a matter of principle, namely whether the union had the right to exist and to protect its members from retaliation for union activity despite an employer's refusal to grant recognition.[69] SCAP and the Japanese leadership agreed that the unions had gone too far and had become too political, but their notions of what constituted a responsible union movement were still far apart. SCAP still aimed at building an independent union movement, while the old guard was still set on establishing the closest thing to company unions it could get.

These basic issues of labor policy were partially obscured in the *Yomiuri* dispute because of the transcendent importance SCAP attached to purging communists from the press. Thus, when the chips were down and the independence of the union was at stake, Labor Division alone came to the *Yomiuri* workers' defense—only to be slapped down for its trouble. In the instance of the *Yomiuri*, SCAP played right into the hands of the conservatives, and Allied labor policy took second place to anti-communism in a housebreaking that foreshadowed events to come in 1947.

When the *Yomiuri* dispute flared up again in early July, there was no longer any question about who managed the paper and controlled editorial policy. Workers' control had been destroyed and Baba was back in command. The conflict was renewed over the union's claim to legitimacy and its attempts to protect its members. The blue-collar workers in the engineering bureau and a part of the editorial staff who had been the mainstay of the *Yomiuri* union revived the dispute out of concern over job security and attainment of an adequate livelihood. They demanded conclusion of an effective collective bargaining contract, but owing to company encouragement of the anti-union faction a stalemate appeared in the offing, one that eventually might have ended with the reunification of the two factions of the employees into a reorganized and moderate union.[70]

At this point Labor Division became alarmed about the tactics being used against the *Yomiuri*, and its chief, Theodore Cohen, encouraged the union side to fight for its rights. Cohen summoned all the principals to the *Yomiuri* dispute to meet with him on 29 June in order to advise them of Labor Division's interests. Cohen informed Baba, Kikunami and the discharged men (including Suzuki) that the provisions of the Trade Union Law protected union members from discharge and other kinds of retaliation for union activity, that it was illegal to suppress labor unions, and that any agreements an employer obtained under duress had no legal force. On the other hand, both sides were legally bound to observe the terms of the original collective labor agreement signed in December 1945. He further encouraged

them to make use of the machinery of the Labor Relations Committees to achieve a settlement.[71]

Cohen had every reason to be concerned about the direction labor
relations in Japan was taking. MacArthur's statement on mass violence
on 20 May had already emboldened the government authorities. According to a Labor Division study which Cohen prepared in late June,
not only was the Home Ministry already talking openly of "rigid control" by the police over labor disputes and mass actions deemed to be
violating democratic principles, but also "presurrender practices of
police surveillance and interference in labor union activity have reappeared."[72]

Cohen cited the fact that the Metropolitan Police Bureau had issued
a strong directive signed by the chief of the Marunouchi police station
to all labor organizations and political groups in the Tokyo area on 19
June restricting the right to demonstrate.

In case a movement (including demonstration, and any movement to be made
by a group with the object of presenting a petition or having an interview at
an official or public institution) is to be accomplished, authorization will not
be granted unless its objective, the time and date, place, route, the name of
sponsoring organizations and responsible individuals are reported to the Pro-
vost Marshal Office 48 hours prior to the time it will be effective through the
police station which has jurisdiction at the place the movement is to be accomplished.[73]

This same police chief, two days after release of the directive, in coordination with the chief of the Criminal Affairs Department in the
Home Ministry had carried out the raid and arrests at the *Yomiuri*.
When called to account by Labor Division and the press, he justified
his acts on the grounds that authorization had not been obtained in
advance for the demonstration as required by "SCAP directive."[74] Cohen
viewed the *Yomiuri* raid in quite a different light:

No court order had been issued to support such action, nor had any warrants
been issued for arrest. No violence, attempted or actual bodily harm or significant destruction of property had taken place. No public demonstration
was being held. In the ensuing activities, Japanese were arrested and held
four hours without charges, among them several bystanders outside the building
who were arrested for cheering the union.[75]

Cohen may well have informed the JNRU and the *Yomiuri* local that
the raid had been illegal when he called them in on the 29 June meeting. At any rate, the JNRU prepared to press charges against the authorities for illegal arrest.[76]

Only then were the four leaders still being held in jail released, by order of the Department of Justice. This intervention angered the Home Ministry and police authorities enough to cause them to refuse for some time to take decisive action to protect Baba and the pro-management faction at the *Yomiuri* from dispute activities by the union.[77] No doubt the authorities were reluctant to send the police into action not only because of resentment, but also because of fear engendered by Labor Division's strong reaction to the previous raid and the adverse publicity it attracted. Police were stationed outside the *Yomiuri*, nonetheless, and their presence lent considerable support to Baba.

The JNRU filed a complaint in the name of its *Yomiuri* local with the Central Labor Relations Committee on 2 July. On the same day, the standing executive committee of the local met and served a new set of demands on Baba. These included demands for wages and allowances, but the basic ones were for conclusion of a collective bargaining agreement with the union and submission of the issue of the dismissals to an organ authorized to represent the union, presumably the management council.[78]

Baba struck back against these union moves on 3 July by transferring seventeen union leaders in the editorial bureau out of Tokyo to remote offices. A week later a "Council for the Reconstruction of the *Yomiuri*" was organized through the joint efforts of the company and the pro-management faction of the *Yomiuri* union. This was done as a preliminary to the setting up of a "second union" that could undermine and displace the *Yomiuri* local. Indeed, Baba had been ignoring the proposals of the union for some time, and now indicated he would negotiate with the employees only through the reconstruction council.[79]

The *Yomiuri* local held a general meeting on 11 July, at which the members decided to go out on strike on the next day if their demands were not met. When the company ignored this ultimatum, the printers and other workers in the engineering bureau seized the printing plant, stopping publication of the paper. The pro-management faction swung into action, and over the next three days set up the reconstruction council as a second union claiming to be the legitimate *Yomiuri* local. Reorganized and functioning openly as a company union, the reconstruction council proceeded on 15 July to "expel" forty union members who had been key figures in the strike. The company immediately fired thirty-one of those expelled.[80]

The sit-down strike by the engineering bureau put Baba in a fix from which he tried to extricate himself by asking the police to break the strike as they had in June by removing the strikers by force. When they would not do so without a directive from SCAP, Baba went to

CIE to ask that they order the Japanese police in, but Nugent did not move fast enough for Baba.[81]

Despairing of police action in time to prevent the pieing of the type—dumping of the type into a heap on the floor—and throwing of sand into the rotary presses—which would have done tremendous damage—the company organized a group of strikebreakers around the reconstruction council. This group attacked the sit-down strikers in strength on 16 July and threw them out by force while the Japanese police stood by watching. The strikers had been following a policy of nonviolent resistance, and took no steps either to fight off the company men or to sabotage the printing plant.[82]

When Baba reported to CIE on the 17th, Nugent congratulated him personally on resuming publication, and asked for daily reports. At the end of a sympathetic interview, Nugent stated that he wanted to be able to make a report to the Chief of Staff "that the paper is going to be published tomorrow and that in your opinion you will be able to continue to publish it."[83]

Nugent did his part to stabilize the situation for Baba by sending a memo to the Chief of Staff on 20 July recommending that "The Japanese Government be ordered to furnish protection to the personnel and property of the *Yomiuri* Shimbun."[84] After this the Japanese authorities became bolder about the open use of police force to suppress the actions of the *Yomiuri* strikers.

Baba had characterized the strike faction as part of a communist conspiracy to take over the paper when he met with Nugent, and Nugent fully agreed. Baba's attitude was expressed quite clearly in the lead editorial in the *Yomiuri* when it resumed publication. Baba wrote: "The *Yomiuri* is one of the important targets of the left who wish to take over Japan. The *Yomiuri*, in a sense, is the point which will decide the fate of Japan. Should the *Yomiuri* fall into their hands, all other papers will be in danger and Japan herself will face the crisis of Bolshevization."[85] General MacArthur must have agreed. On 25 July he called in the heads of the *Yomiuri*, *Asahi*, *Mainichi*, and *Jiji* newspapers for a conference, and told them to "kick out" the communists.[86]

The help extended to the *Yomiuri* management thereafter by SCAP and the Japanese government, and the pressure exerted on the *Yomiuri* local and the JNRU, left little hope for a union victory.[87] Although the struggle went on for some months to come, the strike had been broken when the sit-down strikers were driven out of the print shop. The reorganization of the company union into the *Yomiuri* Employees' Union on 30 July, and its secession from the JNRU, merely formalized that fact.

Even though their sit-down had been broken and the *Yomiuri* was back in publication—now as the most conservative of the major papers—the remaining members of the original *Yomiuri* union struggled on, basing their hopes for eventual victory on either a national press strike by the JNRU or a favorable ruling from the Central Labor Relations Committee. The JNRU organized a coalition of powerful national unions behind the *Yomiuri* which promptly began carrying out mass demonstrations ranging up to 4,000 participants almost daily before the *Yomiuri* from 19 June to 2 August.[88]

The demonstration on 2 August was stopped by police order despite the fact that the demonstrators had notified the police beforehand as required. While the organizers were arguing with the police authorities over the reasons, a Lieutenant Thurston of the Public Safety Division of Civil Intelligence Section in SCAP appeared on the scene. According to the demonstrators' account, Thurston told them to disperse in ten minutes or he would call in the Military Police. When asked under what authority he was acting, Thurston said the Metropolitan Police Board had General Headquarters' backing to cancel the demonstration. While all this was going on, a large force of armed Japanese police stood by, as well as a contingent of U.S. military policemen.[89]

Then on 3 August the Central Labor Relations Committee handed down its ruling on the *Yomiuri* dispute. The ruling said in essence that the initial discharge of the six men had been justifiable in order for the management to regain control over editorial policy. But, it went on, the succeeding transfers and dismissals were potentially in violation of the Trade Union Law in that Baba had apparently used these means to punish employees for legitimate union activities and to weaken the union. Accordingly, these would have to be reviewed case by case and the company would have to show cause for the steps taken.[90]

The striking *Yomiuri* local accepted the ruling and requested compliance, but Baba ignored it, denying that the Central Labor Relations Committee had jurisdiction. Baba's intransigence eventually led to a decision by the JNRU in mid-September to carry out a general strike of the press for early October. Since there was a great deal of support for the *Yomiuri* strikers among the employees of the other major Tokyo papers—the *Asahi* and *Mainichi*—it began to seem that a general strike might well succeed in bringing Baba around.[91]

While preparations were going on for the general strike, a collection of opinions on the arbitration ruling was printed in the *Asahi* on 29 September. In them a spokesman for Yoshida openly supported Baba's viewpoint, stating that decisions by the committee were not legally binding as a basis for settlement of labor disputes. The Tokyo Procurator's Office gave a similar opinion. The director of Keidanren agreed and added that Baba's acceptance of the arbitration ruling would threaten his establishment of unchallenged editorial authority and that he should not do so.

The Yoshida government indicated it would intervene against the union if the threatened general press strike resulted in disturbances,[92] and intervene it did. The strike failed because of the combined pressure by SCAP and the Japanese authorities,[93] and the *Yomiuri* affiliate of the JNRU finally admitted defeat in mid-October when it accepted the company's terms unconditionally. The union was dissolved, and those who rejoined the paper were brought into the company union. Subsequently, the head of the JNRU, Kikunami Katsumi, accepted responsibility for the failure of the general press strike and resigned the chairmanship in late October. The federation became seriously divided over the issue of left-wing influence, and was not very effective thereafter. It split openly in 1947, and a new national press union was formed in 1948.[94]

The dramatic events at the *Yomiuri* alerted workers in other sectors of the economy to the fact that the balance of power within Japan was beginning to change against the labor movement. In this respect, the anti-labor offensive of business and government did not have the hoped-for effect, but resulted in a rising tide of labor militance that nearly swept the government from power six months later.

8

The Unions Fight Back

Sanbetsu Takes the Lead

Even while the *Yomiuri* union was heading towards total defeat, the labor policies of the Yoshida cabinet sustained a stunning setback in the failure of the government to enforce personnel reductions and to hold the line on wage increases in the national railways and maritime shipping. The setback came at the hands of Sanbetsu (Zen Nihon Sangyōbetsu Rōdō Kumiai Kaigi, Congress of Industrial Unions) as part of the offensive it mounted in the second half of 1946 to establish the power of national union federations built upon a foundation of subordinate enterprise locals.[1]

The Anti-Dismissal Fight

The National Railways were already state-operated, and shipping had been put under the control of the Marine Transport Control Council during the war. The government's policy in these industries as elsewhere had long been the maximum possible substitution of labor for capital. Consequently, labor provided by the emergency training and employment of youth and women was used to compensate for wartime deterioration and destruction of equipment, shortages of materials and fuels, and losses of experienced workers to conscription. One consequence was that when the postwar demobilization and repatriation freed many of the former workers to reclaim their old jobs, there were soon many more workers than needed to keep the few decrepit ships and the run-down railroads going.[2]

The Shidehara government had tried with a degree of success to make large-scale dismissals—over 24,000 in shipping, about one-third of the work force. No doubt the government feared to go as far as it wanted in transportation at a time when workers were resorting to production control to save their livelihoods, an eventuality that must have made even a swelling wage bill look infinitely preferable. Now, when the tide was turning against the working class and the government was preparing to try to bring organized labor to heel as part of Ishibashi's financial policies, mass dismissals were in the wind. It was logical that the government chose to make its first move in transportation; if a case could be made for surplus employment in any industry, it was in railroads and shipping.

At about the time of Ishibashi's speech to the Diet, the government was already preparing immediate personnel reductions totalling 118,000. On 24 July, the authorities announced that 75,000 dismissals were to take place in the National Railways, and on 7 August announced 43,000 in shipping. Ishibashi had promised positive measures to cushion the shock for the workers thrown out of their jobs, but this was a dead letter from the start. When the Ministry of Transportation notified the railway workers' union of the impending dismissals, it openly admitted that making a significant effort to aid the workers through on unemployment policy would be difficult.[3] These government moves brought to a head the conflicts that had been brewing between the executives of the unions in these industries and the rank and file.

The first union notified, the General Federation of National Railway Workers' Unions (Kokutetsu Rōdō Kumiai Sōrengo Kai, 530,000 members),[4] was as yet loosely organized and closer to being a liaison council of autonomous railroad unions than the national industrial union it aspired to be. Otherwise, it was run by executives unresponsive to the rank and file and anxious to find grounds for accommodation with management.[5] The other union involved, the Seamen's Union, was run by labor bosses equally anxious for accommodation, and was the next thing to being a company union (see chapter 2). Nevertheless, the government's plan to dismiss well over half of the union's 75,000 members produced a rank-and-file rebellion that could not be contained.

The official announcements of personnel reductions brought about a spontaneous uprising of seamen and railroad workers in anti-dismissal struggles spearheaded by the young men and women who were slated to be the first to go. Union members in ports and railroad centers all over Japan expressed their total opposition to discharges, demanded wage increases, and showed their readiness to go out on a nationwide strike for their unions if necessary. The union leaders, far from being swayed by the workers' militance, condemned the idea of a strike and hastily promoted agreements with the authorities compromising the workers' demands by omitting concrete guarantees not to carry out personnel reductions. The rank and file rallied behind opposition factions in both unions, which shouldered aside the old leaders for a time and put together organizations capable of assuming the leadership of the anti-dismissal movement.[6]

The SCAP and government crackdown in May and June against working-class radicalism had enabled the right-wing union leaders to stave off the growing pressure for the unification of the labor movement under the leadership of the left-wing unions. Yet, the anti-labor offensive of the Yoshida cabinet also made it imperative to hasten the inauguration of a central organization for labor unions. So August 1946 saw the formation of two competing national federations: Sōdōmei (Nihon Rōdō Kumiai Sōdōmei, Japan General Federation of Labor, carrying on the name and the tradition of the prewar Sōdōmei) on 1–3 August with about 850,000 members, and Sanbetsu on 19–21 August with about 1,600,000 members, together accounting for two-thirds of organized labor. This actually amounted to a three-way split. Since most of the remaining unions opposed both the bosses' control over Sōdōmei and JCP influence in Sanbetsu, they set up their own organization two months later, Nichirō Kaigi (Nihon Rōdō Kumiai Kaigi, All Japan Council of Labor Unions). Sanbetsu and Nichirō Kaigi were loose councils of autonomous unions and had much less power over their affiliates than Sōdōmei, which had a centralized and authoritarian structure.

From the moment of its birth, Sanbetsu began marshalling its strength in support of the *Yomiuri* strike and the anti-dismissal fights of the seamen's and railway workers' unions; although neither of the latter was an affiliate, Sanbetsu leaders regarded the victory of each as crucial to the realization of a unified labor movement for Japan, and felt that unification could only be achieved by organizing powerful joint struggles drawing in as many unions as possible. In this way they would be able to repel the capitalist counterattack and at the same time increase the pressure on Sōdōmei enough so that it could refuse a Sanbetsu offer of unconditional merger only at considerable cost, perhaps an internal revolt or mass disaffection.[7]

While the seamen and railway workers prepared for nationwide strikes, Sanbetsu did succeed in putting together an imposing joint struggle which must be given considerable credit for forcing the government to back down and retract the dismissals in mid-September and to grant sizeable wage increases. These concessions were gained only by means of a ten-day strike by the seamen and the fixing of a deadline for a combined railroad walkout and sympathy strike by a number of Sanbetsu affiliates. Sōdōmei, understandably, gave only nominal backing to the joint struggle and in actuality opposed the railroad and shipping strikes as political, as did the Socialist party. Unfortunately for the *Yomiuri* strikers, they were unable to use the joint struggle to bring about a satisfactory settlement of their dispute.

The lesson of these three major disputes of summer 1946 was clear to all—the key to a worker victory was solidarity and industry-wide organization. To the extent that Sanbetsu could achieve this combination in other unions and industries, business and government leaders would be confronted by a formidable labor movement able to wreck their regressive economic plans by halting their plans to make personnel reductions and peg wages. Sanbetsu had right at the outset based itself solidly on the principle of industrial unionism adopted by the World Federation of Trade Unions, that is, one local union in each enterprise, one national federation in each industry, and one central labor organization for the country.[8] Real power to negotiate contracts and take dispute actions was to be located with the national federations, not the enterprise local as was the case for most of the new unions.

This placed it in eye-to-eye confrontation with the business leaders who looked for leadership in labor matters to Kankeikyō; the writing of contracts at the enterprise level and not with the national labor federations was already an article of faith with this association.[9] The employers associated with Kankeikyō were strong backers of the Yoshida cabinet's free-labor policies, and stood for a business line of encouraging company unions and straightforward union busting. The contrast to Dōyūkai's call for enlisting labor's cooperation in a capitalist economic recovery and tolerating business unionism was sharp, but somewhat deceptive nonetheless. In truth, both wings of big business, whatever their philosophical disagreements over labor's basic rights, had an aversion to labor organization transcending the bounds of the individual enterprise, as did the government.[10] This was unlike the situation in the United States, where at the critical time of formation industrial unions were favored by state policy and by a part of big business. The result was that when employers in Japan had to sign an industry-wide contract due to overwhelming union strength—for example, in coal mining and electric power, as will be seen below—

constant pressure thereafter to decentralize and downwardly relocate
the main arena for relations between labor and capital almost always
succeeded in undermining the authority of the national union federation and in enhancing the autonomous powers of the enterprise union.[11]

A strong, united labor movement might well have overcome big-
business and government hostility and forced an acceptance of industrial unionism that would have transformed labor relations in Japan.
But that was not to be; for if Sanbetsu had provided a focus for the
desire of the majority of the working class to see strong industrial unions
established, it also reflected the formal division of labor and the left-
wing parties into the same two warring camps that had fatally weakened the working class in the past.

The injurious effect of disunity was readily apparent. The *Yomiuri*
union was destroyed by an internal split, and the authority of the national press union was badly compromised when the *Asahi, Mainichi,*
and other newspapers bowed to outside pressure and withdrew from
the planned national strike. More discouraging was the fact that in
spite of the successes of the rank-and-file–supported dissidents in the
railroad and shipping disputes, boss control was soon reestablished in
the Seamen's Union and vicious infighting plagued the National Railway Workers' Union for years thereafter. Internal divisions such as
these would eventually make it possible for employers to succeed in
breaking militant unions by the tactics of playing off white-collar staff
against lower-level workers (both blue and white-collar) and abetting
the formation of "second" unions entirely within the enterprise. This
had happened first at the *Yomiuri.*

In the fall of 1946, it looked as if the trend of the labor movement
was in the other direction, toward an even higher percentage of
unionization, even greater solidarity, and ever more successful struggles.
The October offensive sponsored by Sanbetsu seemed to confirm this.

The October Offensive

The October offensive began in the electrical industry with the prolonged and arduous Tōshiba strike, reached a high point in mid-October in the coal mines of Hokkaidō, and culminated in the renowned
struggle of the workers in the electrical power industry for a guaranteed minimum wage. Though the emphasis of union demands varied
from industry to industry, the offensive was primarily a continuation
of those demands which had first come to the fore that summer. Sanbetsu and many participating unions adopted radical demands for a
revival of production by the people themselves and for immediate
overthrow of the "mass firing" Yoshida cabinet, but the real fight—as

before—centered upon turning back employer plans for mass dismissals, gaining permanent increases in real wages, and getting a contract.[12]

In 1946 there were three regional labor federations organized within the Tōkyō Shibaura Denki Kabushiki Kaisha (Tōshiba), in Kantō, Kansai, and Tōhoku. The Kantō federation (the Tōshiba Kantō Rōdō Kumiai Rengōkai, Tōshiba Kantō Federation of Electric Equipment Workers' Unions) had become the acknowledged leader in disputes with the company. Thus, when the Kantō Federation held an emergency meeting at the Tōshiba Horikawa-chō factory on 14 September to put together demands to present to the company, the other federations quickly adopted them also.

The Tōshiba unions wanted a company pledge not to make dismissals—as yet unannounced but expected to involve well over 10,000 workers—a minimum wage based on the cost of living, and extensive rights of worker participation in a revival of production at Tōshiba.[13] The company rejected all demands, and, in what was an obvious attempt to avoid negotiating with the union, insisted that the first two items must be deliberated in the joint labor-management council set up in accord with the existing agreement. It refused to respond to the third item on the grounds that the union proposal was too vague.[14] In response to the company's hard line, the union set 1 October as the date for a strike. On the day before, SCAP issued a strong warning that it would intervene if the dispute led to results counter to occupation objectives.[15]

The Tōshiba strike on 1 October kicked off the fall labor offensive. All but four of the sixty-three locals belonging to the Tōshiba union (50,000 members) in the national federation for the electrical industry went out on schedule.[16] They were led by a struggle committee system, and the dispute was greatly stimulated by the activities of the radical youth action groups.[17]

The company's attitude was unyielding throughout, and management showed the will to close down individual factories if necessary. This was a move perhaps intended to bring about government and SCAP intervention, since Tōshiba had a large number of orders for goods for the occupation forces. The Central Labor Relations Committee chaired by Suehiro Izutarō quickly initiated mediation of the dispute at government request, but found no easy solution.[18]

The union defied official orders to resume production for the occupation, and the strike dragged on. Then, in early November, in a desperate bid to force a solution, the strikers occupied the Horikawa-chō factory, forcibly detained the company executives, and subjected them to mass negotiations. At that point the police and the American military police were used against them.[19]

Under tremendous pressure from all sides, the union was compelled to settle for a partial victory that entailed a weaker company pledge on dismissals than the union wanted and a stipulation that future pay raises would be by an efficiency wage tied to increased productivity. Worker participation came to nothing more than the establishment of a company-controlled committee for increasing production, the opposite of what had been intended.[20] Yet, although the unions had hardly achieved a complete victory, they had gained major concessions on dismissals and wages. More important, the fierce resistance of the Tōshiba workers discouraged other private employers from making mass dismissals for some time to come.

Major coal strikes had broken out in Kyūshū during the summer of 1946, but the inherent weakness of the enterprise-based unions there made it next to impossible for the mine workers to defeat the well-coordinated and determined regional federations of management in the coal industry, particularly since they were bolstered by SCAP intervention and police action. Management tactics for dealing with mine worker demands for wages and contracts were simple and effective. They insisted on negotiations at the local level in the joint labor-management committees and played upon the fears of temporizing labor leaders that a long fight and a split would strengthen the influence of the left wing in the Kyūshū mines. The result was a defeat for the mine workers.[21]

Wages and contracts were also the major demands of the Hokkaidō mine workers that fall, but in contrast to the failure of the enterprise-based unions in Kyūshū, Zentan (Zen Nihon Tankō Rōdō Kumiai, the All-Japan Federation of Coal Miners' Unions) won its Hokkaidō strike in October. The management federation initially insisted on negotiations at each mine individually and refused to bargain with the regional Zentan body, the Hokkaidō Coal Miners' Federation (Hokkaidō Sekitan Kōgyō Renmei), but the fixing of a 10 October strike deadline brought them around. Bargaining began 30 September, followed by government attempts at mediation, but with no positive results, so on the 10th, forty-six of the fifty-three Hokkaidō mines, involving 66,000 of the more than 71,000 mine workers, went on strike. As in Kyūshū and in other disputes at the time, the women's and youth action groups played a major part.[22]

It is significant that the Hokkaidō mine workers, who had carried out some of the most radical and successful production control struggles after the war, adopted the strike as their weapon for the October of-

fensive. In part they were following Sanbetsu's lead, but the real reason was that production control *as a dispute tactic* was less effective
under the changed economic and political situation after Yoshida came
to power with SCAP's support.[23] Winning concessions from the operators, who had come under great pressure from all sides to produce,
was now more likely by shutting the mines down than by taking them
over and continuing operations.

In this judgment the Coal Miners' Federation proved correct. The
shutdown in the Hokkaidō mines was felt almost immediately in such
critical areas as the iron and steel industry, and soon became a major
political and economic problem for the Yoshida cabinet. The management federation contributed to the politicization of the dispute by accusing Zentan of trying to destroy the wage-price system put into effect under the Shidehara cabinet by demanding baseless wage increases,
thereby endangering the whole effort for a revival of production. The
Yoshida cabinet charged the strikers with illegal political ends and
threatened to institute national control and issue a production order.
Fears of a wider shutdown and other unpleasant consequences brought
about another effort at mediation, and the management settled on 15
October, signing a full contract with Zentan on 11 December. The
management and the government achieved little beyond union acceptance of the concept of an "efficiency wage," a goal proclaimed during the strike by Zen Keinosuke, the head of the Economic Stabilization Board.[24]

The significance of the coal miners' strike in Hokkaidō was twofold;
it broke the wage framework the government was trying to fasten on
the labor movement nationally, and it demonstrated conclusively the
power of a national federation of unions to gain victories that enterprise unions could not achieve.

The October offensive ended on 30 November with the provisional
settlement of the long struggle by Densan (Zen Nihon Denki Sangyō
Rōdō Kumiai Kyōgikai, 100,000 members), the national federation of
the electric power workers' unions. In early October, Densan had presented its demands to the government, the private companies in the
industry having been put under state control during the war. Its main
demands were for a minimum wage system keyed to the cost of living,
a reform of the retirement-pension system, and abolition of bureaucratic control over the industry. Densan wanted the private companies
to be centralized into one public enterprise and the industry to be
democratized through establishment of organs for popular control over
policy and for worker participation in management. These demands

had been thoroughly discussed among the membership, as were all major issues in the dispute.[25]

The Yoshida government tried by every means at its disposal to defeat Densan, including the sudden promulgation of the Labor Relations Adjustment Law on 13 October, breaking a government commitment to delay enactment until passage of the companion Labor Standards Law. The reason for the government's hasty action was that the law provided for a thirty-day cooling-off period in disputes in public utilities when put to the Labor Relations Committee for mediation. The Committee's mediation under Chairman Suehiro strongly favored the Densan position, but the authorities rejected it out of hand in November on the usual grounds that the wage increases endangered the revival of Japan's economy. Next, the Home Minister threatened criminal prosecution for any interference with the operations of the power industry. Densan stood firm throughout—secure in having both internal solidarity and strong public support—and used the weapon of selective and temporary suspension of power service to industry with great effectiveness, always being careful not to run afoul of SCAP. Finally Densan scheduled a massive power shutdown for 2 December and the Yoshida cabinet, its back to the wall, gave in and settled.[26]

Densan, like the national federation of railroad unions, was set up as a loose council of enterprise unions based on the various plants around the country. Yet none of the national unions organized after the war approached the solidarity that distinguished Densan. The council structure of Densan was, in effect, a transitional form bridging the gap between the enterprise-based unions that power workers had formed just after the war and the industrial union that came into being in May 1947. Densan's evolution shows that enterprise unionism was not inevitable and that industrial unions could be and were established above a lower structure of originally autonomous unions at the enterprise level.[27]

Japanese workers understood full well why the *Yomiuri* strikers and the Kyūshū coal miners had gone down to defeat, and why the railway workers and the Hokkaidō coal miners had won victories over equally powerful opponents. Organization and worker solidarity paid off. Although the October offensive was a nationwide effort and the working class made considerable gains in pay and organization, the benefits were unevenly distributed. Workers in private industry had gained wage raises of about 20 percent, but wages for public and government employees were now at the very low level of 45–60 percent of those for private industry employees. The struggle of public and government employees was next—a winter offensive that would come to a climax in a powerful movement to topple the Yoshida cabinet by the widest general strike in the history of Japan.[28]

Chairman Suehiro of the Central Labor Relations Committee, a man intimately involved with the labor policy of the Yoshida cabinet of 1946, later succinctly summed up the significance of the labor offensive:

> Thus, the labor offensive staged beginning in August generally attained a considerable success. What is to be pointed out was [sic] the fact that the economic rehabilitation program carelessly drafted by the Government mainly for the interests of capital experienced a setback in the face of labor's opposition. As a result of the opposition from the Seamen's Union and the Government Railway Workers' Union, the Government's plan to carry out industrial adjustment by discharging a large number of workers completely failed. The Densan workers' offensive made it impossible for the Government to maintain its low-wage policy.
>
> In a sense, the labor offensive at this time was largely responsible for the delay in the economic rebuilding of post-war Japan. The Government virtually had no unemployment relief measures, to say nothing of unemployment insurance. In other words, the Government attempted to carry out the industrial adjustment merely from the standpoint of protecting capital. It was only natural that such an attempt should have failed to win the support of the working class.[29]

Staving Off a March Crisis

A Reluctant Government Conversion to Economic Planning

Ishibashi's financial program had prevented a financial panic in summer 1946, a considerable achievement given SCAP's demand for action on cancellation of wartime indemnities and the imposition of a stiff capital levy. But that was its only success. The government's financial and labor policies did not come up to expectations. Far from being a first step toward a general economic recovery by providing funds for increasing the output of producer goods, red-ink finance of big business merely increased the flow of essential materials and capital into the flourishing—and parasitic—black market in consumer goods. Instead of stabilizing prices and wages, Ishibashi's program brought about a second burst of inflation. Instead of creating a cheap and tractable labor force, the attempt to peg wages and make dismissals goaded workers to organize and to take action in strikes led by powerful national union federations. The economic policies of the Yoshida cabinet were incapable of getting production moving again, above all because they encouraged profit-taking in speculation and black market operations, and discouraged the risky but crucial business of making massive, long-term investments in basic industry.[30]

According to official figures, Japan's economic performance was dismal. Output of producer goods rose from 26.7 percent of the 1935–37 average in May when the Yoshida cabinet came to office to a high of 31.1 percent in October, a mere 4.4 percent increase. In contrast, production of consumer goods had risen from 14 percent to a high of 48.9 percent for September.[31]

In September, note issue by the Bank of Japan exceeded 64 billion yen, surpassing the previous high of 61.8 billion reached on the eve of the Shidehara currency revaluation in February. By December, note issue was approaching 100 billion yen, while the official figures for output of both producer and consumer goods had fallen back to approximately their May levels, and would fall yet more.[32]

More ominous was the fact that as a percentage of the 1935–37 average steel industry production was stagnating at about 7 percent and output in coal mining had stalled at a little over 50 percent. Since 70–80 percent of iron and steel consumed as raw materials for production from October 1945 through September 1946 had come from private stockpiles or the black market, and since exhaustion of remaining stocks seemed likely in the first half of 1947, a grim prospect of economic collapse began to emerge.[33]

Fear of economic collapse in the spring of 1947, a "March Crisis," spread in government ranks in late October and compelled the Yoshida cabinet to begin a painful reevaluation of its conventional conservative economic wisdom of dismantling controls, giving financial handouts to big business, and extending a free hand to private enterprise. With their financial and labor policies in ruins by the end of October, big-business and government leaders had to reckon with three imperatives if they were not to lose control of the situation entirely.[34] First, they had to avert the looming economic collapse. Second, they had to find an alternative to basing industrial revival on cheap, "free" labor. Third, they had to mobilize the now thoroughly alienated workers behind whatever alternative plan they made.

These goals, which were part of the Priority Production Plan (Keisha Seisan Hōshiki) advocated by Arisawa Hiromi and the Council for Economic Reconstruction (Keizai Fukkō Kaigi) supported by Dōyūkai, would be adopted as government policy in the wake of the October offensive. However, the Yoshida cabinet had to be converted first. SCAP had previously forced the government's hand in regard to its handling of the economy, a prime example being the emergency economic measures grudgingly enacted by the Shidehara cabinet. Ad hoc and sporadic controls, however, forced upon the government by SCAP and economic circumstances, were not at all equivalent to a policy of comprehensive and coordinated controls adopted as the heart of centralized economic planning for recovery.[35]

In the absence of any effort by either Shidehara or Yoshida to erect effective economic controls, it took strong SCAP pressure to push through the setting up of the Economic Stabilization Board (Keizai Antei Honbu)—which was finally organized in August 1946 after months of delay—and the enactment on 1 October of the Temporary Supply and Demand Adjustment Act. This act in effect replaced the National General Mobilization Act and provided the legal basis for the "public corporations" which soon assumed control over allocation of essential goods and services, becoming the peacetime counterparts of the control associations of the war years. Since SCAP had intended the Japanese government to establish the Economic Stabilization Board as the key government agency in full control of economic planning, it was given responsibility for the operation of the new control machinery.[36]

This role for the Economic Stabilization Board had been clear from the outset. On 31 May, Captain W. Soren Egekvist, chief of the Price Control and Rationing Division, Economic and Scientific Section, gave a press interview at which he explained SCAP's assessment of the powers and purposes of the newly established board. Egekvist said that the crisis of the economy demanded sound economic planning. Since the Economic Stabilization Board was set up for this purpose, it had binding power over the economic activities of every ministry equivalent to those held by the cabinet. The board was only to have the short term of life of one year, because such a powerful organ posed a threat to democratic political institutions.[37]

Whatever SCAP might have intended for the Economic Stabilization Board, there is no indication that the Yoshida cabinet had any intention of engaging in comprehensive economic planning until late October or early November, about the time that talk of a "March crisis" could be heard on all sides.[38] By then the government must have been grateful for SCAP's persistence in erecting a framework for planning.

The Yoshida cabinet's reluctance to initiate comprehensive economic planning was still evident in its announcement on 1 November of its plan for supply and demand of commodities for the third quarter of fiscal 1946 (October–December). This announcement was no less than an official notification that the stocks remaining in government hands were virtually exhausted and that shortages of critical materials like steel threatened the nation's economic and social stability. The plan placed highest priority on increasing production of coal and chemical fertilizers together with securing minimum requirements for railroads, communications, and production of export goods, meaning textiles.[39] The commitment to controls on the supply of essential commodities and their planned allocation on a priority basis was a reversal of the cabinet's previous policy.[40] Yet the stress upon increasing production of food, coal, and export commodities showed a reluctance to abandon the idea of a revival of heavy industry fueled by cheap labor and textile exports.[41]

The second step in the Yoshida cabinet's conversion to comprehensive planning came in early December when the Commerce Minister announced in the Diet that SCAP was approving the government's request for the import of significant quantities of petroleum, anthracite, and coking coal. The imports were to be allocated to the iron and steel industry and to coal mining in order to overcome the stagnation in coal production, which (it was hoped) would be stepped up to 30 million tons in 1947.[42] With the singling out of the iron and steel industry and coal mining as the main priorities in the allocation of raw materials, the stage was now set for the cabinet's formal adoption on 24 December of the epoch-making Priority Production Plan formulated by Professor Arisawa Hiromi.

The Priority Production Plan was an exceedingly simple, not to say simpleminded, approach to economic recovery that proposed diverting all possible resources into expansion of coal production, the increased output to be allocated to the iron and steel industry. The increased output of iron and steel would be allocated to coal mining, thereby providing yet greater production of coal for allocation back to iron and steel. This would be kept up until the desired levels of production were reached and allocations could be made to other industries. Arisawa recognized that this was a circular approach, but argued that the two industries were both short of raw materials and must recover mutually if there was to be a general economic revival before all remaining stockpiles ran out.[43] The new policy was embodied in the government plan for supply and demand of commodities for the fourth quarter of fiscal 1946, January through March 1947. The plan received cabinet approval on 24 December and went into effect immediately.[44]

Arisawa based his argument upon the actual situation in the mines, where the deterioration of surface and underground equipment during the war had been overcome by the usual expedient of employing more manual labor. The resultant lowering of productivity was compounded by shortages that still obtained in late 1946 of timber, explosives, cement, cast-iron pipe, wire rope, and above all, rolled steel materials. Accordingly, Arisawa argued, there was no way that a further intensification of labor and a longer work day could produce a great increase in output, unless enough materials were supplied to the mines to permit, at the same time, an elongation and an increased rate of advance of the coal face (the exposed surface of the coal veins being mined).[45] The upgrading of mining facilities and labor conditions, Arisawa made clear, implied the transformation of the mine work force from low-paid and exploited manual workers into highly efficient and much better-paid skilled mine workers.[46]

By the same reasoning, labor conditions in the iron and steel industry would need to be improved, followed by improved conditions in other industrial sectors, for this was a policy that could not be implemented selectively without arousing wide-scale labor protests. In the guise of the Priority Production Plan, Arisawa was arguing the case he and other academics had made ten months earlier for creating an efficient, well-paid and highly motivated work force as one of the mainstays of economic reconstruction. To him, it was clear that the Allied policy of economic and political democratization had fundamentally altered the terms for capitalism in Japan. Like it or not, labor was now a force to be reckoned with, and its cooperation would have to be sought.[47]

Worker cooperation would not be forthcoming as a matter of course. It would require a positive effort by big-business and government leaders, an effort that not all were prepared to make. The Yoshida cabinet adopted the Priority Production Plan in late December, but Yoshida showed no readiness to seek accommodation with organized labor as a result. On the contrary, in December and January he seemed to be deliberately antagonizing the labor movement, intending to provoke another SCAP clampdown on what he was trying to portray as the excesses of communist leaders in the militant unions affiliated with Sanbetsu. On the other hand, the more progressive business leaders associated with Dōyūkai were working hard to find grounds for accommodation with the labor movement. Their attempt would soon be crowned with success in the establishment of the Council for Economic Reconstruction.

Mobilizing the Workers for a Planned Capitalist Reconstruction

As the second winter of occupation came on with no industrial revival in sight—a winter promising even greater privation than the one before—two distinct movements appeared within organized labor for tackling the problem of reconstruction. Sōdōmei approached economic revival as a problem transcending class interests. Japan's need was so great and so pervasive that the only question before the working class was how to get production going again, regardless of method. Labor's duty was to cooperate with the existing business leaders and put off questions of socialism to the morrow.[48] Sanbetsu proposed instead an industrial revival by the workers themselves and popular control of industry in a manner reminiscent of the production control movement of the preceding spring. Its program called for a thoroughgoing democratization of management alongside a movement to establish a popular-based democratic government. Socialization could not be put off to the morrow, since it was the only possible means for overcoming capitalist footdragging and getting production going again.[49]

Big-business and government leaders were also divided into two camps on the question, but all had become more intent upon reviving the economy for fear of a March crisis in 1947 that might see social upheaval in the wake of the descent of Japan's shattered economy into chaos. Compelled to shelve their differences, they backed the Priority Production Plan as an emergency measure to stimulate output in the vital producer goods sector of the economy.

The better wages, working conditions, and benefits envisaged in the plan might well have enlisted the cooperation of coal miners and steel workers in achieving great increases in output. But the idea of creating a core labor force of well-paid, skilled, and highly productive workers as the driving force behind capitalist recovery was not realizable all at once throughout the producer goods sector, not to speak of other areas of the economy. To the extent that scarce resources were diverted to coal and iron and steel, other industries would suffer even more severe shortages of both materials and capital, which would be felt by workers in the form of dismissals and low wages.

Taking heed of the various plans for industrial revival then being advanced in the labor movement, Dōyūkai and some of the other business associations began to move in October to forge a national movement for reconstruction built upon an alliance of capital and organized labor. This was to bear fruit in the Council for Economic Reconstruction. The link between the Council for Economic Reconstruction and the Priority Production Plan would be close. Some measure of worker cooperation was indispensable if the plan was not to be disrupted by a continuation of the strike wave of fall. Plans were useless, no matter how well conceived, if they further aroused the hostility of the labor movement. The council looked to be the answer. Its goal was the ideological mobilization of the working class behind a capitalist reconstruction and the tapping of the long-standing desire of the working class to increase output that had had its most radical expression in production control.

Labor Movement Plans for Industrial Revival

As early as May, Sōdōmei had proclaimed a movement for industrial reconstruction as a central goal for the federation. The inspiration had come from Takano Minoru, a leading left-wing activist within the federation. Takano approached the task of reconstruction as one transcending narrow class interests, because the goals of securing basic material necessities and furthering the country's democratization were held in common by most Japanese. Given the divisions within big business and government and the inaction of industrialists, Takano believed the most important duty for the labor movement was to take responsibility for the revival of industry. This was to be done through the cooperation of workers, technicans, and progressive managers— in brief, through labor's participation in management.[50] Takano no doubt expected a union-led revival of industry to contribute greatly toward the ultimate goal of socialism in Japan by enabling the working class to take the initiative decisively in its contest with capital.

Whatever Takano's expectations, the movement for industrial reconstruction took another turn in the hands of the right-wing socialists leading Sōdōmei. Sōdōmei's program for the movement as adopted in late May called for a centralized organization to be built upon the joint labor-management councils already in existence in many industries. At the top was to be a national council made up of representatives of Sōdōmei, the business associations, government officials, and also individual experts. A hierarchy of similarly constituted councils was to provide the link down to the enterprise.[51]

Sōdōmei's choice of the joint labor-management council as the foundation for its reconstruction movement meant that the leaders of the federation had rejected the goal of rank-and-file participation in management that lay at the heart of Takano's original proposal. Rather, the structure they devised was eminently suited to the type of top-down leadership characteristic of Sōdōmei unions. Indeed, Sōdōmei had been using the existing councils in the enterprises they had unionized as an appropriate place for applying the provisions of labor contracts, for taking up workplace issues that needed resolution day by day, and for cooperating in increasing production.[52]

Although the first joint labor-management councils after the war had been set up against the will of business as a result of worker efforts to achieve some degree of workers' control, in practice, as noted above, such councils almost always became organs for consultation that possessed no significant control over company policy. In a strange reversal, by late spring of 1946, many big-business and government leaders saw them as a vehicle for deflecting workers from anti-capitalist actions like production control by conceding token rights of participation in management. Management was soon using the councils as a place for resolving labor grievances before they erupted into full-fledged disputes and—an equally valuable function—for increasing worker productivity by gaining employee support for the enterprise production plan. In short, the councils held out many possibilities to employers for manipulation of the work force.[53]

The Sanbetsu policy of an industrial reconstruction "by the workers themselves" owed much to steps taken in July by Zentan and seven union federations in industries dependent upon coal to set up a council for reviving the coal industry. They proposed to take the mines out of the hands of the bureaucracy and the zaibatsu owners and to put them under the direct control of the coal mine workers, technicians, and other progressive groups. Sanbetsu developed the policy further, and on 7 October held a preparatory conference for the purpose of forming an Industrial Reconstruction Council (Sangyō Fukkō Kaigi) which would undertake the task of industrial recovery.[54]

The Sanbetsu policy included not only a thoroughgoing democratization of management but also the establishment of a people's government. Accordingly, when Sanbetsu issued a plan on 4 December spelling out basic policy for the Industrial Reconstruction Council, this called for the formation of a united front in industry to be composed of workers, peasants, proprietors of medium- and small-scale businesses, intellectuals, and other progressive elements. The working class was to play the leading role in the front, and toward this end the plan contained provisions for workers to organize their own hierarchy of "reconstruction committees" within industry starting from a factory-floor base. Through the system of reconstruction committees they were to participate in formulating a working-class plan for economic revival. Yet, as Sanbetsu laid it out, the real authority to decide upon a final plan and to implement it lay in the very same joint labor-management councils which Sōdōmei had made the foundation of its movement for industrial reconstruction. Furthermore, the Sanbetsu policy statement had defined the joint councils as having equality of representation between labor and capital and as making decisions by majority vote.[55] Such moderate proposals clearly belied the radical rhetoric of Sanbetsu about reconstruction "by the workers themselves." Similarly, the Sanbetsu demands for overthrow of the reactionary Yoshida cabinet and for the establishment of a people's government were very equivocal.[56]

The JCP was making similar demands, but JCP policy was still solidly grounded on the program adopted at the Fifth Congress in February 1946 when the party had renounced the goal of immediate social revolution and endorsed a bourgeois-democratic revolution by peaceful and democratic methods.[57] The Sanbetsu and JCP commitment to the parliamentary road to socialism would be tested twice in the near future: once over Sanbetsu participation in the Council for Economic Reconstruction and again during the general strike movement.

The Council for Economic Reconstruction

In the middle of November Sōdōmei and Dōyūkai began working together to hammer out a joint plan for mobilizing the working class behind economic revival that would appeal to the broadest possible spectrum among both business and labor. A series of intensive discussions which also involved Nissankyō (Nihon Sangyō Kyōgikai, Japan Industry Council) and the neutralist union federation Nichirō Kaigi concluded in a Sōdōmei-Dōyūkai agreement to join hands in pursuit of national reconstruction.[58] They issued their basic statement of policy on 6 December.

This remarkable document began by stating that "democratic managers and the working class, burning with zeal for national salvation, are conscious of their mission to take charge in economic reconstruction,"[59] and would cooperate toward that end by developing one great national movement. How that would be done was explained in the six sections that followed, of which the most important were sections 3 and 4.

Section 3 stipulated that management was to respect labor's basic rights to organize, bargain collectively, and strike; the workers were to recognize management's rights over the enterprise. It singled out the joint labor-management council as the essential organ for cooperation in reaching the primary goal of increasing production in the enterprise, and spelled out in some detail rules for the councils' operations.[60]

The councils were to "deliberate upon and decide" matters concerning working conditions, that is, hours of work, wage-payment systems, conditions of employment, and the like. Personnel problems affecting union members would be decided on the basis of "consultation" in the councils, and proposals regarding the production plan, output standards, work processes, rationalization measures, increases of efficiency, and wages would be "explained" in the council and decided "with due respect for the opinions of the union." Concerning company finances, these too would be "explained" to the council and thrown open to it as necessary. Minor concessions indeed, if they can be called concessions at all, particularly in the light of the concluding article in the same section. Here the union was enjoined "voluntarily to discipline union members" and to enact regulations enabling it to assume its "responsibility for worker discipline," in exchange for a vague management commitment to the betterment of the workers' welfare.[61]

Section 4 addressed itself to the relationship between increased productivity and the creation of a well-paid and highly motivated work force. A rational wage system linked to the cost of living but allowing for incentive payments for increased productivity was held up as the method to avoid unnecessary disputes between capital and labor. The direction labor policy must take for the construction of a new Japan was a system based on "high wages" and "high efficiency."[62]

After brief acknowledgement of the role of education in industrial democracy, the policy statement closed with a proposal for management and labor to mount a "movement for breaking through the production crisis" using the joint labor-management council as its basic organizational unit. The intent was to use mass communications in a patriotic campaign to mobilize the people behind the goals of the Priority Production Plan.[63] Given its aims, it is no surprise that the Council for Economic Reconstruction bore a certain resemblance to the corporatism of the wartime labor front, Sanpō. For example, the focus on joint organization in the enterprise, the stress on the mutuality of interests between capital and labor, the appeals to a national consensus transcending local and class interests, and the presumption of worker readiness to repay managerial paternalism with loyalty and hard work all resounded with the Sanpō philosophy of labor-capital collaboration. These same ideas were later to become traits of the enterprise union, itself a corporate approach to labor relations.

Sōdōmei and Dōyūkai might have proclaimed the inauguration of a great national movement for economic reconstruction, but because it lacked full support from either Nissankyō or Sanbetsu, it was as yet nothing of the kind. Understanding full well that the movement's usefulness for business would be minimal without Sanbetsu, since it was by far the largest and strongest of the national labor federations, Nissankyō had made Sanbetsu's participation the condition for its own joining. Discussions began with Sanbetsu, and on 23 December, Nissankyō, Sanbetsu, and Dōyūkai agreed to four articles that Sanbetsu had insisted on as conditions for its participation, the gist of which was that the movement was not a Sanpō-like truce between capital and labor, that cooperation between capital and labor was to be on a level of equality, and that there was to be nothing in it that denied to the workers their right to strike.[64] Nissankyō resolved formally to participate the next day, and Sanbetsu followed on the 27th.[65]

Sanbetsu's misgivings about the Council for Economic Reconstruction were more than borne out subsequently. The council produced no positive results, even on the admission of its Dōyūkai sponsor.[66] Takano Minoru, the active spirit behind the whole movement, concluded later that in this case he and the others on the left wing of Sōdōmei, far from contributing to the advance of the labor movement, "fell into the quagmire of labor-capital collaboration."[67]

Tokuda Kyūichi of the JCP was one of those who at the time had noted this tendency toward labor-capital collaboration in the movement.[68] Yet, he argued, due to working-class support for the reconstruction movement, Sanbetsu's refusal to participate might look like a sectarian move, running the risk of alienating the federation from the masses.[69] Sanbetsu evaded facing the contradiction of a militant labor organization backing an avowedly collaborationist movement by the weak rationalization that it regarded the council as a forum for exposing the schemes of the government, bureaucrats, and big business, and that participation was therefore useful for preparing the masses for the political struggle for a people's government.[70]

Neither of these reasons is particularly convincing. Economic reconstruction was first on everyone's list of priorities, but there is no evidence that workers were solidly united behind the council. Rather, the labor movement was exhibiting another great outburst of rank-and-file militance in the joint struggle of government employees against the Yoshida cabinet. Indeed, the very effort to create a reconstruction movement from the top strongly suggests that workers had other ideas about how to achieve industrial revival. As for using the council for propaganda purposes, Sanbetsu was the one that ended up being used, not the other way around. The best explanation for Sanbetsu's participation in the movement is that the radical demand for economic reconstruction by the workers themselves was mostly rhetoric, and that Sanbetsu in practice operated on conventional trade union principles. This is strongly supported by the decision to use the joint labor-management councils as the primary building blocks for the reconstruction movement.

Such a gap between union rhetoric and practice is neither exceptional nor surprising; it is a common reality of trade unionism. Leaders of left-wing unions must also produce economic benefits for their members and find enough common ground for cooperation with capitalist employers to allow the negotiation of contracts regularizing and protecting those benefits. This means that a "revolutionary union" is a contradiction in terms, despite the fact that unions engage in political action from time to time in order to achieve their demands.

Sanbetsu could not escape the limitations inherent in trade unionism. Once the decision had been made to reject workers' control and to operate within the framework of capitalism, and once concessions had been extracted from big business, pressures built up for the routinization of labor relations. Recognition by the Council for Economic Reconstruction of labor's right to have adequate pay and conditions and to organize in pursuit of these interests was just such a concession in that it amounted to a big-business retreat from the "free labor" policies of the old guard. Because the conditions requiring business recognition of labor's rights turned out to be inadequate and because the sincerity of conservative business and government leaders turned out to be lacking, the Sanbetsu decision to participate might well have been an error of judgement. Nevertheless, the decision at the time was entirely consistent with Sanbetsu's character as a federation of trade unions. In the end, the radicalism of the left-wing leaders in the federation gave way—as it had to—before the need to regularize the unions' place within the forthcoming capitalist reconstruction.

A similar need to make labor relations stable and manageable had compelled Nissankyō and other employer organizations to abandon their insistence on returning to the past for their model for reconstruction. The futility of battling with powerful unions had been convincingly demonstrated in the October offensive.

To sum up, the formation of the Council for Economic Reconstruction signaled that a new stage had arrived in the struggle between capital and labor in postwar Japan. From left to right, the national leaders of labor and big business were now in tentative agreement that high efficiency and high wages would be the two pillars upon which revival of production in modern industry would be built.

General Strike

In January 1946 big business and the working class in factories and offices had been locked in struggle over whether Japan was to have a worker-led socialist reconstruction. In January 1947 left-wing labor unions were mounting a massive general strike which proclaimed as its major goal the overthrow of the Yoshida cabinet and the installation of a people's government. Yet in the preceding twelve months the conflict over Japan's reconstruction had greatly moderated; first narrowing to the question of what kind of capitalist revival there was to be—a conservative or a progressive one—and then resolving with a tentative consensus in favor of the latter. The contradiction between the political aims of the general strike movement and the emergence of a consensus on a liberal capitalist reconstruction is apparent.

The vehemence of the political struggle of January 1947 had much more to do with the die-hard conservatism of the Yoshida cabinet than with a resurgence of revolutionary radicalism. Yoshida might have agreed to economic planning in hopes of breaking through the economic stagnation and staving off a March crisis, but he was not prepared to go very far with concessions to labor, especially to government and public workers. He rejected the progressives' view that the working class had a responsible role in recovery and deserved to be well rewarded for its willing cooperation. Yoshida insisted that the workers' main duty was to work hard, be content with their lot, and loyally obey their employers who had the responsibility of effecting recovery. He stigmatized the union leaders on the left as cynical and self-serving men who would fan class hatred and prevent labor from fulfilling its patriotic duty of increasing output.[71] Such had been the content of his Declaration on Social Order of 13 June, and such was his New Year's message for 1947, in which he castigated "rebellious elements" in the labor movement.

Yoshida's intransigence on labor brought him face to face with the millions of government workers in Japan whose wages were among the lowest in the country by the end of 1946. These workers embarked on a campaign in December, a winter offensive designed to enable them to catch up with the gains made in private industry during the October offensive. The task before the government workers was to force government recognition of their right to independent labor organizations of their own and to obtain wages in the public sector comparable to those in private industry. The Yoshida cabinet resisted those ends, and the struggle inevitably became politicized. Although the overthrow of the Yoshida cabinet was a political goal, it was not a revolutionary one. What the left-wing leaders of the general strike had uppermost in their minds was no more than the installation of a left-of-center coalition cabinet within the existing framework of parliamentary democracy.

A Winter Offensive for Government Workers

The main strength behind the general strike movement came from the unions of government workers whose members had not gained much during the October offensive. Government workers not only had low wages, averaging 50 percent of the wages of their private industry counterparts, they had other serious grievances against their common employer, the government, which provided a firm foundation for the joint struggle that would be waged against the Yoshida cabinet in December 1946 and January 1947.[72]

The October offensive had adopted the slogan of overthrowing the reactionary Yoshida cabinet, but it had remained a slogan despite labor's antipathy toward Yoshida. Sōdōmei had resisted adopting this slogan at the time, but as the offensive was winding down in early

November the federation issued a statement urging the Yoshida cabinet to make way for a government more representative of labor. Sanbetsu for its part announced shortly thereafter a political offensive against the Yoshida cabinet and offered unconditional merger to Sōdōmei in the interest of creating a united labor movement.[73] These steps proved to be the harbinger of closer cooperation between the two federations in the months ahead, and in this sense they mark the earliest beginnings of the general strike that in January would unite the entire labor movement behind the objective of toppling the Yoshida cabinet.

The first organizational step toward the consolidation of a winter offensive was taken on 26 November when a group of government unions formed Kyōtō (Zen Kankōchō Kyōdō Tōsō Iinkai, Joint Struggle Committee of Public Employees' Unions). The pillars of Kyōtō throughout the coming struggle were the three most important of these unions, those of the national railway workers, communications workers, and teachers, which had a combined membership of 1.25 million, approximately half of Kyōtō's total membership of 2.6 million.[74] Ii Yashirō, vice-chairman of the railway workers' union, was chosen chairman.

On 3 December Kyōtō presented a package of ten joint demands to the government. Their primary economic goal was to defeat the government's attempt to keep wages of government workers at a low level and to peg wages generally. Their foremost demands, therefore, were for large wage increases, establishment of a minimum wage system, payment of all wages and allowances in cash, prevention of dismissals, and conclusion of collective contracts. Despite the stress on economic benefits, much of the fire behind the joint struggle sprang from the government workers' desire to democratize the authoritarian bureaucracy pervasive in public enterprises and offices. The heart of the system of bureaucratic control in the workplace was the traditional status system. Its rigidities and inequities were galling socially and unfair economically, and lay behind the general demand presented by Kyōtō for abolition of discriminatory treatment.[75]

While Kyōtō was opening the economic struggle against the government, the left wings of the JSP and Sanbetsu were busy with the task of forging a political united front against the Yoshida cabinet. Katō Kanjū and other sympathetic left-wing socialists like Takano Minoru organized a meeting on 29 November under the sponsorship of the trade union department of the JSP at which Sōdōmei, Sanbetsu, Nichirō Kaigi, and a number of independent national unions formed the National Labor Union Conference (Zenkoku Rōsō Kondankai). This was to be the political arm of the government workers' offensive, and advanced three central objectives: securing the workers' right to a minimum livelihood, overthrowing the Yoshida cabinet, and forming a democratic government centered upon the JSP.[76]

The government rejected the Kyōtō demands on 10 December in a point-by-point reply couched in the arrogant tone which Yoshida habitually used in reference to organized labor. Yoshida, far from showing an inclination to compromise, had engineered the promulgation on 9 December of Imperial Ordinance No. 591, which denied pay to government employees while out on strike.[77] He also prohibited participation of government employees in the mass political demonstrations against the government being organized by the National Labor Union Conference for 7 December.

The Union Conference planned to advance the political struggle by a two-pronged offensive staged simultaneously within and outside the Diet. That is, the JSP would lead the attack in the Diet and present on 17 December a resolution calling upon the government to recognize the aspirations of working people and make way for a new regime. The Union Conference hoped to exert maximum pressure upon the government by scheduling anti-Yoshida political demonstrations throughout Japan on the same day. The JSP resolution was voted down, as expected, but the demonstrations were massive, with a turnout of millions and with 500,000 gathering in Tokyo alone. SCAP described the Tokyo demonstration as the biggest since surrender.[78]

The original initiative for the political movement had been taken by the left wing of the JSP, but Sanbetsu and the JCP quickly assumed the lead in the Union Conference, just as they did in Kyōtō, eclipsing both Sōdōmei and the JSP. (The latter still found it expedient to cooperate since the conference was calling for a government to be led by the Socialist party.) This unusual degree of cooperation was possible because Sanbetsu and the JCP had adopted the middle-of-the-road political program of the left-wing socialists which Takano characterized as appealing for the support—and the vote—of the "broad middle classes."[79] The speech by Tokuda for the JCP before the mass meeting on 17 December endorsing the objectives of the Union Conference clearly indicated this.[80]

This was a kind of negative unity reflecting the need for combined action against a common opponent. The goal of a government centered on the Socialist party was sufficiently vague and flexible to admit of various possibilities. The socialist left wing hoped to organize a government with the backing of the JCP, while the right wing hoped to come to power through coalition with any willing conservative factions, Yoshida's included. These deep disagreements surfaced later when the winter offensive began to reach its critical stage. It was, of course, the very success of Kyōtō and the Union Conference in undermining Yoshida's political credibility that encouraged the maneuvering of early January when all sides were bargaining over allotment of seats in a successor cabinet.

The demonstrations on 17 December shook Yoshida, for the Union Conference had brought together with the common purpose of his overthrow the two left-wing parties, all three of the national labor federations, and the major independent unions as well as the farmers' union and many urban groups. Nonetheless, the cabinet determined to stick it out, insisting that it would not be dictated to by non-parliamentary agitation or pressure.[81]

As if to add to Yoshida's woes by underscoring the legitimacy of labor's political activities, the Far Eastern Commission saw fit to announce on the next day the sixteen principles for Japanese labor unions it had approved on 6 December. These principles spelled out a political role for labor:

6. Trade unions should be allowed to take part in political activities and to support political parties.
7. Encouragement should be given to organized participation by trade unions and their officials in the democratization process in Japan and in measures taken to achieve the objectives of the occupation, such as the elimination of militaristic and monopolistic practices.[82]

The issuance of this announcement encouraged the leaders of the winter offensive, but also led them to take much too lightly the possibility of SCAP intervention.[83]

Toward February

December ended with two weeks of relative calm. The government made a few minor economic concessions to the government workers, but that did not mean that Yoshida had moderated his anti-labor stance. In his New Year's speech to the nation he made that clear by accusing the leaders of the government workers of being a subversive minority, in words echoing those used by the authorities and the right wing in previous decades.[84] Yoshida's speech created more enemies than ever in the labor movement, and was followed by heightened activity in the direction of a nationwide general strike.

The first evidence of this trend came out of the Second National Consultative Conference of the JCP which began on 6 January. On the 8th it issued a declaration of support for the demands of Kyōtō and for the tactic being discussed within Kyōtō of securing their demands through a general strike that would bring about a change of government. The JCP declared it would marshall its strength behind a general strike aimed at establishing a democratic people's government, by which it meant that it would support a strike to demand the formation of a socialist-led coalition cabinet and new elections, not one dedicated to bringing on a revolutionary seizure of power. The conference also expressed its confidence that SCAP would not suppress a political strike of this nature and criticized the trend in the labor movement toward direct action and a frontal attack upon the rights of the capitalist owners of the means of production.[85]

In short, the JCP was once again rejecting production control and affirming its commitment to the parliamentary road to socialism, secure in its belief that such a policy was within the limits of SCAP tolerance. It believed this strongly enough to propose specific names for a projected JSP-JCP coalition cabinet. It was to have a socialist premier, with Tokuda as Home Minister and Nosaka as Foreign Minister.[86]

The idea of a general strike had been in the air for some time, having first been proposed by the railway workers' union in late November at the Union Conference as a last recourse in the government workers' struggle. This idea had been favorably received. The government had shown little inclination thereafter to compromise and settle the dispute, so Kyōtō had organized a conference for 11 January to prepare for a strike. Things began to take on a much more definite shape on 9 January when the Kyōtō leadership made the decision to prepare for a nationwide general strike to begin on 1 February. The Kyōtō conference on the 11th resubmitted its demands to the government with minor changes and added new demands for the abrogation of Imperial Ordinance No. 591 and for an apology from Yoshida for his New Year's greeting. They also added the statement that they would resist suppression by the authorities.[87] The threat of a general strike for February was not made, but left hanging, ready to be made should the government reply be unsatisfactory.

The reply on the 15th was unsatisfactory, and the next move was up to Kyōtō and its political arm, the Union Conference. First, on that same day the Union Conference was expanded and reorganized as Zentō (Zenkoku Rōdō Kumiai Kyōdō Tōsō Iinkai, the Joint Struggle Committee of National Labor Unions). This organization had Sanbetsu as its center and was a national labor front combining virtually all unions of both public and private workers. Zentō represented at least 4,000,000 workers, if not the 6,000,000 it claimed. The founding declaration optimistically asserted that these unions would rise up to-gether behind the impending general strike by the unions of govern-ment workers in Kyōtō. Zentō formalized its policy and organization in a document issued five days later which in fact left the constituent unions free to make their own decisions on what actions to take if a general strike erupted.[88] Zentō was less united than it looked, but was still a formidable organization capable of coordinating a nationwide general strike combining unions of both public and private workers.

Next, Kyōtō—now expanded to include several more unions and at the peak of its strength—held a mass meeting in Tokyo on 18 January at which it challenged the Yoshida cabinet by formally setting 1 Feb-ruary as the date on which it would call a general strike if its demands were not accepted by the government. It also stated that if there was an attempt at suppression before that date, the unions would auto-matically call a general strike at once.[89]

As the general strike movement brought increasing pressure to bear upon the government in early January, Yoshida and the right-wing socialists made common cause in trying to put together a three-party coalition cabinet of the Liberal, Progressive, and Socialist parties. They hoped by this stratagem to undermine the unity of the popular move-ment and block the formation of a government in which the left-wing socialists and the JCP would have a major role. It was too late to save the situation by such temporizing, and the several attempts at coali-tion all failed because of the fierce antagonism they aroused from labor and its allies. The cost for the JSP leadership of pushing through and joining a conservative cabinet would have been too high—a secession of the party's left wing and a loss of popular confidence in the integrity of the JSP as the major opposition party.[90]

SCAP Makes Its Move

At this point it dawned on SCAP that Yoshida was not going to act to extricate his government from the difficulty it was in,[91] and prepa-rations began to force a solution to the impasse. The commanding general of the occupying U.S. Eighth Army, Lt. General Robert L. Eichelberger, wrote in his diary on 16 and 23 January that he believed a railroad strike or sabotage of the railways by strikers could "ruin the occupation."[92] Eichelberger so warned MacArthur on 25 January in a strongly worded letter[93] to which MacArthur responded on the 26th through his Chief of Staff, Major General Paul J. Mueller. "Mueller told me in confidence that General MacArthur had told him to tell Eichelberger that following receipt of my letter on the dangers of the railroad strike that 'He doesn't intend to allow that strike to occur.'"[94]

Brigadier General William F. Marquat, chief of Economic and Scientific Division, on 21 January sent a memorandum to General MacArthur on how to deal with the general strike threat. The memo began by recognizing that Kyōtō was proceeding within the letter of the law and was making provisions "to avoid interfering with services required by the Occupation."[95] It noted next that the unions' demands were primarily economic and directly related to the government's inability to control inflation and the black market and to remedy scarcities of consumer goods. Moreover, it continued, the result of the long period in which wages had been below subsistence was serious worker unrest and an unwillingness by even conservative union leaders to postpone resolution of the issue beyond 1 February. Yet the government was simply appealing to SCAP for rescue and not displaying adequate initiative toward effecting a realistic resolution of the problem.[96]

Marquat recommended that the Japanese government be directed to respond effectively and immediately to the basic economic demands put forth by the general strike movement; to carry out a longer range policy to destroy the black market, increase employment, and increase production of basic necessities; to "complete the purge of undesirable persons from political, government and labor circles"; and to "announce plans and commitments for the local and national elections."[97] In conjunction with this, Marquat recommended that SCAP take action to limit the extent of the strike as much as possible by making it clear to both the government and the leaders of the strike movement that "work stoppages in transportation, communications and other services required by the Occupation are considered directly prejudicial to the objectives and needs of the Occupation" and would be prohibited.[98] In sum, Marquat recognized the validity of the major accusations that had long been made by organized labor and the left wing against the Yoshida cabinet and the justice of their current demands. Yet he proposed to emasculate the general strike by a sweeping prohibition of strikes in "transportation, communications and other services," that is, by the very unions that were the mainstay of Kyōtō and Sanbetsu.

The next morning, Marquat called in representatives of the Yoshida government and asked them to implement reforms. Marquat described the government concessions that came out of that meeting in a later memo to MacArthur as ". . . including an average raise of about 50 percent in pay for the government workers, raising of the 500 yen limit on the cash payment of wages to 700 yen, invocation of the long awaited tripartite Wage Investigation Commissions and resumption of negotiations through the good offices of the Central Labor Relations Committee."[99] Minimal concessions indeed, as Marquat well knew before he warned the labor leaders to call off the general strike.[100] The contrast is striking between this and the root-and-branch reforms the earlier memo had urged MacArthur to direct the Yoshida cabinet to carry out.

In the afternoon, Marquat called in Ii Yashirō, Chairman of Kyōtō, the heads of its constituent unions, and Sōdōmei to inform them in strict confidence of the concessions made by the government and to warn them that:

Any action on the part of union personnel, either in the form of a general strike or other coordinated work stoppage which interrupts the continued service of national communication or transportation facilities or which curtails production of commodities necessary to prevent disease, unrest and human suffering, will be considered as endangering the objectives of the Occupation and will be summarily dealt with by the Occupying powers.[101]

Yoshida had won. Marquat's actions of 22 January revealed that SCAP was ready to act harshly against labor militance and the left wing in order to shore up the prestige of a conservative government, but was unprepared to force that government to make adequate concessions to labor's demands. Once again SCAP was allowing its fear of communism to assume precedence over the Allied policy of encouragement of a strong and independent union movement. Sōdōmei responded to the warning in a way that recognized that the tide had turned against the Sanbetsu forces. It sent a letter to MacArthur on 25 January stating that the federation solemnly pledged to abide by Marquat's instructions and would do its best to prevent the general strike from taking place.[102] But the leaders of Kyōtō met and decided to reject the SCAP warning, so notifying SCAP on 26 January. Marquat reported to MacArthur that the responsibility for the decision to go ahead lay with "Communists and 'fellow travellers.'"[103]

Plans were being made in Economic and Scientific Section for actions to be taken should a general strike break out, and the measures under consideration were drastic. First would be a SCAP order to terminate the strike within twenty-four hours, but: "If the strike does not terminate within the 24 hours military police and CIC teams are released under an existing plan to arrest persons responsible for the situation."[104] Secondly, the Japanese government was to be directed as follows:

1. For a period of one year, strikes and work stoppages in public welfare work, and any work the stoppage of which will seriously affect the national economy or seriously endanger the daily life of the general public, as defined in Article 8 of the Labor Relations Adjustment Law are deemed prejudicial to the objectives and needs of the Occupation, and are prohibited.
2. The Imperial Japanese government is directed to take appropriate actions to effect the prohibition.[105]

Such actions included revision of the Labor Relations Adjustment Law to forbid strikes in designated services and to set up machinery for compulsory arbitration in those industries. Furthermore, the government was to be "directed informally to undertake a comprehensive program of exposing to the Japanese workers those who precipitate strikes, contrary to SCAP interests and to Japanese national interests, for their own ulterior purposes."[106] How much of this draft plan was communicated to the Japanese government is unclear, but paragraphs 1 and 2 above apparently were sent on 31 January. At any rate, SCAP's intent was unmistakable.

On 29 January Eichelberger wrote in his diary that it looked as if the "railroad strike" was going through, then bemoaned the encouragement given to unions in Japan by the U.S. as promoting democracy backwards: "After nearly 150 years of democracy in the United States we have not been able to surmount the problem of power without responsibility concentrated in the union heads. . . . There is little doubt in my mind that the Reds are controlling the unions to a large extent and Reds are also infiltrating into our own SCAP offices to some extent."[107] The entry for 30 January noted that at a dinner party given by the Muellers his host had told him that MacArthur had ordered the union heads (through Marquat) not to carry out the general strike. MacArthur had also said, according to Mueller, "If they start anything I am going to have Eichelberger arrest them and that includes those lower down also."[108]

Marquat called in the representatives of the labor unions and the strike organizations on the evening of 30 January to transmit an order from MacArthur to call off the strike at once and to give proof that orders to that effect had been sent to their member unions within six hours, that is, by 2:00 A.M. on the 31st.

If the prohibited strike results, those responsible for the action of the unions in opposition to instructions and all others implicated in inciting or participating in such action will be arrested and charged with direct disobedience of orders of the Supreme Commander. Consequence [sic] can reach proportions of maximum seriousness.

Defiance of the Supreme Commander for the Allied Powers can only provoke action of the most drastic nature against individual and organized labor interests. Responsibility for the consequences rests squarely upon the shoulders of the leaders who either fail to accept or who directly oppose the instructions of the Supreme Commander. Defiance by force obviously will be the height of futility.[109]

Another version of this memo included in the second paragraph quoted above, "If necessary the entire power of the Occupation Forces will be employed to carry out his orders."[110]

Of the thirteen unions whose leaders had been called in by Marquat, eight—including the three central unions in the general strike movement, the railway workers', communications workers', and teachers' unions—reported just before the deadline that they were unable to comply with this order. Later in the day they were summoned to explain this. The reasons given for non-compliance boiled down to the refusal of most of the executive committees of the unions and branches involved to cancel the proposed strike or to admit that the strike was lost without a written directive from SCAP prohibiting it.[111]

General MacArthur publicly issued such a directive the afternoon of 31 January, and the leaders of the eight unions and the chairman of Kyōtō were summoned once again to headquarters to be ordered by Marquat to dictate a message on the spot for immediate transmission to their organizations calling off the strike. They were in effect under informal arrest until a message of cancellation was sent.[112] All the unions complied, and Chairman Ii of Kyōtō made a radio broadcast at 8:00 P.M. calling off the general strike. Ii concluded with the words of Lenin, calling for one step backward and two steps forward, and exhorting the workers and peasants to organize.[113]

The Yoshida cabinet took immediate advantage of MacArthur's action. The Soviet delegate to the Allied Council stated in a letter to MacArthur on 20 February that the Home Minister on 2 February had made a statement to the effect that any strikes called in the wake of the banned general strike would also be prohibited. The letter also stated that the next day the Ministry "clarified" MacArthur's order by construing it to mean that all future strikes would be prohibited, even strikes by individual labor unions. The Soviet delegate urged that in view of this SCAP should take steps to protect the rights of Japanese labor unions.[114] Though SCAP prepared a reply denying the validity of the Soviet allegations,[115] checking by Labor Division revealed that the government had made the statements substantially as reported in the Soviet letter.[116] The upshot of the matter was that SCAP reaffirmed the rights of labor, but nonetheless the strike wave that had been gathering momentum for six months was stopped dead in its tracks.

The general strike movement contained the possibility of turning into a general crisis for capitalism in Japan, but not for the reason commonly cited of a left-wing government coming to power. There have been numerous examples of socialist or labor governments that have failed to effect a socialist transformation of their countries under much more advantageous circumstances than existed in occupied Japan. It was entirely unlikely that any socialist-led coalition cabinet brought to power by the general strike movement, regardless of JCP participation, would have been much more successful at this task than the Katayama cabinet subsequently was during its brief life. The danger to a capitalist reconstruction in Japan would not, therefore, have come from a "democratic people's government," of the type envisaged. If it had materialized at all, its main impetus was likely to have been the spontaneous anti-capitalist radicalism just beginning to be visible among the working class, particularly the unionized workers participating in the general strike movement.

The impulse was far weaker and less widespread in January 1947 than it had been nine months earlier, and the links with farmers' organizations and city groups of spring 1946 had no real counterpart in the winter of 1947. For one thing, the food needed to feed the Japanese people was now available. For another, the land reform was in process and had taken much of the initiative from the radical farmers' organizations.

Even so, the Japanese government—unpopular and, having been disarmed by SCAP, still very weak in terms of its police power—could not have withstood on its own a general strike of anywhere near the magnitude of the one being planned for February 1. SCAP had realized as much and was now playing the role of policeman vis-à-vis the workers' movement. This was not an unwelcome role, since the pro-labor sentiment that had prevailed during the early months had given way rapidly during the tenure of the Yoshida cabinet to an increasingly overt anti-communism. Labor Division had been one of the last holdouts, but its sympathy no longer counted for much by the time the general strike movement reached its peak. While SCAP's capability in the spring of 1946 to act decisively in putting down a working-class challenge to the old order might have been open to question, there was no longer any doubt by January 1947 that the will and the means for action were there.

Oddly enough, certain Sanbetsu leaders had been less dismissive than the JCP about the possibility of SCAP repression, and the federation and some of its constituent unions had made hesitant preparations for just that eventuality. A part of the leadership of Sanbetsu was to go underground at the time of the outbreak of the strike, in readiness for the SCAP military suppression that they thought would open the eyes of the Japanese people and create conditions for a new stage in the evolution of the working-class movement in postwar Japan—a struggle for national liberation.[117] They expected SCAP to be exposed as the agent of American imperialism and that the high hopes which workers, farmers, and others had held for the future would be transferred to a national liberation movement led by the organs of the working class. Though they had some reason to believe that a revolutionary spirit was emerging among the union rank and file, the radical leaders in Sanbetsu by no means had a comprehensive strategy and tactics worked out for transforming the general strike movement into a revolutionary struggle.[118]

That some leaders within Sanbetsu, a federation of labor unions, should have been contemplating actions typical of a political party engaged in a struggle for power did not mean that they were doing so at the behest of the JCP, although Tokuda apparently had thoughts that workers would take over industry through production control after the cabinet fell.[119] On the contrary, this strange reversal of roles reflects the fact that they were dissatisfied with the JCP and its commitment to the parliamentary road to socialism for postwar Japan.

The JCP had been counting on the basic good will of SCAP as the liberation army of the Western democracies fully as much as the old guard had been banking on the essential conservatism of SCAP as the representative of the interests of a capitalist America. JCP confidence in SCAP's tolerance of left-wing activism seems misplaced given MacArthur's blunt warning to labor and the left in May 1946, and in view of the part SCAP played in crushing the *Yomiuri* strike and housebreaking the national press union. Be that as it may, Yoshida had a better grasp of the situation, and the left lost the general strike. Instead of marking the commencement of the peaceful transformation of Japan into a socialist country, the general strike was broken, and the

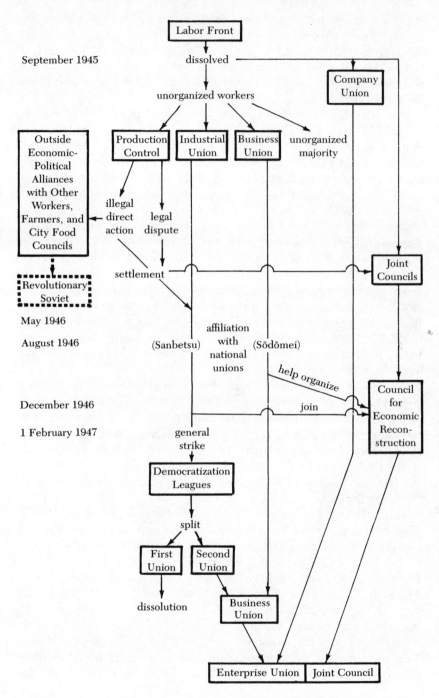

Figure 8.1. Course of the Postwar Workers' Movement at the Enterprise Level.

initiative in the postwar conflict between labor and capital passed definitely to the latter with disastrous consequences for the union movement and for the working class.

Labor unity and industrial unionism were the two major casualties of the general strike. The discrediting of Sanbetsu permitted the right-wing leaders of Sōdōmei to reassert their independence, and it brought internal division to Sanbetsu affiliates, making them vulnerable to big-business and government efforts to drive labor organization back within the confines of the enterprise. Sōdōmei raiding—which went so far as deliberate attempts to split and destroy Sanbetsu affiliates—accelerated this process immensely, since the successor Sōdōmei "second" union was almost always an enterprise union. The defeat of the left, therefore, cleared the way for the institutionalization of the enterprise union, that weakened form of workers' organization that replaced the militant industrial unions of Sanbetsu (see figure 8.1)

From the beginning of the occupation to the end, SCAP pursued the elusive goal of creating an industrial relations system in Japan built on the moderate unionism characteristic of the American labor movement. Once the legal framework was erected, however, SCAP found itself all but powerless to make American-style unionism flourish. The conflict of classes in postwar Japan blocked that middle way. There were but two alternatives before SCAP—industrial unions too deeply involved in politics to be acceptable or collaborationist unions too closely tied to management to be comfortable. In the end SCAP lent its support to the old guard's destruction of the militant industrial unions.

A working-class democratization of postwar Japan was not to be. Too much was against it—the early surrender, the retention in power of the old guard, the divisions on the left, the presence of SCAP. The fight for a new Japan during the early occupation must be seen, nevertheless, as one of the peaks in the history of the Japanese working class.

Reference Material

Notes

Abbreviations Used in the Notes

NTRK   Nihon Tankō Rōdō Kumiai
RSCK   Rōdō Sōgi Chōsa Kai
TDSKK   Tōkyō Daigaku Shakai Kagaku Kenkyū-jo

Chapter 1: The Old Guard Digs In

1 John W. Dower, *Empire and Aftermath: Yoshida Shigeru and the Japanese Experience, 1878–1954* (Cambridge: Council on East Asian Studies, Harvard University, 1979), p. 260.

2 Jon Halliday, *A Political History of Japanese Capitalism* (New York: Pantheon Books, 1975), pp. 162–63, 167. In any case, American policy at the outset leaned further toward the "China hands" in the State Department, who argued for a hard peace and radical economic and political reforms, than it did toward the conciliatory Japan crowd. See Dower, *Empire and Aftermath*, pp. 106, 110, 229; and John G. Roberts, "The 'Japan Crowd' and the Zaibatsu Restoration," *Japan Interpreter* 12:3–4 (summer 1979): 384–415.

3 Halliday, *A Political History*, p. 372; Hugh Borton, *Japan's Modern Century* (New York: Ronald Press, 1955), p. 393.

4 James W. Morley, "The First Seven Weeks," *Japan Interpreter* 6:2 (summer 1970): 154; Thomas A. Bisson, *Prospects for Democracy in Japan* (New York: MacMillan, 1949), pp. 22–23; "Winning the Peace in Japan," *Amerasia* 9:16 (Sept. 1945): 246–47.

5 Theodore McNelly, ed., *Sources in Modern East Asian History and Politics* (New York: Appleton-Century-Crofts, 1967), pp. 169–70; Tsuji Kiyoaki, ed., *Shiryō Sengo Nijū Nen Shi* (Tokyo: Nihon Hyōronsha, 1966), vol. 1, *Seiji*, p. 6.

6 Morley, "The First Seven Weeks," p. 155; Roberts, "The 'Japan Crowd.'"

7 Bisson, "Winning the Peace," p. 246.

8 Supreme Command for the Allied Powers (hereafter cited as SCAP), General Headquarters, *Summation: Non-Military Activities in Japan*, no. 1, p. 26.

9 Shinobu Seizaburō, *Sengo Nihon Seiji Shi* (Tokyo: Keisō Shobō, 1965), vol. 1, pp. 117–21.

10 Ibid., p. 119.

11 Ibid., pp. 117–21; Morley, "The First Seven Weeks," p. 155.

12 Theoretically, the Finance and Munitions Ministries and the control associations were responsible for economic policy planning and implementation, but zaibatsu executives filled the top positions in those agencies. There, in coordination with other leading zaibatsu executives, they made the important decisions regarding production, distribution of finished goods, and allocation of materials, capital, and labor. See Jerome B. Cohen, *Japan's Economy in War and Reconstruction* (Minneapolis: University of Minnesota Press, 1949), pp. 59ff., 74ff.

13 SCAP, General Headquarters, *Summation,* no. 2, charts 1–2; SCAP, Government Section, *Political Reorientation of Japan: September 1945 to September 1948* (Washington, D.C.: Government Printing Office, 1949), pp. 135–38, 292–93.

14 Kurt Steiner, *Local Government in Japan* (Stanford: Stanford University Press, 1965), pp. 55–60, 71–75.

15 Bisson, *Prospects,* pp. 38–39; SCAP, Government Section, *Political Reorientation,* p. 413.

16 Fukutake Tadashi, *Japanese Rural Society* (Ithaca: Cornell University Press, 1967), pp. 16–17; Andrew J. Grad, *Land and Peasant in Japan: An Introductory Survey* (New York: Institute of Pacific Relations, 1952), pp. 30–31, 34–35, 39–40; Lawrence Hewes, *Japan—Land and Men* (Ames: Iowa State College Press, 1955), pp. 38–39; Steiner, *Local Government,* pp. 55–60, 71–75; E. Herbert Norman, British Commonwealth Conference on a Japanese Peace Settlement, 27 Aug. 1947, Verbatim Minutes (Australian Archives, CP-104, Far Eastern Commission Records, bundle 3, set 2), pp. j1, k1.

17 Cohen, *Japan's Economy,* pp. 278–81.

18 Suehiro Izutaro, *Japanese Trade Unionism: Past and Present* (Tokyo: mimeographed, 1950), pp. 130–31, 141–45; Cohen, *Japan's Economy,* pp. 276–82, 318.

19 Cohen, *Japan's Economy,* pp. 282–86; SCAP, General Headquarters, *History of the Non-Military Activities of the Occupation of Japan,* monograph 28, *Development of the Trade Union Movement: 1945 through June 1951* (30 Nov. 1951), pp. 10–14; George O. Totten, "Collective Bargaining and Works Councils as Innovations in Industrial Relations in Japan during the 1920's," in *Aspects of Social Change in Modern Japan,* ed. Ronald P. Dore (Princeton: Princeton University Press, 1967), pp. 216–33.

20 Okochi Kazuo, *Labor in Modern Japan,* Economic Series 18, Commerce and Business Administration, Science Council of Japan (Tokyo: 1958), p. 67.

21 SCAP, General Headquarters, *History of the Non-Military Activities of the Occupation of Japan,* monograph 29, *Working Conditions: 1945 through September 1950* (30 Nov. 1951), p. 41; Cohen, *Japan's Economy,* pp. 304–6.

22 SCAP, General Headquarters, monograph 29, pp. 35–38; Suehiro, *Japanese Trade Unionism*, pp. 130–31, 142–43; Cohen, *Japan's Economy*, pp. 304–6.

23 Suehiro, *Japanese Trade Unionism*, pp. 145–47; Cohen, *Japan's Economy*, pp. 287–93.

24 Robert A. Scalapino, "Japan," in *Labor and Economic Development*, ed. Walter Galenson (New York: John Wiley & Sons, 1959), pp. 114–16; Suehiro, *Japanese Trade Unionism*, pp. 141–45; Cohen, *Japan's Economy*, pp. 282–86.

25 Miriam S. Farley, *Aspects of Japan's Labor Problems* (New York: John Day, 1950), pp. 31–33; SCAP, General Headquarters, monograph 28, pp. 10–11.

26 Tōyama Shigeki, "Sengo Nijū Nen no Gaikan," in *Shiryō Sengo Nijū Nen Shi*, ed. Tōyama Shigeki (Tokyo: Nihon Hyōronsha, 1967), vol. 6, *Nenpyō*, p. 3; U.S., Department of State, Interim Foreign Economic and Liquidation Service, *Labor Developments in Japan Since Surrender: August 15–November 15, 1945* (U.S. National Archives Record Group [hereafter cited as RG] 226, Office of Strategic Services, XL 37772, 30 Nov. 1945), p. 8; Rodger Swearingen and Paul Langer, *Red Flag in Japan: International Communism in Action 1919–1951* (Cambridge: Harvard University Press, 1952), pp. 77–78, 87–88, 258; Takayanagi Mitsutoshi and Rizō Takeuchi, eds., *Kadogawa Nihon-shi Jiten* (Tokyo: Kadogawa Shoten, 1966), p. 816.

27 Tōyama, "Sengo," p. 3.

28 U.S., Department of State, *Labor Developments*, pp. 9–10.

29 Watanabe Tōru, *Gendai Rōnō Undōshi Nenpyō* (Tokyo: Sanichi Shobō, 1961), p. 156; U.S. Department of State, *Labor Developments*, pp. 6–8.

30 SCAP, General Headquarters, monograph 28, appendix, pp. 16–19.

31 Yamamoto Kiyoshi, "Sengo Kiki no Tenkai Katei," in *Sengo Kaikaku* (Tokyo: Tōkyō Daigaku Shakai Kagaku Kenkyū-jo, 1974), vol. 5, *Rōdō Kaikaku*, p. 84.

32 U.S., Department of State, *Labor Developments*, p. 8; SCAP, General Headquarters, *Summation*, no. 1, p. 38; Morley, "The First Seven Weeks," pp. 160–62.

33 Morley, "The First Seven Weeks," pp. 162.

34 U.S., Department of State, *Labor Developments*, pp. 8–9; Daily Labor Press, ed., *The Labor Union Movement in Postwar Japan* (Tokyo: Daily Labor Press, 1954), p. 23; Halliday, *A Political History*, p. 171; *Nihon Shihonshugi Kōza: Sengo Nihon no Seiji to Keizai* (Tokyo: Iwanami Shoten, 1954), vol. 7, *Bekkan*, p. 14.

35 U.S., Department of State, *Labor Developments*, pp. 8–9.

36 Borton, *Japan's Modern Century*, pp. 393–94; Far Eastern Commission, Australian Delegation, "Japanese Attitudes to Occupation," p. 2, in "Interim Report" on visit of Far Eastern Commission to Japan in Jan. 1946, classified "Top Secret" (Australian Archives, CP-104, bundle 15, item 2).

37 Bisson, *Prospects*, p. 12; Thomas A. Bisson, "Are We Winning the Peace

in Japan?" *Amerasia* 10:2 (Feb. 1946): 44–45; SCAP, General Headquarters, *Summation*, no. 1, p. 28, and no. 2, p. 29; Mark Gayn, *Japan Diary* (New York: William Sloane, 1948), pp. 51–52, 71, 91.

38 Gayn, *Japan Diary*, pp. 457–59; Morley, "The First Seven Weeks," pp. 162–63; Richard L. G. Deverall, memoranda to Chief, Labor Division, Economic and Scientific Section, SCAP, in regard to background of Japanese labor officials, 13 June, 14 and 25 July 1946 (Deverall Papers, Catholic University, Washington, D.C., C8-38, vol. 2, p. 400; C8-39, vol. 3, pp. 529, 584).

39 Gayn, *Japan Diary*, p. 458.

40 Morley, "The First Seven Weeks," pp. 156–58.

41 SCAP, General Headquarters, *Summation*, no. 1, p. 5.

42 Morley, "The First Seven Weeks," p. 158.

43 Bisson, "Are We Winning the Peace?" p. 70.

44 SCAP, General Headquarters, *Selected Data on the Occupation of Japan: Organization and Activities of General Headquarters* (June 1950), p. 5.

45 Ibid., p. 6.

46 John Maki, "The Role of the Bureaucracy in Japan," *Pacific Affairs* 20:4 (Dec. 1947): 398–99.

47 Steiner, *Local Government*, pp. 55, 71; Cohen, *Japan's Economy*, pp. 69, 72, 316–17.

48 SCAP, General Headquarters, *Summation*, no. 1, pp. 26–27; Steiner, *Local Government*, p. 71.

49 SCAP, General Headquarters, *Summation*, no. 1, p. 27.

50 Steiner, *Local Government*, p. 71.

51 U.S., Department of State, *Labor Developments*, pp. 9–10.

52 Bisson, *Prospects*, pp. 38–43; SCAP, Government Section, *Political Reorientation*, pp. 286–88.

53 SCAP, Government Section, *Political Reorientation*, pp. 135–38.

54 Thomas A. Bisson, "The Zaibatsu's Wartime Role," *Pacific Affairs* 18 (Dec. 1945): 356.

55 Ibid., p. 358; Eric E. Ward, "Economic Problems of Japan Affecting the Peace Settlement" (3 June 1947), doc. I/48 for the British Commonwealth Conference on a Japanese Peace Settlement (Australian Archives, CP-104, Far Eastern Commission Records, bundles 51–52), pp. 14–15.

56 Ibid., pp. 362–63.

57 Ibid.

58 Sherwood M. Fine, *Japan's Post-war Industrial Recovery*, Eastern Economist pamphlet 13, ed. E. P. W. Da Costa (New Delhi: 1952), pp. 12–13.

59 Horikoshi Teizō, ed., *Keizai Dantai Rengō Kai Jūnen Shi* (Tokyo: Keizai Dantai Rengō Kai, 1962), vol. 1, pp. 25–26, and vol. 2, pp. 490–91; SCAP, General Headquarters, *Summation*, no. 1, p. 104.

60 Horikoshi, *Keizai*, vol. 1, pp. 25–26, and vol. 2, pp. 490–91.

61 SCAP, Government Section, *Political Reorientation*, p. 413.
62 McNelly, *Sources*, pp. 144–51.
63 U.S., State-War-Navy Coordinating-Committee, Subcommittee for the Far East, *Treatment of Japanese Workers' Organizations*, JCS 1575 (Washington: [Aug.] 1945) RG 218, box 138, folder: CCAC 014 Japan secs. 1–5, appendix, pp. 13–16.
64 Yoshida Shigeru, *The Yoshida Memoirs: The Story of Japan in Crisis* (Boston: Houghton Mifflin, 1962), p. 225.
65 SCAP, General Headquarters, *Summation*, no. 1, p. 15.
66 Ibid., pp. 15–16.
67 Martin Bronfenbrenner, "The American Occupation of Japan: Economic Retrospect," in *The American Occupation of Japan: A Retrospective View*, ed. Grant K. Goodman (University of Kansas: Center for East Asian Studies, 1968), pp. 15, 24.
68 Horikoshi, *Keizai*, vol. 1, pp. 4–6; Bisson, *Prospects*, p. 117.
69 Horikoshi, *Keizai*, vol. 1, pp. 6–10.
70 Ibid., p. 7, item 3.
71 Ibid., vol. 3, p. 305.
72 Ibid., pp. 304–5, 547–48.
73 Ibid., pp. 304–5; Miwa Yoshikazu, "Keizai Dantai Ron," in *Gendai Nihon no Dokusen Shihon*, ed. Imai Noriyoshi (Tokyo: Shiseidō, 1964), vol. 1, *Dokusen Keitai*, pp. 215–16; Noda Kazuo, ed., *Sengo Keiei Shi*, vol. 1 of *Nihon Keiei Shi*, ed. Nihon Seisan-sei Honbu (Tokyo: Nihon Seisan-sei Honbu, 1965), p. 51.
74 John D. Montgomery, *Forced to Be Free: The Artificial Revolution in Germany and Japan* (Chicago: University of Chicago Press, 1957), pp. 106–7.
75 Horikoshi, *Keizai*, vol. 2, pp. 495–96.
76 Thomas A. Bisson, *Zaibatsu Dissolution in Japan* (Berkeley: University of California Press, 1954), pp. 191–92; Cohen, *Japan's Economy*, p. 431; Bisson, *Prospects*, pp. 98, 104, 111.
77 Fine, *Japan's Post-war*, p. 21; Yamamoto Kiyoshi, "'Sangyō Saiken' to Sho-seiji Shutai," in *Sengo Kaikaku* (Tokyo: Tōkyō Daigaku Shakai Kagaku Kenkyū-jo, 1974), vol. 5, *Rōdō Kaikaku*, p. 194.
78 William McMahon Ball, British Commonwealth Member, Allied Council for Japan, to Australian Secretary of External Affairs, "Monthly Report, April, 1947, Transition Controls," extracted in doc. I/47 for the British Commonwealth Conference on a Japanese Peace Settlement (Australian Archives, CP-104, Far Eastern Commission Records, bundles 51–52).
79 Japan, House of Representatives Special Committee for the Investigation of Concealed and Hoarded Goods, *Supplementary Report* (Tokyo: Dec. 1947), in SCAP, General Headquarters, *Summation*, no. 27, pp. 25–29, and SCAP, Government Section, *Political Reorientation*, pp. 307–13; William Costello, *Democracy vs Feudalism in Post-War Japan* (Tokyo: Itagaki Shoten, 1948), pp. 152–57; Bisson, *Prospects*, p. 98.

80 SCAP, General Headquarters, *Summation,* no. 27, pp. 25–26.
81 Gayn, *Japan Diary,* p. 496; Costello, *Democracy,* p. 153; Bisson, *Prospects,* pp. 12–13, 114.
82 SCAP, General Headquarters, *Summation,* no. 1, pp. 154–55, and no. 2, p. 204; SCAP, Government Section, *Political Reorientation,* pp. 307–8; Gayn, *Japan Diary,* p. 156; Bisson, *Prospects,* p. 14.
83 SCAP, General Headquarters, *Summation,* no. 27, pp. 24, 27, 31; Bisson, *Prospects,* p. 115; Costello, *Democracy,* p. 154.
84 SCAP, Government Section, *Political Reorientation,* p. 722.
85 Ibid., p. 309.
86 Costello, *Democracy,* pp. 156–57.
87 Bisson, *Zaibatsu,* p. 66; Bisson, *Prospects,* p. 117.
88 SCAP, General Headquarters, *Summation,* no. 27, pp. 30–33.
89 Cohen, *Japan's Economy,* p. 417; Ōuchi Hyōe, "Keizai," in *Sengo Nihon Shōshi,* ed. Yanaihara Tadao (Tokyo: Tōkyō Daigaku Shuppan-kai, 1958), vol. 1, p. 82; Mainichi Daily News Staff, *Fifty Years of Light and Dark: The Hirohito Era* (Tokyo: Mainichi Newspapers, 1975), p. 215.
90 SCAP, General Headquarters, *Summation,* no. 1, p. 55.
91 Horikoshi, *Keizai,* vol. 3, p. 692.
92 SCAP, General Headquarters, monograph 28, pp. 10–11; Totten, "Collective Bargaining," pp. 216–33.
93 SCAP, General Headquarters, monograph 28, p. 12.
94 SCAP, Economic and Scientific Section, Advisory Committee on Labor, *Final Report: Labor Policies and Programs in Japan* (Tokyo: 1946), p. 98; Farley, *Aspects,* p. 31; U.S., Department of State, *Labor Developments,* pp. 6–7, 22–23.

Chapter 2: The Workers Stand Up

1 Nihon Tankō Rōdō Kumiai (hereafter cited as NTRK), ed., *Tanrō Jūnen Shi* (Tokyo: Rōdō Junpōsha, 1964), p. 48; Rōdō Sōgi Chōsa Kai (hereafter cited as RSCK), ed., *Sengo Rōdō Sōgi Jittai Chōsa* (Tokyo: Chūō Kōron Sha, 1957), vol. 1, *Sekitan Sōgi,* p. 51.
2 RSCK, *Sekitan,* p. 49.
3 NTRK, *Tanrō,* pp. 47, 51; RSCK, *Sekitan,* p. 49.
4 Tagawa Kazuo, *Sengo Kakumei no Haiboku* (Tokyo: Gendai Shichō Sha, 1970), vol. 1, *Sengo Nihon Kakumei Undō Shi,* pp. 24, 26–28.
5 RSCK, *Sekitan,* p. 51.
6 NTRK, *Tanrō,* pp. 47, 49.
7 The following discussion of the Chinese and Korean miners is based on: NTRK, *Tanrō,* pp. 52–60; RSCK, *Sekitan,* pp. 50–51; Tagawa, *Sengo Kakumei,* p. 26.
8 NTRK, *Tanrō,* p. 60.
9 The following discussion is based on: NTRK, *Tanrō,* pp. 43–44; RSCK, *Sekitan,* pp. 54–59; Ōkōchi Kazuo and Matsuo Hiroshi, *Nihon Rōdō Ku-*

miai Monogatari (Tokyo: Chikuma Shobō, 1969), vol. 1, *Sengo*, p. 98.

10 Mizutani Takashi, one of the Mitsubishi Bibai workers involved, played a key role not only in organizing the militant union at Mitsubishi Bibai but also in leading the first worker takeover and operation of a mine at nearby Mitsui Bibai in December. Later on, after taking the lead in setting up a federation of coal miners' unions in Hokkaidō, he would help organize and become the first president of the leftist national federation of coal miners' unions founded in February 1946.

11 SCAP, General Headquarters, *Summation*, no. 5, p. 192.

12 NTRK, *Tanrō*, pp. 41, 44–45; RSCK, *Sekitan*, pp. 61–64.

13 RSCK, *Sekitan*, pp. 76–82; NTRK, *Tanrō*, pp. 72–75.

14 Watanabe, *Gendai*, p. 155; Saitō Ichirō, *Ni Ichi Suto Zengo* (Tokyo: Shakai Hyōron Sha, 1972), p. 50; Farley, *Aspects*, p. 132; Ōkōchi and Matsuo, *Sengo*, p. 87; Yamamoto Kiyoshi, *Sengo Rōdō Undō Shiron* (Tokyo: O-Cha no Mizu Shobō, 1977), vol. 1, *Sengo Kiki ni okeru Rōdō Undō*, p. 248.

15 Suehiro, *Japanese Trade Unionism*, p. 3 of insert following p. 377.

16 Noda, *Sengo Keiei*, p. 243.

17 Nikkeiren Sōritsu Jūnen Kinen Jigyō Iinkai, ed., *Jūnen no Ayumi* (Tokyo: Nikkeiren Sōritsu Jūnen Kinen Jigyō Iinkai, 1958), pp. 7–9.

18 RSCK, *Sekitan*, pp. 85–86; NTRK, *Tanrō*, pp. 34–38.

19 SCAP, General Headquarters, *Summation*, no. 4, p. 179.

20 NTRK, *Tanrō*, pp. 34–38.

21 U.S., Department of State, Division of Research for Far East, Office of Intelligence Research, Report 4247, "The Yomiuri Shimbun Case: A Significant Development in the Post-Surrender Japanese Press" (10 Mar. 1947) (RG 331, box 8499, folder: Labor Relations: Disputes—Newspapers, Yomiuri Case [Confidential]), pp. 5–6. SCAP, International Prosecution Section, Case 181, Shōriki Matsutarō (RG 331). I am indebted to Gavan McCormack for this document. Despite Shōriki's release from prosecution, this voluminous file substantiates his extreme right-wing views and activities, including use of the *Yomiuri* to promote them, which continued even after the surrender.

22 Tōkyō Daigaku Shakai Kagaku Kenkyū-jo (hereafter cited as TDSKK), ed., *Shiryō* (Tokyo: Tōkyō Daigaku Shakai Kagaku Kenkyū-jo, 1973–74), pt. 1, vol. 6, *Sengo Kiki ni okeru Rōdō Sōgi: Yomiuri Shinbun Sōgi 1945–1946*, pp. 9–11, 26–27, 75; Edward Uhlan and Dana L. Thomas, *Shoriki, Miracle Man of Japan: A Biography* (New York: Exposition Press, 1957), pp. 61–67; TDSKK, Yomiuri, pt. 2, pp. 18–20.

23 TDSKK, *Yomiuri*, pt. 1, pp. 19, 23–25; Takano Minoru, *Nihon no Rōdō Undō* (Tokyo: Iwanami Shoten, 1958), pp. 30–31.

24 U.S., Department of State, "The Yomiuri Shimbun Case," p. 9; Rōdōshō, ed., *Shiryō: Rōdō Undō Shi—Shōwa 20–21-nen* (Tokyo: Rōmu Gyōsei Kenkyū-jo, 1951), p. 7; TDSKK, *Yomiuri*, pt. 1, pp. 9–10, 22; Ōkōchi and Matsuo, *Sengo*, p. 93; Masuyama Taisuke, "Dai Ichiji Yomiuri Sōgi Shi," in *Rōdō Undō Shi Kenkyū*, ed. Rōdō Undō Shi Kenkyū Kai (Tokyo:

Rōdō Junpōsha, 1970), vol. 53, *Sanbetsu Kaigi: Sono Seiritsu to Undō no Tenkai*, pp. 26–30; RSCK, ed., *Sengo Rōdō Sōgi Jittai Chōsa* (Tokyo: Chūō Kōron Sha, 1957), vol. 6, *Rōdō Sōgi ni okeru Tokushu Kēsu*, p. 16.

25 Masuyama, "Dai Ichiji," p. 22; RSCK, *Tokushu Kēsu*, pp. 13–14; Uhlan and Thomas, *Shoriki*, p. 169.

26 Masuyama, "Dai Ichiji," p. 22; RSCK, *Tokushu Kēsu*, pp. 13–14.

27 TDSKK, *Yomiuri*, pt. 1, pp. 9–10, 22.

28 Fujiwara was one of the great business magnates in Japan. He had been invited as the representative for Japanese business to the Nazi Party Congress in 1939, and had been active in government through the war years, serving as Home Minister under Tōjō. At the time that he was Munitions Minister under Koiso, Shōriki had himself become one of the seven representatives of business among the fourteen advisers to the Koiso cabinet, and no doubt had frequent dealings with Fujiwara. RSCK, *Tokushu Kēsu*, p. 16; TDSKK, *Yomiuri*, pt. 1, pp. 9–10.

29 RSCK, *Tokushu Kēsu*, p. 27; Uhlan and Thomas, *Shoriki*, pp. 170, 172; TDSKK, *Yomiuri*, pt. 1, pp. 9–10.

30 TDSKK, *Yomiuri*, pt. 1, pp. 5–6.

31 Masuyama, "Dai Ichiji," p. 28.

32 Ibid., p. 29.

33 RSCK, *Tokushu Kēsu*, pp. 15–16.

34 Ibid., pp. 21–22; Masuyama, "Dai Ichiji," pp. 27, 29; U.S., Department of State, "The Yomiuri Shimbun Case," p. 73–78.

35 Masuyama, "Dai Ichiji," p. 46; RSCK, *Tokushu Kēsu*, pp. 15–16.

36 U.S., Department of State, "The Yomiuri Shimbun Case," pp. v, 74.

37 TDSKK, *Yomiuri*, p. 1, pp. 33–35, 38–39; Yamamoto, *Sengo Kiki*, vol. 1, pp. 262–65.

38 Gayn, *Japan Diary*, p. 23.

39 Ōkōchi and Matsuo, *Sengo*, p. 95; TDSKK, *Yomiuri*, pt. 1, p. 44; U.S., Department of State, "The Yomiuri Shimbun Case," pp. 10–15; RSCK, *Tokushu Kēsu*, pp. 23–26.

40 Rōdōshō, *Shiryō 20–21-nen*, pp. 7–8; RSCK, *Tokushu Kēsu*, pp. 23, 29–33; U.S., Department of State, "The Yomiuri Shimbun Case," pp. 17–18.

41 Arthur Behrstock, "Snafu in Tokyo," *Nisei Weekender*, 1 Jan. 1947, enclosure to: John K. Emmerson to JCV, HB, et al. office memorandum: "Article 'Snafu in Tokyo'" (RG 59: 740.00119/1–847).

42 Rōdōshō, *Shiryō 20–21-nen*, pp. 7–8; RSCK, *Tokushu Kēsu*, pp. 29–33; U.S., Department of State, "The Yomiuri Shimbun Case," pp. 47–48; Far Eastern Commission, Australian Delegation, "Interim Report," annex 7 (D), entry for 25 Jan. 1946.

43 TDSKK, *Yomiuri*, pt. 1, pp. 55–58.

44 Ibid., pp. 56–57; RSCK, *Tokushu Kēsu*, pp. 26–27; Masuyama, "Dai Ichiji," pp. 47–48.

45 Masuyama, "Dai Ichiji," pp. 47–48; TDSKK, *Yomiuri*, pt. 1, pp. 54–58; RSCK, *Tokushu Kēsu*, p. 31.

46 U.S., Department of State, "The Yomiuri Shimbun Case," pp. 19–21; TDSKK, *Yomiuri*, pt. 1, pp. 54–58.

47 Rōdōshō, *Shiryō 20–21-nen*, pp. 7–8; U.S., Department of State, "The Yomiuri Shimbun Case," pp. 17–18.

48 The following discussion is based on: Keisei Dentetsu Rōdō Kumiai, ed., *Waga Tatakai to Kensetsu no Rekishi: Keisei Dentetsu Rōdō Kumiai 16-nen Shi* (Tokyo: Keisei Dentetsu Rōdō Kumiai, 1962), pp. 41–51; Rōdōshō, *Shiryō 20–21-nen*, pp. 14–15; Sengo Kakumei Shiryō Hensan Iinkai, ed., *Seisan Kanri Tōsō: Shiryō Sengo Kakumei* (Tokyo: Jōkyō Shuppan, 1 Oct. 1974), Rinji Zōkan, *Jōkyō*, pp. 82–98; Ōkōchi and Matsuo, *Sengo*, p. 100.

49 The following discussion is based on: Sumiya Mikio, "Mitsubishi Bibai Sōgi," in *Chōsa Hōkoku*, ed. Tōkyō Daigaku Shakai Kagaku Kenkyū-jo (Tokyo: Tōkyō Daigaku Shakai Kagaku Kenkyū-jo, 1971), vol. 13, *Sengo Shoki Rōdō Sōgi Chōsa*, pp. 15–32; RSCK, *Sekitan*, pp. 65–66.

50 Sumiya, "Mitsubishi Bibai," p. 24.

51 Ibid., p. 25.

52 Bronfenbrenner, "American Occupation," pp. 21–22.

53 Theodore Cohen, "The U.S. Occupation Policies for Japan," interview by Takemae Eiji, *Tokyo Metropolitan University Journal of Law and Politics* 14:1 (1973): 4–5.

54 Gayn, *Japan Diary*, p. 331. Cohen's self-assessment is borne out by his correspondence from Japan on labor matters with Jay Lovestone of the rabidly anti-communist Free Trade Union Committee of the American Federation of Labor. It is unclear whether this dated back to his tenure as chief of Labor Division. Valery Burati, Labor Division, Economic and Scientific Section, SCAP, to Jay Lovestone, Free Trade Union Committee, 11 Oct. 1949 (RG 331, box 8477, folder: Chrono. File July '49–Oct. '49).

55 T. Cohen, "Occupation Policies," p. 8.

56 Joyce Kolko and Gabriel Kolko, *The Limits of Power: The World and United States Foreign Policy, 1949–1954* (New York: Harper & Row, 1972), pp. 441, 450.

57 T. Cohen, "Occupation Policies," pp. 9–10.

58 Ibid., pp. 5, 8–9; Theodore Cohen, "Labor Democratization in Japan: The First Years," in *The Occupation of Japan: Economic Policy and Reform*, ed. Lawrence H. Redford (Norfolk, Va.: MacArthur Memorial, 1980), p. 164.

59 State-War-Navy Coordinating Committee, *Treatment*, p. 3; T. Cohen, "Labor Democratization," pp. 163–64, 191.

60 State-War-Navy Coordinating Committee, *Treatment*, pp. 11, 13, 16–17.

61 Ibid., pp. 13–15.

62 SCAP, Economic and Scientific Section, Advisory Committee on Labor, *First Interim Report on Treatment of Workers' Organizations since the Surrender*, 30 June 1946, appendix A to SCAP, Economic and Scientific

Section, Advisory Committee on Labor, *Final Report;* Far Eastern Commission, Report by the Secretary General, *Activities of the Far Eastern
Commission, February 26, 1946–July 10, 1947* (Washington: Government Printing Office, 1947); Theodore Cohen, Foreign Economic Administration, Enemy Branch, *Trade Unions and Collective Bargaining in
Japan* (July 1945) (RG 407).

63　SCAP, Government Section, *Political Reorientation,* pp. 463–65.
64　William Karpinsky, in "Session Four: Labor," *The Occupation of Japan:
Economic Policy and Reform,* ed. Lawrence H. Redford (Norfolk, Va.:
MacArthur Memorial, 1980), pp. 192–96; Cohen, "Labor Democratization," p. 166.
65　Philip B. Sullivan, Committee on Economic Policy, Department of State,
to Mr. Mulliken, Department of State, memorandum: "Revised Directive to the CINC, USAF, PAC for the Military Government of Japan"
(RG 59: 740.00119/8–2845).
66　SCAP, General Headquarters, *Summation,* no. 8, p. 29.
67　Ibid., no. 2, p. 103.
68　Kolko, *The Limits of Power,* p. 312; Far Eastern Commission, Australian
Delegation, "Political Parties," pp. 2–3, in "Interim Report."
69　SCAP, Government Section, *Political Reorientation,* p. 436.
70　SCAP, *Economic and Scientific Section, Advisory Committee on Labor,
First Interim Report,* pp. 2–3, 6–7.
71　Ibid., p. 6.
72　SCAP, General Headquarters, *Summation,* no. 3, pp. 112–13.

Chapter 3: Capitalist Sabotage
and the Winter Crisis

1　Morinaga Eizaburō, *Seisan Kanri no Hōritsu Mondai,* no. 2 of *Sanrō
Gyōsho,* ed. Nihon Sangyō Rōdō Chōsa-kyoku (Tokyo: Kenshin Sha, 1948),
pp. 28ff.; Sanbetsu Kaigi Hōritsu-bu, ed., "Seisan Kanri no Gōhōsei to
Senjutsu" (pamphlet) (Tokyo: Sanbetsu Kaigi Hōritsu-bu, Jan. 1947);
Tsuchida Mitsuyasu, *Seisan Kanri no Tatakai* (Tokyo: Nihon Rōnō Kyūen
Kai, 1948); Yanase Tetsuya, "Genka Sekitan Mondai no Shozai," *Jinmin*
2:3 (Mar. 1946): 30–36; Thomas A. Bisson, "Reparations and Reform in
Japan," *Far Eastern Survey* 16:21 (Dec. 1947): 241–47.
2　SCAP, General Headquarters, *Summation,* no. 27, pp. 24–32.
3　Shidehara Heiwa Zaidan, ed., *Shidehara Kijūrō* (Tokyo: Shidehara Heiwa
Zaidan, 1955), pp. 567–69.
4　Ibid.; Shinobu, *Sengo Nihon,* vol. 1, p. 184.
5　SCAP, Government Section, *Political Reorientation,* p. 741.
6　Shidehara Heiwa Zaida, *Shidehara,* p. 601.
7　Tsuji, *Seiji,* p. 334.
8　Ibid., p. 336.
9　Ibid.

10 Ibid.

11 Horikoshi, *Keizai*, vol. 1, pp. 6–10; vol. 2, pp. 495–96; vol. 3, pp. 304–5, 309.

12 Japan, Economic Stabilization Board, "A Report on Economic Conditions of Japan," 3 July 1947 (hereafter cited as "White Paper"), (personal papers of Eric E. Ward), ch. 2, pt. 3, sec. A.

13 Cohen, *Japan's Economy*, p. 353.

14 Ibid., pp. 108, 386; Japan, Economic Stabilization Board, "White Paper," ch. 2, pt. 3, sec. A.

15 Ibid., ch. 4 *passim;* ch. 5, pp. 201–8. SCAP, General Headquarters, *Summation,* no. 1, pp. 44–68; no. 2, pp. 59–97.

16 SCAP, General Headquarters, *Summation,* no. 1, p. 52; no. 3, charts 10, 13. Japan Ministry of Finance and Bank of Japan, *Statistical Year-Book of Finance and Economy of Japan, 1948* (Tokyo: Ministry of Finance Printing Office, 1948), p. 670.

17 SCAP, Economic and Scientific Section, Programs and Statistics Division, *Missions and Accomplishments of the Supreme Commander for the Allied Powers in the Economic, Scientific, and Natural Resources Fields* (Tokyo: 1952), p. 21. SCAP, General Headquarters, *Summation,* no. 1, p. 51; no. 2, p. 70.

18 SCAP, General Headquarters, *Summation,* no. 4, p. 7.

19 Robert B. Textor, *Failure in Japan: With Keystones for a Positive Policy* (New York: John Day, 1951), p. 48; Gayn, *Japan Diary,* p. 496; Costello, *Democracy,* pp. 150–57; Suehiro, *Japanese Trade Unionism,* pp. 209–10.

20 SCAP, General Headquarters, *Summation,* no. 1, pp. 51–52; no. 2, p. 70. U.S. Strategic Bombing Survey, *Japanese War Production Industries* (Military Supplies Division, 1946), p. 10.

21 Arisawa Hiromi, "Senki/Sengo no Kōgyō Seisaku," in *Sengo Nihon Keizai no Shomondai,* ed. Yanaihara Tadao (Tokyo: Yūhikaku, 1949), pp. 104ff.

22 Fine, *Japan's Post-war,* pp. 31–32; SCAP, General Headquarters, Economic and Scientific Section, *Outlook for the Japanese Cotton Industry, 1948–1949* (1948), p. 6.

23 SCAP, General Headquarters, *Summation,* no. 1, p. 65; Cohen, *Japan's Economy,* pp. 249–50, 266–67.

24 Yanase, "Genka Sekitan."

25 Fine, *Japan's Post-war,* p. 22; Japan, Economic Stabilization Board, "White Paper," ch. 2, pt. 3, sec. B.

26 Cohen, *Japan's Economy,* p. 162.

27 SCAP, General Headquarters, *Summation,* no. 2, p. 100.

28 Ibid., no. 3, p. 67.

29 U.S., Department of State, Foreign Economic Administration, Enemy Branch, *Working Conditions Other Than Wages and Hours in Japan* (Sept. 1945), pp. 20–21 (RG 407).

30 SCAP, General Headquarters, *Summation,* no. 1, p. 85.

31 Ibid., no. 2, pp. 100–101.

32 Ibid.

33 Ibid., no. 3, pp. 114–15.
34 SCAP, General Headquarters, monograph 29, pp. 16–17.
35 SCAP, General Headquarters, *Summation*, no. 10, pp. 77–78; Farley, *Aspects*, p. 18.
36 Fine, *Japan's Post-war*, p. 24.
37 Ibid., pp. 24–25.
38 Ōhara Shakai Mondai Kenkyū-jo, ed., *Saitei Chingin-sei no Igi*, Ōhara Shakai Mondai Kenkyū-jo series, no. 3 (Tokyo: Daiichi Publishing, 1949), p. 37; Japan, Economic Stabilization Board, "White Paper," ch. 2, pt. 1, sec. E.
39 SCAP, General Headquarters, *Summation*, no. 4, p. 176.
40 Cohen, *Japan's Economy*, pp. 407–8.
41 Ibid.
42 SCAP, General Headquarters, Economic and Scientific Section, Research and Statistics Division, *Annual Changes in Population of Japan Proper: 1 October 1920–1 October 1947* (1948), p. 10.
43 It is impossible to set a figure for unemployment with certainty, because this is an area in which government and SCAP statistics alike are next to worthless. They do not measure the totally unemployed correctly, much less hidden and partial unemployment. When all factors are accounted for—such as the mass shift of population out of the cities and the near stoppage of industrial production—it seems quite likely that unemployment might have reached thirteen million in the worst days of the first winter. Even the big-business association Dōyūkai estimated it at twelve million. Japan Ministry of Finance and Bank of Japan, *Statistical Year-Book*, p. 589; Keizai Dōyūkai, *Keizai Dōyūkai Jūnen Shi* (Tokyo: Keizai Dōyūkai, 1956), p. 14; Ōkōchi and Matsuo, *Sengo*, p. 63; SCAP, Economic and Scientific Section, Programs and Statistics Division, *Missions and Accomplishments*, 1952, p. 37; "Japan's Postwar Labor Movement," *Amerasia* 10:6 (Dec. 1946): 181; Norman, British Commonwealth Conference, Verbatim Minutes, pp. j1, k3–4. Unemployment remained at least as high as five to six million well into 1947.
44 Shiota Shōbei, "Senryōka no Rōdō Undō," in *Nihon Rōdō Undō no Rekishi to Kadai*, ed. Rōdō Undōshi Kenkyū-kai (Rōdō Undō Shi Kenkyū no. 50, Tokyo: Rōdō Junpōsha, 1969), p. 79; U.S., Department of State, *Labor Developments*, p. 16; SCAP, General Headquarters, Economic and Scientific Section, Research and Statistics Division, *Summary Tables: Population of Japan April 26, 1946* (1946), table 7; Japan Ministry of Finance and Bank of Japan, *Statistical Year-Book*, p. 589.
45 Mainichi Daily News Staff, *Fifty Years*, p. 226.
46 Ibid., p. 227.
47 Ibid.; Gayn, *Japan Diary*, pp. 232–34, 212–16.
48 Gayn, *Japan Diary*, p. 212.
49 Mainichi Daily News Staff, *Fifty Years*, pp. 212–13.
50 Interview with William McMahon Ball and Eric Ward, 4 June 1980.
51 SCAP, General Headquarters, *Summation*, no. 7, p. 199; no. 8, pp. 181–

84; no. 9, pp. 217–20. For a detailed study of the food situation in post-war Japan, see Tanabe Katsumasa, *Gendai Shokuryō Seisaku Shi* (Tokyo: Nihon Shūhō Sha, 1948).
52 SCAP, General Headquarters, *Summation*, no. 2, p. 118.
53 Ouchi Hyoe, *Financial and Monetary Situation in Postwar Japan* (Tokyo: Japan Institute of Pacific Studies, International Publishing," 1948), p. 40; Japan, Economic Stabilization Board, "White Paper," ch. 1, para. 16.
54 A letter from a housewife to the *Ashai Shinbun* on 2 Nov. 1945 sounded a note of despair common to city families:

"With two children, one 11 and the other 8, ours is a family of four. My husband is working for the city office. For us, it's a forbidden spiritual luxury to think about the future. We are so preoccupied with daily life; our only concern is how to survive today—and hopefully tomorrow.

"We consume 10 days' food rations in five days, supplementing the deficiency with costly food sold in the black market. People say we should also go and see the farmers in Chiba and buy agricultural products from them. They say even if we pay the train fare to Chiba, it more than pays off. But the trouble is we have no extra hand who can travel. We cannot afford the train ticket in the first place.

"We have no other choice but to go and find food in the black market. We have to eat somehow. My husband's monthly salary is ¥200, while our livelihood costs are about ¥600 every month. To make both ends meet, we sell everything we can. I know we cannot get along much longer this way."

As serious as this white-collar family's plight was, it could not compare to the misery endured by others. The husband did have a job and they at least had a place to live and something to sell. Mainichi Daily News Staff, *Fifty Years*, p. 211.
55 SCAP, General Headquarters, *Summation*, no. 5, p. 204; no. 6, pp. 183–85. SCAP, Natural Resources Section, *Preliminary Studies*, no. 4, "Food Position of Japan for the 1947 Rice Year," p. 56; no. 6, "Japanese Food Collection Program with Emphasis on Collection of the 1946 Rice Crop," pp. 10–11.
56 SCAP, Government Section, *Political Reorientation*, p. 749.
57 Interview with William McMahon Ball and Eric Ward, 4 June 1980.
58 Ibid.; William McMahon Ball to William F. Marquat, Chief, Economic and Scientific Section, SCAP, in regard to food situation, 20 Feb. 1947 (personal papers of Eric E. Ward); [Eric E. Ward], "The Food Situation in Japan During the 1946 Rice Year" (Dec. 1946) (personal papers of Eric E. Ward).
59 Tanabe, *Gendai Shokuryō*, pp. 319–28.
60 SCAP, General Headquarters, *Summation*, no. 4, pp. 56–57; Bisson, *Prospects*, pp. 105–7; Major J. Plimsoll, "Report on Visit to Japan with the Far Eastern Advisory Committee, January 1946" (Australian Archives, CP-104, Far Eastern Commission Records, bundle 15), paras. 13–28.

61 SCAP, General Headquarters, *Summation*, no. 8, p. 181; no. 4, p. 56, no. 3, p. 45. SCAP, Civil Information and Education Section, Analysis and Research Division, Publications Analysis no. 81, 29 Oct. 1946, "Food Distribution and Food Supply" (personal papers of Eric E. Ward); SCAP, Allied Translator and Interpreter Section, Press Translations, no. 1691, 7 Mar. 1946, Editorial Series: 552, items 1–3.

62 SCAP, General Headquarters, *Summation*, no. 4, pp. 57–58.

Chapter 4: Workers' Control, Unions, and the Left

1 TDSKK, *Yomiuri*, pt. 1, p. 80.
2 Ibid.
3 Ibid., p. 81.
4 TDSKK, *Yomiuri*, pt. 2, p. 12.
5 Ibid., pp. 10–11.
6 The following discussion is based on: Rōdōshō, *Shiryō 20–21-nen*, pp. 23–24; Sanbetsu Kaigi Shiryō Seiri Iinkai (hereafter cited as Sanbetsu), ed., *Sanbetsu Kaigi Shōshi*, in *Sanbetsu Kaigi: Sono Seiritsu to Undō no Tenkai*, ed. Rōdō Undō Shi Kenkyū Kai (Rōdō Undō Shi Kenkyū no. 53, Tokyo: Rōdō Junpōsha, 1970), pp. 59–60; Ōkōchi and Matsuo, *Sengo*, pp. 124–25; Watanabe, *Gendai*, p. 157.
7 The following discussion is based on: Rōdōshō, *Shiryō 20–21-nen*, pp. 29–32; Sengo Kakumei Shiryō Hensan Iinkai, *Seisan Kanri*, pp. 115–40; Ōkōchi and Matsuo, *Sengo*, p. 122.
8 Harry Braverman, *Labor and Monopoly Capital: The Degradation of Work in the Twentieth Century* (New York: Monthly Review, 1974), p. 151.
9 SCAP, Economic and Scientific Section, Advisory Committee on Labor, *Final Report*, p. 36; RSCK, *Sengo Rōdō Sōgi Jittai Chōsa* (Tokyo: Chūō Kōron Sha, 1958), vol. 7, *Tekkō Sōgi*, pp. 89–90.
10 Japan, Prime Minister's Office, Cabinet Bureau of Statistics, *Japan Statistical Year-book* (Tokyo: Cabinet Bureau of Statistics, 1949), pp. 734–35; for examples, see Rōdōshō, *Shiryō 20–21-nen*, pp. 7, 14, 23, 44, 82–83.
11 Suehiro Izutaro, "The State's Policy in Respect to Production Management," *Mainichi*, 15 Apr. 1946, translation in SCAP, Economic and Scientific Section, Labor Division (RG 331, box 8481, folder: Production Control).
12 Numata Inajirō, *Seisan Kanri Ron* (Tokyo: Nihon Kagaku Sha, 1946), pp. 27–31. In this theoretical treatment of the legality of production control written in the fall of 1946, the author argues in a short chapter on "permanent" production control that three conditions in Japan prohibit the appearance of revolutionary councils such as those the Russian workers established in 1917: the stage of capitalism, the strength of the working class, and the occupation army. Other sections of the book make clear

what tremendous obstacles faced any attempt to make production control a legal dispute tactic. Other works cite similar difficulties for "legal" production control, without doubt because Japan's big-business and government leaders realized that, however circumscribed, production control was still in essence an anti-capitalist action. Morinaga, *Seisan Kanri;* Sanbetsu Kaigi, "Seisan Kanri no Gōhōsei"; Tsuchida, *Seisan Kanri no Tatakai.*

13 Koike Hiroshi, "Rōdōsha Seisan Kanri no Genkai—Seisan Kanri ni Tomonau Shokonnan to sono Kaiketsu no Hōkō," *Minshū Hyōron* 2:3 (Mar. 1946): 9–11.

14 Yanase, "Genka Sekitan"; Koike, "Rōdōsha Seisan Kanri."

15 Nihon Keieisha Dantai Renmei, ed., *Seisan Kanri to sono Taisaku,* Keieisha series no. 2 (Tokyo: Nikkeiren, 1948); Beatrice G. Reubens, "'Production Control' in Japan," *Far Eastern Survey* 15:22 (6 Nov. 1946): 345.

16 Keizai Hyōron Henshū-bu, ed., "Keiei Kanri wa Kōshite Okonawareru," *Keizai Hyōron* (Apr. 1946): 30–31.

17 Shiota Shōbei, *Nihon Rōdō Undō no Rekishi* (Tokyo: Rōdō Junpōsha, 1964), pp. 82–84; [British Mission to SCAP], "Labour Activity in Japan (from the Surrender to 31st October, 1946)" (personal papers of Eric E. Ward), p. 5.

18 U.S., Department of State, *Labor Developments,* pp. 37–38, 39–41; Rekishi Kagaku Kenkyū Kai, *Sengo Nihon Shi* (Tokyo: Aoki Shoten, 1961), vol. 1, p. 92; Shinobu, *Sengo Nihon,* vol. 2, p. 11; "Are We Winning the Peace in Japan?" *Amerasia* 10:2 (Feb. 1946): 44–45.

19 Kaneko Kenta, "Sanbetsu Kaigi no Shoki Katsudō," in *Sanbetsu Kaigi: Sono Seiritsu to Undō no Tenkai,* ed. Rōdō Undō Shi Kenkyū-kai (Rōdō Undō Shi Kenkyū no. 53, Tokyo: Rōdō Junpōsha, 1970), p. 58; Tagawa, *Sengo Kakumei,* p. 57.

20 Ōkōchi and Matsuo, *Sengo,* p. 82; Ōkōchi Kazuo, ed., *Shiryō Sengo Nijū Nen Shi* (Tokyo: Nihon Hyōron Sha, 1966), vol. 4, *Rōdō,* p. 12.

21 Grad, *Land and Peasant,* p. 140.

22 Ōkōchi and Matsuo, *Sengo,* pp. 83–84.

23 Nihon Shakaitō Nijū Nen Kinen Jigyō Shikkō Iinkai (hereafter cited as Nihon Shakaito), ed., *Nihon Shakaitō Nijū Nen no Kiroku* (Tokyo: Nihon Shakaitō Kikanshi Shuppan Kyoku, 1965), p. 25.

24 Yamamoto, "'Sangyō Saiken,'" pp. 186–87.

25 Ōkōchi and Matsuo, *Sengo,* p. 82.

26 Nihon Rōdō Kyōkai, ed., *Sengo no Rōdō Rippō to Rōdō Undō* (Tokyo: Nihon Rōdō Kyōkai, 1950), vol. 1, p. 51.

27 Watanabe, *Gendai,* p. 157.

28 Takano, *Nihon,* p. 11.

29 Ōkōchi and Matsuo, *Sengo,* p. 85; Takano, *Nihon,* p. 10.

30 Nihon Rōdō Kyōkai, *Sengo no Rōdō,* vol. 1, p. 12.

31 Ōkōchi, *Rōdō,* p. 12.

32 Aihara Shigeru, ed., *Gendai Nihon Shihonshugi Taikei* (Tokyo: Kōbundō, 1958), vol. 4, *Rōdō,* pp. 276–77.

33 Rekishi Kagaku Kenkyūkai, *Sengo Nihon,* vol. 1, p. 99.

34 Shiota Shōbei, "Zen Sen'i Sangyō Rōdō Kumiai Dōmei," in *Nihon Rōdō Kumiai Ron*, ed. Ōkōchi Kazuo (Tokyo: Yūhikaku, 1954), p. 289; Kaneko, "Sanbetsu," p. 58.

35 Kaneko, "Sanbetsu," p. 58; Shiota, "Zen Sen'i," pp. 288–89; Nihon Shakaitō, *Nihon Shakaitō*, p. 559.

36 George M. Beckmann and Genji Okubo, *The Japanese Communist Party: 1922–1945* (Stanford: Stanford University Press, 1969), p. 341.

37 Ibid., pp. 336–41, 343, 346.

38 Sumiya Mikio, *Social Impact of Industrialization in Japan* (Japan: Government Printing Bureau, Ministry of Finance, 1963), chs. 4–5 *passim;* Shinobu, *Sengo Nihon*, vol. 1, p. 188.

39 Shakai Undō Shiryō Kankō Kai, ed., *Nihon Kyōsantō Shiryō Taisei* (Tokyo: Ōdosha Shoten, 1951), pp. 3–10.

40 Beckmann and Okubo, *Communist Party*, p. 339.

41 Shakai Undō Shiryō Kankō Kai, *Kyōsantō*, pp. 3–4; Tokuda Kyuichi, Shiga Yoshio, et al., "An Appeal to the People," appendix 2, despatch 31, 27 Oct. 1945, from George Atcheson, Acting Political Adviser to SCAP, "Periodic Report: Developments of Political Parties and Movements for the Week Ending October 26, 1945" (RG 59: 894.00/10–2745).

42 Nihon Kyōsantō Chūō (hereafter cited as Kyōsantō), ed., "Nihon Kyōsantō no Gojū Nen," *Zen'ei*, Rinji Zōkan, no. 342 (Aug. 1972): 114–16.

43 Shakai Undō Shiryō Kankō Kai, *Kyōsantō*, pp. 6–7; Beckmann and Okubo, *Communist Party*, p. 275.

44 Tokuda Kyuichi, E. Herbert Norman, and John K. Emmerson, "Communist Party Policy and Current Japanese Problems," memorandum of conversation, despatch 51, 15 Nov. 1945, Atcheson to the Secretary of State, "Political and Economic Policies of the Japanese Communist Party" (RG 59: 894.00/11–1345); Saitō, *Ni Ichi*, p. 31.

45 SCAP, Government Section, *Political Reorientation*, pp. 424, 430.

46 Watanabe, *Gendai;* Tsukahira Toshio, *The Postwar Evolution of Communist Strategy in Japan* (Cambridge: Center for International Studies, Massachusetts Institute of Technology, 1954), pp. 8–9.

47 George Atcheson, despatch 92, 11 Dec. 1945, "Political Parties in Japan: Developments During Week Ending December 8, 1945" (RG 59: 894.00/12–1145), pp. 4–5; Tsukahira, *Postwar Evolution*, p. 7; Kyōsantō, *Kyōsantō*, p. 114; Watanabe, *Gendai*, p. 156.

48 U.S., Department of State, Division of Research for Far East, Office of Intelligence Research, report 2530, 1 Jan. 1947, "Left-Wing Groups in Japanese Politics, 1918–46," pp. 157–58.

49 Shakai Undō Shiryō Kankō Kai, *Kyōsantō*, pp. 6–8, 36–38.

50 Tokuda, Norman, and Emmerson, "Communist Party Policy," p. 2–3.

51 Shiga, for one, took much the same position as Tokuda. Shiga Yoshio, "The Present Policy of the Japanese Communist Party," enclosure 1, despatch 306, 14 Mar. 1946, from Max Bishop, Office of the Political Adviser, to SCAP, "Translation of November 22, 1945, *Akahata* (Red Flag)" (RG 59: 740.00119/3–1446), p. 1.

52 Shakai Undō Shiryō Kankō Kai, *Kyōsantō*, pp. 36–37.
53 Kyōsantō, ed., *Nihon Kyōsantō Kōryōshū* (Tokyo: Nihon Kyōsantō Chūō Iinkai Shuppan Kyoku, 1962), pp. 100–104.
54 Shakai Undō Shiryō Kankō Kai, *Kyōsantō*, pp. 23–25.
55 Yamamoto, "'Sangyō Saiken,'" pp. 209–11.
56 Unno Yukitaka, Kobayashi Hideo, and Shiba Hiroshi, eds., *Sengo Nihon Rōdō Undō Shi* (Tokyo: San'ichi Shobō, 1961), vol. 1, p. 42.

Chapter 5: "Modified" Capitalism and the Co-optation of Workers' Control

1 Nikkeiren Sōritsu Jūnen Kinen Jigyō Iinkai (hereafter cited as Nikkeiren), ed., *Jūnen no Ayumi* (Tokyo: Nikkeiren Sōritsu Shūnen Kinen Jigyō Iinkai, 1958), pp. 100–102. Horikoshi, *Keizai*, vol. 1, p. 38; vol. 2, pp. 498–99; vol. 3, p. 689. Keizai Dōyūkai, *Jūnen*, pp. 34–36.
2 Asahi Shinbun Sha, ed., *Asahi Shinbun ni Miru Nihon no Ayumi* (Tokyo: Asahi Shinbun Sha, 1973), vol. 1, *Shōdo ni Kizuku Minshushugi*, p. 153; Noda, *Sengo Keiei*, p. 243; Horikoshi, *Keizai*, vol. 3, p. 689.
3 Yamamoto, *Sengo Kiki*, vol. 1, p. 168.
4 Ōkōchi, *Rōdō*, p. 8.
5 Chūō Rōdō Gakuen, ed., *Rōdō Nenkan: Shōwa 22* (Tokyo: Chūō Rōdō Gakuen, 1947), pp. 292–93; Max Bishop, Office of the Political Adviser to SCAP, despatch 250, "Political Parties in Japan: Developments During the Week Ending February 9, 1946" (RG 59: 740.00119/2–1346), pp. 3–4; Noda, *Sengo Keiei*, pp. 242–43; Horikoshi, *Keizai*, vol. 1, appendix, p. 136.
6 SCAP, Economic and Scientific Section, Advisory Committee on Labor, *Final Report*, p. 37; Theodore Cohen, Chief, Labor Division, Economic and Scientific Section, SCAP, conference with Mr. Iguchi, Chief, General Affairs Bureau, Central Liaison Office, in regard to issuance of Japanese government statement on legality of production control [4 April 1946] (RG 331, box 8481, folder: Production Control); Rōdōshō, *Shiryō 20–21-nen*, pp. 33–34; Keizai Dōyūkai, *Jūnen*, p. 32.
7 Rōdōshō, *Shiryō 20–21-nen*, p. 34; SCAP, General Headquarters, *Summation*, no. 5, p. 194; Farley, *Aspects*, p. 30.
8 Horikoshi, *Keizai*, vol. 1, appendix, p. 136; Nagata Masaomi, *Keizai Dantai Hatten Shi* (Tokyo: Kotō Shoten, 1956), pp. 189–90.
9 Noda, *Sengo Keiei*, p. 243; Horikoshi, *Keizai*, vol. 1, p. 39; appendix, p. 136; vol. 3, p. 688.
10 Noda, *Sengo Keiei*, p. 244; Nikkeiren, *Jūnen*, p. 8.
11 Yamamoto, "'Sangyō Saiken,'" p. 201.
12 Bishop, despatch 250.
13 RSCK, *Tekkō Sōgi*, pp. 106–7; Yamamoto, "'Sangyō Saiken,'" p. 222.
14 Takano, *Nihon*, p. 11.
15 Yamamoto, "'Sangyō Saiken,'" pp. 221–29.

16 RSCK, *Sengo Rōdō Sōgi Jittai Chōsa* (Tokyo: Chūō Kōron Sha, 1958), vol. 8, *Kagaku Kōgyō no Sōgi to Kumiai Undō*, p. 267.
17 Shakai Undō Shiryō Kankō Kai, *Kyōsantō*, p. 53.
18 Ibid., pp. 53–54; Ōkōchi and Matsuo, *Sengo*, p. 115.
19 Tsukahira, *Postwar Evolution*, p. 16; U.S. Army, Pacific Forces, General Headquarters, Office of the Chief of Counter-Intelligence, Research and Analysis, "Strategy of the KYOSANTO (Communist Party)," memorandum of interrogation of Nosaka Sanzo, 31 Jan. 1946, p. 2, enclosure to despatch 243, Max Bishop, Office of the Political Adviser to SCAP (RG 59: 740.00119/2–946).
20 Tsukahira, *Postwar Evolution*, pp. 18–19.
21 Kyōsantō, *Kōryōshū*, pp. 105–7.
22 Yamamoto, "'Sangyō Saiken,'" pp. 212–15; Shiino Etsurō, "Jōban Sōgi ni okeru Ni San no Keiken," *Zen'ei* 1:5 (May 1946).
23 Kyōsantō, *Kōryōshū*, pp. 106–7.
24 SCAP, Government Section, Harry E. Wildes et al., report of interview with Nosaka Sanzo, 19 Feb. 1946, enclosure to despatch 265, Max Bishop, Office of the Political Adviser to SCAP (RG 59: 740.00119/2–1946), pp. 2–3.
25 Harry Emerson Wildes, "Communist Party" (24 July 1946), enclosure to despatch 529, William J. Sebald, Office of the Political Adviser to SCAP (RG 59: 894.00/8–146), p. 15.
26 Yamamoto, "'Sangyō Saiken,'" pp. 215, 219–20.
27 The following discussion is based on: Rōdōshō, *Shiryō 20–21-nen*, pp. 44–58; Sumiya, "Mitsubishi Bibai," pp. 22–30; NTRK, *Tanrō*, pp. 68–69; RSCK, *Sekitan*, pp. 66–69.
28 Sumiya, "Mitsubishi Bibai," p. 25.
29 Rōdōshō, *Shiryō 20–21-nen*, pp. 46–47; Sengo Kakumei Shiryō Hensan Iinkai, *Seisan Kanri*, p. 171.
30 Sengo Kakumei Shiryō Hensan Iinkai, *Seisan Kanri*, p. 172; Rōdōshō, *Shiryō 20–21-nen*, pp. 46–47; Sumiya, "Mitsubishi Bibai," pp. 25–26.
31 Sengo Kakumei Shiryō Hensan Iinkai, *Seisan Kanri*, p. 153; Sumiya, "Mitsubishi Bibai," pp. 25–26.
32 Rōdōshō, *Shiryō 20–21-nen*, pp. 47 ff.; Sengo Kakumei Shiryō Hensan Iinkai, *Seisan Kanri*, p. 172; RSCK, *Sekitan*, pp. 68–69; NTRK, *Tanrō*, pp. 68–69; Sumiya, "Mitsubishi Bibai," pp. 27–29.
33 Nishimura Takeo, "Jinmin Saiban no Shinsō" (pamphlet) (15 Apr. 1946), p. 33. I am indebted to Professor Yamamoto Kiyoshi for this document. Sumiya, "Mitsubishi Bibai," p. 29.
34 Sumiya, "Mitsuibishi Bibai," p. 29.
35 Nishimura, "Jinmin Saiban no Shinsō," pp. 43–44.
36 Sengo Kakumei Shiryō Hensan Iinkai, *Seisan Kanri*, p. 184.
37 William J. Sebald, memorandum of conversation with leading Japanese businessmen, 12 Feb. 1946, enclosure to despatch 258, Max Bishop, Office of the Political Adviser to SCAP (RG 59: 740.00119/2–1546), pp. 1, 3.
38 Ibid.

39 Horikoshi, *Keizai*, vol. 1, appendix, p. 136.
40 Keizai Dōyūkai, ed., *Keizai Dōyūkai Gonen Shi* (Tokyo: Keizai Dōyūkai, 1951), p. 2; Horikoshi, *Keizai*, vol. 1, pp. 453–56.
41 Horikoshi, *Keizai*, vol. 1, p. 309.
42 Ibid.
43 Yamamoto, "'Sangyō Saiken,'" pp. 195–96; Horikoshi, *Keizai*, vol. 3, p. 309.
44 Keizai Kikaku Chō, Sengo Keizai Shi Hensanshitsu (hereafter cited as Keizai Kikaku Chō), ed., *Sengo Keizai Shi: Keizai Seisaku Hen* (Tokyo: Ōkurashō Insatsu-kyoku, 1964), pp. 66–68; Ouchi Hyoe, *Financial and Monetary Situation in Postwar Japan* (Tokyo: Japan Institute of Pacific Studies, International Publishing, 1948), pp. 22–24; SCAP, General Headquarters, *Summation*, no. 5, pp. 203–23, 225–26.
45 Arisawa Hiromi and Inaba Hidezō, eds., *Shiryō Sengo Nijū Nen Shi* (Tokyo: Nihon Hyōron Sha, 1966) vol. 2, *Keizai*, pp. 21–22.
46 Ibid.
47 Ibid., p. 22. Japanese Foreign Office, Research Bureau, Special Research Committee, *The Basic Problems for the Reconstruction of Japan's Economy* (Tokyo: Mar. 1946), pt. 2, p. 4. I am indebted to Eric Ward for this document. It is a translation of the entire document cited in note 44 above.
48 SCAP, General Headquarters, monograph 28, p. 20.
49 Suehiro, *Japanese Trade Unionism*, p. 469.
50 Ibid., p. 470.
51 Suehiro Izutaro, "The Legality and the Limitations of Labor's Exercise of Management Controls," translation of 7–8 Feb. 1946 *Mainichi* article in appendix to Thomas L. Blakemore, "Suggested Legal Justification of Labor's Assertion of Managerial Powers in Japanese Labor Disputes," enclosure to despatch 319, Max Bishop, Office of the Political Adviser to SCAP (RG 59: 894.504/3–2346), p. 2.
52 Ibid., pp. 3–4.
53 Ibid., p. 5.
54 Suehiro, "The State's Policy," p. 1.
55 Ibid., pp. 2–3.
56 Ibid., p. 3.
57 Ibid.
58 Keizai Dōyūkai, *Gonen*, p. 2.
59 Keizai Dōyūkai, *Jūnen*, p. 27.
60 Keizai Dōyūkai, *Gonen*, pp. 4, 9; Miwa, "Keizai Dantai," pp. 223, 225.
61 Yamamoto, "'Sangyō Saiken,'" p. 199; Nagata, *Keizai Dantai*, pp. 190–91.
62 Ibid., pp. 21–22.
63 Keizai Dōyūkai, *Jūnen*, p. 35.
64 Miwa, "Keizai Dantai," p. 223.
65 Arisawa and Inaba, *Keizai*, p. 116; Horikoshi, *Keizai*, vol. 3, pp. 309–10.
66 Keizai Dōyūkai, *Jūnen*, p. 22; Arisawa and Inaba, *Keizai*, p. 116.
67 Keizai Dōyūkai, *Jūnen*, pp. 32–34.

68 Ibid., p. 36.
69 Ibid., pp. 3, 32.
70 Ibid., p. 34.
71 Gōshi Kōhei, "Seisan Kanri no Keizaiteki Seiyaku," *Keiei Hyōron* 1:2 (May 1946): 6-9

Chapter 6: The Working Class Crosses the Line

1 The following discussion is based on: Rōdōshō, *Shiryō 20-21-nen*, pp. 90-99; NTRK, *Tanrō*, pp. 68-69; RSCK, *Sekitan*, pp. 66-69.
2 Rōdōshō, *Shiryō 20-21-nen*, p. 97.
3 Sengo Kakumei Shiryō Hensan Iinkai, *Seisan Kanri*, p. 184.
4 Ibid.
5 Ibid., p. 186.
6 Rōdōshō, *Shiryō 20-21-nen*, p. 95.
7 T. Cohen, conference with Iguchi.
8 Rōdōshō, *Shiryō 20-21-nen*, pp. 98-99.
9 SCAP, General Headquarters, *Summation*, no. 7, p. 184.
10 Sengo Kakumei Shiryō Hensan Iinkai, *Seisan Kanri*, pp. 187-88; Yamamoto, *Sengo Kiki*, pp. 148-50.
11 Rōdōshō, *Shiryō 20-21-nen*, p. 99.
12 The following discussion is based on: Rōdōshō, *Shiryō 20-21-nen*, pp. 96, 111-15; RSCK, *Sekitan*, pp. 69-73; Sengo Kakumei Shiryō Hensan Iinkai, *Seisan Kanri*, pp. 184-87; NTRK, *Tanrō*, p. 66.
13 Rōdōshō, *Shiryō 20-21-nen*, p. 23.
14 Ibid., p. 15.
15 Sengo Kakumei Shiryō Hensan Iinkai, *Seisan Kanri*, pp. 184-87.
16 The following discussion is based on: Rōdōshō, *Shiryō 20-21-nen*, pp. 83-84; Yamamoto, *Sengo Kiki*, pp. 147-50; RSCK, *Kagaku Kōgyō*, p. 266.
17 Nihon Sangyō Rōdō Chōsa-kyoku, ed., "Sōgi Shudan toshite no Seisan Kanri," in *Chōsa Hōkoku*, ed. Tōkyō Daigaku Shakai Kagaku Kenkyū-jo (Tokyo: Tōkyō Daigaku Shakai Kagaku Kenkyū-jo, 1971), vol. 13, *Sengo Shoki Rōdō Sōgi Chōsa*, pp. 286-87; Yamamoto, *Sengo Kiki*, pp. 147-50.
18 Nihon Sangyō Rōdō Chōsa-kyoku, "Sōgi Shudan," p. 287. The following discussion is based on: ibid., pp. 286-91; Yamamoto, *Sengo Kiki*, pp. 147-50; RSCK, *Kagaku Kōgyō*, p. 279.
19 [British Mission], "Labour Activity," pp. 8-9.
20 Matsumoto Kenji et al., "Shokuryō Kiki Toppa no Tame ni," *Jinmin*, special issue, vol. 1, no. 3 (Mar. 1946): 19-23; Harold Wakefield, *New Paths for Japan* (London: Royal Institute of International Affairs, 1948), pp. 132-33.
21 Ronald P. Dore, *Land Reform in Japan* (London: Oxford University Press, 1959), ch. 5 *passim*; Grad, *Land and Peasant*, ch. 4 *passim*.
22 Grad, *Land and Peasant*, pp. 134-35; Chūō Rōdō Gakuen, *Rōdō Nen-*

kan, pp. 391–92; Tagawa, *Sengo Kakumei*, p. 101.

23 Grad, *Land and Peasant*, pp. 135–36.

24 Chūō Rōdō Gakuen, *Rōdō Nenkan*, pp. 391–92; Tagawa, *Sengo Kakumei*, p. 101.

25 SCAP, General Headquarters, *Summation*, no. 5, pp. 203–4.

26 Ibid.

27 Unno, Kobayashi, and Shiba, *Sengo Nihon*, vol. 1, pp. 82–83.

28 Ibid., p. 92.

29 George Atcheson, U.S. Political Adviser to SCAP, despatch 453; "Demonstrations and Growing Tendency towards Violence in Japan," enclosure 4: "Summaries of 20 incidents in Japan involving violence or threatened violence (September 12, 1945 to May 19, 1946)," pp. 4–5 (RG 59: 740.00119/6–1046).

30 Chūō Rōdō Gakuen, *Rōdō Nenkan*, pp. 394–95.

31 Atcheson, despatch 453, enclosure 4, "Summaries," p. 8.

32 Yamamoto, *Sengo Kiki*, pp. 182–83.

33 The following discussion is based on: Rōdōshō, *Shiryō 20–21-nen*, pp. 920–21; Yamamoto, *Sengo Kiki*, pp. 172–76.

34 Rōdōshō, *Shiryō 20–21-nen*, pp. 62–64; Watanabe, *Gendai*, p. 159.

35 Rōdōshō, *Shiryō 20–21-nen*, p. 62.

36 Ibid., p. 921.

37 Okada Bunkichi, "Haikyū o Guai Yoku Suru ni wa—Shimin Shokuryō Kanri Iinkai to wa Nani ka," *Minshū no Hata* 1:3 (May 1946): 42–45; Matsumoto, "Shokuryō Kiki," pp. 19–23.

38 SCAP, Government Section, *Political Reorientation*, p. 719.

39 Tatsuki Yasuo, *General Trend of Japanese Opinion Following the End of War* (Tokyo: Japan Institute of Pacific Studies, International Publishing, 1948), pp. 5–6.

40 William McMahon Ball, "Interim Report," 16 May 1946 (Australian Archives, CRS A518, Prime Minister's Department: Correspondence File, item N.815/1/1).

41 Ōkōchi Kazuo and Ōtomo Fukuo, "Sengo Rōdō Undō Shi," in *Nihon Shihonshugi Kōza: Sengo Nihon no Seiji to Keizai* (Tokyo: Iwanami Shoten, 1954), vol. 7, *Rōdōsha to Nōmin*, pp. 36–37; *Rekishi Kagaku Kenkyū Kai, Sengo Nihon*, vol. 1, p. 100; Unno, Kobayashi, and Shiba, *Sengo Nihon*, vol. 1, pp. 80–81; Max Bishop, despatch 250, p. 2.

42 Tagawa, *Sengo Kakumei*, p. 79; Rekishi Kagaku Kenkyū Kai, *Sengo Nihon*, vol. 1, p. 100; Max Bishop, Office of the Political Adviser to SCAP, despatch 314: "Political Parties in Japan: Developments During the Week Ending March 16, 1946" (RG 59: 740.00119/3–1946), p. 2.

43 SCAP, General Headquarters, *Summation*, no. 6, pp. 38–39.

44 Max Bishop, despatch 314, p. 4.

45 Yamamoto, *Sengo Kiki*, p. 177.

46 Far Eastern Commission, U.S. Delegation, "A Brief Survey of the Growth of Japanese Labor Sentiment Against the Government" (14 Feb. 1947) (RG 287, box 228), p. 1. I am indebted to Kim Stege for this document.

Also see Atcheson, despatch 453, p. 3; Yamamoto, *Sengo Kiki*, pp. 177–78; Tagawa, *Sengo Kakumei*, pp. 79–81.

47 Yamamoto, *Sengo Kiki*, p. 178.
48 Gayn, *Japan Diary*, pp. 164–65; Tagawa, *Sengo Kakumei*, pp. 80–81.
49 Gayn, *Japan Diary*, pp. 165–66.
50 Rekishi Kagaku Kenkyū Kai, *Sengo Nihon*, vol. 1, p. 119.
51 Gayn, *Japan Diary*, pp. 166–67.
52 Ibid., p. 168.
53 Ibid., pp. 170–71.
54 Ibid., p. 171.
55 Ibid, p. 169; Rekishi Kagaku Kenkyū Kai, *Sengo Nihon*, vol. 1, p. 119; Tagawa, *Sengo Kakumei*, pp. 81–82.
56 Yamamoto, *Sengo Kiki*, pp. 179–80; Tagawa, *Sengo Kakumei*, pp. 81–82.
57 SCAP, General Headquarters, *Summation*, no. 7, pp. 42–43; Watanabe, *Gendai*, p. 159; Rekishi Kagaku Kenkyū Kai, *Sengo Nihon*, vol. 1, pp. 123–24.
58 SCAP, Government Section, "Counter-Measures Against the Subversive Potential in Japan—1946 to 1951 Inclusive," tab C (RG 331, box 8497, folder: Communism: Miscellaneous Data on Communist Counter-Measures Committee).
59 SCAP, General Headquarters, *Summation*, no. 8, p. 29; Far Eastern Commission, "A Brief Survey," pp. 1–2.
60 Gayn, *Japan Diary*, p. 199.
61 Ibid., p. 197.
62 Allied Council for Japan, Meeting 4, 15 May 1946, afternoon session, Verbatim Minutes, pp. 10–12 (RG 43, Allied Council for Japan, box 70).
63 Ibid., pp. 15–16; Gayn, *Japan Diary*, p. 218.
64 Allied Council for Japan, Verbatim Minutes, p. 13; Atcheson, despatch 453, enclosure 4.
65 Tōkyō Daigaku Shakai Kagaku Kenkyū Kai, ed., "Seijiteki Kaikyū Ishiki no Shinten," in *Chōsa Hōkoku*, ed. Tokyo Daigaku Shakai Kagaku Kenkyū-jo (Tokyo: Tōkyō Daigaku Shakai Kagaku Kenkyū-jo, 1971), vol. 13, *Sengo Shoki Rōdō Sōgi Chōsa*, pp. 298–304; Yamamoto, *Sengo Kiki*, pp. 193–94.
66 Yamamoto, *Sengo Kiki*, p. 169; Atcheson, despatch 453, enclosure 4, p. 2; Gayn, *Japan Diary*, p. 226; Tagawa, *Sengo Kakumei*, pp. 84–85.
67 SCAP, General Headquarters, *Summation*, no. 8, pp. 29–30; Atcheson, despatch 453, enclosure 4, p. 3; FEC, "A Brief Survey," p. 2; Gayn, *Japan Diary*, pp. 222–26.
68 Yamamoto, *Sengo Kiki*, pp. 169, 183–85; Unno, Kobayashi, and Shiba, *Sengo Nihon*, vol. 1, pp. 102–3.
69 Atcheson, despatch 453, enclosure 4, p. 1; Rekishi Kagaku Kenkyū Kai, *Sengo Nihon*, vol. 1, p. 129; Gayn, *Japan Diary*, p. 227.
70 Tagawa, *Sengo Kakumei*, p. 86; Rekishi Kagaku Kenkyū Kai, *Sengo Nihon*, vol. 1, p. 130.
71 Gayn, *Japan Diary*, p. 223.

72 SCAP, General Headquarters, *Summation*, no. 8, pp. 21–26; Gayn, *Japan Diary*, pp. 225–28.
73 Ōkōchi and Matsuo, *Sengo*, p. 143.
74 Atcheson, despatch 453, enclosure 4, p. 2; Gayn, *Japan Diary*, p. 230; Ogura Takekazu, *Can Japanese Agriculture Survive?—A Historical and Comparative Approach*, 2nd ed. (Tokyo: Agricultural Policy Research Center, 1980), pp. 198–99.
75 Lt. General Robert Lawrence Eichelberger, Commander of the Eighth Army, to wife, 29 May 1946 (Eichelberger Papers, Duke University: Letters [personal], 1946, 22-A, box 14, folder: "Personal Correspondence to Miss Em"); Eichelberger, diary, 23 May 1946 (Eichelberger Papers: Diaries, 22-D, box 180, Diary 24 Oct. 1945–26 Dec. 1946).
76 Gayn, *Japan Diary*, p. 229; Atcheson, despatch 453, enclosure 4, pp. 1–2.
77 Sengo Kakumei Shiryō Hensan Iinkai, *Seisan Kanri*, p. 229.
78 Yamamoto, *Sengo Kiki*, pp. 186–87; Atcheson, despatch 453, enclosure 1.
79 Atcheson, despatch 453, enclosure 1.

Chapter 7: The Conservative Reaction

1 SCAP, General Headquarters, *Summation*, no. 8, p. 31; Ogura, *Japanese Agriculture*, p. 199.
2 Far Eastern Commission, "A Brief Survey," p. 2.
3 SCAP, General Headquarters, *Summation*, no. 10, pp. 183–90; no. 11, pp. 181–86.
4 SCAP, Government Section, "Counter-Measures," tab C.
5 SCAP, General Headquarters, *Summation*, no. 9, pp. 24–25; Ōkōchi, *Rōdō*, pp. 8–9.
6 Rōdōshō, *Shiryō 20–21-nen*, pp. 662–65, 804; [British Mission], "Labour Activity," p. 10; Minobe Ryōkichi, "Seisan Kanri no Hinin to Keiei Kyōgikai no Setchi," *Jinmin Sensen* 5 (Aug. 1946): 11–14.
7 Ibid. See also the special number of *Keiei Hyōron*, which makes it clear that the joint labor-management councils were intended to take the place of production control and domesticate it, so to speak, by purging it of its class content and bringing to the fore the production content by coopting it into consultative councils established on the principle of production first. Gōshi Kōhei et al., *Keiei Hyōron*, pp. 3–17.
8 William McMahon Ball, "Monthly Report, May 1946, pt. 2, Political Developments," 4 June 1946 (CRS A518, item N.815/1/1).
9 William J. Coughlin, *Conquered Press: The MacArthur Era in Japanese Journalism* (Palo Alto: Pacific Books, 1952), p. 85; Samuel Romer, Labor Relations Branch, Labor Division, Economic and Scientific Section, SCAP, "Summary of Communist Infiltration and Influence in Japanese Labor Movement," 19 Nov. 1948 (RG 331: box 8497, folder: Communist Activ-

ities June '48–Dec. '49); SCAP, General Headquarters, Military Intelligence Section, General Staff, "Special Report: Communist Leadership of National Congress of Industrial Unions," 13 Mar. 1948 (RG 331, box 8497, folder: Communist Activities 1945–May '48), p. 2; Morita Yoshio, *Nihon Keieisha Dantai Hatten Shi* (Tokyo: Nikkan Rōdō Tsūshin Sha, 1958), p. 330; [British Mission], "Labour Activity," pp. 16–17.

10 SCAP, Government Section, "Counter-Measures," tab C.

11 RSCK, *Tokushu Kēsu*, pp. 49–53; TDSKK, *Yomiuri*, pt. 1, pp. 240–42.

12 Gayn, *Japan Diary*, pp. 331–32.

13 U.S., Department of State, "The Yomiuri Shimbun Case," pp. 73–78; [British Mission], "Labour Activity," pp. 16–17; Deverall to Chief, Labor Division, Economic and Scientific Section, SCAP, memoranda, 21 May 1946 and 4 June 1946 (Deverall Papers: C8-38, vol. 2), pp. 359–62, 403–5.

14 TDSKK, *Yomiuri*, pt. 2, pp. 9–11; Masuyama Taisuke, *Yomiuri Sōgi (1945–46)* (Tokyo: Aki Shobo, 1976), ch. 2 *passim*.

15 Sanbetsu, *Shōshi*, pp. 123–28; Masuyama, *Yomiuri Sōgi*, ch. 2.

16 Behrstock, "Snafu in Tokyo."

17 TDSKK, *Yomiuri*, pt. 2, pp. 10–11; U.S., Department of State, "The Yomiuri Shimbun Case," pp. 20–21, 25–27, 32–34.

18 The abrupt imposition of censorship of left-wing publications is readily apparent in the files of the Civil Censorship Detachment, Press Publication and Broadcasting Section of SCAP, now held in the Gordon W. Prange Collection in the East Asia Collection of McKeldin Library at the University of Maryland.

19 Major Daniel C. Imboden, Chief of Press Division, Civil Information and Education Section, SCAP, report of special conference with Tokyo public procurators on the *Yomiuri* newspaper labor-management dispute, 2 July 1946 (RG 331, box 8499, folder: Labor Relations Disputes, Newspaper, Yomiuri Case [Confidential]), p. 2; TDSKK, *Yomiuri*, pt. 1, p. 145.

20 Gayn, *Japan Diary*, pp. 235–36.

21 Ibid.

22 SCAP, Government Section, "Counter-Measures," tab C; Ōkōchi, *Rōdō*, pp. 8–9.

23 U.S., Department of State, "The Yomiuri Shimbun Case," pp. iv–v; Howard Schonberger, "American Labor's Cold War in Occupied Japan," *Diplomatic History* (1979): 253.

24 Takano, *Nihon*, p. 32.

25 Rōdōshō, *Shiryō 20–21-nen*, p. 140; TDSKK, *Yomiuri*, pt. 2, p. 29; Ōkōchi and Matsuo, *Sengo*, p. 161.

26 Rōdōshō, *Shiryō 20–21-nen*, pp. 140–41; Takano, *Nihon*, p. 32.

27 TDSKK, *Yomiuri*, pt. 1, p. 145.

28 Ibid., pt. 2, p. 30; U.S., Department of State, "The Yomiuri Shimbun Case," p. 27; Rōdōshō, *Shiryō 20–21-nen*, pp. 144–46.

29 TDSKK, *Yomiuri*, pt. 2, p. 32.

30 Ibid., pt. 1, pp. 14–15.
31 Ibid., pt. 2, p. 32; Gayn, *Japan Diary*, p. 253.
32 TDSKK, *Yomiuri*, pt. 2, p. 9; Gayn, *Japan Diary*, p. 254.
33 TDSKK, *Yomiuri*, pt. 2, p. 21.
34 Ibid., pp. 30, 257.
35 Imboden, report of special conference (2 July 1946), pp. 2–3.
36 U.S., Department of State, "The Yomiuri Shimbun Case," p. 28.
37 Rōdōshō, *Shiryō 20–21-nen*, p. 146.
38 Ibid., pp. 141–42.
39 Ibid., pp. 142–43; TDSKK, *Yomiuri*, pt. 2, pp. 26, 43, 47.
40 Rōdōshō, *Shiryō 20–21-nen*, p. 145; TDSKK, *Yomiuri*, pt. 2, pp. 26–27.
41 Rōdōshō, *Shiryō 20–21-nen*, p. 143; TDSKK, *Yomiuri*, pt. 2, p. 257.
42 Rōdōshō, *Shiryō 20–21-nen*, p. 143; TDSKK, *Yomiuri*, pt. 2, p. 43.
43 Shūkan Shinchō Henshū-bu, ed., *Makkāsā no Nihon* (Tokyo: Shinchō Sha, 1970), pp. 130–31; TDSKK, *Yomiuri*, pt. 2, p. 47.
44 U.S., Department of State, "The Yomiuri Shimbun Case," p. 35.
45 TDSKK, *Yomiuri*, pt. 2, pp. 47–48, 258.
46 Ibid., p. 48.
47 Ibid.
48 Ibid., p. 22.
49 Ibid., p. 49.
50 Rōdōshō, *Shiryō 20–21-nen*, pp. 149–51.
51 TDSKK, *Yomiuri*, pt. 2, p. 49.
52 SCAP, Government Section, *Political Reorientation*, p. 413; State-War-Navy Coordinating Committee, *Treatment*, appendix, pp. 13–16.
53 Horikoshi, *Keizai*, vol. 1, pp. 4–14, 25–26; vol. 3, pp. 304–7, 547–48. Miwa, "Keizai Dantai," pp. 215–16; Noda, *Sengo Keiei*, p. 51.
54 Keizai Dōyūkai, *Gonen*, p. 2; Keizai Dōyūkai, *Jūnen*, pp. 21–22, 27; Miwa, "Keizai Dantai," pp. 223, 225.
55 Keizai Dōyūkai, *Gonen*, pp. 4, 9; Keizai Dōyūkai, *Jūnen*, pp. 32, 25; Arisawa and Inaba, *Keizai*, pp. 21–22.
56 Ball, "Monthly Report, Jan. 1947, Economic Developments," extracted in doc. I/47 for the British Commonwealth Conference on a Japanese Peace Settlement (Australian Archives, CP-104, Far Eastern Commission Records, bundles 51–52).
57 Keizai Kikaku Chō, Sengo Keizai Shi Hensanshitsu, ed., *Sengo Keizai Shi: Keizai Antei Honbu Shi* (Tokyo: Ōkurashō Insatsu-kyoku, 1964), pp. 12–13.
58 Ouchi, *Financial*, p. 26; Ball, "Monthly Report, May 1946, Political Developments."
59 Arisawa and Inaba, *Keizai*, pp. 46–47.
60 Keizai Kikaku Chō, *Keizai Seisaku*, pp. 70–71; Keizai Kikaku Chō, *Keizai Antei*, p. 18; Inaba and Arisawa, *Keizai*, pp. 46–47; Ball, "Monthly Report, Jan. 1947, Economic Developments."
61 Inaba and Arisawa, *Keizai*, pp. 46–47.
62 The legislation effecting the cancellation of the indemnities was delayed

until October, by which time many had already been paid by the government. The assets of the corporations involved had increased many fold during the wartime and postwar inflation; thus, the damage done to the capital structure of big business was far less than anticipated. On the capital levy, Ishibashi more than pleased the zaibatsu, not only by excluding non-juridical persons, but also by raising the exemption margin to 100,000 yen, drastically reducing the tax rate to 50 percent of the value of property, and deferring payment until after April 1947. See Ouchi, *Financial*, pp. 27–29; Cohen, *Japan's Economy*, pp. 428–29.

63 U.S., Department of State, Division of Research for the Far East, Office of Intelligence Research, report 3479.15, "The Japanese Cancellation of Wartime Indemnities" (27 Sept. 1946), in *A Guide to O.S.S./State Department Intelligence and Research Reports*, ed. Paul Kesaris (Washington, D.C.: University Publications of America, 1977), vol. 2, *Postwar Japan, Korea and Southeast Asia*, reel 3, no. 18; Tagawa, *Sengo Kakumei*, p. 125.

64 Shibagaki Kazuo, "Dissolution of Zaibatsu and Deconcentration of Economic Power," Tokyo University Institute of Social Science, *Annals of the Institute of Social Science* 20 (1979): 42–52; Pacific Basin Reports, *1972 Handbook of Japanese Financial/Industrial Combines* (San Francisco: Pacific Basin Reports, 1972), pp. 1–8; Tracy Dahlby, "The Japanese Supertraders," *Far Eastern Economic Review* 107:5 (1 Feb. 1980).

65 For partially conflicting analyses of "Ishibashi finance" see the following: Keizai Kikaku Chō, *Keizai Seisaku*, pp. 70–74; Takeda Takao, "Senji Sengo no Zaisei Seisaku," in *Sengo Nihon Keizai no Shomondai*, ed. Yanaihara Tadao (Tokyo: Yūhikaku, 1949), pp. 272–78; Kawazaki Misaburō, *Sengo Keizai no Kihon Mondai* (Tokyo: Kaizō Sha, 1948), pp. 120–24; Nonomura Kazuo, *Nihon Sengo Keizai no Gendankai: "Kiki" yori "Antei" e* (Tokyo: Ran Shobō, 1948), pp. 123 ff.

66 Ishibashi Tanzan, *Infureshon ka Defureshon?* (Tokyo: Tōkyō Kōen Kai, July 1946), p. 26.

67 Ibid., pp. 25–26.

68 Suehiro, *Japanese Trade Unionism*, p. 254.

69 U.S., Department of State, "The Yomiuri Shimbun Case," pp. 41–42.

70 Rōdōshō, *Shiryō 20–21-nen*, p. 152; TDSKK, *Yomiuri*, pt. 2, pp. 49–51; U.S., Department of State, "The Yomiuri Shimbun Case," p. 38.

71 Rōdōshō, *Shiryō 20–21-nen*, p. 152; U.S., Department of State, "The Yomiuri Shimbun Case," p. 39.

72 Theodore Cohen, Labor Division, Economic and Scientific Section, SCAP, "Staff Study: Clarification of General MacArthur's 20th of May Statement on Mob Violence as Affecting Labor Unions, Meetings and Demonstrations" (26 June 1946) (RG 331, box 8497, folder: Labor Relations Demonstrations), pp. 2–4, appendices B, C; Shūkan Shinchō Henshū-bu, *Makkāsā*, pp. 129–31; Deverall to Chief, Labor Division, Economic and Scientific Section, SCAP, memoranda, 3, 13, and 14 June 1946 (Deverall Papers: C8-38, vol. 2), pp. 400–401, 439–41.

73 T. Cohen, "Staff Study," appendix B.
74 Ibid., p. 3; Shūkan Shinchō Henshū-bu, *Makkāsā*, pp. 129–31.
75 T. Cohen, "Staff Study," p. 3.
76 U.S., Department of State, "The Yomiuri Shimbun Case," p. 41.
77 Lt. Colonel Donald R. Nugent, Chief of Civil Information and Education Section, SCAP, reports concerning the situation at the *Yomiuri* newspaper, 17–18 July 1946 (RG 331, box 8499, folder: Labor Relations Disputes, Newspaper, Yomiuri Case [Confidential]).
78 Rōdōshō, *Shiryō 20–21-nen*, p. 153; TDSKK, *Yomiuri*, pt. 2, p. 27.
79 U.S., Department of State, "The Yomiuri Shimbun Case," p. 44.
80 TDSKK, *Yomiuri*, pt. 2, p. 40.
81 Nugent, reports concerning the *Yomiuri*.
82 Ibid.; TDSKK, *Yomiuri*, pt. 2, pp. 56–57; Gayn, *Japan Diary*, p. 265.
83 Nugent, reports concerning the *Yomiuri*.
84 Ibid.
85 Uhlan and Thomas, *Shoriki*, p. 191.
86 TDSKK, *Yomiuri*, pt. 2, pp. 40, 81, 258.
87 Shūkan Shinchō Henshū-bu, *Makkāsā*, pp. 133–34; Brig. General William F. Marquat, Chief, Economic and Scientific Section, SCAP, memorandum for Chief of Staff, "Coordination of Staff Sections in Labor Relations" (2 Aug. 1946) (RG 331, box 8498, folder: Labor Relations, Demonstrations).
88 TDSKK, *Yomiuri*, pt. 2, p. 72.
89 Masuyama Taisuke, Kikunami Katsumi, Nakahara Jūnkichi, and Kameta Tōgo, "Appeal to Gen. MacArthur on the Question of Interference into August 2nd Demonstration" (2 Aug. 1946) (RG 331, box 8498, folder: Labor Relations, Demonstrations).
90 Rōdōshō, *Shiryō 20–21-nen*, pp. 154–55; SCAP, General Headquarters, *Summation*, no. 11, p. 171; U.S., Department of State, "The Yomiuri Shimbun Case," pp. 50–51.
91 Rōdōshō, *Shiryō 20–21-nen*, pp. 156–57; U.S., Department of State, "The Yomiuri Shimbun Case," p. 63.
92 U.S., Department of State, "The Yomiuri Shimbun Case," p. 64.
93 Gayn, *Japan Diary*, pp. 33–35.
94 TDSKK, *Yomiuri*, pt. 2, pp. 74–80; U.S., Department of State, "The Yomiuri Shimbun Case," pp. 63, 66; Gayn, *Japan Diary*, pp. 334–35; Farley, *Aspects*, p. 113.

Chapter 8: The Unions Fight Back

1 Shiota, "Senryōka," p. 85.
2 Ōkōchi and Matsuo, *Sengo*, p. 163.
3 RSCK, *Sengo Rōdō Sōgi Jittai Chōsa* (Tokyo: Chūō Kōron Sha, 1959), vol. 13, *Kokutetsu Sōgi*, pp. 76–77.
4 Watanabe, *Gendai*, p. 163.

5 Ii Yashirō, "Kokutetsu Kugatsu Tōsō to Ni Ichi Zene Suto," in *Rōdō Undō Shi Kenkyū*, ed. Rōdō Undō Shi Kenkyū Kai (Tokyo: Rōdō Junpōsha, 1972), vol. 54, *Senryōka no Rōdō Sōgi*, pp. 10–11.

6 Ibid., pp. 11–13; Saitō Ichirō, *Sengo Rōdō Undō Shi* (Tokyo: Shakai Hyōron Sha, 1974), pp. 37–38; Rōdōshō, *Shiryō 20–21-nen*, pp. 213–15; Shiota, "Senryōka," pp. 85–86; Ōkōchi and Ōtomo, "Sengo Rōdō," p. 45.

7 Sanbetsu, *Shōshi*, pp. 127–28.

8 Sanbetsu Kinen Kai, ed., *Sanbetsu Kaigi/Zenrōren Kikanshi* (Tokyo: Rōdō Junpōsha, 1973), pp. 1, 11, 751–52; Rōdōshō, *Shiryō 20–21-nen*, pp. 658–59; Saitō, *Ni Ichi*, p. 107; Ōkōchi and Ōtomo, "Sengo Rōdō," pp. 42–43.

9 Rōdōshō, *Shiryō 20–21-nen*, pp. 659–60. SCAP, General Headquarters, *Summation*, no. 11, p. 171; no. 12, p. 151; no. 13, pp. 165–66; no. 14, p. 212; no. 15, p. 163; no. 17, p. 181.

10 Yamamoto, *Sengo Kiki*, pp. 104–7, 282–86; Tagawa, *Sengo Kakumei*, p. 125; Keizai Dōyūkai, *Jūnen*, pp. 51–55; Deverall, letter (15 Nov. 1946) (Deverall Papers: C8-2, vol. 4, series 3, letter 1).

11 Okochi Kazuo, Bernard Karsh, and Solomon B. Levine, eds., *Workers and Employers in Japan: The Japanese Employment Relations System* (Tokyo: University of Tokyo Press, 1973), pp. 293–301; Kishimoto Eitarō, "Labour-Management Relations and the Trade Unions in Post-War Japan (1)," *Kyoto University Economic Review* 38:1 (Apr. 1968), no. 84, p. 4.

12 Saitō, *Sengo Rōdō*, p. 38; Shiota Shōbei, "Sengo no Rōdō Sōgi," in *Chōsa Hōkoku*, ed. Tōkyō Daigaku Shakai Kagaku Kenkyū-jo (Tokyo: Tōkyō Daigaku Shakai Kagaku Kenkyū-jo, 1971), vol. 13, *Sengo Shoki Rōdō Sōgi Chōsa*, p. 4; SCAP, General Headquarters, *Summation*, no. 13, pp. 166–67.

13 RSCK, *Tokushu Kēsu*, pp. 35–38; Shiota, "Sengo no Rōdō Sōgi," p. 5.

14 RSCK, *Tokushu Kēsu*, pp. 38–40.

15 Ibid., p. 41.

16 Saitō, *Ni Ichi*, p. 113; Ōkōchi and Ōtomo, "Sengo Rōdō," pp. 47–48.

17 RSCK, *Tokushu Kēsu*, p. 42.

18 Ibid., pp. 43 ff.

19 Ibid., pp. 42–43, 50–53.

20 Ibid., p. 54.

21 RSCK, *Sekitan*, pp. 90–94; NTRK, *Tanrō*, pp. 97–99.

22 RSCK, *Sekitan*, pp. 94–97; Nihon Sekitan Kōgyō Renmei and Nihon Sekitan Kōgyō Kai, eds., *Sekitan Rōdō Nenkan* (Tokyo: Nihon Sekitan Kōgyō Renmei, 1947), pp. 358–63; NTRK, *Tanrō*, pp. 100–102.

23 NTRK, *Tanrō*, pp. 101–4.

24 RSCK, *Sekitan*, pp. 97–99; Nihon Sekitan Kōgyō Renmei, *Sekitan Rōdō*, pp. 365–68.

25 Aizumi Kyō et al., "Densan Jūgatsu Sōgi (1946)," in *Chōsa Hōkoku*, ed. Tōkyō Daigaku Shakai Kagaku Kenkyū-jo (Tokyo: Tōkyō Daigaku Shakai Kagaku Kenkyū-jo, 1971), vol. 13, *Sengo Shoki Rōdō Sōgi Chōsa*, pp. 48–50.

26 Ibid., pp. 50–53; Farley, *Aspects*, ch. 8, pp. 114–125; Sanbetsu, *Shōshi*, pp. 131–32.

27 Aizumi, "Densan," pp. 43–44.

28 Tōyama, "Sengo Nijū Nen," p. 12; Shiota, "Senryōka," p. 88.

29 Suehiro, *Japanese Trade Unionism*, p. 254. Numerous errors in spelling in the copy have been corrected.

30 Arisawa, "Senki/Sengo," pp. 90–93; Kawazaki Misaburō, *Sengo Keizai no Kihon Mondai* (Tokyo: Kaizō Sha, 1948), pp. 120–26; Ball, "Monthly Report, Feb. 1947, Economic Development" (personal papers of Eric E. Ward).

31 The situation was actually even worse, for production for the black market (primarily consumer goods) was excluded from the official figures, but might have accounted for as much as 50 percent of total production. See Arisawa, "Senki/Sengo," p. 91; Kawazaki, *Sengo Keizai*, p. 125.

32 Arisawa, "Senki/Sengo," p. 91; Bisson, *Prospects*, p. 100.

33 Arisawa, "Senki/Sengo," p. 91, 104–11.

34 Ibid., pp. 121–22; Keizai Kikaku Chō, *Keizai Antei*, p. 19; Keizai Kikaku Chō, *Keizai Seisaku*, pp. 33–39.

35 Keizai Kikaku Chō, *Keizai Seisaku*, pp. 36, 43, 64 ff.

36 Ibid., pp. 74, 80–83; Keizai Kikaku Chō, *Keizai Antei*, pp. 11–14; Cohen, *Japan's Economy*, p. 431; Bisson, *Prospects*, pp. 103–4; Ball, "Monthly Report, April 1947, Transition Controls."

37 Keizai Kikaku Chō, *Keizai Antei*, p. 12.

38 Ibid., p. 19; Keizai Kikaku Chō, *Keizai Seisaku*, pp. 39–40.

39 Keizai Kikaku Chō, *Keizai Seisaku*, pp. 39–40; Arisawa, "Senki/Sengo," pp. 11–14.

40 Keizai Kikaku Chō, *Keizai Seisaku*, pp. 81 ff.

41 Yamamoto, "'Sangyō Saiken,'" pp. 233–35.

42 Keizai Kikaku Chō, *Keizai Seisaku*, p. 40; Keizai Kikaku Chō, *Keizai Antei*, p. 26; Ball, "Monthly Report, April 1947, Transition Controls."

43 Arisawa, "Senki/Sengo," pp. 125–27; Matsuo Hiroshi and Yamaoka Kikuji, eds., *Sengo Nihon Keizai Seisaku Shi Nenpyō* (Tokyo: Keisō Shobō, 1962), p. 25.

44 Keizai Kikaku Chō, *Keizai Antei*, p. 26.

45 Arisawa, "Senki/Sengo," pp. 93–103, 122–23, 128.

46 Yamamoto, "'Sangyō Saiken,'" p. 236.

47 Arisawa and Inaba, *Keizai*, pp. 21–22.

48 Takano, *Nihon*, pp. 55–58; Rōdōshō, ed.; *Shiryō: Rōdō Undō Shi—Shōwa 22-nen* (Tokyo: Rōmu Gyōsei Kenkyū-jo), pp. 393–97.

49 Ōkōchi, *Rōdō*, pp. 41–42; Sanbetsu, *Shōshi*, pp. 130–35; Rōdōshō, *Shiryō 22-nen*, pp. 397–401.

50 Takano, *Nihon*, pp. 55–58; Yamamoto, "'Sangyō Saiken,'" p. 227.

51 Yamamoto, "'Sangyō Saiken,'" p. 227.

52 RSCK, *Sekitan*, pp. 103–4.

53 Ibid., pp. 102–5.

54 Ibid., p. 104; Unno, Kobayashi, and Shiba, *Sengo Nihon*, vol. 1, p. 188; Ōkōchi and Ōtomo, "Sengo Rōdō," pp. 50–51.
55 Ōkōchi, *Rōdō*, pp. 41–42.
56 Unno, Kobayashi, and Shiba, *Sengo Nihon*, vol. 1, p. 189; Sanbetsu, *Shōshi*, pp. 134–35.
57 Kyōsantō, *Kōryōshū*, pp. 105–9.
58 Keizai Dantai Rengōkai, ed., *Keidanren no Nijū Nen* (Tokyo: Keizai Dantai Rengōkai, 1969), p. 214; Horikoshi, *Keizai*, vol. 2, appendix, p. 154; Rōdōshō, *Shiryō 22-nen*, pp. 401–2; Keizai Dōyūkai, *Jūnen*, pp. 55–70.
59 Ōkōchi, *Rōdō*, p. 40.
60 Ibid.
61 Ibid.
62 Ibid.
63 Ibid., pp. 40–41.
64 Saitō, *Sengo Rōdō;* Ōkōchi, *Rōdō*, p. 42.
65 Ōkōchi, *Rōdō*, pp. 39, 42.
66 Keizai Dōyūkai, *Jūnen*, p. 167.
67 Takano, *Nihon*, p. 60.
68 Saitō, *Sengo Rōdō*, p. 45; Ii Yashirō, *Ni Ichi Zene Suto no Shinsō—Ippo Kōtai, Nihon Zenshin* (Tokyo: Tetsudō Nihon Sha, Feb. 1947), pp. 17–28. In this assessment of the general strike written immediately afterwards, Ii specifically rejected this imputation against the Keizai Fukkō Kaigi. The Civil Censorship Detachment in the Press Publication and Broadcasting Section of SCAP suppressed this book before publication. The page proofs are located in the Gordon S. Prange Collection, McKeldin Library, University of Maryland.
69 Saitō, *Ni Ichi*, pp. 174–75.
70 Sanbetsu, *Shōshi*, pp. 135.
71 SCAP, General Headquarters, *Summation*, no. 15, p. 47; no. 16, pp. 23–24. Far Eastern Commission, "A Brief Survey," p. 8; Shinobu, *Sengo Nihon*, vol. 2, p. 446; Dower, *Empire and Aftermath*, pp. 333–37.
72 Shiota, "Senryoka," pp. 88–89.
73 Far Eastern Commission, "A Brief Survey," p. 8; Labor Division, Economic and Scientific Section, SCAP, "Reports Concerning Activities of the Labor Movement Culminating in the 1 February 1947 General Strike Threat in Japan," 1 April 1947 (RG 331, box 8498, folder: Labor Relations Disputes: General Strike 1947, Jan.–Feb.), p. 3.
74 SCAP, Economic and Scientific Section, list of labor organizations attending meeting with Chief, Economic and Scientific Section (30 Jan. 1947) (RG 331, box 8498, folder: Labor Relations Disputes: General Strike 1947, Jan.–Feb.); Saitō, *Ni Ichi*, pp. 189–90.
75 Ōkōchi, *Rōdō*, p. 45; Saitō, *Sengo Rōdō*, pp. 47–48; Ōkōchi and Ōtomo, "Sengo Rōdō," pp. 52–53.
76 Takano, *Nihon*, p. 53.
77 SCAP, General Headquarters, *Summation*, no. 15, p. 165.

78 Takano, *Nihon*, pp. 52–53; Saitō, *Sengo Rōdō* pp. 49–50; Far Eastern Commission, "A Brief Survey," p. 8.

79 Takano, *Nihon*, pp. 53–54.

80 Ibid., p. 54.

81 SCAP, General Headquarters, *Summation*, no. 15, p. 27; S. M., "Seisan Kanri Dan'atsu ni Hantai Suru," *Jinmin Hyōron* 2:6 (June 1946), "Shuchō," pp. 4–5; Higuchi Kōki, *Saikin no Rōdō Undō—Rōdō Kumiai Undō no Shin Chōryū* (Tokyo: Chūō Rōdō Gakuen, 1949), pp. 6–7.

82 Far Eastern Commission, *Activities of the Far Eastern Commission, February 26, 1946–July 10, 1947* (Washington, D.C.: Government Printing Office, 1947), p. 92.

83 Maj. General Charles Willoughby, Chief of Military Intelligence Section, General Staff, Spot Intelligence memorandum for Chief of Staff, "Communists Incite Labor Leaders to Strike" (30 Jan. 1947) (RG 331, box 8499, folder: Labor Relations [Secret] Disputes: General Strike 1947, Jan.–Feb.).

84 SCAP, General Headquarters, *Summation*, no. 16, pp. 23–24; Dower, *Empire and Aftermath*, p. 337.

85 Rōdōshō, *Shiryō 22-nen*, pp. 63–66; Saitō, *Sengo Rōdō*, p. 52.

86 Saitō, *Sengo Rōdō*, p. 47.

87 Ōkōchi, *Rōdō*, p. 47.

88 Ibid., pp. 47–48; Farley, *Aspects*, p. 146.

89 Ōkōchi, *Rōdō*, p. 47.

90 SCAP, General Headquarters, *Summation*, no. 16, pp. 24–25; Watanabe, *Gendai*, p. 165.

91 For a thorough account from the Japanese perspective, see Saitō, *Ni Ichi*, ch. 9. For discussions of SCAP's role, see also: Takemae Eiji, *Amerika Tainichi Rōdō Seisaku no Kenkyū* (Tokyo: Nihon Hyōronsha, 1970), pp. 174–92; and Shūkan Shinchō Henshū-bu, *Makkāsā*, pp. 136–43.

92 Eichelberger, diary, 16 and 23 Jan. 1947 (Eichelberger Papers: Diaries, 22-D, box 181, Diaries, 1 Jan.–20 Dec. 1947).

93 Eichelberger to MacArthur, letter in regard to threatened general strike [25 Jan. 1947] (Eichelberger Papers: Memoranda, Occupation of Japan, 22-D, box 171, folder: "Memoranda on the Occupation of Japan").

94 Eichelberger, diary, 26 Jan. 1947 (Eichelberger Papers: Diaries, 22-D, box 181, Diaries, 1 Jan.–20 Dec. 1947).

95 Marquat, Economic and Scientific Section, SCAP, memorandum for General Douglas MacArthur, "Plan to Deal with Strike Threat of Government Employees, 1 Feb. 47" (21 Jan. 1947) (RG 331, box 8498, folder: Labor Relations Disputes: General Strike 1947, Jan.–Feb.), p. 1.

96 Ibid., pp. 1–2.

97 Ibid., pp. 3–4.

98 Ibid., pp. 4–5.

99 Marquat, memorandum for MacArthur, "The General Strike Scheduled for 1 February 1947" (29 Jan. 1947) (RG 331, box 8498, folder: Labor

Relations Disputes: General Strike 1947, Jan.–Feb.); Ōkōchi, *Rōdō*, p. 48.
100 Saitō, *Sengo Rōdō*, p. 53.
101 Marquat, informal memorandum given orally to representatives of Janpanese trade unions, 22 Jan. 1947 (RG 331, box 8498, folder: Labor Relations Disputes: General Strike 1947, Jan.–Feb.).
102 Matsuoka Komakichi, President, Sōdōmei, to MacArthur, 25 Jan. 1947 (RG 331, box 8498, folder: Labor Relations Disputes: General Strike 1947, Jan.–Feb.).
103 Marquat, memorandum for MacArthur, "The General Strike," 29 Jan. 1947.
104 SCAP, Economic and Scientific Section, draft of memorandum on actions to be taken in regard to the general strike, undated (RG 331, box 8498, folder: Labor Relations Disputes: General Strike 1947, Jan.–Feb.). This memorandum was never sent out of Economic and Scientific Section, apparently because the strike was banned without incident.
105 Ibid.
106 Ibid.
107 Eichelberger, diary, 29 Jan. 1947 (Eichelberger Papers: Diaries, 22-D, box 181, Diaries, 1 Jan.–20 Dec. 1947).
108 Eichelberger, diary, 30 Jan. 1947 (Eichelberger Papers: Diaries, 22-D, box 181, Diaries, 1 Jan.–20 Dec. 1947).
109 Marquat, informal memorandum to representatives of Japanese trade unions, 30 Jan. 1947 (RG 331, box 8498, folder: Labor Relations Disputes: General Strike 1947, Jan.–Feb.).
110 Ibid.
111 Anthony Constantino, Economic and Scientific Section, memorandum to Marquat, "Answer of Labor Union Leaders" (31 Jan. 1947) (RG 331, box 8498, folder: Labor Relations Disputes: General Strike 1947, Jan.–Feb.); Constantino, memorandum to Marquat, "Reports of Representatives of Labor Organizations" (31 Jan. 1947) (same RG, box, and folder); Constantino, memorandum for record, "Conference with Union Leaders 31 January 1947" (31 Jan. 1947) (same RG, box, and folder).
112 SCAP, Economic and Scientific Section, handwritten questions for Marquat to ask representatives of labor organizations, 31 Jan. 1947 (RG 331, box 8498, folder: Labor Relations Disputes: General Strike 1947, Jan.–Feb.); Marquat, transcripts of interviews with representatives of labor organizations in regard to cancellation of the general strike, 31 Jan. 1947 (same RG, box, and folder); Marquat, memorandum for Maj. General Paul J. Mueller, Chief of Staff, "Incidents of 31 January in Connection with General Strike" (1 Feb. 1947) (same RG, box, and folder).
113 Ii, "Kokutetsu," pp. 54–55.
114 Willoughby to Labor Division, Economic and Scientific Section, "Transmittal of Soviet Letter" (21 Feb. 1947), and letter from Lt. General Kuzma Derevyanko, Allied Council for Japan, to MacArthur and Members, Al-

lied Council for Japan (RG 331, box 8498, folder: Labor Relations Disputes: General Strike 1947, Jan.–Feb.).

115 T. Cohen, draft of "Memo for Record" regarding reply to Derevyanko letter, undated (RG 331, box 8498, folder: Labor Relations Disputes: General Strike 1947, Jan.–Feb.); SCAP, Economic and Scientific Section, Labor Affairs, draft memorandum for Member, Allied Council for Japan, from U.S.S.R., "Communication Regarding General Strike," undated (same RG, box, and folder).

116 T. Cohen, memorandum for Marquat, "Letter from Lieutenant General Derevyanko, Soviet Member of Allied Council for Japan" (25 Feb. 1947) (RG 331, box 8498, folder: Labor Relations Disputes: General Strike 1947. Jan.–Feb.); T. Cohen, routing slip to Marquat regarding reply to Derevyanko letter, 26 Feb. 1947 (same RG, box, and folder).

117 Saitō, Sengo Rōdō, p. 52; Sanbetsu, Shōshi, p. 137.

118 Ōkōchi and Ōtomo, "Sengo Rōdō," pp. 55–56. Ii Yashirō was apparently not one of these. He did not believe Japan was ready for a proletarian revolution, but that it still had to complete the bourgeois-democratic one. Dobashi Kazuyoshi, in his contribution to Ii's book, seconded Ii's view that the strike was to complete Japan's democratic revolution. Ii, Ni Ichi Zene Suto no Shinso, pp. 6, 17–18, 83.

119 SCAP, Press Publication and Broadcasting Section, Civil Censorship Detachment, Press, Pictorial, and Broadcast Division, District I, News Agency Sub-section, censored conversations on the general strike, pt. 3, Tokuda Kyūichi, Nishio Suehirō, et al., Mainichi, 10 March 1947 (Prange Collection, McKeldin Library, University of Maryland, folder: "Radio Censorship: 9 Nov. 1947 Foreign"), pp. 9–17. Here again Ii disagreed with Tokuda's stand. He evaluated production control as no more than a dispute tactic suited to the particular conditions of Japan during the early part of the occupation. See Ii Yashirō, Tenkanki no Rōdō Undō (Tokyo: Saiwai Shobō, 1948), pp. 41–42.

Bibliography

Japanese

Aihara Shigeru, ed. *Rōdō*. Vol. 4 of *Gendai Nihon Shihonshugi Taikei*. Tokyo: Kōbundō, 1958.

Aizumi Kyō et al. "Densan Jūgatsu Sōgi (1946)." In *Sengo Shoki Rōdō Sōgi Chōsa*, edited by Tōkyō Daigaku Shakai Kagaku Kenkyū-jo. Vol. 13 of *Chōsa Hōkoku*. Tokyo: Tōkyō Daigaku Shakai Kagaku Kenkyū-jo, 1971.

Arisawa Hiromi. "Senki/Sengo no Kōgyō Seisaku." In *Sengo Nihon Keizai no Shomondai*, edited by Yanaihara Tadao. Tokyo: Yūhikaku, 1949.

Arisawa Hiromi and Inaba Hidezō, eds. *Keizai*. Vol. 2 of *Shiryō: Sengo Nijū Nen Shi*. Tokyo: Nihon Hyōron Sha, 1966.

Asahi Shinbun Sha, ed. *Shōdo ni Kizuku Minshūshugi*. Vol. 1 of *Asahi Shinbun ni Miru Nihon no Ayumi*. Tokyo: Asahi Shinbun Sha, 1973.

Bekkan. Vol. 7 of *Nihon Shihonshugi Kōza: Sengo Nihon no Seiji to Keizai*. Tokyo: Iwanami Shoten, 1954.

Chūō Rōdō Gakuen, ed. *Rōdō Nenkan: Shōwa 22*. Tokyo: Chūō Rōdō Gakuen, 1947.

Gōshi Kōhei. "Seisan Kanri no Keizaiteki Seiyaku." *Keiei Hyōron* 1:2 (May 1946): 6–9.

Higuchi Kōki. *Saikin no Rōdō Undō—Rōdō Kumiai Undō no Shin Chōryū*. Tokyo: Chūō Rōdō Gakuen, 1949.

Horikoshi Teizō, ed. *Keizai Dantai Rengō Kai Jūnen Shi*. 3 vols. Tokyo: Keizai Dantai Rengō Kai, 1962.

Ii Yashirō. "Kokutetsu Kugatsu Tōsō to Ni Ichi Zene Suto." In *Senryōka no Rōdō Sōgi*, edited by Rōdō Undō Shi Kenkyū Kai. Vol. 54 of *Rōdō Undō Shi Kenkyū*. Tokyo: Rōdō Junpōsha, 1972.

Ii Yashirō. *Ni Ichi Zene Suto no Shinsō—Ippo Kōtai, Nihon Zenshin*. Tokyo: Tetsudō Nihon Sha, Feb. 1947. Suppressed by SCAP. Page proofs in Gordon S. Prange Collection, McKeldin Library, University of Maryland.

Ii Yashirō. *Tenkanki no Rōdō Undō*. Tokyo: Saiwai Shobō, 1948.

Ishibashi Tanzan. *Infureshon ka Defureshon?* Tokyo: Tōkyō Kōen Kai, July 1946.

Kaneko Kenta. "Sanbetsu Kaigi no Shoki Katsudō." In *Sanbetsu Kaigi: Sono Seiritsu to Undō no Tenkai*, edited by Rōdō Undō Shi Kenkyū Kai. Vol. 53 of *Rōdō Undō Shi Kenkyū*. Tokyo: Rōdō Junpōsha, 1970.

Kawazaki Misaburō. *Sengo Keizai no Kihon Mondai*. Tokyo: Kaizō Sha, 1948.

Keisei Dentetsu Rōdō Kumiai, ed. *Waga Tatakai to Kensetsu no Rekishi: Keisei Dentetsu Rōdō Kumiai 16-nen Shi*. Tokyo: Keisei Dentetsu Rōdō Kumiai, 1962.

Keizai Dantai Rengō Kai, ed. *Keidanren no Nijū Nen*. Tokyo: Keizai Dantai Rengō Kai, 1969.

Keizai Dōyūkai, ed. *Keizai Dōyūkai Gonen Shi*. Tokyo: Keizai Dōyūkai, 1951.

Keizai Dōyūkai, ed. *Keizai Dōyūkai Jūnen Shi*. Tokyo: Keizai Dōyūkai, 1956.

Keizai Hyōron Henshū-bu, ed. "Keiei Kanri wa Kōshite Okonawareru." *Keizai Hyōron* (April 1946): 30–31.

Keizai Kikaku Chō, Sengo Keizai Shi Hensanshitsu, ed. *Sengo Keizai Shi: Keizai Antei Honbu Shi*. Tokyo: Ōkurashō Insatsu-kyoku, 1964.

Keizai Kikaku Chō, Sengo Keizai Shi Hensanshitsu, ed. *Sengo Keizai Shi: Keizai Seisaku Hen*. Tokyo: Ōkurashō Insatsu-kyoku, 1964.

Koike Hiroshi. "Rōdōsha Seisan Kanri no Genkai—Seisan Kanri ni Tomonau Shokonnan to sono Kaiketsu no Hōkō." *Minshū Hyōron* 2:3 (March 1946): 9–11.

Masuyama Taisuke. "Dai Ichiji Yomiuri Sōgi Shi." In *Sanbetsu Kaigi: Sono Seiritsu to Undō no Tenkai*, edited by Rōdō Undō Shi Kenkyū Kai. Vol. 53 of *Rōdō Undō Shi Kenkyū*. Tokyo: Rōdō Junpōsha, 1970.

Masuyama Taisuke. *Yomiuri Sōgi (1945–46)*. Tokyo: Aki Shobō, 1976.

Matsuo Hiroshi and Yamaoka Kikuji, eds. *Sengo Nihon Keizai Seisaku Shi Nenpyō*. Tokyo: Keisō Shobō, 1962.

Minobe Ryōkichi. "Seisan Kanri no Hinin to Keiei Kyōgikai no Setchi." *Jinmin Sensen* 5 (August 1946): 11–14.

Miwa Yoshikazu. "Keizai Dantai Ron." In *Dokusen Keitai*, edited by Imai Noriyoshi. Vol. 1 of *Gendai Nihon no Dokusen Shihon*. Tokyo: Shiseidō, 1964.

Morinaga Eizaburō. *Seisan Kanri no Hōritsu Mondai*. No. 2 of *Sanrō Gyōsho*, edited by Nihon Sangyō Rōdō Chōsa-kyoku. Tokyo: Kenshin Sha, 1948.

Morita Yoshio. *Nihon Keieisha Dantai Hatten Shi*. Tokyo: Nikkan Rōdō Tsūshin Sha, 1958.

Nagata Masaomi. *Keizai Dantai Hatten Shi*. Tokyo: Kotō Shoten, 1956.

Nihon Keieisha Dantai Renmei, ed. *Seisan Kanri to sono Taisaku*. Keieisha series no. 2. Tokyo: Nihon Keieisha Dantai Renmei, 1948.

Nihon Kyōsantō Chūō Iinkai, ed. *Nihon Kyōsantō Kōryōshū*. Tokyo: Nihon Kyōsantō Chūō Iinkai Shuppan-kyoku, 1962.

Nihon Kyōsantō Chūō Iinkai, ed. "Nihon Kyōsantō no Gojū Nen." *Zen'ei*, Rinji Zōkan, no. 342 (August 1972): 70–183.

Nihon Rōdō Kyōkai, ed. *Sengo no Rōdō Rippō to Rōdō Undō*. 2 vols. Tokyo: Nihon Rōdō Kyōkai, 1960.

Nihon Sangyō Rōdō Chōsa-kyoku, ed. "Sōgi Shudan toshite no Seisan Kanri." In *Sengo Shoki Rōdō Sōgi Chōsa*, edited by Tōkyō Daigaku Shakai Kagaku

Kenkyū-jo. Vol. 13 of *Chōsa Hōkoku*. Tokyo: Tōkyō Daigaku Shakai Kagaku Kenkyū-jo, 1971.

Nihon Sekitan Kōgyō Renmei and Nihon Sekitan Kōgyō Kai, eds. *Sekitan Rōdō Nenkan*. Tokyo: Nihon Sekitan Kōgyō Renmei, 1947.

Nihon Shakaitō Nijū Nen Kinen Jigyō Shikkō Iinkai, ed. *Nihon Shakaitō Nijū Nen no Kiroku*. Tokyo: Nihon Shakaitō, 1965.

Nihon Tankō Rōdō Kumiai, ed. *Tanrō Jūnen Shi*. Tokyo: Rōdō Junpōsha, 1964.

Nikkeiren Sōritsu Jūnen Kinen Jigyō Iinkai, ed. *Jūnen no Ayumi*. Tokyo: Nikkeiren Sōritsu Jūnen Kinen Jigyō Iinkai, 1958.

Nishimura Takeo. "Jinmin Saiban no Shinsō" (15 April 1946). Document provided by Professor Yamamoto Kiyoshi.

Noda Kazuo, ed. *Sengo Keiei Shi*. Vol. 1 of *Nihon Keiei Shi*, edited by Nihon Seisan-sei Honbu. Tokyo: Nihon Seisan-sei Honbu, 1965.

Nonomura Kazuo. *Nihon Sengo Keizai no Gendankai: "Kiki" yori "Antei" e*. Tokyo: Ran Shobō, 1948.

Numata Inajirō. *Seisan Kanri Ron*. Tokyo: Nihon Kagaku Sha, 1946.

Ōhara Shakai Mondai Kenkyū-jo, ed. *Saitei Chingin-sei no Igi*. No. 3 of Ōhara Shakai Mondai Kenkyū-jo series. Tokyo: Daiichi Shuppan Kabushiki Kaisha, 1949.

Okada Bunkichi. "Haikyū o Guai Yoku Suru ni wa—Shimin Shokuryō Kanri Iinkai to wa Nani ka." *Minshū no Hata* 1:3 (May 1946): 42–45.

Ōkōchi Kazuo, ed. *Rōdō*. Vol. 4 of *Shiryō: Sengo Nijū Nen Shi*. Tokyo: Nihon Hyōron Sha, 1966.

Ōkōchi Kazuo and Matsuo Hiroshi. *Sengo*. Vol. 1 of *Nihon Rōdō Kumiai Monogatari*. Tokyo: Chikuma Shobō, 1969.

Ōkōchi Kazuo and Ōtomo Fukuo. "Sengo Rōdō Undō Shi." In *Rōdōsha to Nōmin*. Vol. 7 of *Nihon Shihonshugi Kōza: Sengo Nihon no Seiji to Keizai*. Tokyo: Iwanami Shoten, 1954.

Ōuchi Hyōe. "Keizai." In *Sengo Nihon Shōshi*, edited by Yanaihara Tadao. Vol. 1. Tokyo: Tōkyō Daigaku Shuppan-kai, 1958.

Rekishi Kagaku Kenkyū Kai, ed. *Sengo Nihon Shi*. Vol. 1. Tokyo: Aoki Shoten, 1961.

Rōdōshō, ed. *Shiryō: Rōdō Undō Shi—Shōwa 20–21-nen*. Tokyo: Rōmu Gyōsei Kenkyū-jo, 1951.

Rōdōshō, ed. *Shiryō: Rōdō Undō Shi—Shōwa 22-nen*. Tokyo: Rōmu Gyōsei Kenkyū-jo, 1951.

Rōdō Sōgi Chōsa Kai, ed. *Kagaku Kōgyō no Sōgi to Kumiai Undō*. Vol. 8 of *Sengo Rōdō Sōgi Jittai Chōsa*. Tokyo: Chūō Kōron Sha, 1958.

Rōdō Sōgi Chōsa Kai, ed. *Kokutetsu Sōgi*. Vol. 13 of *Sengo Rōdō Sōgi Jittai Chōsa*. Tokyo: Chūō Kōron Sha, 1959.

Rōdō Sōgi Chōsa Kai, ed. *Rōdō Sōgi ni okeru Tokushu Kēsu*. Vol. 6 of *Sengo Rōdō Sōgi Jittai Chōsa*. Tokyo: Chūō Kōron Sha, 1956.

Rōdō Sōgi Chōsa Kai, ed. *Sekitan Sōgi*. Vol. 1 of *Sengo Rōdō Sōgi Jittai Chōsa*. Tokyo: Chūō Kōron Sha, 1957.

Rōdō Sōgi Chōsa Kai, ed. *Tekkō Sogi*. Vol. 7 of *Sengo Rōdō Sōgi Jittai Chōsa*. Tokyo: Chūō Kōron Sha, 1958.

Saitō Ichirō. *Ni Ichi Suto Zengo*. Tokyo: Shakai Hyōron Sha, 1972.

Saitō Ichirō. *Sengo Rōdō Undō Shi*. Tokyo: Shakai Hyōron Sha, 1974.

Sanbetsu Kaigi Hōritsu-bu, ed. "Seisan Kanri no Gōhōsei to Senjutsu" (pamphlet). Tokyo: Sanbetsu Kaigi Hōritsu-bu, January 1947.

Sanbetsu Kaigi Shiryō Seiri Iinkai, ed. *Sanbetsu Kaigi Shōshi*. In *Sanbetsu Kaigi: Sono Seiritsu to Undō no Tenkai*, edited by Rōdō Undō Shi Kenkyū Kai. Vol. 53 of *Rōdō Undō Shi Kenkyū*. Tokyo: Rōdō Junpōsha, 1970.

Sanbetsu Kinen Kai, ed. *Sanbetsu Kaigi/Zenrōren Kikanshi*. Tokyo: Rōdō Junpōsha, 1973.

"Seisan Kanri Mondai." *Keiei Hyōron* 1:2, special issue (May 1946): 3–17.

Sengo Kakumei Shiryō Hensan Iinkai, ed. *Seisan Kanri Tōsō: Shiryō Sengo Kakumei*. *Jōkyō*, special issue (1 October 1974).

Shakai Undō Shiryō Kankō Kai, ed. *Nihon Kyōsantō Shiryō Taisei*. Tokyo: Ōdosha Shoten, 1951.

Shidehara Heiwa Zaidan, ed. *Shidehara Kijūrō*. Tokyo: Shidehara Heiwa Zaidan, 1954.

Shiino Etsurō. "Jōban Sōgi ni okeru Ni San no Keiken." *Zen'ei* 1:5 (May 1946): 23–24.

Shinobu Seizaburō. *Sengo Nihon Seiji Shi*. Vols. 1–2. Tokyo: Keisō Shobō, 1965, 1966.

Shiota Shōbei. *Nihon Rōdō Undō no Rekishi*. Tokyo: Rōdō Junpōsha, 1964.

Shiota Shōbei. "Sengo no Rōdō Sōgi." In *Sengo Shoki Rōdō Sōgi Chōsa*, edited by Tōkyō Daigaku Shakai Kagaku Kenkyū-jo. Vol. 13 of *Chōsa Hōkoku*. Tokyo: Tōkyō Daigaku Shakai Kagaku Kenkyū-jo, 1971.

Shiota Shōbei. "Senryōka no Rōdō Undō." In *Nihon Rōdō Undō no Rekishi to Kadai*, edited by Rōdō Undō Shi Kenkyū Kai. Vol. 50 of *Rōdō Undō Shi Kenkyū*. Tokyo: Rōdō Junpōsha, 1969.

Shiota Shōbei. "Zen Sen'i Sangyō Rōdō Kumiai Dōmei." In *Nihon Rōdō Kumiai Ron*, edited by Ōkōchi Kazuo. Tokyo: Yūhikaku, 1954.

"Shokuryō Kiki Toppa no Tame ni." *Jinmin* 1:3, special issue (March 1946): 19–23.

Shūkan Shinchō Henshū-bu, ed. *Makkāsā no Nihon*. Tokyo: Shinchō Sha, 1970.

S. M. "Seisan Kanri Dan'atsu ni Hantai Suru." *Jinmin Hyōron* 2:6 (June 1946), "Shuchō," pp. 4–5.

Sumiya Mikio. "Mitsubishi Bibai Sōgi." In *Sengo Shoki Rōdō Sōgi Chōsa*, edited by Tōkyō Daigaku Shakai Kagaku Kenkyū-jo. Vol. 13 of *Chōsa Hōkoku*. Tokyo: Tōkyō Daigaku Shakai Kagaku Kenkyū-jo, 1971.

Tagawa Kazuo. *Sengo Nihon Kakumei Undō Shi*. Vol. 1 of *Sengo Kakumei no Haiboku*. Tokyo: Gendai Shichō Sha, 1970.

Takano Minoru. *Nihon no Rōdō Undō*. Tokyo: Iwanami Shoten, 1958.

Takayanagi Mitsutoshi and Takeuchi Rizō, eds. *Kadogawa Nihon Shi Jiten*. Tokyo: Kadogawa Shoten, 1966.

Takeda Takao. "Senji Sengo no Zaisei Seisaku." In *Sengo Nihon Keizai no Shomondai*, edited by Yanaihara Tadao. Tokyo: Yūhikaku, 1949.

Takemae Eiji. *Amerika Tainichi Rōdō Seisaku no Kenkyū*. Tokyo: Nihon Hy-ōron Sha, 1970.

Takemae Eiji. "Sanbetsu Kaigi to CIO—Hicks Chūi ni Kiku." *Nihon Rōdō Kyōkai Zasshi* 22:4 (April 1980): 49–57.

Tanabe Katsumasa. *Gendai Shokuryō Seisaku Shi*. Tokyo: Nihon Shūhō Sha, 1948.

Tōkyō Daigaku Shakai Kagaku Kenkyū-jo, ed. *Sengo Kiki ni okeru Rōdō Sōgi: Yomiuri Shinbun Sōgi*. Vols. 6–7 of *Shiryō*. Tokyo: Tōkyō Daigaku Shakai Kagaku Kenkyū-jo, 1973, 1974.

Tōkyō Daigaku Shakai Kagaku Kenkyū Kai, ed. "Seijiteki Kaikyū Ishiki no Shinten." In *Sengo Shoki Rōdō Sōgi Chōsa*, edited by Tōkyō Daigaku Shakai Kagaku Kenkyū Kai. Vol. 13 of *Chōsa Hōkoku*. Tokyo: Tōkyō Daigaku Shakai Kagaku Kenkyū-jo, 1971.

Tōyama Shigeki. "Senryōka no Nihon." In *Nenpyō*, edited by Tōyama Shigeki. Vol. 6 of *Shiryō: Sengo Nijū Nen Shi*. Tokyo: Nihon Hyōron Sha, 1967.

Tsuchida Mitsuyasu. *Seisan Kanri no Tatakai*. Tokyo: Nihon Rōnō Kyūen Kai, 1948.

Tsuji Kiyoaki, ed. *Seiji*. Vol. 1 of *Shiryō: Sengo Nijū Nen Shi*. Tokyo: Nihon Hyōron Sha, 1966.

Unno Yukitaka, Kobayashi Hideo, and Shiba Hiroshi, eds. *Sengo Nihon Rōdō Undō Shi*. Vol. 1. Tokyo: San'ichi Shobō, 1961.

Watanabe Tōru, ed. *Gendai Rōnō Undō Shi Nenpyō*. Tokyo: San'ichi Shobō, 1961.

Yamamoto Kiyoshi. "'Sangyō Saiken' to Sho-seiji Shutai." In *Rōdō Kaikaku*, edited by Tokyo Daigaku Shakai Kagaku Kenkyū-jo. Vol. 5 of *Sengo Kaikaku*. Tokyo: Tōkyō Daigaku Shakai Kagaku Kenkyū-jo, 1974.

Yamamoto Kiyoshi. *Sengo Kiki ni okeru Rōdō Undō*. Vol. 1 of *Sengo Rōdō Undō Shiron*. Tokyo: O-Cha no Mizu Shobō, 1977.

Yamamoto Kiyoshi. "Sengo Kiki no Tenkai Katei." In *Rōdō Kaikaku*, edited by Tōkyō Daigaku Shakai Kagaku Kenkyū-jo. Vol. 5 of *Sengo Kaikaku*. To-kyo: Tōkyō Daigaku Shakai Kagaku Kenkyū-jo, 1974.

Yamamoto Kiyoshi. *Yomiuri Sōgi (1945–46)*. Vol. 2 of *Sengo Rōdō Undō Shi-ron*. Tokyo: O-Cha no Mizu Shobō, 1973.

Yanase Tetsuya. "Genka Sekitan Mondai no Shozai." *Jinmin* 2:3 (March 1946): 30–36.

English

Allied Council for Japan. Meeting 4, 15 May 1946, Afternoon Session, Ver-batim Minutes. U.S. National Archives, Record Group 43: Allied Council for Japan, box 70.

"Are We Winning the Peace in Japan?" *Amerasia* 10:2 (February 1946): 43–71.

Atcheson, George, U.S. State Department Political Adviser to the Supreme Commander for the Allied Powers. Despatch 92, 11 December 1945. "Political Parties in Japan: Developments During Week Ending December 8, 1945." U.S. National Archives Record Group 59: 894.00/12–1145.

Atcheson, George. Despatch 453: "Demonstrations and Growing Tendency towards Violence in Japan." Enclosure 4: "Summaries of 20 incidents in Japan involving violence or threatened violence (September 12, 1945 to May 19, 1946)." U.S. National Archives Record Group 59: 740.00119/6–1046.

Ayusawa Iwao. A History of Labor in Modern Japan. Honolulu: East-West Center Press, 1966.

Ball, William McMahon, British Commonwealth Member, Allied Council for Japan. "Interim Report," 16 May 1946, to Australian Secretary of External Affairs. Australian Archives, CRS A518, Prime Minister's Department: Correspondence file, item N.815/1/1.

Ball, William McMahon. "Monthly Report, May 1946, pt. 2, Political Developments" (4 June 1946). Australian Archives, CRS A518, item N.815/1/1.

Ball, William McMahon. "Monthly Report, January 1947, Economic Developments." Extracted in document I/47 for the 1947 British Commonwealth Conference on a Japanese Peace Settlement. Australian Archives, CP-104, Far Eastern Commission Records, bundles 51–52.

Ball, William McMahon. "Monthly Report, February 1947, Economic Developments." Personal papers of Eric E. Ward.

Ball to William F. Marquat, Economic and Scientific Section, SCAP, in regard to food situation, 20 February 1947. Personal papers of Eric E. Ward.

Ball, William McMahon. "Monthly Report, April 1947, Transition Controls." Extracted in document I/47 for the British Commonwealth Conference on a Japanese Peace Settlement. Australian Archives, Far Eastern Commission Records, bundles 51–52.

Ball, William McMahon. Japan: Enemy or Ally? New York: Day, 1949.

Beckmann, George M., and Okubo Genji. The Japanese Communist Party: 1922–1945. Stanford: Stanford University Press, 1969.

Behrstock, Arthur. "Snafu in Tokyo." Nisei Weekender, 1 January 1947. Enclosure to: John K. Emmerson to JCV [John Carter Vincent], HB [Hugh Borton], et al., office memorandum: "Article 'Snafu in Tokyo.'" U.S., National Archives Record Group 59: 740.00119/1–847.

Berkov, Robert H. "The Press in Postwar Japan." Far Eastern Survey 16:14 (23 July 1947): 162–66.

Bishop, Max. Office of the U.S. State Department Political Adviser to the Supreme Commander for the Allied Powers. Despatch 250: "Political Parties in Japan: Developments During the Week Ending February 9, 1946." U.S. National Archives Record Group 59: 740.00119/2–1346.

Bishop, Max. Despatch 314: "Political Parties in Japan: Developments During the Week Ending March 16, 1946." U.S. National Archives Record Group 59: 740.00119/3–1946.

Bisson, Thomas A. *Prospects for Democracy in Japan*. New York: MacMillan, 1949.

Bisson, Thomas A. "Reparations and Reform in Japan." *Far Eastern Survey* 16:21 (17 December 1947): 241–47.

Bisson, Thomas A. *Zaibatsu Dissolution in Japan*. Berkeley: University of California Press, 1954.

Bisson, Thomas A. "The Zaibatsu's Wartime Role." *Pacific Affairs* 18:4 (December 1945): 355–68.

Borton, Hugh. *Japan's Modern Century*. New York: Ronald Press, 1955.

Braverman, Harry. *Labor and Monopoly Capital: The Degradation of Work in the Twentieth Century*. New York: Monthly Review Press, 1974.

[British Mission to SCAP]. "Labour Activity in Japan (from the surrender to 31st October, 1946)." Personal papers of Eric E. Ward.

Bronfenbrenner, Martin. "The American Occupation of Japan: Economic Retrospect." In *The American Occupation of Japan: A Retrospective View*, edited by Grant K. Goodman. University of Kansas: Center for East Asian Studies, 1968.

Bronfenbrenner, Martin. "The Road Not Taken: Reflections on the Minseitō-Zaibatsu Alternative in Japan." Harry Johnson Memorial Lecture, York, England, March 1978.

Burati, Valery, Labor Division, Economic and Scientific Section, SCAP, to Jay Lovestone, Free Trade Union Committee, in regard to labor developments in Japan, 11 October 1949. U.S. National Archives Record Group 331, box 8477, folder: Chrono. File July '49–Oct. '49.

Cohen, Jerome B. *Japan's Economy in War and Reconstruction*. Minneapolis: University of Minnesota Press, 1949.

Cohen, Theodore. "Memo for Record" (draft), regarding reply to Derevyanko letter (undated). U.S. National Archives Record Group 331, box 8498, folder: Labor Relations Disputes: General Strike 1947, Jan.–Feb.

Cohen, Theodore, Chief, Labor Division, Economic and Scientific Section, SCAP. Conference with Mr. Iguchi, Chief, General Affairs Bureau, Central Liaison Office, in regard to issuance of Japanese government statement on legality of production control [4 April 1946]. U.S. National Archives Record Group 331, box 8481, folder: Production Control.

Cohen, Theodore. "Staff Study: Clarification of General MacArthur's 20th of May Statement on Mob Violence as Affecting Labor Unions, Meetings and Demonstrations" (26 June 1946). U.S. National Archives Record Group 331, box 8497, folder: Labor Relations Demonstrations.

Cohen, Theodore. Memorandum for William F. Marquat, Chief, Economic and Scientific Section. "Letter from Lieutenant General Derevyanko, Soviet Member of Allied Council for Japan" (25 February 1947). U.S. National Archives Record Group 331, box 8498, folder: Labor Relations Disputes: General Strike 1947, Jan.–Feb.

Cohen, Theodore. Routing slip to Marquat, regarding reply to Derevyanko letter (26 February 1947). U.S. National Archives Record Group 331, box

8498, folder: Labor Relations Disputes: General Strike 1947, Jan.–Feb.

Cohen, Theodore. "Labor Democratization in Japan: The First Years." In *The Occupation of Japan: Economic Policy and Reform*, edited by Lawrence H. Redford. Norfolk, Va.: MacArthur Memorial, 1980.

[Cohen, Theodore.] Foreign Economic Administration, Enemy Branch. *Trade Unions and Collective Bargaining in Japan* (July 1945). U.S. National Archives Record Group 407: Records of the Adjutant General's Office, 1917–.

Cohen, Theodore. "The U.S. Occupation Policies for Japan." Interview by Takemae Eiji. *Tokyo Metropolitan University Journal of Law and Politics* 14:1 (1973): 1–39.

Colbert, Evelyn S. *The Left Wing in Japanese Politics*. New York: Institute of Pacific Relations, 1952.

Constantino, Anthony. Memo for record. "Conference with Union Leaders, 31 January 1947" (31 January 1947). U.S. National Archives Record Group 331, box 8498, folder: Labor Relations Disputes: General Strike 1947, Jan.– Feb.

Constantino, Anthony. Labor Division, Economic and Scientific Section, SCAP. Memo to Marquat. "Answer of Labor Union Leaders" (31 January 1947). U.S. National Archives Record Group 331, box 8498, folder: Labor Relations Disputes: General Strike 1947, Jan.–Feb.

Constantino, Anthony. Memo to Marquat. "Reports of Representatives of Labor Organizations" (31 January 1947). U.S. National Archives Record Group 331, box 8498, folder: Labor Relations Disputes: General Strike 1947, Jan.– Feb.

Costello, William. *Democracy vs Feudalism in Post-War Japan*. Tokyo: Itagaki Shoten, 1948.

Coughlin, William J. *Conquered Press: The MacArthur Era in Japanese Journalism*. Palo Alto: Pacific Books, 1952.

Dahlby, Tracy. "The Japanese Supertraders." *Far Eastern Economic Review* 197:5 (1 February 1980): 39–40.

Daily Labor Press, ed. *The Labor Union Movement in Postwar Japan*. Tokyo: The Daily Labor Press, 1954.

Deverall, Richard L. G. Letter in regard to employers and unions. Deverall Papers, Catholic University, Washington, D.C.: C8-2, vol. 4, series 3, letter 1.

Deverall to Chief, Labor Division, Economic and Scientific Section, SCAP, 21 May and 4 June 1946. Deverall Papers, Catholic University, Washington, D.C.: C8-38, vol. 2, pp. 359–62, 403–5.

Deverall to Chief, Labor Division, Economic and Scientific Section, SCAP, 3, 13, 14 June 1946. Deverall Papers, Catholic University, Washington, D.C.: C8-38, vol. 2, pp. 400–401, 439–41.

Deverall to Chief, Labor Division, Economic and Scientific Section, SCAP, 13 June and 14, 25 July 1946. Deverall Papers, Catholic University, Washington, D.C.: C8-38, vol. 2, p. 400; C8-39, vol. 3, pp. 529, 584.

Dore, Ronald P. *Land Reform in Japan*. London: Oxford University Press, 1959.

Dower, John W. *Empire and Aftermath: Yoshida Shigeru and the Japanese Experience, 1872–1954.* Harvard University: Council on East Asian Studies, 1979.

Eichelberger, Lt. General Robert Lawrence. Diary, 23 May 1946. Eichelberger Papers, Duke University: Diaries, 22-D, box 180, vol.: Diary 24 Oct. 1945–26 Dec. 1946.

Eichelberger to wife, 29 May 1946. Eichelberger Papers, Duke University: Letters (Personal), 1946, 22-A, box 14, folder: "Personal Correspondence to Miss Em."

Eichelberger, Lt. General Robert Lawrence. Diary, 16, 23, 26, 29, and 30 January 1947. Eichelberger Papers, Duke University: Diaries, 22-D, box 181, Diaries, 1947, Jan. 1–1947, Dec. 20.

Eichelberger to MacArthur [25 January 1947]. Eichelberger Papers, Duke University: memoranda, Occupation of Japan, 22-D, box 171, folder: "Memoranda on the Occupation of Japan."

"Ersatz Democracy for Japan." *Amerasia* 10:4 (October 1946): 111–24.

Far Eastern Commission. *Activities of the Far Eastern Commission, February 26, 1946–July 10, 1947.* Report by the Secretary General. Washington, D.C.: Government Printing Office, 1947.

Far Eastern Commission. Australian Delegation. "Interim Report," on visit to Japan in January 1946. Australian Archives, CP-104, Far Eastern Commission Records, bundles 51–52.

Far Eastern Commission. U.S. Delegation. "A Brief Survey of the Growth of Japanese Labor Sentiment Against the Government" (14 February 1947). RG 287, box 228.

Farley, Miriam S. *Aspects of Japan's Labor Problems.* New York: John Day, 1950.

Farley, Miriam S. "Labor Policy in Occupied Japan." *Pacific Affairs* 20 (June 1947): 131–40.

Fine, Sherwood M. *Japan's Post-war Industrial Recovery.* Eastern Economist pamphlet 13, edited by E. P. W. Da Costa. New Delhi, 1952.

Fukutake Tadashi. *Japanese Rural Society.* Ithaca: Cornell University Press, 1967.

Gayn, Mark. *Japan Diary.* New York: William Sloane, 1948.

Grad, Andrew J. *Land and Peasant in Japan: An Introductory Survey.* New York: Institute of Pacific Relations, 1952.

Hadley, Eleanor M. *Antitrust in Japan.* Princeton: Princeton University Press, 1970.

Halliday, Jon. *A Political History of Japanese Capitalism.* New York: Pantheon Books, 1975.

Hewes, Lawrence. *Japan—Land and Men.* Ames: Iowa State College Press, 1955.

Imboden, Major Daniel C., Head of Press Division, Civil Information and Education Section, SCAP. Report of Special Conference with Tokyo public procurators on the Yomiuri Newspaper labor-management dispute (2 July 1946). U.S. National Archives Record Group 331, box 8499, folder: Labor

Relations Disputes—Newspaper, Yomiuri Case (Confidential).

Japan, Economic Stabilization Board. "A Report on Economic Conditions of Japan," 3 July 1947 (the "White Paper"). Personal papers of Eric E. Ward.

Japan. Foreign Office, Research Bureau, Special Research Committee. *The Basic Problems for the Reconstruction of Japan's Economy.* 2 parts. Tokyo, March 1946. Personal papers of Eric E. Ward.

Japan. House of Representatives Special Committee for the Investigation of Concealed and Hoarded Goods. *Supplementary Report* (Tokyo, December 1947). In SCAP, Government Section, *Political Reorientation of Japan: September 1945 to September 1948.* Washington, D.C.: Government Printing Office, 1949.

Japan. Ministry of Finance and Bank of Japan. *Statistical Year-Book of Finance and Economy of Japan.* Tokyo: Ministry of Finance Printing Office, 1948.

Japan. Prime Minister's Office. Cabinet Bureau of Statistics. *Japan Statistical Year-book.* Tokyo: Cabinet Bureau of Statistics, 1949.

Kishimoto Eitarō. "Labour-Management Relations and the Trade Unions in Post-War Japan (1)." *Kyoto University Economic Review* 38:1 (April 1968): 1–35.

Kolko, Joyce, and Gabriel Kolko. *The Limits of Power: The World and United States Foreign Policy, 1945–1954.* New York: Harper and Row, 1972.

Levine, Solomon B. *Industrial Relations in Postwar Japan.* Urbana: University of Illinois Press, 1958.

McNelly, Theodore, ed. *Sources in Modern East Asian History and Politics.* New York: Appleton-Century-Crofts, 1967.

Mainichi Daily News Staff. *Fifty Years of Light and Dark: The Hirohito Era.* Tokyo: Mainichi Newspapers, 1975.

Maki, John. "The Role of the Bureaucracy in Japan." *Pacific Affairs* 20:4 (December 1947): 391–406.

Marquat, Brig. General William F., Chief, Economic and Scientific Section, SCAP. Memorandum for Chief of Staff. "Coordination of Staff Sections in Labor Relations" (2 August 1946). U.S. National Archives Record Group 331, box 8499, folder: Labor Relations Disputes: Newspaper, Yomiuri Case.

Marquat, William F. Memorandum for General Douglas MacArthur. "Plan to Deal with Strike Threat of Government Employees, 1 Feb. 47" (21 January 1947). U.S. National Archives Record Group 331, box 8498, folder: Labor Relations Disputes: General Strike 1947, Jan.–Feb.

Marquat, William F., Informal memorandum given orally to representatives of Japanese trade unions (22 January 1947). U.S. National Archives Record Group 331, box 8498, folder: Labor Relations Disputes: General Strike 1947, Jan.–Feb.

Marquat, William F. Memorandum for General Douglas MacArthur. "The General Strike Scheduled for 1 February 1947" (29 January 1947). U.S. National Archives Record Group 331, box 8498, folder: Labor Relations Disputes: General Strike 1947, Jan.–Feb.

Marquat, William F. Informal memorandum to representatives of Japanese trade unions (30 January 1947). U.S. National Archives Record Group 331, box 8498, folder: Labor Relations Disputes: General Strike 1947. Jan.–Feb.

Marquat, William F. Transcripts of interviews with representatives of labor organizations in regard to cancellation of the general strike (31 January 1947). U.S. National Archives Record Group 331, box 8498, folder: Labor Relations Disputes: General Strike 1947, Jan.–Feb.

Marquat, William F. Memorandum for Maj. General Paul J. Mueller, Chief of Staff. "Incidents of 31 January in Connection with General Strike" (1 February 1947). U.S. National Archives Record Group 331, box 8498, folder: Labor Relations Disputes, General Strike 1947, Jan.–Feb.

Masuyama Taisuke, Kikunami Katsumi, Nakahara Jūnkichi, and Kameta Tōgo. "Appeal to Gen. MacArthur on the Question of Interference into August 2nd Demonstration" (2 August 1946). U.S. National Archives Record Group 331, box 8498, folder: Labor Relations, Demonstrations.

Matsuoka Komakichi, President, Japan Federation of Labor Unions, to MacArthur, 25 January 1947. U.S. National Archives Record Group 331: box 8498, folder: Labor Relations Disputes: General Strike 1947, Jan.–Feb.

Mills, C. Wright. *The New Men of Power: America's Labor Leaders.* New York: Harcourt, Brace and Co., 1948.

Montgomery, John D. *Forced to Be Free: The Artificial Revolution in Germany and Japan.* Chicago: University of Chicago Press, 1967.

Moran, William T. "Labor Unions in Postwar Japan." *Far Eastern Survey* 18:21 (19 October 1949): 241–48.

Morley, James W. "The First Seven Weeks." *Japan Interpreter* 6:2 (summer 1970): 151–64.

Norman, E. Herbert. British Commonwealth Conference on a Japanese Peace Settlement, 27 August 1947, Verbatim Minutes. Australian Archives, CP-104, Far Eastern Commission Records, bundle 3, set 2.

Nugent, Lt. Colonel D. R., Chief, Civil Information and Education Section, SCAP. Reports concerning the situation at the Yomiuri newspaper (17–18 July 1946). U.S. National Archives Record Group 331, box 8499, folder: Labor Relations Disputes, Newspaper, Yomiuri Case [Confidential].

Ogura Takekazu. *Can Japanese Agriculture Survive?—A Historical and Comparative Approach* ——. 2nd ed. Tokyo: Agricultural Policy Research Center, 1980.

Okochi Kazuo. *Labor in Modern Japan.* Economic Series 18, Commerce and Business Administration, Science Council of Japan. Tokyo, 1958.

Okochi Kazuo, Bernard Karsh, and Solomon B. Levine, eds. *Workers and Employers in Japan: The Japanese Employment Relations System.* Tokyo: University of Tokyo Press, 1973.

Ouchi Hyoe. *Financial and Monetary Situation in Postwar Japan.* Tokyo: Japan Institute of Pacific Studies, International Publishing, 1948.

Pacific Basin Reports. *1972 Handbook of Japanese Financial/Industrial Combines.* San Francisco: Pacific Basin Reports, 1972.

Plimsoll, Major J. "Report on Visit to Japan with the Far Eastern Advisory Committee, January 1946." Australian Archives, CP-104, Far Eastern Commission Records, bundle 15.

Reubens, Beatrice G. "'Production Control' in Japan." *Far Eastern Survey* 15:22 (6 November 1949): 344–47.

Roberts, John G. "The 'Japan Crowd' and the Zaibatsu Restoration." *Japan Interpreter* 12:3–4 (summer 1979): 384–415.

Romer, Samuel. Labor Relations Branch, Labor Division, Economic and Scientific Section, SCAP. "Summary of Communist Infiltration and Influence in Japanese Labor Movement" (19 November 1948). U.S. National Archives Record Group 331, box 8497, folder: Communist Activities June '48–Dec. '49.

Scalapino, Robert A. "Japan." In *Labor and Economic Development,* edited by Walter Galenson. New York: John Wiley & Sons, 1959.

Schonberger, Howard. "American Labor's Cold War in Occupied Japan." *Diplomatic History* (1979).

Sebald, William J. Office of the U.S. State Department Political Adviser to SCAP. Memorandum of conversation with leading Japanese businessmen (12 February 1946). Enclosure to: Max Bishop, Office of the Political Advires, despatch 258. U.S. National Archives Record Group 59:740.00119/2–1546.

Shibagaki Kazuo. "Dissolution of Zaibatsu and Deconcentration of Economic Power." Tokyo University Institute of Social Science, *Annals of the Institute of Social Science* 20 (1979).

Shiga Yoshio. "The Present Policy of the Japanese Communist Party." Enclosure 1, despatch 306, 14 March 1946, from Max Bishop, Office of the Political Adviser, to SCAP. "Translation of November 22, 1945 *Akahata* (Red Flag)." U.S. National Archives Record Group 59: 740.00119/3–1446.

Steiner, Kurt. *Local Government in Japan.* Stanford: Stanford University Press, 1965.

Suehiro Izutaro. *Japanese Trade Unionism: Past and Present.* Mimeographed. Tokyo, 1950.

Suehiro Izutaro. "The Legality and the Limitations of Labor's Exercise of Management Controls." Appendix of enclosure to: Max Bishop, Office of the Political Adviser to SCAP despatch 319. U.S. National Archives Record Group 59: 894.504/3–2346.

Suehiro, Izutaro. "The State's Policy in Respect to Production Management." *Mainichi,* 15 April 1946. U.S. National Archives Record Group 331, box 8481, folder: Production Control.

Sullivan, Philip B. Committee on Economic Policy, U.S. State Department. Memorandum to Mr. Mulliken, State Department. "Revised Directive to CINC, USAF, PAC for the Military Government of Japan." U.S. National Archives Record Group 59: 740.00119/8–2845.

Sumiya Mikio. *Social Impact of Industrialization in Japan.* Tokyo: Government Printing Office, Ministry of Finance, 1963.

SCAP. Allied Translator and Interpreter Section. Press Translations, no. 1497,

24 February 1946. Economic Series: 346, item 1. McKeldin Library, University of Maryland.

SCAP. Allied Translator and Interpreter Section. Press Translations, no. 1692, 7 March 1946. Editorial Series: 552, items 1–3. McKeldin Library, University of Maryland.

SCAP. Civil Information and Education Section, Analysis and Research Division. Publications Analysis no. 81, 29 October 1946, "Food Distribution and Food Supply." Personal papers of Eric E. Ward.

SCAP. Economic and Scientific Section. Draft of memorandum on actions to be taken in regard to the general strike (undated). U.S. National Archives Record Group 331, box 8498, folder: Labor Relations Disputes: General Strike 1947, Jan.–Feb.

SCAP. Economic and Scientific Section. Handwritten questions for Marquat to ask representatives of labor organizations (31 January 1947). U.S. National Archives Record Group 331, box 8498, folder: Labor Relations Disputes: General Strike 1947, Jan.–Feb.

SCAP. Economic and Scientific Section. List of labor organizations attending meeting with Marquat (30 January 1947). U.S. National Archives Record Group 331, box 8498, folder: Labor Relations Disputes: General Strike 1947, Jan.–Feb.

SCAP. Economic and Scientific Section. *Outlook for the Japanese Cotton Industry, 1948–1949.* 1948. U.S. National Archives Record Group, 331.

SCAP. Economic and Scientific Section. Advisory Committee on Labor. *Final Report: Labor Policies and Programs in Japan.* Tokyo: 1946.

SCAP. Economic and Scientific Section. Advisory Committee on Labor. *First Interim Report on Treatment of Workers' Organizations since the Surrender.* Appendix A to SCAP, Economic and Scientific Section, Advisory Committee on Labor, *Final Report.* Tokyo: 30 June 1946.

SCAP. Economic and Scientific Section. Labor Affairs. Draft memorandum for Member, Allied Council for Japan from U.S.S.R. "Communication Regarding General Strike" (undated). U.S. National Archives Record Group 331, box 8498, folder: Labor Relations Disputes: General Strike 1947, Jan.–Feb.

SCAP. Economic and Scientific Section. Labor Division, "Reports Concerning Activities of the Labor Movement Culminating in the 1 February 1947 General Strike Threat in Japan" (1 April 1947). U.S. National Archives Record Group 331, box 8498, folder: Labor Relations Disputes: General Strike 1947, Jan.–Feb.

SCAP. General Headquarters. *History of the Non-Military Activities of the Occupation of Japan.* Monograph 28, *Development of the Trade Union Movement: 1945 through June 1951* (30 November 1951). U.S. National Archives Record Group 331.

SCAP. General Headquarters. *History of the Non-Military Activities of the Occupation of Japan.* Monograph 29, *Working Conditions* (30 November 1951). U.S. National Archives Record Group 331.

SCAP. General Headquarters. *Selected Data on the Occupation of Japan:*

Organization and Activities of General Headquarters. June 1950. Memorial Library, University of Wisconsin.

SCAP. General Headquarters. Military Intelligence Section, General Staff. "Special Report: Communist Leadership of National Congress of Industrial Unions" (13 March 1948). U.S. National Archives Record Group 331, box 8497, folder: Communist Activities 1945–May '48.

SCAP. Government Section. "Counter-Measures Against the Subversive Potential in Japan—1946 to 1951 Inclusive." U.S. National Archives Record Group 331, box 8497, folder: Communism: Miscellaneous Data on Communist Counter-measures Committee.

SCAP. Government Section. *Political Reorientation of Japan: September 1945 to September 1948.* Washington, D.C.: Government Printing Office, 1949.

SCAP. Government Section. (Harry E. Wildes et al.) Report of interview with Nosaka Sanzo (19 February 1946), enclosure to: Max Bishop, Office of the Political Adviser to SCAP, despatch 265. U.S. National Archives Record Group 59: 740.00119/2–1946.

SCAP. International Prosecution Section. Case 181, Shōriki Matsutarō. U.S. National Archives Record Group 331. Document provided by Gavan McCormack.

SCAP. Natural Resources Section. *Preliminary Studies.* No. 4, "Food Position of Japan for the 1947 Rice Year," and No. 6, "Japanese Food Collection Program with Emphasis on Collection of the 1946 Rice Crop." Memorial Library, University of Wisconsin.

SCAP. Press Publication and Broadcasting Section. Civil Censorship Detachment. Press, Pictorial, and Broadcast Division. District I, News Agency Sub-section. Censored conversations on the general strike, pt. 3. *Mainichi,* 10 March 1947. Gordon S. Prange Collection, McKeldin Library, University of Maryland. Folder: "Radio Censorship: 9 Nov. 1947 Foreign."

Swearingen, Rodger, and Paul Langer. *Red Flag in Japan: International Communism in Action 1919–1951.* Cambridge: Harvard University Press, 1952.

Taira Koji. *Economic Development and the Labor Market in Japan.* New York: Columbia University Press, 1970.

Taira Koji. "Unions, Ideologies, and Revolutions in Japanese Enterprise during the Occupation." In *The Occupation of Japan: Economic Policy and Reform,* edited by Lawrence H. Redford. Norfolk, Va.: MacArthur Memorial, 1980.

Tatsuki Yasuo. *General Trend of Japanese Opinion Following the End of the War.* Tokyo: Japan Institute of Pacific Studies, International Publishing, 1951.

Textor, Robert B. *Failure in Japan: With Keystones for a Positive Policy.* New York: John Day, 1951.

Tokuda Kyuichi, E. Herbert Norman, and John K. Emmerson. "Communist Party Policy and Current Japanese Problems." Memorandum of conversation, enclosure to: George Atcheson, U.S. Political Adviser to SCAP, despatch 51. U.S. National Archives Record Group 59: 849.00/11–1345.

Tokuda Kyuichi, Shiga Yoshio, et al. "An Appeal to the People." Appendix 2 of enclosure to: George Atcheson, U.S. Political Adviser to SCAP, despatch 31. U.S. National Archives Record Group 59: 894.00/10–2745.

Totten, George O. "Collective Bargaining and Works Councils as Innovations in Industrial Relations in Japan during the 1920's." In *Aspects of Social Change in Modern Japan*, edited by Ronald P. Dore. Princeton: Princeton University Press, 1967.

Tsukahira Toshio. *The Postwar Evolution of Communist Strategy in Japan*. Cambridge: Center for International Studies, Massachusetts Institute of Technology, 1954.

Uhlan, Edward, and Dana L. Thomas. *Shoriki, Miracle Man of Japan: A Biography*. New York: Exposition Press, 1957.

U.S. Army. Pacific Forces. General Headquarters. Office of the Chief of Counter-Intelligence, Research and Analysis. "Strategy of the Kyosanto (Communist Party)." Memorandum of interrogation of Nosaka Sanzo (31 January 1946), enclosure to: Max Bishop, Office of the Political Adviser to SCAP, despatch 243. U.S. National Archives Record Group 59: 740.00119/2–946.

U.S. Department of State. Division of Research for Far East, Office of Intelligence Research. Report 2530, 1 January 1947. "Left-Wing Groups in Japanese Politics, 1918–46." In *A Guide to O.S.S./State Department Intelligence and Research Reports*, edited by Paul Kesaris. Vol. 2, *Postwar Japan, Korea and Southeast Asia*. Washington, D.C.: University Publications of America, 1977, reel 3, no. 31.

U.S. Department of State. Division of Research for Far East, Office of Intelligence Research. Report 3479.15, "The Japanese Cancellation of Wartime Indemnities" (27 September 1946). In *A Guide to O.S.S./State Department Intelligence and Research Reports*, edited by Paul Kesaris. Vol. 2, *Postwar Japan, Korea and Southeast Asia*. Washington, D.C.: University Publications of America, 1977, reel 3, no. 18.

U.S. Department of State. Division of Research for Far East, Office of Intelligence Research. Report 4247, "The Yomiuri Shimbun Case: A Significant Development in the Post-Surrender Japanese Press" (10 March 1947). U.S. National Archives Record Group 331, box 8499, folder: Labor Relations: Disputes—Newspaper, Yomiuri Case (Confidential).

U.S. Department of State. Foreign Economic Administration, Enemy Branch. *Working Conditions Other Than Wages and Hours in Japan* (September 1945 Civil Affairs Guide). U.S. National Archives Record Group 407.

U.S. Department of State. Interim Foreign Economic and Liquidation Service. *Labor Developments in Japan Since Surrender: August 15–November 15, 1945*. U.S. National Archives Record Group 226: Office of Strategic Services, X. 37772, 30 November 1945.

U.S. State-War-Navy Coordinating Committee. Subcommittee for the Far East. *Treatment of Japanese Workers' Organizations*. JCS 1575, August 1945. U.S. National Archives Record Group 218, box 138, folder: CCAS 014 Japan secs. 1–5.

U.S. Strategic Bombing Survey. *Japanese War Production Industries*. Military Supplies Division, 1946.

Wakefield, Harold. *New Paths for Japan*. London: Royal Institute of International Affairs, 1948.

Ward, Eric E. "Economic Problems of Japan Affecting the Peace Settlement" (3 June 1947). Document I/48 for the British Commonwealth Conference on a Japanese Peace Settlement. Australian Archives, CP-104, Far Eastern Commission Records, bundles 51–52.

[Ward, Eric E.] "The Food Situation in Japan During the 1946 Rice Year" [December 1946]. Personal papers of Eric E. Ward.

Wildes, Harry Emerson. "Communist Party" (24 July 1946). Enclosure to: William J. Sebald, Office of the Political Adviser to SCAP, despatch 529. U.S. National Archives Record Group 59: 894.00/8–146.

Willoughby, Maj. General Charles, Chief of Military Intelligence, G-2, to Labor Division, Economic and Scientific Section, SCAP. "Transmittal of Soviet Letter" (21 February 1947). U.S. National Archives Record Group 331, box 8498, folder: Labor Relations Disputes: General Strike 1947, Jan.–Feb.

"Winning the Peace in Japan." *Amerasia* 9:16 (September 1945): 243–51.

Yoshida Shigeru. *The Yoshida Memoirs: The Story of Japan in Crisis*. Boston: Houghton Mifflin, 1962.

Index

JACKET DESIGNED BY RICHARD HENDEL
COMPOSED BY GRAPHIC COMPOSITION, INC., ATHENS, GEORGIA
MANUFACTURED BY FAIRFIELD GRAPHICS, FAIRFIELD, PENNSYLVANIA
TEXT AND DISPLAY LINES ARE SET IN CALEDONIA

Library of Congress Cataloging in Publication Data
Moore, Joe, 1939–
Japanese workers and the struggle for power 1945–1947.
Bibliography: pp. 281–296.
Includes index.
1. Industrial relations—Japan—History—20th century.
2. Trade-unions—Japan—History—20th century. 3. Labor
and laboring classes—Japan—Political activity—History
—20th century. I. Title.
HD8726.5.M58 1983   322'.2'0952   82–70552
ISBN 0-299-09320-4